Political Opposition and Dissent

Political Opposition and Dissent

Barbara N. McLennan, Editor

DUNELLEN PUBLISHING COMPANY, INC.
New York • London

First Edition

Library of Congress Catalog Card # 74-91993

ISBN # 0-8424-0070-2 (hard)
0-8424-0095-8 (soft)

Martin Robertson & Company Ltd — London

iv

Contributors

Robert J. Alexander
Department of Economics
Rutgers, The State University of New Jersey

Angela S. Burger
Department of Political Science
University of Wisconsin

Ardath W. Burks
Department of Political Science
Rutgers, The State University of New Jersey

John T. Deiner
Department of Political Science
University of Delaware

Arthur B. Gunlicks
Department of Political Science
University of Richmond

Erik P. Hoffman
Department of Political Science
State University of New York at Albany

Raymond F. Hopkins
Department of Political Science
Swarthmore College

Ellis Katz
Departments of Political Science and
Foundations of Education
Temple University

Roy C. Macridis
Department of Politics
Brandeis University

Barbara N. McLennan
Department of Political Science
Temple University

Table of Contents

Political Opposition and Dissent

1 Approaches to the Concept of Political Opposition: An Historical Overview

Barbara N. McLennan
Temple University

For as long as politics has been viewed as a system including more than one participant, each competing for scarce resources, there has been a concept of legitimate political opposition. Although it has roots in the ancient past, this concept has been applied in practice only recently in historical terms, largely since the eighteenth century with its emerging modern concepts of representative democracy. Before this period, opposition may have been recognized—but as immoral, dangerous, and threatening to the established political order. Such an assessment would have included opposition of all types, whether in established institutional groups, in factions of politically ambitious men, or in latent social discontent. The premodern treatment of critics of the established order, in western and nonwestern regions, was arbitrary and brutal.

In recent years much interest has been focused on the development of types of political opposition in various political systems. Several new journals of comparative politics have been established, one in fact entitled *Government and Opposition,* and many books and articles have appeared dealing with facets of the concept. The present volume presents a series of studies of types of opposition in different modern political systems. The systems dealt with here are quite varied, representing many different approaches to the appearance of political opposition. The countries include several established representative democracies (Great Britain,

France, West Germany, the United States, Chile, India, and Japan), a series of communist systems (The USSR), one nationalist dictatorship (Tanzania), and one notoriously unstable system (Argentina). By presenting so many contrasting approaches to the phenomenon, we hope to underline the basic similarities and fundamental differences among these different approaches to political opposition. However, there are a large literature and a long history to the development of these approaches, and all of these systems draw on this history to some degree.

Some Traditional Concepts of Opposition

The word "opposition" is vague and difficult to apply in a rigorous manner. It can refer to a theoretical condition or to a practical application of it. When discussing political "opposition" one can be referring to total systemic opposition, as that of revolutionary groups; to moderate differences in policy among institutionalized groups such as courts, legislatures, and political parties; or to the more informal oppositions of interest groups or generalized social groupings. One can also include intellectual critiques of the regime or "cultural opposition" of a theoretical type.

Traditionally, theories of political opposition in the West have been inferred from the development of concepts of political democracy and representation. The earliest theoretical inferences to the concept can be found in the political literature and practices of ancient Greece.

Physically, Greek civilization was spread out over the rugged, hilly Greek coastline and islands in the Aegean Sea. The Greek peninsula was invaded perhaps several times[1] by Acheans, Ionians, and Dorians; the latter Dorian Greeks established the city-states from which Hellenic civilization later developed. Early Greek political organization was tribal, with kings depending on the advice of the heads of aristocratic families. The people in this early period subsisted in a simple agricultural and pastoral economy. Successive changes of government began to take place with the rise of commerce in city-states located along the Aegean Sea. The appearance of a wealthy merchant class, as well as large groups of foreigners ("metics"), within the Greek population, undermined the simple tribal political organization which had supported the old monarchies; henceforth the wealthy classes, or aristocracy, played a major role in Greek politics. Later, economic exploitation of the lower classes by large landowners in the new economy led to strife and revolution, and the aristocrats eventually experienced the rise of the mass of the citizens led by some popular leader—that is, the democracy.[2] Thus, the three classic forms of government categorized by Plato: monarchy (tyranny), aristocracy (oligarchy), and democracy.

The ancient Greeks developed their political concepts in this state of great political fluidity: the Greeks were in a position to compare many different, independent, and competitive forms of government. It is also noteworthy that Greek religion was not a restraining influence on Greek inquisitiveness at this time. It allowed the possibility of many interpretations, just as the political system allowed for many different types of polis. Greek gods were more like perfect human beings than the fearful deities of Oriental religions of the period: the goal of the ancient Greek was the achievement of the perfect life or ideal state of affairs here on earth and not in some imaginary afterlife. Also, the ancient Greek relied on his own imagination, curiosity, and intelligence—not on the guidance of some special priestly class.

Within this context, the Greeks developed the notion of citizenship within the polis, although this was restricted to Greeks and was not applied to slaves and foreigners. To the Greeks citizenship meant *participation* in the life of the state. The polis was a small unit by modern standards, but it was the normal and ideal unit to the Greeks—even Aristotle, writing on the eve of Alexander the Great's imperial conquests, could not visualize a more perfect unit than the polis.[3] The polis had to be small enough, so that every Greek could give full direct service to the state.

Closely related to this concept of citizenship was the Greek concept of the life of the state, that is, the *constitution:* it was viewed as the totality of all the social customs and practices and traditions of Greek society. The Greek constitution was a mode of life rather than a legal institution. The constitution, or customs of the state, was seen as the limitation on the arbitrary will of rulers, and reflected the Greek conception of law: that is, the law and the constitution were seen as coequal with the "will" (i.e., mores) of the people. The Greeks never differentiated private from public law,[4] as they never really viewed politics as a vocation, by itself, separate from other occupational roles in the society.

Despite this lack of differentiation of politics from other social relations within the polis, the Greeks were vere well aware of the impact of economic forces on the life of the state and were also conscious of the effect of economic changes on the "form" or structure of the state. Thus, both Plato and Aristotle categorized states according to the number and wealth of the ruling members.[5] Both, also, saw that there were corrupt as well as "healthy" versions of the three major types of state (monarchy, aristocracy, and democracy) —and that the essense of corruption of a state is the inability or unwillingness of its ruling class to abide by the constitution. The concept to them, as to the Greeks generally, was that when the people's mores were being violated the state had taken an improper turn; the Greeks detested government that depended only on force.

In spite of their recognition of the various economic and social groups comprising the polis, the Greeks never could maintain an institutionalized recognition of political opposition for very long. Democracies tended to degenerate quickly into tyrannies, and for this reason were not highly regarded by Plato and Aristotle.

Plato's ideal state presented in the *Republic* put great emphasis on achieving the correct division of labor. Each class was to do its own work and not interfere with others, and the statesman "philosopher-king" was to have the task of supervising the whole state. Plato had no desire to institutionalize methods by which political opposition might thrive. Justice in the state was seen as the achievement of harmony among the classes, a haromony ruled by reason and achieved through education, not by mutual competition or argument.[6] Plato realized the need for many different kinds of labor in the state and he would have had all of them play their essential roles just as the different parts of the body did their tasks in completing the human organism.

Closely paralleling this theory of division of labor within the state was Plato's concept of the "mixed state" which he discussed in the *Laws*. The polity presented in this work was supposed to combine the two "pure" principles of democracy and monarchy by allowing freedom of the masses and rule by a wise ruler: each tendency was to balance and offset the excesses of the other,[7] with contradictory claims and interests being mutually adjusted. Plato's view of opposition was of a necessary evil that must be minimized and controlled; when it opposed the established order it had to be repressed by the knowing ruler.

Taking a somewhat different approach, Aristotle contributed a concept of the proper state which was based more on observed reality than on the creation of an abstract model. Though he temperamentally and intellectually preferred a small, leisured, and highly cultivated aristocracy,[8] he still viewed a "middle-class" government as probably the best attainable. He viewed it as best, because political opposition in it would be more moderate and restricted than in other systems. In this concept of the middle class can be found the germs of a later more universal concept of popular equality, while Plato's view of the worth of each part of society within the organic unity of the state is carried over:

> . . . a city ought to be composed, as far as possible, of equals and similars, and these are generally the middle classes. Wherefore the

5

city which is composed of middle-class citizens is necessarily best constituted in respect of the elements of which we say the fabric of the state naturally consists. And this is the class of citizens which is most secure in the state, for they do not, like the poor, covet their neighbor's goods; nor do others covet theirs, as the poor covet the goods of the rich; and as they neither plot against others, nor are themselves plotted against, they pass through life safely.[9]

Thus, even though both Plato and Aristotle accepted the prevailing Greek concept of direct participation of all citizens in their polis, and did not conceive of a system of political representation and institutionalized opposition, they did contribute certain ideas which served as the basis for later representational theories. The recognition of different economic classes and of the possibility of a "mixed state" later was taken as the rationale for establishing different branches of government as representative of these different classes. The recognition of the need for different kinds of labor in a polity also was taken as a basis for later functional theories of representation.

The Contributions of Ancient Rome

The Roman concept of opposition and representation can be traced back to the traditions and practices of the Roman republic which predated the rise of the empire. In this early political unit the Romans had created a city-state, in some respects similar to the Greek polis. In Rome, as in Greece, the city-state originally was led by a king who derived his power from the people in theory, but who governed with the advice of the landed aristocracy in practice. In 509 B.C. the aristocrats staged a rebellion overthrowing the Etruscan royal dynasty and vested the major power of the government in the Senate—the king's former advisory council whose membership was restricted to the patrician class.[10]

From the establishment of the aristocratic republic, the

plebians, the lower class of Roman citizens composed of nonnoble freeman (mostly small farmers and tradesmen), attempted to raise their political position in the state. In this attempt they used the characteristically Roman method of collective action by a corporate group within Roman society. The Roman plebians did not, as the Greeks had done, turn to a tyrant to overthrow the form of state; they rather set up councils to represent them within the context of the prevailing system. These councils (the Concilium Plebis, Comitia Tributa, and Comitia Centuriata) were all designed to safeguard the interests of the plebians and to negotiate with the aristocrats' chosen representatives, the consuls.[11] Eventually the plebians were successful by this means in attaining high political offices and greater political power for themselves, but this was only a temporary success: with the expansion of Rome, the upper classes became wealthy and more powerful, while the lower classes lost their land and became impoverished. This situation led eventually to revolution and civil war, with the eventual establishment of a military dictatorship and then the empire. Through all these changes, the theoretical underpinning of the Roman state stayed the same: the government was still, under the empire, conceived of as deriving its power from the consent of the people, as a corporate body.

With the demise of the city-state and the rise of the Roman Empire encompassing many different peoples, political theory in the Mediterranean world underwent appropriate changes. No longer was the political unit so small and intimate that citizenship could be taken to imply direct participation. The coexistence of many different ethnic and tribal groups on equal terms within the same large imperial organization implied a more universal concept of the rights of citizenship: no longer could one small ethnic group claim all the virtues of civilization while allotting to the others a status of "barbarianism." These political realities were accounted for by the political philosophy of the Stoics, particularly in their concept of natural law, which was transmitted to Rome.

The ideas of the Stoics formed part of the later evolving Roman concepts of opposition and representation.[12]

Roman Stoicism accepted the ideas of Polybius and Greek Stoicism and is exemplified in the writings of Cicero. The existence of universal law, eternal in duration and divine in character, was a presupposition of Cicero's theory of state. It followed that the whole world was the home of its subjects. Cicero held that human beings were naturally equal, a belief implicit in his conception of reason as a natural and universal attribute of man. It followed, in the Roman concept of representation, that *all men* were represented in the government—not just one tribal group or class.

Cicero believed that nothing matched the law of a state in importance; it was the bond that held political society together—without law the state could not exist; the state by definition was a group of men united by law. However, the magistrates played a role so important that Cicero regarded the state as held together by magistrates; he considered its type as determined by the system in which its magistracies were arranged.[13]

Cicero thus gave voice to a permanent contribution of the Romans to later theories of representation and legitimate opposition: the distinction made between public and private law. In Roman legal theory the difference between the public and private spheres of law lay in the fact that private rights affected private individuals only (a notion foreign to the ancient Greek conception of citizenship), while all individuals alike participated in the public sphere (similar to the Greek view). The primary notion in each of the two spheres was the independence of the individual. The early Romans found that the most effective safeguard of the rights of man against man lay in the guarantee of the people to protect these rights. The whole people were therefore in theory made responsible for the maintenance of individual rights—via the development of public law.[14]

The recognition of a public sphere of law separate from the private interests of average citizens made possible the conception of the role of a magistrate as a public official: politics, unlike in the Greek situation, was seen as a separate sphere of activity—though still dependent *theoretically* on the will of the people. Now the magistrates and judges were allowed to act for and symbolize the will of the population—that is, to represent them. This was impossible in Greece where the existence of a separate public sphere of life was never recognized theoretically.

This new approach to politics and the role of the public official can be seen in the evolution of the *jus gentium*—the Roman system of common law. This body of law gradually expanded to incorporate the varied local customs and legal principles of the Italian states, which in time became general and common throughout the empire. Roman law was "judge-made" law and contained a great many legal fictions[15] necessary to the process of accommodating so many different customs and traditions. Implicit in this legal development was the continuing concept that law was the common possession of a people in its corporate capacity and that customary law has the consent of the people even though it must be interpreted by judges and magistrates. In a sense, the magistrates were viewed as mere representatives of the popular will, an element which required interpretation.

In Cicero's ideal state, likewise, even though the rulings of the people theoretically were the chief source of law, constitutional flexibility could be attained by the appointment of a dictator in times of crisis. To Cicero, even though a law had to be universally applied to all individuals, recognizing no privileged class, in the ideal state, the people met only at the bidding of the magistrate, and then only to consider such proposals as he chose to submit to them. The people's actions in practice would have been subordinated to the judgment of the ruling officials.[16] Representation of the people therefore was achieved, but in theory only—as another kind of legal fiction. Political opposition was permitted in the Roman Empire also, but only as a legal fiction.

When Rome ceased to be a city-state and became a world

empire, the republican form of government (involving direct participation of the lower classes) could no longer cope with political realities. Although the republican constitution fell into disuse (power became lodged first in the hands of the Senate and later in the emperor), the theory continued that all powers were ultimately derived from the people. The theoretical legal powers of the people never were formally abolished—not even at the height of the empire.[17] It was the peculiar flexibility of the Roman constitution and legal system which made possible the fiction of the people's delegation of legislative authority to the emperor as was stated in Justinian's Code—that is, the concept that law was the will of the emperor even though each emperor received his authority from the people by delegation at the inauguration of his reign. This double-sided conception of the emperor's legal sovereignty—on the one hand, that his pleasure had the force of law, and on the other, that his powers were ultimately derived from, and therefore representative of, the people—persisted for many centuries.[18]

The Medieval Contribution

The Roman Empire in the West went into eclipse during the 5th century A.D., when Rome succumbed to the invasions of Germanic tribes. The one-time great universal empire in which all men could claim citizenship was broken up into many different, practically autonomous, feudally organized provinces. Only a shadow of the old Roman imperium remained in the person of the Holy Roman Emperor; the real connecting link among the successor states to Rome was the belief in Christianity as expounded by the single authority of the Roman Church.

The Middle Ages was characterized politically by a series of conflicts between the Roman Catholic Pope and the Holy Roman Emperor, during the course of which the Church first attained its independence of the emperor and then gradually attained enough stature to challenge his temporal authority. However, corruption within the Church in the latter part of the period led to severe criticisms of the form of Church government itself—and these criticisms eventually culminated in the Reformation. The latter movement, which coincided with the rise of the modern nation-state, signalled the end of even the theoretical unity of Europe.

Between the sixth and ninth centuries, after the decline of Roman imperial power, the political framework of Western Europe became established and determined by the German tribes. The ideas of these peoples, containing traces of Roman thought, developed within a political and economic environment which was much the same throughout Europe, and, together with the teachings of the Christian Church Fathers, they made their way into the political thought of the Middle Ages and became commonly accepted.[19] These commonly held beliefs contained certain elements making for the further development of the Western concept of representation and political opposition.

In the Middle Ages it was generally believed that the law belonged to the people, or folk, and was to be found in the customs of the community. Law was thought to belong to the people and to be applied or modified with their consent. However, there were almost no means of accurately defining any constitutional authority. No one doubted, for example, that there were limits beyond which the king could not exceed without violating both law and morals; on the other hand no one doubted that he ought to have powers not equalled by those of any subject. The king, therefore, both represented the will of the community, but was elevated above it: like a Roman emperor in theory, but not as absolute in practice—due to political realities.

Law in the Middle Ages was largely customary law and was conceived as theoretically changeless. It was agreed in early times that the king promulgated the law assisted by a council representing the community's best knowledge of the law. Feudal lawyers called the king's orders administrative acts, temporary and changeable, designed to supplement and enforce the permanent law itself. Eventually more philosophical and scholarly minds demanded a rational and uniform standard by which human laws and institutions might be measured. These more sophisticated minds turned to the natural law doctrine of the Stoics, which was transmitted to the Middle Ages through the Code of Justinian and the writings of the Fathers of the Church.[20]

From Roman ideas of natural law, medieval thinkers learned to conceive of positive law as based on the human recognition of norms of morality and justice which did not depend on human inventiveness, but which were a product of the very nature of the universe. Continuing familiarity with Roman law also increased the emphasis on the importance of authoritative promulgation of a law, a process not conceived as the creation of a law, but as the formal discovery of a law that already existed and as the formal declaration of what the law already was. Roman law also introduced the idea that the Roman people had enjoyed, originally, the legislative authority which the emperor later exercised by their delegation, an idea that coincided with prevailing medieval views. Also, the Roman distinction between public law, which dealt with the interests of the commonwealth, and private law, which dealt with the separate interests of individuals, provided a basis for the conception of the ruler as an officer or magistrate in whom a corporate community had voluntarily focused a governing authority.

Feudalism, the typically medieval system of land tenure, created the conditions which made possible the most important medieval contribution to representative theory: that is, the creation of parliaments. Feudalism established as the normal form of landholding a tenure in which the original holder of the land did not relinquish his "lordship" of that land, although his actual relations to the land were very slight:

If the land system were logically worked out the king would be

12

the sole landowner. His barons would be tenants upon lands granted to them for specified services, and the barons would have tenants under them, until the bottom is reached in the serfs, upon whose labor the whole system rests.[21]

Feudalism tended to construe all authority as proprietary and to treat the rights of the king as simply an agglomeration of property rights, established within the same framework of legal principles as that governing the property rights of his subjects. The feudal court, or parliament, was a council in which the lord (or king) and his vassals could settle the disputes that arose among them within the context of their feudal relationships. Theoretically, the feudal court provided every vassal a trial by his peers in accordance with customary law; it followed from this, theoretically again, that the king was merely *primus inter pares* and could legally be bound by a decision of his court. The king and his barons throughout this period therefore shared power over the judicial, executive, and legislative aspects of government, because the contractual aspect of the feudal relationship had transformed the kingdom into a network of personal proprietary relationships among the king and the barons which made up his council and had prevented authority from becoming concentrated in any one place.[22] The feudal council institutionalized this sharing of power by means of a species of representation: it produced a forum in which the king's vassals, as proprietors of the realm, could voice their grievances and resolve them while bound by the same legal principles that bound the king and their peers.

The Middle Ages also saw the development of corporate forms of social organization, particularly in the Northern Italian city-states. Here techniques were discovered by which a number of men could arrive at the unity of decision and consistency of action which characterize the human individual. Here, the principle of majority rule was developed. Although few of these representative institutions lasted, the theories developed to support them were important for later political theory.

During the course of the Middle Ages, most of the political views advanced were in criticism, or in support, of one or another parties in the Papal-Imperial controversy. Although the theorists involved were part of the medieval tradition and maintained many prevailing attitudes of the time, they generally presented the arguments supporting their points of view in their most logically extreme form. The concepts presented, therefore, constituted critiques or additions to the prevailing medieval theories of representation and did not reflect the mainstream of medieval thought; their repercussions for the future were, however, very great.[23]

Modern Western Democratic Approaches to Opposition

Any discussion of the development of modern Western democratic approaches to opposition logically begins in England where the first fully developed modern Western concepts of government appeared. In addition, English political theory evolved gradually: modern central government in England developed from foundations laid in the medieval period, and English constitutional history may be described as a series of changes in the balance of power and principles among and within the fundamental institutions of national government that were established before the end of the Middle Ages.[24] The exceptional phenomenon in the history of England that distinguished it from the development of continental political systems was the evolution of Parliament from the king's baronial court (such an institution existed in many parts of Europe) into a representative assembly in the political sense.[25] Parliament in England evolved a political consciousness and an authority not deriving from the king's majesty, but from the nation. Where continental countries attempted to limit the secular ruler's power by appealing to the Pope, the British succeeded in setting up a secular institution whose function it would be to decide the limits of the king's

14

jurisdiction. Thus when the Pope fell into disrepute, the new nation-states on the continent had no effective institution to combat the claims to absolute power by the national monarchs. While the Tudors in England were powerful monarchs, they never dispensed with Parliament. England thus developed an institutional embodiment of a representative system with enough of a recognized function to enable it to withstand the vicissitudes of the ages.

The English king in the Middle Ages was compelled to act through his council, and the court retained aspects of its feudal right to be consulted down to the modern era. The king was bound to proceed by law and not otherwise. Though the judges were appointed by him and acted only in his name, they were bound by their oaths to determine the rights of the subject not according to the king's will but according to the law. In England the right to legislate could not be settled ultimately in the king, but in the king in Parliament.[26] In the other emerging nation-states of Europe where constitutional theory had not been so institutionalized, the breakdown of Papal authority set the stage for the rise, in the modern period, of monarchical absolutism at the expense of medieval representative institutions. In England the medieval baronial court, the Parliament, became so universally accepted that it was able to evolve, in the modern period, into a constitutional device representing the will of the nation.

The development of British representational concepts in the period following the Middle Ages followed the course of British and European political history. As noted above, the Tudor monarchs had never found it necessary to dispense with Parliament; indeed, the Tudors had found the Parliament to be a source of strength and support when they needed it.[27] Only when the Stuarts with their belief in the divine right of kings acceded to the throne, did the king and Parliament openly come into conflict. The conflict was compounded by the problems of religious dissension and economic disruption: when the king could no longer support himself financially and Parliament refused to issue funds sufficient to support him, civil war between the pro-monarchy and pro-Parliamentary factions became the inevitable result. The victory of the Puritan Parliamentary faction led by Cromwell signalled the passage of political power in England to the moneyed classes represented in Parliament. Parliamentary supremacy was finally made legitimate in the Bill of Rights of 1689, issued as a result of the "Glorious Revolution"—the act by which Parliament had forced out King James II, without a fight, because of differences with his religious policy.

English Views of Opposition

In the English medieval theory, as stated by Henry de Bracton, the king was seen both as a party to a contractual relation with his vassals and as head of the commonwealth On the one hand the king was conceived as created by the law, and on the other hand it was admitted that he could not be coerced by the ordinary processes of his own courts. In Bracton's view if the king exceeded his authority, it was the duty of his court of barons (Parliament) to restrain him. Thus both the king and court had a twofold capacity: in the one the king was the chief landowner of the realm, while the court comprised his tenants; as an institution the court existed to dispose of the difficulties that arose among them in this contractual relation. In the other the king stood as the chief bearer of public authority inherent in the realm or folk, which he shared in some vague way with his court. In the first relationship the king may have proceeded against like others of the court; in the second his responsibility to law rested ultimately on his own conscience. The one view represents the tendency of feudalism to submerge public authority in private relationships; the other represents the continuing tradition of a commonwealth in which the king was the chief magistrate.[28] It should be remembered that in the feudal theory the members of Parliament represented the property interests of landed estates and corporations, not the abstract political will of a popular constituency.

Much later, in the course of the 17th century in Britain, the concept of representation in Parliament, largely due to the stimulation of conflicting views, became crystalized. The medieval view of life (that is, the emphasis on social oneness and the preeminence of the Church-ordered community) had given way to a conception of the world as ordered by a reason ("Natural Law") which each *individual*, under proper conditions, could perceive. This change in outlook had been influenced by the rediscovery of ancient Greek and Roman scientific and political texts, by the humanism of Renaissance writers and artists who looked to the glorification of man and not the Church, to the Reformation which preached the "priesthood" of all believers (the responsibility of each individual in interpreting the word of God, rather than depending on the Church), and by the scientific and mathematical revolution begun by Copernicus, Galileo, Descartes and later Newton, which revealed the power of the individual's deductive reasoning in comprehending the seemingly well-ordered mechanical universe. The British rationalist philosopher Thomas Hobbes applied this new mechanistic and individualistic conception to the problems of British politics and social stability in the 17th century.[29]

Hobbes began with the assumption of the equality of all men in a prepolitical society. Due to the inconveniences of this "state of nature" (inconveniences due to the natural selfishness of men who both fear and try to get the best of one another), the "people" by a fictional contract enter into a society by setting up a sovereign whose function would be to restrain the natural competitiveness of themselves and to prevent civil war. This sovereign (which for Hobbes would most preferably have been a king, but might also have been an assembly) kept absolute power by virtue of the contract and was not limited by it. The sovereign was the source and executor of all law and mores in every party of society; in a

17

sense the sovereign "created" society by establishing the legal and moral system. The people by entering into the contract gave up all their rights to the sovereign, i.e., they retained no "natural" rights but kept only those privileges which the sovereign allowed. Only if the sovereign did not perform its function (thus returning them to a state of nature) could the people revert to their own self-protection. Opposition thus naturally existed, but no one should want it and it must be repressed.

The sovereign, to Hobbes, was representative of the people in the sense that a corporation is representative of its shareholders: the people compose the state and set up the sovereign, just as shareholders make up the corporation and set up the corporate head; however, a corporation (and Hobbes' state) could be conceived of as a single legal person with a single will—that of its leadership or sovereign. Thus the will of the sovereign was taken by Hobbes to be the will of the people in all their pursuits and, in this sense, was representative of them. This sovereign "will" was in no sense accountable to the people and depended more on force than on anything else for its legitimacy.

Hobbes' philosophy was very influential in the years to come, but it always remained in the realm of science and scholarship. James Harrington, in the same period, provided a more complete analysis of the economic basis of republicanism. It was his view that real power in government is always a reflection of the distribution of property, especially the ownership of land. Like the ancients, Harrington's theory described three basic forms of government—monarchy, aristocracy, and democracy—each reflecting the land distribution in the population.[30] Harrington's ideal was an aristocratic republic, and he made great efforts to devise an agrarian law which would have kept landed property from becoming either too concentrated in one person's hands or becoming too fragmented.

The government structure, in Harrington's conception, represented the power balance of the community. In order to

18

keep the government responsive to the popular will, he advocated the use of such devices as rotation in office, election by ballot, and separation of powers. In Harrington's theory, each function of government was conducted by and representative of a separate portion of the community: the senate for the nobility who have the wisdom, the assembly for the people who have the interests, and the magistracy for the king who has the authority.

The British theory of representation in Parliament, while in some sense based on the writings of Hobbes and Harrington, received its clearest statement as a result of the Glorious Revolution of 1689. John Locke, acting as an apologist for the primarily merchant interests in the Parliament who overthrew the king, developed the concept of Parliamentary supremacy based on the will of the people. In Locke's theory[31] the population retained certain natural indefeasible rights (to life, liberty, and property) which no governmental authority could abridge. These natural rights formed the customs of the community which arose in a state of nature; government was responsible to the community for protecting these rights. The government was therefore limited by moral law and tradition, and if it overstepped these bounds, it could rightfully be resisted. Opposition was finally conceived of as legitimate, moral, and entirely desirable.

Locke, like Hobbes, depended on a contract theory. In a state of nature the people (theoretically) by contract were supposed to have set up a government. By this contract each individual became a member of society, but did not lose his traditional "natural" rights; the contract merely required the individual became a member of society but did not lose his Parliament supreme, postulating that the legislative power is overriding in the commonwealth. The people who set up the legislature for the purpose of directing the best interests of the community were theoretically empowered, according to Locke, to change any legislature or executive who interfered with this end. To Locke the legislative power could only be placed in the hands of the people's representatives, "diverse persons who, duly assembled, have by themselves, or jointly with others, a power to make laws, which when they have done, being separated again, they are themselves subject to the laws they have made."[3][2] In time this came to mean that political parties, the bearers of representation in Parliament, would be the institutions empowered to carry on the functions of opposition. The party in power became the government, the party out of power became His Majesty's loyal opposition, and the stable two-party system became established on a strong theoretical foundation.

American Variations on the British Theme

Approaches to political opposition in the United States were derived from the theories of John Locke and the British Revolution of the 17th century. From this period were derived the characteristically American beliefs in the worth of written constitutions, bills of rights, emphasis on the worth of the individual, separation of powers, and checks and balances. Though originating in Britain, certain of these beliefs became more institutionalized in the American colonies than they ever did in the mother country. The theoretical basis for American concepts was always considered in Britain to be more radical than in the mainstream of British political theory. In Britain restoration of the monarchy, even if only temporarily, meant a continuation of the British evolutionary process of political thought; the new British concept of government could find roots in a rich and commonly accepted medieval past. In contrast, new colonies settled by emigrants from monarchical Britain who in many cases had been persecuted for political and/or religious beliefs allowed the more radical theories much greater opportunity to take root. The colonies were thousands of miles away from the mother country in an age of primitive transportation. Even though politically and economically tied to Britain and nominally allegiant to the British monarchy, the American colonies had ample opportunity to develop their own individual approaches to aspects of their personal political theory and practice. In the real sense the American colonies, from their inception, were self-governing political units. The British were not able either physically or conceptually to closely supervise local politics so far away from home; the Americans therefore were required by necessity to develop their own political practices. They did this by relying mainly on their British heritage, including the more extreme contributions made by Milton, Cromwell, Winstanley, and others.

The immediately postrevolutionary concept of representation in the United States which was incorporated into the 1787 Constitution was most clearly stated by Hamilton, Madison, and Jay in *The Federalist Papers.*[33] The underlying assumptions of this early American theory were derived from the 17th century British; the framers (that is, the Federalist faction), like Hobbes, feared the natural selfishness of citizens and hoped to restrain them but, like Locke, a portion of them (the republicans) also believed in the natural rights of all men and hoped to protect these. As a result, the 1787 Constitution was a compromise: though established by "We, the People," it includes almost every method possible to prevent any temporary majority from taking control of the government and pushing a radical program through. In a sense representation was for all the people, but the early Federalist framers still hoped and believed that leadership would be provided by the rich and educated.

The early Federalist concept was contradictory to the contemporary republican one: the republican framers had an intellectual belief in the equality of man establishing the concept of popular sovereignty as the ideological basis of the Constitution; in contrast, the Federalist farmers wanted to safeguard the rights of property. A compromise was reached by the two factions by incorporating such devices as indirect election, a federal system, separation of powers, and judicial review in order to prevent any radical majority interest from taking control of the government. The function of the representative to the Federalists, even though they agreed to the ideal of popular sovereignty, was to provide wise and enlightened leadership, not to cater to the wishes of the population.[34]

The popular republican trend in American thought, starting with Jefferson, tended to believe in the unconditional equality of men and wanted to remove all obstacles to the popular will. Jefferson wanted the representative to be bound by his constituents and to act by their instructions and be their agent.[35]

From Jefferson's ideological basis, the 19th century populistic concept of representation finally emerged. This was the view that all branches of government are responsible to and representative of the majority will in the community. Political equality and popular sovereignty were the basic assumptions forming the underpinning of Jacksonian democracy and produced what Toqueville later described as the "tyranny of the majority."[36]

The equality and majority-rule concepts that prevailed in the United States during the early 19th century were part of the general laissez-faire theory of politics and economics. As in Britain, the Americans in this period sought to do away with government restrictions on the economic and political life of the country: the theory, following Adam Smith, Bentham, and Mill, was that if each individual was allowed to be unrestrained in pursuit of his own interests, the whole community would automatically benefit. For the concept of representation this implied the end of all property qualifications for political participation: the idea was that all men were equal in the possession of certain natural rights (as stated in the Declaration of Independence) and that no individual, despite his wealth, had a greater "stake in society" than any other.[37]

The laissez-faire theory was a purely logical and abstract one, not based on any real observation of how the political and economic system operated. When, by the end of the 19th century, there had emerged a small group of powerful business monopolies who were unchecked by the government in their exploitation of the general population, new, more active theories of government were developed. The concepts of popular sovereignty and political equality were as potent as ever but the concept of political participation was considerably broadened; no longer was it thought sufficient that the government keep from interfering with property rights: now popular movements insisted that representatives in state and federal government actively stop the exploitation of the people by the large corporations. These movements favored greater direct accountability of the government to the people through such mechanisms as the referendum, initiative, and recall. Representatives, according to the Populists and others, were to be no more than agents of the people and were to actively carry out the people's wishes.[38] Representation was to be made as "representative" as possible, that is, democracy was to be as direct a reflection of popular sentiment as possible, and the possibility for legitimate opposition was to be maximized.

The 19th and 20th centuries also saw the growth of more empirical political concepts. Studies were made and theories were presented that were based on a more realistic and systematic observation of the political process. It became recognized that majority rule was something of a fiction: that people actually were members of minorities, or interest groups, which processed raw desires and converted them into pressures on government which the representative process had to resolve.[39] It was recognized that leadership could be exercised only by a minority, that "the people" as a whole were not really able or even interested in running the government in all its various functions.

These concepts have, in the United States, been incorporated into a more empirical theory of democracy and representation. This theory, labeled by Dahl as "Polyarchal,"[40] involves a continued belief in the equality of citizens as an abstract ideal, but describes representative democracy as a system of "minorities rule" rather than "majority rule."

Historical and traditional habits of politics have served to maintain devices that actually make it more difficult for any majority (i.e., coalition of minorities) from getting its way—such practices as judicial review, the seniority system in Congress, etc. Great emphasis has become focused on the need for, and methods of, achieving the necessary social consensus that underlies the political system. Representation in this context has been taken to mean that mechanism by which the leaders of the country are controlled, to a relatively high degree, by the ordinary citizens.[41] This generally implies a system of elections in which all citizens have an approximately equal opportunity to participate. Representation of the general population occurs at different levels—by officials elected to public office and by the leaders of the particular legitimate interest groups in society who themselves are the politically active members of the community.[42]

Through all of this, the ideals of popular sovereignty and political equality are still taken as ideal goals to be maximized, but to be brought into the context of observed social reality. This has been described as the basic difference between the British and American concepts of government:

> ...in the U.S. is the strong tradition—which finds no real counterpart in Britain—that "we, the people" are sovereign. With us [the British], sovereignty rests with "the Queen in Parliament" and so long as Parliament is held to be accountable to the people at general elections that is the beginning and end of the formal participation by "the people" in the political process.[43]

Concepts of Political Opposition in Continental Europe: France

As noted above, the British were one of the very few European nations that managed to avoid the establishment of absolute monarchy by developing Parliament as an institutional restraint on the monarchy; in Britain, Parliament as much as the king could claim to embody the will of the nation and a form of opposition was engrained in the system. In much of continental Europe, for example in France, this was not the case: there the king in many cases became absolute in the political and ideological sense. When Louis XIV said, *"L'etat c'est moi,"* he was stating a well-known political reality: the monarchy was the only political institution in France that could claim any real political power. It was immoral and dangerous to oppose his will in any sense.

However, France and other European nations were not so isolated from Britain that their intellectuals could not read the works of Locke and Hobbes and the other British theorists. Taking France as an example of a continental European nation's experience with political opposition, it is clear that France's ancient and medieval traditions were similar to Britain's; only the representative institutions of the Middle Ages had become atrophied through disuse: the king was all-powerful, but scholars could hark back to a past when *parlements* existed. Montesquieu and Voltaire, each important in the French Enlightenment, both lived in England in the early 18th century; their acceptance and reinterpretation of Locke's theories and their admiration of English government became commonly accepted among French intellectuals who opposed the absolutism of the monarchy.[44]

In developing their own concept of representative political opposition the French could not claim to have inalienable rights derived directly from natural law doctrines and an unbroken medieval tradition as could Locke and the English. The French instead resorted to the use of unbridled reason: rather than the rights of Frenchmen, they set up the rights of man as their ideological basis. In a sense the French were forced to fall back on their intellectual prowess: they were not apologists, as was Locke, for a power shift that had already taken place peacefully. The French in order to criticize the monarchy had to preach a wholesale overhaul of the class system and the social order; this in fact took place as a result of the French Revolution.[45]

The French concept as stated by the revolutionaries was a republican one, similar to Jefferson's. It was built upon the contributions of intellectuals, especially of Montesquieu and Rousseau. Montesquieu based his theory on Locke and Harrington, but his central theme was the relativity of laws and institutions as conditioned by experience; he concluded that systems of government (which he classified as republics, monarchies, and despotisms) were the product of historical conditions and the physical environment. Montesquieu believed that the British separation of powers safeguarded the liberty of the people; he proposed, in consequence, the adoption of a system of separation of powers by incorporating legal checks and balances into a constitutional system. The Americans did just this, but the French did not.[46]

Montesquieu's emphasis on environment as a factor in political development led directly into Rousseau's concept of the society being the source and cause of all values. It was Rousseau's belief that all values and rights are received by individuals from the society in which they live. Rousseau's theory was thus a revolt against the rationalism of the earlier philosophers: he denied the ancient and medieval tradition of natural law as a body of moral principles which all right-thinking people could perceive; in its place, he substituted his own concepts, which made rights derivative from particular social arrangements. Rousseau's view was at once narrower (that is, bound to the concept of the community rather than being universal) but closer to empirical reality. His concept of the polity as a social whole was far different from the rationally ordered mechanical view of government and society developed by Hobbes and Locke.

Rousseau's concept of opposition is tied to his theory of politics. In Rousseau's view the ideal community was a small city-state within which all citizens surrendered their individual desires to a "general will." Sovereignty rested with the people and government derived its authority from them; the government was an executive officer designed to execute this "general will." In Rousseau's theory the "general will" represented the collective good of all the citizens; it was his idea that individuals, by consenting to live in a community (which they do by convention and habit, not by rational choice), also consented to live by the wishes of the general populace. According to Rousseau the "general will" was always right and should never be restrained. Rousseau's emphasis on the importance of the intimacy of the group led him to the idea that there could be no representative of the "general will": it had to embody all the individual wills of the society.

Rousseau was thus the father of the two conflicting traditions in French politics: that of the strong man and that of the omnipotent legislature. If the "general will" was always right, whichever body of people or individual which claimed to *represent* the "general will" would have to be unrestrained: this implied the lack of any checks and balances in French government, whether democratic or aristocratic in structure. In a sense, he regarded political criticism and opposition as fundamentally immoral.

Rousseau's concept of the rights and morals of individuals deriving from the community was an inspiration for the later important French contribution to Western concepts of representation which spread throughout Europe in the 19th century and to Asia and Africa in the 20th—the idea of nationalism. This was basically an emotional and romantic sentiment (in contrast to the rationalism of preceding authors) which tied individuals of a common cultural heritage together so that the creation of a "general will" could become possible. In the years following the French Revolution, the "will of the nation" became the overriding appeal throughout Europe.

Transitional States and the Concept of Political Opposition

There are currently a large number of independent countries

in the world which have not directly participated in the development of Western democratic theory. The states of Asia and Africa have developed from a variety of traditional systems—nomadic, village, centralized kingdom—and have produced political forms based on their own respective backgrounds. Many, because of a colonial heritage, have reinterpreted Western political theories to fit their own situations.

Many countries have in the past been governed by urban-based centralized monarchies buttressed by religious sanctions, ruling over an extended rural population. This tradition emphasized the importance of the community being in harmony with the greater cosmos as defined in the religious texts. In such countries there generally exists an emphasis on the need to unite "all the people" as an undifferentiated mass behind the government in the new age of nationalism. Thus, for example, in Indonesia, Burma, and the various African states the concepts of Rousseau (as later reinterpreted in the West by various socialists and other philosophers) have been generally accepted; these countries have concepts of representation which place great emphasis on the community as a harmonious whole giving rise to the government. These countries do not give much weight to the importance of free interaction of competing groups (even in Parliamentary periods); rather, they emphasize a tutelary approach—the people, they argue, must be led into their new representative system of government by that group, as stated in the nationalist ideology, which is best qualified to do the leading. As in traditional times the idea persists that society is hierarchically structured with the leading class rightfully, on the basis of an accepted ideology, determining the direction of the state as a whole. There is no real emphasis or respect given to the concept of free, independent opposition.

In some states, (e.g., Thailand, Ethiopia) the hierarchical view of society has persisted in an extreme form, mainly due to the fact that traditional attitudes here have developed on their own—without the impact of a superimposed colonial experience. Here, political concepts have been stated pretty much in traditional rather than in Western terms—society is still openly viewed as a hierarchy led from the top. Though "popular sovereignty" has been proclaimed, it has had little impact on actual governmental practice; it has rather been a slogan used by those men who overthrew the absolute monarchy (in Thailand) or utilize it (in Ethiopia).

The particular colonial experiences of these countries has had a substantial impact on their respective approaches to opposition. In countries where there has been substantial colonial impact, Western concepts have been brought closer to the people, especially to the leading class. Where the basic principle of colonial administration was to preserve the traditional way of life (e.g., the Dutch in Indonesia), such impact has been minimized.

Nevertheless, it should be emphasized that even in a country such as Indonesia an attempt was made after independence to establish a representative system of government as it was believed to be practiced in the West. A Parliament was created, parties formed, and, eventually, elections held. However, the traditional Indonesian political attitudes which survived Dutch colonialism hindered the full acceptance and understanding of Western political concepts, even though Western institutions had been copied. Thus, even though Indonesia had a Parliament, political parties and elections, there was no clear idea that these were methods of receiving a popular mandate from below to politicians serving as representatives of the people who would elect them. The Indonesian leadership group felt themselves to be qualified for leadership by virtue of their role in the nationalist movement and not because the people elected them. The Indonesian leaders were therefore torn between two sources of thought— their own tradition and that of the West. When what they thought was the Western concept of representative government had failed to operate effectively, the Western institutions were criticized for being out of step with Indonesia's customary way of life. As a result the Indonesian leadership

29

fell back on its traditions and established an autocratic government called "guided democracy." Sukarno personally blamed the West's concept of party ("opposition for opposition's sake") for the problems of his country. The concept of opposition, as it is known in the West, has been a difficult concept for newly independent countries either to understand or to imitate, especially when their traditions and political conditions differ markedly from Western experience. A concept of representation apparently must be a product of conditions that can make representative government possible; these conditions must include the existence of a coherent political society, the absence of absolute dictatorial political power in a single political institution, and the existence of a periodic mandate from the mass of the people to their representatives. These conditions have existed in the West where, on the whole, political theory has not supported the legitimacy of the concentration of absolute political power in one place in the community; there, the whole course of political philosophy has stressed the idea that "the people" are the source of all sovereignty. In Africa and Southeast Asia, this is an idea often stated vocally but rarely understood or put into practice. In these countries the people could not logically have been regarded as sovereign since they still, for the most part, expected to be led by an upper-class elite. A concept of representation apparently cannot exist for long in societies that do not have populations that wish to be "represented." In addition, such a concept will not long be accepted in societies where representative institutions (ostensibly based on the concept of representation) seem to have been a failure in carrying out the tasks of government. However, it should be emphasized that, even with these given differences in political reality and social organization, every country in the world, without exception, still claims to respect some sort of concept of representation and opposition.

Soviet Communism: A Totalitarian Approach to Opposition

Like Germany, the political history of Soviet Russia developed in a manner distinctly different from that of Western Europe. Germany, however, at least had shared in the heritage of Graeco-Roman philosophy and had gone through a medieval period roughly similar to that of Britain and France; German traditional absolutism was a European-style authoritarianism. In prerevolutionary Russia, autocracy and centralized rule could be traced to historic accidents which no Western European country had experienced.

Russian Czarism was in many ways similar to continental European absolutisms in that the monarch was viewed as a semidivine head of state whose will could not be checked by any competing national institution. The Russian system was different in that traditionally and constitutionally the Russian Czar was a total autocrat and there had not existed in Russian history some strong representative institution, like a national court or parliament, which at some time had challenged or shared Czarist political authority.

Between the 13th and 15th centuries, when the rest of Europe saw the emergence of courts, parliaments, and city councils as legitimate representative institutions, Russia was isolated from the rest of Europe and dominated by the Tartars, a Mongol tribe with highly autocratic political practices. Though there did exist several political bodies which have been compared to European representative institutions (there was a Russian Assembly of the Land and a Council of Magnates), these medieval coucils were much weaker than in the rest of Europe and lacked a strong social basis.[48]

The unification of Russia into a modern nation-state was carried out by absolute monarchs like Ivan the Terrible (1533-1584) and later Peter the Great (1682-1725), not by councils or committees which in some way could claim to speak for a "popular will." Though the monarchy did bring important reforms into Russia, at the same it destroyed the weak popular institutions and restricted much private initiative. Thus, the monarch introduced modern technology and industry into Russia, not private entrepreneurs. The Russian noble classes, Western educated and trained, were incorporated into the state bureaucracy and became estranged from, rather than responsible to, the mass of the population. The Russian nobility spoke different languages (French and German) and lived lives completely separate from the life of the average Russian peasant. There was no class in Russia comparable to the British middle class of the 17th century, which could maintain some kind of independent power based on economic activities and could, at the same time, claim to speak for "the people." The powerful groups in Russia were part of a foreign-educated upper class allied to the Czar's government: they did not see the need for appealing to the immobilized and, in a sense, alien and primitive Russian popular will.

Popular revolutionary movements crept into Russia during the 19th century, beginning with the unsuccessful rebellion by the Decembrists against Czar Nicholas I in 1825. The government responded to this attack by instituting as thorough a police state as was possible at the time, including the use of secret police, severe censorship, and the general denial of civil rights. Further underground revolutionary activity followed during the course of the 19th century, maintained mainly by dissatisfied elements within the Russian upper class. However, even though Alexander II instituted several important social reforms (as for example abolishing serfdom, making judges independent of administrative officials, and making jury trials public,[49] the government remained substantially the same form of autocracy. Finally, during the reign of Nicholas II, at the beginning of the 20th century, some concessions were made to the effort to establish popular representative institutions. In 1905, Nicholas allowed the establishment of a Duma, or national representative assembly; this proved to be ineffective as a legislative body but was important as a public forum in which demands for reform could be heard. In essence, the Czarist government retained its autocratic traditions down to the day it was overthrown in March 1917. However, it had allowed the creation of a movement which desired at least some form of popular representation, even if the government had suppressed the achievement of the Western understanding of such representation in practice.

The March Revolution of 1917 ostensibly was carried out for the purposes of overthrowing the Czar and of creating a democratic form of government which would be based on a constitution drawn up by a freely elected assembly responsible to all the people. Moderate leaders thought of the new government as some form of parliamentary republic; more radical groups hoped to establish a government of soviets (councils) which would represent workers, peasants, and soldiers. The more extreme groups led by Lenin and his Bolsheviks finally took over the government in November 1917. Russia had experienced only seven months of "representative government" when the Communists took over the leadership of the state.[50]

Early communist political thought thus developed in the hands of revolutionaries who had little opportunity for actual political experience. These men considered themselves to be socialists and followers of Karl Marx, but they found themselves operating in an environment quite different from the one in which Marx's theory had emerged. They therefore found it necessary to adapt Marx's theories to their own needs.

Marx's political theory was secondary in important respects to his economic theory—Marx was primarily an abstract thinker and ideologist rather than a political organizer. Marx's contribution to Western concepts of democracy and representation lay in his writing, particularly in his criticism of the sham of political democracy in an economic system which allowed for gross inequalities. Marx gave very little interest and attention to actual problems of political organi-

33

zation and administration, gaps in his theory which Russians later filled in.

In Marx's theory, economic organization was the single most important factor determining political organization. Reinterpreting the writings of Hegel, Marx described the evolution of history as a series of class (rather than national) conflicts in which the more progressive class inevitably defeated the less progressive. Class membership was determined by a person's relationship to the ownership of the means of production. In general, Marx saw society as a place where only two classes conflicted at a time: the exploiters, who owned the means of production, vs. the exploited, who, by economic necessity, had to serve the upper class. History, according to this theory, was characterized by the inevitable widening of membership of the ruling class—absolute kings were overthrown by the feudal nobility, feudal barons gave way to bourgeois capitalists, and now, according to Marx, it is inevitable that the proletariat will overthrow the bourgeoisie.

The purpose of the state, or government, in all of this, according to Marx, is to act as an instrument in the hands of the ruling class in its natural class struggle. This is Marx's commentary on Western, particularly 19th century German, practices of political democracy and representation: the bourgeoisie, because it is the ruling class, determines all the mores and practices of society. The capitalists control the schools, the churches, all the media of communication, and all of political life, and in so doing they stamp their values on the whole system—even those they exploit come to accept the capitalist way of looking at things. Thus, a capitalist state—even the most democratic republic characterized by universal direct suffrage and free speech and press—serves the bourgeoisie by keeping the instruments of oppression (the police and the military) in bourgeois hands. No matter which party wins in a capitalist system, the bourgeoisie keeps control—because they have the money to wage successful election campaigns and to publicize their views. Thus, even though the capitalist state was historically a step forward when compared to the feudal state it superseded, it still was not Marx's idea of the ideal state of the future.

Marx's utopian future, which would be achieved when the proletariat overthrew the capitalists, would be characterized by a classless society. Marx saw the revolution of the proletariat as the revolution of the immense majority of the people who, once they took over the state, would through education and the change in value systems (the "dictatorship of the proletariat") do away with the class struggle. Since by definition the state was an instrument of class suppression, the end of the class struggle (by the elimination of classes entirely) would make the state unnecessary. Marx's prediction for the future was therefore "a withering away of the state" and a new system in which all the people would work at what they were best capable of and would receive in return enough to keep them happy. The new society would be characterized by a new culture and new morals, so there would be no need for the state's instruments of violence and suppression—the police and army. This whole theory implied an implicit denial of the possibility of a legitimate system of political representation and opposition as understood in the West. To Marx, as to Rousseau, the ideal system of government was a utopian form of direct democracy in which *every* citizen participated equally. A system of representation, as defined in the West, implied an inevitable leader-follower relationship: politicians were necessary for the direction of the state, though they were bound by their constituents through the election system. To Marx, such a relationship was only a bourgeois fraud foisted on the proletariat: leadership or representation in any form, accompanied by a capitalist economic system, constituted a means by which the bourgeoisie maintained its control over the exploited working classes.[51]

Lenin, though a professed Marxist, was more conscious of the necessity for achieving some form of leadership in a successful revolutionary movement than was Marx. The difference in approach to political thinking between the two can be traced to the different political roles each chose to play: Marx considered himself a spokesman for a revolutionary movement which would inevitably, due to the forces of history, succeed in overthrowing the bourgeois state. To Marx, the Communist party was the most advanced section of the working class, but only because this party could understand the operation of history and could help bring its purposes about. As Marx saw it, the main task of the communists was to educate and persuade the masses to the correct line of thinking; then the success of the proletarian revolution would be assured:

> The Communists . . . are on the other hand, practically, the most advanced and resolute section of the working class parties of every country, that section which pushes forward all others; on the other hand, theoretically, they have over the great mass of the proletariat the advantage of clearly understanding the line of march, the conditions, and the ultimate general results of the proletarian movement.[52]

To Lenin, success in any revolutionary movement depended more on proper organization than on correct thinking and persuasiveness. He accepted Marx's theories of the Communist party's being the advanced section or "vanguard" of the proletariat, but he had no faith in the inevitability of revolutionary success without proper leadership. Thus, Lenin made room in his theory for a Communist party which would act for and symbolize the "will" of its constituents, the working class, but the legitimacy of this party's actions would not be found in some tangible evidence that the working class supported this party, like an open election (an impossibility in prerevolutionary Russia), but in Marxist theory. The Communist party, according to Lenin, was the natural leader because it was most familiar with the purposes of history and, through organization, could best achieve what was best for the proletariat. Communists, coming from all classes including the intelligentsia, were outside the class struggle and were therefore most objective and could bring the masses the most correct interpretations of politics.[53] They could, however, best achieve their status of leadership by following tight principles of organization that Lenin himself stipulated in his tract *What Is To Be Done?*[54]

Lenin's political goals in the early revolutionary period thus led him to reinterpret Marx so that in his view the Communist party would not be composed of the people's "representatives" in the sense of political leaders who could speak for the majority of people because of their ability to persuade them of the correct political course, but by experts who were professionally trained to carry out the purposes of history. Lenin's political organization was not intended to become a mass organization claiming to speak for any popular majority, but a small, tightly organized cadre party which through direction and leadership could undermine the old Czarist regime. This view of political organization later affected Soviet theories of state and government, although much of Marx's assessment of bourgeois democracy was carried over after 1917 as well.

Soviet political ideology after 1917, the date of the establishment of independent communist government, tended to emphasize the weaknesses in "bourgeois"—that is, Western— concepts of democracy and to demonstrate the corresponding strengths of Marxist-Leninist theory. In Soviet parlance, from Lenin to the present day, bourgeois democracy has been labeled as a fraud—much in the same terms Marx himself used so many years earlier.[55]

Similarly, in 1961 a leading Soviet text could declare that "the democratic institutions introduced by the bourgeoisie are of a formal nature and do not really enable the working people to make use of the rights that are proclaimed. . . . Even the most democratic bourgeois state safeguards and sanctifies the capitalist system and private ownership, and suppresses the working people who wage a struggle against it."[56]

In contrast to this false form of democracy, Soviet political ideologists have proposed their own version of "true" democracy—a concept that carries over much of Marx's view with respect to political representation. To Soviet theorists representative government as practiced in the West in parliamentary form is inadequate because it does not allow direct participation in government affairs by all the people. This is because the physical requirements of political participation—press, meeting places, etc.—are not available to everyone equally. The result is that political representatives in the West do not reflect the views of the masses, but only of the ruling classes. In contrast, as proclaimed in the 1961 Draft Program of the Communist Party, "Socialist democracy, unlike bourgeois democracy, does not merely proclaim the rights of the people but makes it really possible for the people to exercise them. . . . Working people take an active part, through the Soviets, trade unions, and other mass organizations, in managing the affairs of state. . . ."[57]

As in Marx's utopian view of a Communist future—a classless society in which *all* citizens will enjoy a form of direct democracy—Soviet theory emphasizes the need for direct participation by all right-thinking people in the government. To this end the Soviet Constitution, on paper, provides for a system of representative government that functions by majority rule, which guarantees civil liberties, provides for universal, equal, and direct suffrage by secret ballot, and allows for an extensive system of accountability by allotting the power of recall to a majority of voters with respect to any elected representative.[58] As in Marx's theory the state is an instrument for spreading the mores and cultural habits of a particular class; in a communist country, true democracy is served because the people learn to become members of one class (through the press, education, communications, etc.) and they learn to contribute directly to government institutions by being in close contact with government bodies. To this end the Soviet theory calls for the abolition of "all the negative features of parliamentarism, especially the separation of legislative and executive powers, the isolation of the representative institutions from the masses. . . ."[59] As direct a form of democracy as possible, not a perfected representative system, is the communist goal in their present stage of the "transition to communism." In this stage it is foreseen that through natural educational processes in the correct environment government will turn more and more into a form of social organization in which the masses will participate "extensively and directly."[60] Obviously this is derived from Marx's theory of the "withering away of the state."

Representation in the Soviet Union is therefore conceived of in entirely different terms than in the West. Since by communist definition a capitalist parliament does not represent the "working people's interests," a common Soviet criticism of Western representative institutions brings up the difference in voting turnout and in the kinds of people elected to each system's respective representative bodies. In Soviet theory, the "best" representative body naturally is elected by as high a proportion of the people as possible and is composed of as many "working people" as possible. In a sense, Soviet theory expects a representative institution to be a miniature picture of communist society at large—as most of the population are workers and peasants, so also should be their representatives. Thus in 1958 Khrushchev noted that in the United States only 57.3% of the people voted in the 1956 American Congressional elections, that only 42.5% voted in 1954, and that in Britain only 26,760,000 out of nearly 35 million voted in the most recent House of Commons elections. His comment was as follows:

> Don't these figures speak for themselves? The voters in those countries see that no matter what representative of the ruling class they elect to Congress or Parliament there will be no change in the state of affairs. It makes no difference whether representatives of the Republican or Democratic Party sit in the United States Congress, they will defend the interests of the ruling classes—the capitalists, bankers, big landowners and big businessmen.[61]

Khrushchev in the same speech went on to note that of 531 American Congressmen in 1958 half were lawyers and 25% were employers and bankers. He cited the fact that even though over 10% of the American population was Negro, only three Negroes sat in Congress, as did only seventeen women. This contrasted with the statistics for the Supreme Soviet were 60% of the candidates were workers and peasants, while the rest represented "the working intelligentsia." In addition, 26.4% of the candidates were women. Khrushchev concluded that in comparison, there were "no real workers in the American Congress":

> The American Congress is actually inaccessible to workers and farmers, to women and to national minorities, who are placed in a position of inequality.
> Here you have the so-called "free world," in which the workers, all the working people, are given the right to vote for this or that representative of the ruling classes, but have no right to take part in the activities of the legislative bodies.[62]

The Soviet approach to representation therefore places great emphasis on the need for a representative body to be as much *like* its constituents as possible. Reflecting the Marxist penchant for direct democracy, Soviet representatives in official state legislative institutions are considered to be one and the same with the people: in a sense, they are not mere representatives, they *are* the people. This contrasts with the leadership function allotted to representatives in traditional Western theory—in the West, a representative was and is supposed to be a political leader bound by his constituents through the free election system. A representative body in the West is supposed to be the arena within which political compromise and conflict take place, with representatives acting for the interests of particular parts of the community; representatives are organized to perform this function through the operation of a party system which nominates candidates, conducts election campaigns, and carries on the government if it wins. Western party systems characteristically claim their legitimate right to perform these functions on the basis of their success in winning popular elections. In the Soviet Union, paraphernalia such as representative institutions and elections have never been confused with the institutions to which the political leadership function has always been reserved—the Communist party. Representative institutions are intended to involve the people with the government and to give them a sense of participation, but behind this facade the Communist party has always remained, following Lenin's original principles, the vanguard or elite cadre of professionals who will make the real political decisions.

The party is conceived of as uniting "the foremost representatives of the working people"[63] while through its proper operations it teaches its ideology, principles and standards to all of society. The goal of the party is to convert every person into a conscious Communist.[64] The admission is made that the party must rely on the working masses and persuade them[65] (a typical concept in Western representational theory), but in the Soviet Union the test of whether the party is expressing the popular will is not really found in the state's elaborate election machinery. The party is still conceived of as the vanguard who proves its skill through its actions. It is claimed that "there is only one way for the party to become a real leader and that is by convincing the masses that it correctly expresses and defends their interests, through its policies, initiative and devotion."[66]

The Soviet state is so organized that the Communist party is given the maximum opportunity to demonstrate its effectiveness as vanguard—rather than any role of mere representative. The aim of almost every communist election on any level is to achieve a unanimous choice behind every candidate. Ballots in the Soviet Union have only one name on them—the communist nominee—and voters may vote only yes or no. To cast a negative ballot a voter must cross out the name, and to do this he must reveal his identity. It would take great courage in the Soviet Union for a citizen either to vote negatively or not to vote at all.[67] Elections are thus just a means for giving people a sense of participation in politics, but political choice and decisions are reserved to those best qualified—Communist party leaders. Communist party members are not "bound" through elections by the masses, but (it is readily admitted) through criticism and self-criticism within the party.[68] The party, it is claimed, must advance the masses in an active way—it cannot "wait passively until reality itself will have taught"[69] them.

Totalitarian Approaches to Political Representation and Opposition

Germany in the 19th century produced several reinterpretations of the Continental concept of representation. Rousseau's mystical attachment to the community was converted by Hegel into a glorification of the nation, or *Volk*. Hegel's mystical *Volksgeist* was defined as a cultural force which dialectically moved the progress of history. In Hegel's concept of the *Volk*, the rights of the individual were completely submerged and the needs of the state were made preeminent. Germany had not had a social revolution like France, and the Germans of this period were more interested in creating and unifying their nation-state than in protecting anything so ephemeral and meaningless as the "rights of man."

Just as the nation swallowed the rights of the individual in Hegel, class swallowed the rights of the individual in Marx. Marx converted the dialectic into a theory of economic determinism—the theory that the proletariat will inevitably overthrow the capitalists that exploit them. Marx viewed Western institutions of representation as just so many "myths" created by the bourgeoisie to keep the masses subordinate and loyal. However, Marx was sure that the inevitable takeover by the proletariat would represent the will of the majority.

Marx and Hegel therefore had no clear concepts of representation themselves, but Lenin and Hitler in their respective theories of communism and national socialism reinterpreted the ideas of the former two. Lenin incorporated into communism the theory of the "vanguard," i.e., the Communist party: as it comprised the most capable and progressive elements of the proletariat, it was to be given the responsibility of directing the revolution. The party was an elite or cadre, in no way accountable to any large mass of people, but merely aiding the inevitable course of history. Lenin was not so much concerned with winning popular support as he was interested in developing an efficient organization under his complete centralized control which would be capable of seizing and maintaining power. In a sense this party would represent the mythical "will of the proletariat"; however, the same party was also supposed to create and manipulate the proletarian "will" so that it would be in step with the inevitable course of history. Lenin's party therefore represented, in his theory, what was good for the people and what was inevitable in history: its ideological support was to be found in the mystical workings of the Marxian dialectic. There was never, in Lenin, an appreciation of the legitimate role of opposition in a state.

The German National Socialists in similar fashion made use of the theories of Hegel, along with other writers such as Nietzsche and Sorel, to develop their concept of elite "representation." The Nazi regime, unlike the communist, was professedly antirational: it glorified the *will* of the nation and sought to harness it for active adventurous purposes. The concept was based on the myth of racial superiority—a reinterpretation of Hegel's *Volk*.

As in communist theory the Nazi concept submerged the individual, but into the mass of the *Volk* rather than into his class; the Nazis, again like the communists, established the ideological basis for leadership by a minority—especially their single "Leader." The mystical folk was seen as having a will, but no brains; the function of the leader and his elite corps was to manipulate this popular will for the benefit of the nation which only they, because of Darwinianlike processes of natural selection, could perceive. Both Lenin and Hitler attacked the Western parliamentary system: both intended to establish elite rule.

In the Nazi and communist theories of government, leadership transcends and overpowers representation.[70] The Germans claimed that they had achieved representation because the will of the people was personified in the leader, who felt himself to be one with the people. In both theories, similar to concepts found in many contemporary developing states, the claim is made of the necessity for popular participation, but the leader (like the Communist party in Russia) was in no way to be held accountable to the masses for his action. The leader was supposed to be, in Max Weber's terms, charismatic:

> Charisma knows only inner determination and inner restraint. The holder of charisma seizes the task that is adequate for him and demands obedience and a following by virtue of his mission. His success determines whether he finds them. . . . he does not derive his "right" from their will, in the manner of an election. Rather, the reverse holds: it is the *duty* of those to whom he addresses his mission to recognize him as their charismatically qualified leader.[71]

Plan of the Book

This volume presents a series of essays on the nature and results of political opposition in a number of contemporary political systems. While all the states draw on a similar theoretical heritage, they evidence important differences both in political structure and in the levels of formal and informal opposition.

The states are arranged not according to region or political structure but in terms of opposition. The book begins with states where political opposition is highly fragmented

(France, Argentina, India), then covers states with moderate political opposition (Chile, Japan, West Germany, the United States), and ends with states where the level of opposition is apparently quite low (Tanzania, Great Britain, the USSR). The concluding chapter is an attempt to compare the various systems of opposition using a comprehensive theoretical framework.

Notes

1. Wallbank TW, Taylor AM: *Civilization Past and Present*. Chicago, Scott, Foresman and Co., 1954, p 128.

2. Ibid., p 131. Wallbank and Taylor note that the city-states "tended to follow a general political pattern in their evolution, though with numerous variations. Power passed by stages from the hands of the clan king to those of the leading families, and finally to the citizens as a whole." (p 131.)

3. Taylor AE: *Aristotle*. New York, Dover, 1955, p 104. (See also Aristotle: *Politics*. Book VII. Jowett tr. New York, Viking Press, 1952.)

4. McIlwain CH: *Constitutionalism, Ancient and Modern*. Ithaca, Great Seal Books, 1958, Ch 1.

5. Plato: *The Republic*. Book VIII. Jowett, tr. New York, Random House; Aristotle: *Politics*. Book III.

6. Plato, *The Republic*. Book IV. Jowett, tr. New York, Random House.

7. Sabine G: *A History of Political Theory*. Ithaca, Cornell University Press, 1955, pp 77-80.

8. Taylor AE: op. cit., p 104; also Aristotle: *Politics*. Book VII, op. cit.

9. Aristotle, op. cit., p 109.

10. Wallbank and Taylor, op. cit. p 161.

11. Ibid.

12. Polybius (204-122 B.C.), a Greek author living at the height of the Roman Republic, represented the views of Panaetius and the Middle Stoa. He did not add very much to the constitutional theory of Aristotle: for his as for the earlier Greeks the unit of political life was still the city-state. However, in his attempt to explain and analyze the greatness of Rome, he did provide a somewhat different outlook on the analysis of government. Polybius recognized that the evolution of one form of state into another was a disease of the Greek city-state. He

believed the "mixed constitution" of Rome, which he said allowed for the representation of monarchical, aristocratic, and democratic elements, had enabled Rome to avoid the destructive cycles of change which had been the experience of the simpler Greek city state. For this achievement he believed that Rome deserved world dominion. See Sabine.

13. Cicero, op. cit., p 76.
14. Sabine, op. cit., p 51.
15. McIlwain, op. cit., p 54.
16. Cicero, op. cit., entire especially pp 21, 22, 32-34, 47-50, 52, 62, 76, 81, 89, 105-269.
17. Strong CF: *Modern Political Constitutions.* London, Sidgwick and Jackson Ltd., 1958, p 19.
18. Ibid., pp 20-21.
19. Sabine, op. cit., p 199.
20. Lewis E: *Medieval Political Ideas.* Vol I. London, Routledge and Paul, 1954, Ch 1.
21. Sabine, op. cit., p 215.
22. Ibid., pp 218-219.
23. See, in particular, the theories of Marsiglio of Padua in Lewis, op. cit., Vol I, Ch 5; see also D'Entreves AP: *The Medieval Contribution to Political Thought.* London, Oxford University Press, 1939, Ch III, IV. Also, the views of conciliarists, such as William of Occam, John of Paris, Pierre D'Ailly, Jean Gerson, and Nicholas of Cusa. See Sabine, Ch XVI; Lewis, Vol II Ch 1, also Coker FW: *Readings in Political Philosophy.* New York, Macmillan Company, 1942, pp 257-273.
24. Chrimes SB: *English Constitutional History.* London, Oxford University Press, 1953, p 69.
25. Ibid., p 109.
26. Sabine, op. cit., p 222.
27. An obvious example of the Tudor use of Parliament can be found in their ecclesiastical policy, i.e., they broke away from the Roman Church and set up their own through the passage of laws through Parliament.
28. McIlwain, op. cit., Ch IV.
29. For a more extensive treatment of Hobbes' theory of representation, utilizing the techniques of linguistic analysis, see Pitkin, H: "Hobbes's Concept of Representation," I and II, *American Political Science Review,* June, 1964 pp 328-340; December, 1964, pp 902-918.
30. Harrington J: *Oceana,* quoted in Coker, op. cit., pp 500-522.
31. Sabine, op. cit., pp 523-540.
32. Locke, J: Book II of the *Two Treatises of Government* (second treatise), quoted in Coker, op. cit., p 552-576. Much of Locke's theory

was incorporated into the final British statement of the supremacy of Parliament in this period, the Bill of Rights of 1689. In a sense it was this document that established the legitimacy of the modern British constitutional monarchy. Among its provisions were the following:

1. The pretended power of suspending of laws, or the execution of laws, by regal authority, without consent of Parliament is illegal.
2. It is the right of subjects to petition the king.
3. Election of members to Parliament ought to be free.
4. Freedom of speech, and debates or proceedings in Parliament, ought not to be impeached or questioned in any court or place out of Parliament.
5. For the redress of all grievances, and for the amending, strengthening, and preserving of the laws, Parliaments ought to be held frequently.

It is noteworthy that the Bill of Rights was issued by the House of Commons using as a base for its legitimacy, its being "pursuant to their respective letters and elections, being now assembled in a full and free representative of this nation."

The whole text of the *Bill of Rights* is in Stearns ES: *Pageant of Europe.* New York, Harcourt, Brace, 1948, pp 235-237.

33. Hamilton, Madison, Jay: *The Federalist Papers.* New York: Mentor Book, New York, 1961.

34. Dahl, op. cit., Ch 1; see *The Federalist Papers, #10 on representation* in a federal system as a brake on the excesses of democracy, pp 81-83.

35. Jefferson T: "Cabinet Opinion, April 28, 1793," *The Political Writings of Thomas Jefferson.* New York, Liberal Arts Press, 1955, p 79. Jefferson wrote:

I consider the people who constitute a society or nation as the source of all authority in that nation; as free to transact their common concerns by any agents they think proper; to change these agents individually or the organization of them in form or function whenever they please; that all the acts done by these agents under the authority of the nation are the acts of the nation, are obligatory on them and enure to their use, and can in no wise be annulled or affected by any change in the form of government, or of the persons administering it.

36. De Toqueville A: *Democracy in America.* Vol I. New York, Vintage Books, 1960, p 269ff. Toqueville notes: "In the United States the omnipotence of the majority, which is favorable to the legal despotism of the legislature, likewise favors the arbitrary authority of

the magistrate. The majority has absolute power both to make laws and to watch over their execution; and as it has equal authority over those who are in power and the community at large, it considers public officers as its passive agents and readily confides to them the task of carrying out its designs." (p 272).

37. For a discussion of the arguments, pro and con, on the issue of property qualifications for voters in the United States see Grimes AP: *American Political Thought*. New York, Holt, Rinehart and Winston, 1960, pp 175-184. It should of course be pointed out that even the populist theory never meant the end of all qualifications for voting. Democratic theory always supposed an informed mature citizenry and both the United States and Britain have, down to modern times, maintained prerequisites for voting based on age, literacy, residence, and the like. These qualifications are not, in this study, considered central to the general concept of a theory of representation; the focus is rather on the concepts governing the adult mass of the population.

38. "The Populist Party Protests," (text of the 1892 Populist Party Platform), in Craven, Johnson, Dunn: *A Documentary History of the American People*. Boston, Ginn and Company, 1951, pp 553-556.

39. Bentley A: *The Progress of Government*. Chicago, University of Chicago Press, 1908. Bentley called the majority will, or "public interest," a "spook."

40. Dahl, op. cit., Ch 3.

41. Ibid., p 3.

42. Dahl R, Lindblom C: *Politics, Economics and Welfare*. New York, Harper and Brothers, 1953, pp 313-314.

43. McKenzie R: "Picking the President." *The Observer*, London, November 1, 1964, pp 14-15.

44. Sabine, op. cit., p 546.

45. Ibid., p 549.

46. Ibid., p 557, and Rousseau JJ: *The Social Contract*. Chicago, Henry Regnery Co., 1954, pp 33-34.

47. Sukarno: "For Liberty and Justice." Speech before the Council for World Affairs, Los Angeles, April 21, 1961 (mimeo.).

48. Ulman AB: "The Russian political system." Beer SH et al: *Patterns of Government*. New York, 1962, pp 603-610.

49. Towster J: "The Soviet Orbit. Union of Soviet Socialist Republics." Cole T: *European Political Systems*. New York, Alfred A. Knopf, 1961, p 55.

50. Meyer AG: *The Soviet Political System*. New York, Random House, 1965, pp 31-35.

51. For Marx's political theories see Marx K, Engels F: "The Communist Manifesto." *Capital and Other Writings*. New York, Modern Library, 1932; also "Critique of the Gotha Program." *The Communist*

Blueprint for the Future, the Complete Text of all Four Communist Manifestoes, 1848-1961. New York, E. P. Dutton, 1962. In the latter, Marx notes (p 79): "A bourgeois republic, even the most democratic, sanctified by such watchwords as 'will of the people'. . . remains in fact, owing to the existence of private property in land and other means of production, the dictatorship of the bourgeoisie, and instrument for exploitation and oppression of the broad masses of workers by a small group of capitalists."

52. From "The Communist Manifesto" (1948). *The Communist Blueprint for the Future*, op. cit., p 23.

53. See for example, Lenin VI: *What Is to Be Done?.* London, Oxford at the Clarendon Press, 1963, pp 62-63, where he says: ". . . the workers could not yet possess Social Democratic consciousness. This consciousness could only be brought to them from the outside. . . . The teaching of Socialism . . . has grown out of the philosophical, historical, and economic theories that were worked out by the educated representatives of the propertied classes-the intelligentsia."

54. Ibid., p 144.

55. Lenin VI: "Democracy and Dictatorship" (December 23, 1918). *On Soviet Socialist Democracy.* Moscow, Foreign Languages Publishing House, p 170.

56. Kuusinen O: *Fundamentals of Marxism-Leninism.* London, Lawrence and Wishart, 1961, pp 195-196.

57. *The Communist Blueprint for the Future*, op. cit., p 115.

58. Meyer AG: *The Soviet Political System.* New York, Random House, 1965, pp 97-104, Ch IV.

59. "Program of the All-Russian Communist Party (Bolsheviks)" (1919). *The Communist Blueprint for the Future*, op. cit., p 81. This idea was rephrased by Khrushchev in a speech to a meeting of electors, Kalinin Constituency, Moscow, on March 14, 1958, when he said: "The strength and merit of our socialist democracy consists not only in the fact that the people themselves take a direct part in determining the composition of the legislative bodies, but also in the fact that all the activities of our state bodies serve the interests of the people." See Khruschev NS: *For Peaceful Victory in Peaceful Competition with Capitalism.* New York, E. P. Dutton, 1960, p 169.

60. "1961 Draft Program of the Communist Party." *The Communist Blueprint for the Future*, op. cit., p 193. This document gives an extensive discussion of what Soviet ideologists conceive to be necessary for the ideal form of democracy they seek to achieve, including improved accountability, publicity, and local self-government. See ibid., p 194.

61. Khrushchev, op. cit., pp 167-168.

62. Ibid., p 168.

63. "1961 Draft Program of the Communist Party," *The Communist Blueprint for the Future*, op. cit., p 224.

64. Kuusinen, op cit., p 846.

65. Ibid., p 647.

66. Ibid., pp 418-419.

67. Meyer, op. cit., p 270.

68. Kuusinen, op. cit., pp 647-648. Party responsibility is a particularly crucial concept in current Russian writings, partly as reaction to the dictatorial methods of Stalin's regime. Though the party still conceives itself as a vanguard governed internally by principles of democratic centralism, great efforts have been made to criticize Stalin's "cult of personality" and to prevent its reemergence. Measures of intraparty democracy have been introduced allowing, on paper, greater freedom of discussion among rank and file members. However, this is an aspect of intraparty evolution—not of the official state representative bodies.

69. Ibid., p 428.

70. Barker E: *Reflections on Government*. New York, Oxford University Press, 1958, p 375.

71. Max Weber, "The Sociology of Charismatic Authority." Gerth, Mills: *From Max Weber*. New York, Oxford University Press, 1958, pp 246-247.

2

Oppositions in France

Roy C. Macridis
Brandeis University

For a variety of reasons, recurrent "oppositions" to all governments and diffuse and pervasive protest against all political regimes and the various constitutions, ranging from disobedience and violence to outright rebellion (verging occasionally upon revolution), have characterized French political history since 1789. To analyze the characteristics of "opposition" therefore is tantamount to attempting an anatomy of the French polity and of power relations associated with it. What is more, the forms of incitement, violence, protests, and opposition have not changed significantly throughout the years. We find an overlap rather than a developmental pattern.

If one were to take "opposition" for what it traditionally means—an organized and structured attempt to replace a government according to certain rules, parliamentary or other—then Grosser's apt characterization "nothing but opposition" obviously doesn't adequately cover the situation.[1] Even if we were to limit ourselves to the French legislative assemblies, "nothing but oppositions" would have been a better characterization. In fact, oppositions not only to governments and policies but to regimes have been formed, dissolved, and reformed in a kaleidoscopic fashion. Not even the venerable distinction between Left and Right can provide us with an orderly way of studying the phenomenon. For

51

instance in the Fourth Republic Communists and Gaullists were against the Constitution and for drastic (though not of course the same) reforms. Communists and Gaullists were also against the EDC. In the same period of time (1946-58) 20 registered or potential "oppositions" accounted for as many cabinet crises. "Opposition" came from every possible combination of political parties, with the Communist Party frequently acting as a pole that was joined in the most promiscuous manner by virtually all the other parties.

It is the purpose of this essay to outline the major forms of oppositions in French political history in the Fourth Republic, relate them to the changing social and political circumstances and arrangements of the Fifth Republic, and provide some hypotheses about the likely course of developments and, relatedly, the likely manifestations and forms of oppositions in the future.

I

The Fourth Republic was born in violence and conceived in opposition. The Resistance movement had exacerbated the latent Jacobin traits of the French political tradition. Primitive violence in the form of vendettas and the settling of long debts and accounts developed side by side with retributions by the collectivity against real or imaginary collaborationists. The possibility of a Paris Commune was averted narrowly thanks to the desperate efforts of the Gaullists. When the latter gained the upper hand, the oppositions began to manifest themselves. The first draft of the Constitution, giving virtually all powers to a unicameral assembly, was rejected. The oppositions won. The second draft providing some modifications in favor of a senate and a somewhat reinforced executive was accepted by default. Only about 35% of the registered voters voted for it. The oppositions were prominent. The conflict over the nature of the regime was born at the very time when a Republican Constitution was put into force. It has yet to cease. Here then is the first observation about the nature of the French oppositions. They relate to the regime. The phenomenon of course was not limited to the Fourth Republic and the post World War II period with which we are primarily concerned. The Third Republic was founded in order to shelter the aspirations of the monarchists; the first president had planned to step down in favor of the pretender; sizeable numbers of die-hard catholic groups rejected it only to rally grudgingly; General Boulanger attacked the Constitution and for a period of time it was believed that he might succeed in toppling it; after the "sacred union" of World War I right-wing *ligues* and the Communists mounted the barricades against it and against each other. The margin of compromise became thinner and thinner as the crisis about the regime and the Constitution mounted. Under the Fourth Republic the Bayeux speech became the Magna Carta of Gaullist revisionism. But Lèon Blum in his *For All Mankind* had also endorsed the idea of strong executive leadership, even of presidential government. The last-minute combination of Communists, MRP, and Socialists in support of the Constitution of the Fourth Republic produced only a minority of the registered vorters. *The majority was again the opposition.* But both majority and minority were internally divided.

It is in the internal division of each and every opposition that one finds the second characteristic of French polity. "Majorities" and "minorities" are internally divided: MRP, Socialists, and Communists founded the Fourth Republic. Within six months, despite the persistence of the Gaullist threat, they were at each other's throats and the Communists were ejected from the government to enter into virtually permanent opposition. By 1953 the Socialists were ready to take the "cure of opposition." In the meantime, the Gaullists had entered Parliament—120 strong—*in opposition.* In fact the array of oppositions was so formidable that the so-called Third Force was nothing else but an adventitious combination of forces formed *in opposition* to the opposition, i.e., to

53

the Gaullists and Communists. Herein lies the third character-istic of French opposition(s). Governments under the Fourth Republic were very often founded to stave off the opposi-tion—opposition real or imaginary. Virtually all governments roughly between 1947 and 1953 were "oppositional" govern-ments. They represented an unsteady coalition of forces that had one and virtually only one thing in common—to stave off the Gaullists and the Communists or, when the Gaullists rallied to a governmental majority, the Communists and their left-wing supporters—including often the Socialists but even right-wing groups.

Here we may then find the fourth trait of French opposi-tion(s). The term negative majority is used to indicate the existence of a numerical combination of forces—usually in a representative assembly, but it can be broadened to apply also to the electorate—that is *against* a government or a policy or the regime but can never be *for* an alternative government, policy, or regime. It was the negative majority (but in fact a negative minority of the registered voters) that was responsible for the adoption of the Constitution of the Fourth Republic. Throughout the Fourth Republic a poten-tially negative majority was ever present in the National Assembly. It averaged between 245 to some 300 deputies out of a total of some 625. Depending on the changing attitudes of the "Algerian deputies" and the position of the Socialists, sometimes the negative majority exceeded the governmental one. Only in the very brief period when Pierre Méndès-France was in power—certainly only during his first two months in office—was there a solid majority for his government. It dissipated. It was a negative majority that overthrew him. Another one overthrew Edgar Faure nine months later.

A corollary to negative majorities is then that of a "nega-tive government"—a topic to which very little attention has been paid as yet. By this I mean something that underlines the oppositional character of the French polity—a govern-ment founded upon multiple *internal* oppositions and surviv-ing only as long as the oppositional forces that surround it

54

appear to be numerically either potentially or actually stronger. This was typically the case of the Third Force roughly between 1948 and 1952. The Gaullist popular appeal was reaching a dangerous crest only comparable to the solidity of the Communist Party. Between them they could command more than half the electoral vote. In the elections of 1951, for instance, the two parties together received over 10 million votes out of a total of some 19 million cast. In 1956 more than 9 million out of some 21 million ballots cast were "oppositional"—Communists, Poujadists, Gaullists. If we take the governments formed between 1951 and the end of the Fourth Republic we shall find the following "oppositional" combinations that accounted either directly or indirectly both for their formations and fall. In almost all cases, the majorities for formation and for overthrow were "negative."

The Pleven cabinet in August, 1951, was endorsed by 390 votes and 222 votes against. The "majority" included some 90 MRP deputies and some of the moderates. They shifted their votes and the cabinet fell. In January, 1953, Rène Meyer was endorsed by 389 votes with 205 (Socialists and Communists) voting against. MRP, Radicals, the USDR, the Independents and Peasants and the Gaullists voted for. Within five months the cabinet fell. To the Communist and Socialist votes, the Gaullist and a few extra votes were added to account for a negative majority of 328. In June, 1953, the Laniel ministry was endorsed with 398 against 206 (Communists and Socialists). Radicals, USDR, MRP, Gaullists, Independents and Peasants voted for. Within a year the cabinet fell. To the Communists and Socialists the bulk of the Radicals and "Gaullists" was added, accounting for 306 votes against the cabinet.

The composition and decomposition of Pierre Méndès-France's cabinet is illustrative. As Table 2.1 shows, he was endorsed by one of the highest votes ever cast for any government—419 votes for, 47 against. All parties including Socialist and Communist voted for. Within about eight

55

months the negative character of the coalition that supported
him became translated into a negative opposition—the

TABLE 2.1: The Vote For Mendes-France

Party	For	Against	Abstaining	Not Voting	Absent
Communists	95				
Progressives	4				
Socialists	104			1	
Radicals	72		3		1
UDSR	19		3	2	
MRP	10	1	74	2	1
Indépendants d'Outre-Mer	15				
Gaullists	64	13	28	2	1
Independents	12	14	25	1	1
Independent Peasants	4	15	7	1	
Peasants	13	4	3	2	
Not Affiliated	7			1	1
TOTAL	419	47	143	12	5

Table 2.2: The Vote Against Mendes-France

Party	For	Against	Abstaining	Not Voting
Communists and Progressives		98		
Socialists	105			
Radicals	52	20	2	2
USDR	18	4	1	
Indépendants d'Outre-Mer	16			
Gaullists	50	44	9	1
MRP	5	73	5	1
Independents	12	40	3	
Independent Peasants	3	21	3	1
Peasants	2	16	3	1
Not Affiliated	10	3	1	
TOTAL	273	319	27	6

Communist Party, virtually all of the MRP, a part of the Radicals, and many of the Independents turned against him on the question of confidence.

Table 2.3: The Vote on the EDC

Parties	Number	Against	For	Ab-staining	Not Voting
Communists	95	95			
Progressives	4	4			
Socialists	105	53	50	1	1
Radical-Socialists	76	34	33	2	7
UDSR	24	10	8	1	5
MRP	86	2	80	4	
Indépendants d'Outre-Mer	15	3	11		1
Independents	54	12	36	1	5
Independent Peasants	27	6	20		1
Peasants	22	10	9		3
Gaullists	106	83	16	2	5
Not Affiliated	12	7	1	1	3
TOTAL	626	319	264	12	31

Every single party in the Fourth Republic was at times a government party and at times an opposition party.[3] In the former capacity it participated in a government and sustained it for a given period of time and in the latter it overthrew it.

Thus far I have identified the following general traits: opposition(s) to the regime; opposition(s) to governments; governments based on a coalition of opposing forces against a similar coalition either in Parliament or in the electorate. I have indicated that the pervasive element of French parliamentary politics was that of opposition(s) to a government or by a government. I have pointed out that the adventitious coalition of opposing forces that founded a government dissolved into its component parts bringing the government down. France under the Fourth Republic was not a multiparty polity; it was a multioppositional one. If one were to align parties and issues, the multioppositional character of the polity becomes apparent:

Economic Liberalism

For: *Radicals*
Independents
"Gaullists"
MRP

Against: *Radicals*
MRP
"Gaullists"
Communists
Socialists

Continuation of War in Indochina

For: *Radicals*
Gaullists
Independents
MRP

Against: Communists
Socialists
Radicals
MRP

Continuation of War in Algeria
(Algerie Francaise)

For: *Radicals*
MRP
Gaullists
Socialists
Independents

Against: *Radicals*
MRP
Gaullists
Socialists
Communists

Subsidy to Catholic Schools

For: Gaullists
MRP
Independents
Radicals

Against: Communists
Socialists
Radicals

European Unity with Supranational Powers

For: MRP
Socialists
Radicals
Independents

Against: Communists
Gaullists

European Defense Community

For: MRP
Socialists
Radicals
Independents

Against: Communists
Gaullists
Socialists
Radicals
Independents

Common Market

For: Socialists   Against: Communists
     MRP   Gaullists
     Radicals   *Radicals*
     Independents   *Independents*

The lack of any stable coalitions as depicted above shows simply, and I must confess, quite crudely that (a) the same party divided on a given issue; (b) that the party alignments for and against constantly shift depending upon the issue; and (c) that finally the alignment for or against consists of a convergence of groups and votes that may not repeat itself—it lacks coherence and predictability.

II

A number of explanations have been offered to account for the configuration of oppositions in the French polity under the Fourth Republic and earlier. Some are ideological; others are institutional; still others relate to the pattern and rate of economic development of the French society. No overall explanatory generalization can be easily produced that accounts for their multiplicity, their lack of internal coherence, and, what is more, the persistence of similar forms and modes of expression that opposition has taken. Not only oppositions in Parliament have had identical political and structural traits. Popular uprisings, violent manifestations, coup d'etats, and organized violence have also continued to manifest themselves. "Communes" were formed in some towns during the recent uprisings of students and workers; the farmers blocked the highways with beets; the generals have risen against all Republics including the Fifth; as late as 1962 the government was defeated by a majority of votes that had all the earmarks of a negative majority. It is generally conceded that one of the reasons De Gaulle was forced to dissolve the National Assembly and call for an election in

59

1968 was that the Independent Republicans under Giscard d'Estaing were ready to bolt the Gaullist majority and vote the motion of censure. In April, 1968, 53% of the electorate defeated De Gaulle's constitutional revision. In the same year a "negative majority" of registered voters abstained or voted against the second President of the Republic, Georges Pompidou.

Despite its apparent stability, the Fifth Republic has experienced virtually every known form of protest, violence, and oppositions reminiscent of the past. The French system reproduces the same forms and manifestations of violence, protest, and opposition with the same virulence. France's history has been rewritten in this sense in the last 12 years.

The ideological explanations go too far and say too little. They describe the phenomenon instead of explaining it. The French are divided in ideological families and the persistence of ideology even when it became a matter of style and form rather than substance is unparalleled in any political system. Ideologies divided sharply; with division comes a breakdown of the fragile bonds on which the system rests. The result is violence. In the thirites or after the Communist Party was ousted from the government between 1947 and 1950—in the year or two before De Gaulle returned to power—France was either in a state of or on the brink of violence. The lines become drawn and the political families resume the ideological war that has never ceased since the French Revolution. Sometimes revolutions or uprisings ensue— witness 1830, 1848, 1870; sometimes a quick settlement follows when a particular grouping of ideological families gains the upper hand—witness 1801, 1851, 1940; sometimes it is a draw—as was the case with 1875 and 1946: the antagonisms are temporarily subdued; they remain in a state of latency. Why this tenacity of ideologies and why do they persist with such virulence in France? No answer is offered.

Another hypothesis is given by those who follow Crozier's analysis,[4] notably Stanley Hoffmann. The French have never come to terms with two of the most generalized aspects of political life: cooperative and associative action and an agreement on a Constitution. Unable to develop grass-roots participatory arrangements, they delegate decision making to higher administrative or political organs—the civil service or the "government" in Paris on condition that the scope of action of such organs remain highly circumscribed. Limitations amount to the protection of the most cherished values of French culture—the individual and individualism. The *citoyen* is dressed *contre l'Etat* in a permanently defiant posture. But the sharp separation between the state and the individual presupposes, in the land of Rousseau, a lack of communitarian values and institutions. Occasionally the quest for community, the yearning for togetherness, overcomes the barriers of individualism. Once in a while, then, the French celebrate with canon and barricade rather than dance the Fourteenth of July. A cleansing breeze of egalitarianism and community rejuvenates the France of *Alain* and *Candide.* This is the basic thesis that some have used to explain the events of May-June 1968.[5] It was the jubilation of the *pays rèel* against the *pays légal.* French men and women were rebelling against the traditional role of citizen in which they had cast themselves for so long and reached out beyond their fences.

The institutional explanation is simpler. Political institutions have legitimized only a temporary state of compromise —they have never legitimized compromise itself. All regimes have represented a temporary victory over a grudging acquiescence. Their performance and their operation have never been fully accepted and their symbolisms and roles internalized by ideological families or by the French citizens. Born always in precarious circumstances, they live a precarious and often short life. To every institutional arrangement that France has experienced ever since the Revolution, two sets of forces were latently or overtly opposed. The first was the pervasive and ever-present force alluded above—that of distrust in the name of individualism. The government—any government; the regime—any regime, was a potential danger. The second involved the ideological families that either in terms of deep-set beliefs or style could not compromise with a given regime or a given government. Catholics, workers, middle classes, farmers, small merchants and artisans, the military, the industrialists found themselves occasionally included or excluded. What matters is that there were always (or so it was perceived) some excluded groups ready to translate their sense of exclusion into opposition and action. Compromise solutions were often reached—as was the case with the Third and the Fourth Republics. But the compromise could not prove viable, and the institutions reflecting it were rejected. This accounts for the Petain regime but more particularly for the return of General De Gaulle in 1958.

We must push our effort further in order to find a more general explanation. Protest and opposition is only the other side of the coin of legitimacy and consensus. It is the lack of the latter that accounts for the former. A "purely" historical explanation might give us the key to the understanding of the French polity. In England when the Industrial Revolution spawned new social groups and classes and produced conflicts, the regime had been fully established. That violence and protest and opposition were rampant throughout the 19th century, as Tilly reminds us, is indisputable.[6] But in the last analysis none of these seriously affected the regime. In fact, the regime was able to develop institutions and governmental services that seemed to most citizens to be appropriate instruments for the satisfaction of wants and interests. Gradually, and to be sure grudgingly, the system became an instrument of the many. They came into the system. It was their own to influence, to hold, and to use. Even as violence occasionally erupted, opposition was channeled along instrumental lines. It became organized, structured, and respected. It revolved around issues rather than the regime; it sought solutions within the regime rather than a recasting of the whole. The lines between violence, revolution, and opposition therefore were clearly drawn. The latter replaced the former. Opposition became a medium that sought new or alternative solutions within a preestablished and agreed-upon frame of rules.

History in France took a different course. Not only the industrial revolution came upon France at a time when no political regime had been fully established, but it also "dragged"—its rate was until War II far behind that of England, Germany, the United States, Japan, and Russia. The lateness and sluggishness of the Industrial Revolution, I think, account for the lack of legitimacy and consensus and for the persistence of diffuse opposition and violence. They further account for the coexistence of so many forms of opposition in France—ranging from violence and revolution to electoral and parliamentary opposition, and for the inability of the French to distinguish clearly between the three. The "regimes" after the end of the Empire reflected a shifting balance of forces in French society. They were the creatures of some combinations never the instrument of the body politic. And as the various combinations of forces alternated throughout the 19th and 20th centuries, each and all of them remained diffident and hostile not only to each other but to the state. The fact that they sought to control it, and occasionally did, made them warier as their opponents could well do the same! What is a potential enemy can never be a trusted and accepted instrument for the expression of one's wishes or interests. Hence the state should be limited. The more the various forces failed to control the state the greater their diffidence to it. A diffident posture on the part of every individual and group became the best protection for all. This has nothing to do with a laissez-faire philosophy or economic individualism which never played a very significant part in French political ideology. In the last analysis economic individualism is based on indifference to the state and on a healthy skepticism of its creative role. French individualism on the contrary was born out of a deep fear of the state and a sober understanding of its immense powers. It was shared by those who used it and those who suffered it—and virtually every group of the French society had a taste of both. Characteristically enough few are the political ideologies in France that concede much to the state—syndicalism and anarchism wish to do away with it; the Catholic ideology of the right or the left sidestep basic issues about politics and the authority of the state; Marxism and socialism strive to wipe it out—ultimately; radicalism is the philosophy of diffidence and protection. Only the Napoleonic tradition extols it, but only when the state has become identified with the Charisma of one man. *Étatism* is more an administrative tradition of performance and efficiency than an all-encompassing ideology about the legitimate role and normative scope of state action. Throughout the 19th century one shall vainly search for the counterpart of T. H. Green or Bosanquet in French political thought. Thus individualism is a reaction against a deeper understanding of the authority of the state and a fear of it. All Frenchmen—even if they have not read the Contrat Social—find in individualism the only possible protection against the general will! The moment the state grows, the individual begins to feel restive. *Ecrasez l'infame* should have been the appropriate slogan of the May-June events of 1968, addressed this time against the Gaullist state.

The lack of organic links between the individual and the state—between the local community and the central authority, between associations of citizens and interests and the administration—protects each and all groups and each and all citizens against the danger that an authoritarian state embodies. It is a trait born out of the long experience of the Ancient Regime and of the 19th-century French political history. It is only one of many manifestations of latent opposition against the state. The others are all ready-made in the political laboratory of the French political history. As industrial development sagged—allowing groups and interests to live long and encrust themselves like living fossils within the society—opposition continued to manifest itself through traditional forms even when times had radically changed. The coup d'etat, the jacquerie, the barricade, the mob violence, terrorism, passive resistance, direct confrontation with the law enforcement agents—all continued to live side by side with party organization, elections, and parliamentary votes. Nor could a given particular form of opposition be exclusively associated with a given group. On the contrary, each and all groups were willing to borrow from the arsenals of the others. Army officers have indulged in coups d'etat, in the OAS, in political organization, and in the more orthodox, even if less dignified for officers, elections and opposition in parliament; only recently the truckers showed they had learned from the peasants. If the latter could use their produce to obstruct their trucks, the truckers can use their machines in turn to obstruct everybody! Every group in France hides Sorelian thoughts of direct action. Despite Marx every French worker remains a syndicalist at heart.

III

The Fifth Republic, like the Fourth, came into being "in opposition"—opposition to the practices of the Fourth and opposition to the manner in which the leadership groups under the Fourth Republic were coping, or rather were unable to cope, with the Algerian War. The overwhelming vote in favor of the Constitution (80%) came from mutually exclusive and oppositional forces—the Radicals, Independents, MRP, and Socialists. In the legislative elections that followed in 1958 all political parties other than the Communists supported General De Gaulle and his policies only to shift gradually away. What appeared to be a positive coalition of forces behind De Gaulle and his government split into its constituent parts. In 1959 Michel Debre was endorsed by all deputies except the Communists; 453 voted for, 56 against, and about 50 abstained or did not take part in the balloting. In 1962 in the vote on the motion of censure against the Gaullist cabinet, now headed by Pompidou, all political parties but the Gaullists, 12 Independents and 7 MRP, joined the Communists. The government was "censured" by 280 deputies out of 480.

The first opposition under the Fifth Republic had, however, the same traits as all oppositions in the past. It was adventitious and ephemeral; it was internally divided; it was a "negative majority." This became abundantly clear in the election that followed. On the first ballot the Gaullists and their allies received about 37% of the vote and on the second over 41%. They gained some 275 seats out of a total of 487. The opposition—280 strong—was cut down to less than 175.

With the election of 1962 and the revision of the Constitution to provide for the direct election of the president the political situation and the traditional game governing the nature of governmental majorities and oppositions appeared to be on the verge of change. The existence of a parliamentary majority, it was argued, would lead irresistibly the opposition parties to coalesce. Also, the manner in which the presidential electoral system was to operate, would force the political parties to unite behind a limited number of candidates on the first ballot and then divide between the only two on the second ballot. The trend was inevitable, it was argued, and many political commentators began to anticipate the simplification of the party system to at least four, and more likely three, major party groups: the Gaullists, the non-Communist Left and Left Center, the Center and the Communists. The Center would be unable to resist the pull from the Left and the Right and France was likely to emerge with three major parties. What concerned primarily those who thought along these lines was the attitude of the Communist Party. A reformist approach, independent of the Moscow line, would make increasingly for the unity of the Left; a militant and staunchly pro-Soviet line, on the other hand, might either prolong the division of the Left or alienate many of its non-Communist voters, i.e., it would condemn the Left to permanent weakness and ineffectiveness.

The development between 1962 and 1967 gave every indication that party simplification was in process of materializing and that a structured and organized "majority-minority"/"government-opposition" pattern was developing. In the presidential election of 1965 there were only two serious candidates. The Left fell behind one candidate—François Mitterand, with full support of the Communists. The Socialists and many of the Radicals and the Republican clubs together with the PSU joined ranks. To the Right the various forces fell in line behind De Gaulle and the Gaullist Party leaders. The last hope of the Center—Lecanuet—made a good showing on the first ballot with some 15% of the votes but was outdistanced by Mitterand with some 34% and by De Gaulle with some 44%. The two leading candidates received almost four out of every five ballots cast! On the second ballot the Left managed to get about one out of every three centrist votes, together with an appreciable number of the anti-De Gaulle protest vote that had been cast on the first ballot for the candidate of the extreme right—Tixier Vignancourt. This was the only anomaly of an election that otherwise followed a classic Left-Right split. The novelty, however, is that for the first time the Left and Right seemed to be represented by one candidate each. The impetus for cooperation and, if possible, unification was obvious—especially in the light of legislative elections scheduled for 1967.

It was the legislative election of 1967 that provides us with the high point of party simplification and close cooperation. To the Right (if we continue to use the Left-Right dichotomy as a convenient landmark) the Gaullists were able to unite the various factions that De Gaulle's long coattails had carried to victory. Even the Independent Republicans, under Giscard d'Estaing, ran under the Gaullist label, while claiming autonomy. Anti-Gaullist candidates from the Right, conservative anti-Gaullist, dissenters from the Gaullist camp, were ruthlessly singled out by the party leadership, with Pompidou, the Prime Minister, playing a key role in the designation of the Gaullist candidates. To the Left the picture was equally impressive. The Communists remained as every disciplined and strong; the Socialists and the Radicals and various left-wing political clubs formed a new coalition that brought them under one single label—the *Fédèration de la Gauche Democrate et Socialiste* the FGDS. The leaders of these three groups, working through an executive committee, managed to agree to designate one candidate in each electoral district. But over and above this, Communists and FGDS reached an agreement according to which while they were free to designate their respective candidates and compete with each other on the first ballot, they would desist on the second ballot in favor of the one of their candidates that had received the highest number of votes. Thus it was hoped that on the second ballot there would be one and only one candidate of "the Left" against somebody from the Right—most likely a Gaullist. The Center was caught in the middle, hoping to get the support both of the Right and the Left on the second ballot in case its candidates ran strong on the first ballot. They did not. The contest was between the Gaullist and the "Left"—a Communist supported by the FGDS or an FGDS candidate supported by the Communists. The Gaullists barely managed to eke out a very slim majority. They gained 245 seats; the Communists and the FGDS together 194 (73 Communists; 121 FGDS); the Center— former MRP, ex-Independents and Moderates and some Radicals—finished with 42 seats.

The new Assembly, *assuming cooperation between Communists and FGDS* was for the first time analogous in its party alignment to that of the British House of Commons. Never before had the configuration of the French Parliament been that simple and never before had a "majority"—supporting the government—and an "opposition" appeared so coherent. Much about the future depended upon the attitude of the Communist Party vis-à-vis the FGDS, upon the ability of the latter to maintain and improve its organization by absorbing the three groups that comprised it and by developing its own organization, membership, and leadership and finally, upon a cooperation between the two based upon a common platform to provide a common ground for parliamentary cooperation and action. The slim majority on which De Gaulle's government was based was not likely to last. A test was expected to come soon and with it the future would be clarified.

Two tests came within less than two years. The May-June, 1968, students and workers uprisings forced the dissolution of the National Assembly and a new election. Within nine months De Gaulle withdrew after losing in a badly conceived and poorly organized referendum and a new presidential election was held.

In both elections—legislative and presidential—the opposition to the Gaullists collapsed. In the legislative election the FGDS split and began to disintegrate; so did the cooperation between Communists and FGDS. The Gaullists and their allies won an unprecedented 345 seats out of 487. They received 44% of the vote on the first ballot and 47% on the second.

The vicotry of the opposition in the referendum of 1969 in which 53% voted against the proposed revision and, at least indirectly, against De Gaulle was not repeated in the presidential election of June, 1969. The Left split and collapsed; the Center experienced a period of unanticipated but fleeting revival, and the Gaullists won by default. Four candidates of the Left faced Pompidou and a Centrist, Alain Poher. The parties of the Left failed to agree on the candidate they would support on the second ballot and the Communist Party, by abstaining, made it possible for the Gaullist to win. After the election the Gaullists were firmly installed in the Elysée with a virtually unshakeable majority in the National Assembly. The Left was divided, the FGDS splintered once more into its constituent parts, and the Center continued to grope for a solution and for the creation of a party that would unite its various fragments.

The new decade therefore seems to usher a government

firmly supported by one party—the Gaullists—that controls *alone* a comfortable majority of some 330 out of 487. Its allies—the Independent Republicans—are no longer needed. The majority makes it virtually impossible for the cabinet to be seriously threatened and in the Elysée the heir to De Gaulle is firmly enthroned until 1976. The Gaullist position looks just as firm as it did in 1969, a few weeks before De Gaulle proceeded with his ill-fated referendum! The basic question therefore is whether this new majority is likely to last—whether, indeed, in the 1970s the secular trends with regard to the multiplicity and heterogeneity of oppositions in the French system and the propensity of majorities to disintegrate are likely to be arrested and reversed.

There are reasons for which one may well argue that we are entering a new phase in French politics and that it will be associated with a reduction in the number of parties, and a "majority-minority" split resulting naturally in a "government"/"opposition" division in the Parliament and the electorate. Outside of the Communists the old parties have been unable to generate enthusiasm, membership, and votes; the Gaullists as a new party have won all three legislative elections; the old ideological splits seem to be on the wane—even the old clerical issue does not divide sharply any more; the state is being viewed with a more utilitarian eye by most of the French groups—the deep-set distrust is waning to be replaced by a growing realization that the state can be used as an instrument for compromise and satisfaction rather than imposition or self-defense; citizens are increasingly losing their distaste or fear of urbanization and grass-roots politics and finally the old status groups are being replaced by new ones spawned by the rapid modernization of the fifties. How is this to effect the political parties? Is it likely to produce a coherence and clarity in the majority/minority, government/opposition configuration? The answer relates to two crucial questions: will the state and its administrative institutions provide for the proper organic links with the citizens through which a constructive dialogue with the various interests can be undertaken and compromise reached? Will the majority—the Gaullist majority of today—become a party, with mass membership, organization, discipline, a platform and leadership? An answer to these questions will require a separate essay. All I can do is outline their importance.

The Gaullist system under De Gaulle undermined the legislature in a favor of the administration and the executive. The links between the citizen and the state were weakened at the very moment when the latter was viewed with tolerance and understanding. The events of May and June, 1968, were in a sense a protest against the continuing aloofness of the state and the remoteness between it and the citizen. Only the future will determine what new relationships will be developed between the administration and the interest groups: intellectuals, teachers, farmers, workers, students, cadres, etc.; it will also determine how sensitive the Gaullist majority in the National Assembly will be to their demands. As for the parties the Gaullist majority today is yet to become a party. It consists of many groups—some of the old notables; some of the former centrists; some for whom fidelity to De Gaulle was the epitome of political commitment and action; some opportunists who simply joined because they thought this was the best way to win. There is no mass membership, no common program. On the contrary the divisions are many: between the Europeans and anti-Europeans; the Atlanticists and those who hope that France will continue a Gaullist foreign policy; those who believe in some neocorporatist arrangements to bridge the conflict between capital and labor and those who believe in economic liberal solutions; those who believe in the old administrative pattern of centralization and those pressing for reforms through consultation and participation of all interests. The Gaullist Party may split. If it does, it will parallel the disarray of the Left, and then we shall return to the old state of things—multipartyism and party fragmentation. The emerging dichotomy between majority and

71

opposition will disappear.

Notes

1. Grosser A: "France—Nothing but Opposition." in Dahl R, ed: *Political Oppositions in Western Democracies*. New Haven, Yale University Press, 1965.
2. The Tables are taken from the *Année Politique* of 1954 and 1955.
3. I have spared the reader the intricate matter of intraparty "opposition(s)." With the exception of the Communist Party all other parties in the Fourth Republic split internally. The EDC vote provides a good illustration. More than half of the Socialists opposed to the EDC. After the end of the war in Indochina the Radicals mounted an increasingly effective opposition against PMF. In 1957 they were divided into three groups. Many of the MRP members rebelled against the Indochina policy and the continuation of the war in Algeria while others supported it. The Moderates and later the National Center of Independents can be defined as a congerie of groupings moving in opposing directions.
4. The table is taken from the *Année Politique* of 1954.
5. Crozier, *The Bureaucratic Phenomenon*. Chicago, University of Chicago Press.
6. See Hoffmann S: *The New Republic*.
7. Tilly: *Violence in America*.
8. For a brief survey and analysis of the elections of 1969 see my "Pompidou and the Communists." *Virginia Quarterly Review*, Vol 45, No 4 (Autumn, 1969).

3   Political Opposition in Argentina

John T. Deiner
University of Delaware

Introduction

The nature and intensity of opposition in Argentina has changed during recent years to reflect more strident criticism of a political system which opposition leaders feel has not served the best interests of Argentines. Increasingly, important sectors of the opposition have called for changes not only in the governments of the nation, but in the very nature of the political system. These opposition leaders are calling for a political system that will allow greater participation in Argentina's political life and will allow the economic and social benefits of the country to be more equitably distributed among its citizens. The military, the traditional political parties, foreigners and foreign interests, and certain "oligarchic" elements in Argentine society are cited as the primary political culprits harming Argentina. Opposition groups say that there is a need for new systematic relationships, and that violence is a legitimate means toward these relationships.

In addition to this new kind of opposition, Argentina also has a goodly share of opposition by groups desiring to bring about changes within the existing system. Although the military leaders who have ruled Argentina since June 1966 banned political party activity, party politicians have remained very active. They have consistently sought a renewal of party activity and a return to elected government. Peronistas, both in labor and in political parties, continue also to want to bring changes, rather than destruction, to the Argentine political system. The Peronistas under General Juan Perón did cause some major alterations in Argentina politics during Perón's occupation of the presidency (1946-55) but never succeeded in completely destroying the preexisting political groups in Argentina.

Argentina, then, is a country where political opposition and dissent currently exist on multiple levels. There is strong opposition to the system itself by several newly active political groups, including factions of students, labor, and the church. Opposition and dissent also come from sectors in society who want a return to civilian political control through elections. Leading politicians of the former parties and some sectors of the armed forces comprise this second group. Still another kind of opposition comes from certain civilian and military sectors who demand that specific policies and people be changed, but do not demand either an entirely new system nor a return to political party activity.

During the 20th century, and particularly since the Perón period, oppositionists of one kind or another have formed a majority in Argentine politics. Since Perón, the country has never had a government that could operate secure in the knowledge that it was backed by a majority and not endangered by powerful opposition. All governments in a sense have been dominated by those who opposed them, and a rapid change in governmental personnel has been a result. Since Perón's ouster in September, 1955, there have been eight governments in Argentina with an average stay in office of two years. No elected president has completed his term, and military governments have been remarkably intolerant of Peronista civilian political activity. Perhaps the major political question facing Argentina today is that one relating to the proper role of the opposition. Since World War II, the opposition has not been a source of constructive criticism for Argentine governments. Indeed, governments have looked upon opposition primarily as a possible source of a government-toppling coup and have attempted to decimate opposition leaders rather than reply to their criticisms and complaints. Such a situation has cast the opposition in Argentina into the role of the enemy. Politically the country has become fragmented, with little hope of an emerging national consensus on political issues. This crisis of fragmentation has been increased in the five years of military rule since 1966, but its roots lie further back in Argentine history.

History of Political Opposition

Since becoming independent Argentina has witnessed opposition centered over a number of issues. At first there was the question of what kind of government the new nation should have. The opponents argued over whether there should be unitary government or federal government. Although this struggle directly involved only a limited number of people (those in the ruling classes), other Argentines were affected by the battles fought to decide the question and by the tyranny of Rosas who governed Argentina from 1832 until defeated in battle in 1852.

Rosas saw his opponents as clear enemies and fought them with repression and terror. His opponents saw a civil war as the only means of defeating Rosas.

With the defeat of Rosas, control of Argentina soon passed into the hands of an "enlightened oligarchy." Such presidents as Sarmiento, Mitre, and Avellaneda brought peace and prosperity to Argentina.

During the years from 1862 to 1890, a succession of representatives from the landholding elite of the nation ruled Argentina and guided its development. Argentina became a great wheat grower and cattle raiser for Europe. The country prospered economically although it did not industrialize. Culturally, Argentina's rulers followed examples set abroad, rather than looking to indigenous cultural leadership.

Although peace reigned, the governments took few political chances, and kept themselves in power by means of fraudulent elections. The national leaders followed a policy of encouraging European immigration so as to populate the large uninhabited expanses of Argentina. Many of the immigrants settled in Buenos Aires or the areas surrounding the national capital. These people brought with them the social and political ideas then current in Europe. An opposition party, the Radical Civic Union (UCR), was formed in 1890. The UCR attempted several unsuccessful coups, and opposed all governments from 1890 on. Its early leaders were Leandro Alem and Hipólito Yrigoyen, two remarkable men. Under these leaders, the party adopted the strategy of not participating in elections as a sign of opposition to the dishonesty of the electoral system.

Finally, the Radicals got their chance. Electoral laws were changed and the secret ballot was introduced during the presidency of Roque Saenz Pena (1910-16). The Radicals participated in the 1916 presidential election, and their leader Yrigoyen was elected and assumed the presidency.

The Radicals had opposed the dishonesty and corruption of Argentine politics, and their platform called for wide changes. In reality, they did not bring such wide-ranging change about, in part because they never had a Senate majority.

Opposition to the Radicals began to develop from within the party and from labor groups. There were several strikes and riots in Buenos Aires in 1919 and and 1922. In the 1922 election, Yrigoyen supported a Radical, Marcelo T. de Alvear. Alvear was elected but by 1924 had formed his own "anti-Personalist" branch of the Radical Party in opposition to Yrigoyen. In 1928 Yrigoyen was reelected to the presidency. By this time, however, he was a very old and incompetent man. Members of his government engaged in corruption on a wide scale, but Yrigoyen himself was not aware of what was going on. He was in no condition to control his own government nor to meet the economic problems of Argentina, caused by the world Depression.

In September 1930 Yrigoyen was ousted from office by a military coup headed by General José F. Uriburu. The coup was organized by military officers, but had wide support among landholding groups, students, and political party leaders. The 1930 coup marked the emergence of the military as a political group actively willing to exercise its opposition to civilian governments. By November 1931 the Uriburu government heeded public pressure and elections were held. The Radicals, however, were barred. The election was won by General Agustín P. Justo, who ran as an anti-Personalist Radical, but had government and conservative backing. The conservative forces were aided by police in carrying out fraudulent electoral practices.

The Justo government ruled Argentina for the next six years. During this period the Radicals began to form factions. The growing working class found no strong political party which it could support. Even the trade union movement was becoming splintered, with socialists being divided, and socialists and communists contending for leadership of the major central trade union organization, the CGT.

In 1938, President Justo's nominee, Roberto Ortiz, became president, again through a fraudulent election. Ortiz seemed to be moving toward the implementation of more honest election practices when his failing health forced him to hand the presidency over to his vice-president, Ramón S. Castillo, in 1940. Castillo was a pro-Axis politician who soon had a state of siege declared, which suspended constitutional guarantees. The Chamber of Deputies, where Radical and Socialist party members represented a majority of the nation's voters, could not effectively oppose Castillo. Although he himself was pro-Axis, it became apparent that Castillo was going to support Robustiano Patrón Costas, a wealthy pro-British sugar plantation owner, for the presidency in 1944.

Groups in the military were unwilling to see Sr. Patrón Costa become president. One of these groups, the GOU (Grupo de Oficiales Unidos), led a coup which deposed Castillo and set up a military government. This 1943 coup was a purely military coup, not having the popular backing among civilians that the 1930 coup had enjoyed. The 1943 coup was led by officers, including Perón, who were primarily from the middle and lower classes. Statements that were circulated showed the coup makers to be pro-Axis, expansionists, and nationalists determined to create a powerful Argentina. They represented a new kind of military opposition in Argentina, and their policies came to fruition under Perón's leadership from 1945 to 1955.

The Perón Period

The military group behind the 1943 coup was interested in creating a stronger Argentina, an Argentina more powerful in world affairs. They were opposed to those Argentines who had collaborated with foreigners at the expense of Argentine development. They opposed civilians who had not brought leadership to Argentina. They were not concerned with the implementation of democratic political practices.

During his ten years in office Perón persecuted all opposition, whether by politicians, trade unionists, industrialists, or the military. Campaigns against opponents of the regime were effective, and political opposition became very dangerous. Some opponents of Perón were jailed, tortured, and killed. Opponents constantly criticized the lack of political freedom under Perón, but did not seem to be aware of the social and economic changes that were taking place, partially as a result of government sponsorship.

Perón began to try to build a new kind of support starting late in 1943. He held meetings with trade unionists and began to promote programs they desired from his post as Secretary of Labor. By aiding trade unionists, Perón was appealing to those people who had been neglected by the established political parties, and whose own labor organizations were unable to help, either because of internal divisions, opposition from government and employers, or failure to appreciate the changing character of the labor force in Argentina. During the decade of the 1930s industrialization and manufacturing had increased markedly, especially in the Buenos Aires area, and there had been a large-scale migration of workers from rural to urban areas. These newly arrived workers were not organized by the existing labor organizations, nor did they share the Europe-derived social and political philosophies of the established labor leaders. Perón used his governmental positions to gain benefits for this new class of workers. His principal efforts were to give aid in organizing previously unorganized workers, such as those in the meat-packing and sugar industries, and to promote and enforce successful collective bargaining agreements for workers. Perón and his wife, Evita, received much publicity for their efforts in behalf of labor, and workers for the first time in Argentina's history began to feel that powerful officials were actively working to provide social and economic benefits for labor.

Struggle for control of the military government continued between 1943 and 1946. Perón rose steadily in importance until finally, in October 1945, a coup was undertaken by a faction of the military which opposed Perón's growing political strength and his strong ties with the labor movement. Perón was ousted and imprisoned on October 10, 1945, but returned victoriously to Buenos Aires seven days later. His triumphant return was brought about by the workers whom he had championed for the preceding two years. Trade unionists who were fearful that Perón's ouster would mean the end of their newly gained benefits began to converge on Buenos Aires to demand the return of their protector. Actions of the trade unionists as well as ineptness by Argentina's civilian politicians and employers and indecision on the part of armed forces leaders all contributed to the successful attempt to bring about Perón's return.

Argentina's politicians apparently assumed that the coup against Perón was a sign of military weakness, and they used the occasion to demand a complete end to military government. They refused to join in a government headed by the military men who had ousted Perón. Employers seized upon Perón's ouster as an excuse to avoid payment of certain bonuses recently negotiated for labor by Perón. This action probably increased worker belief that without Perón the gains he had won for the working man would be lost. In addition, parts of the military were sympathetic to Perón, who was, after all, a military man. This group, plus others who probably did not wish to kill fellow Argentines by firing on the crowds of workers coming to Buenos Aires in support of Perón, played a major role in allowing Perón to return to Buenos Aires to the shouted approval of the massive crowds jammed into the historic Plaza de Mayo in front of the presidential palace.

The Perón Period

Perón's return began a new chapter in Argentina's political history. Although the Perón government that came to power in the elections of 1946 was a new kind of government for Argentina, having active participation by trade unionists, opposition groups did not change their goals or tactics to confront the changed political situation. Because of their lack of adaptation, as well as because of governmental measures, the opposition was rendered ineffective during almost the entire Perón period. In fact, the most bothersome opposition to Perón during most of his tenure in office came from the military, one of the regime's primary sources of support.

From 1943 to 1946 opposition and dissent in Argentina were centered primarily in the political parties opposing military rule and the state of siege that had been declared.

There was also opposition to the government because of its aid to pro-Axis organizations (although Argentina remained officially neutral until almost the very end of the war). Socialist, and to some extent communist, leaders who had dominated the trade union movement also began to form a coherent opposition group during this period. These trade unionists initially welcomed Perón's interest in labor affairs, but soon came to oppose his actions when they saw that control over the labor movement was being taken out of their hands. The government tried to convert, coopt, or coerce those labor leaders it could, but in cases where trade union leaders stood firm against the government, Perón used other methods, such as creating and supporting rival unions which were the only ones to achieve legal standing.

The United States also became a source of opposition during this period. United States policy in the hemisphere had centered on trying to form a united front against a possible Axis threat during the 1930s and early 1940s. Argentina was the primary obstacle to such unity, opposing United States desires at hemispheric conferences, and insisting on a policy of Argentine neutrality until it became obvious that the Axis powers would be defeated. United States politicians publicly expressed their dislike of the military government in Argentina, and Secretary of State Cordell Hull seemed particularly bitter toward Perón and his fellow officers. United States Ambassador Spruille Braden played an active role in leading the opposition to Perón's presidential candidacy while he was stationed in Argentina, and continued actively to oppose Perón after he became Assistant Secretary of State for Inter-American Affairs.

The 1946 presidential campaign showed an interesting alignment of political forces in Argentina. On the one side were almost all the traditional political parties in Argentina, organized in the Unión Democrática coalition. Their candidate was José Tamborini, a rather colorless Radical Party politician. This coalition supported a platform based on an appeal for a return to political democracy and elected

81

decision makers. The coalition leaders did not understand the effects of the changes which had occurred in Argentina. Perón's platform calling for new economic and social policies had more appeal than the coalition's platform based on a call for a return to a discredited political process. Two weeks before the election, the US State Department issued the famous Blue Book on Argentina. The Blue Book purported to document the pro-Fascist activities of Perón and his associates. It was intended to discredit Perón by portraying him as a foe of democracy. The Blue Book perfectly complemented the election campaign appealing for a return to democratic political values.

Juan Perón's campaign emphasized Argentine nationalism and the need to create a new Argentina, free from foreign control, in which all Argentines could take their rightful place in society. He called for basic economic and social change. Perón's support came primarily from trade unionists and the military, but he also received support from a small group of dissident Radical Party members, one of whom appeared on Perón's Partido Laborista ticket as vice-presidential candidate. Argentina's Catholic Church also supported Perón, at least passively. The Church issued a pastoral letter shortly before the election in which it urged voters not to vote for any candidates who supported various policies opposed by the Church. A close reading of the pastoral letter revealed that the Church was actually asking voters not to vote for any candidates except Perón. All others were guilty of supporting one or another of the policies the Church opposed.

The presidential election went smoothly, and both sides issued statements claiming it to be one of the most honest elections in Argentine history. Juan Perón won the election with 55% of the total vote, and his supporters gained control of both houses of the congress. Perón's opposition had lacked dynamism and had been attuned to past issues and conditions. The nationalistic Perón used the US Blue Book publication to depict himself as the target of foreign enemies, and the man who would stand up to those enemies. His nationalism, the overwhelming support given by labor, and the political miscalculations made by his opponents were the major ingredients in Perón's election. During the ten years of the Perón presidency the nature of political opposition in Argentina was altered. The alterations were caused by the fact that the opposition was faced by a new kind of ruler. Much of the opposition was forced underground by the government's tactics. The government used intelligence services to seek out information on opposition activities, it employed force and even torture against its opponents, and the governmental control of communications prevented the opposition from having an effective voice. A law of *desacato*, or disrespect, was passed which could be used to make political criticisms of the government a punishable offense.

Despite governmental measures, opposition to Perón was not completely stifled. It continued to exist in the circumscribed but still legal political parties, and in clandestine or exiled organizations. Under these conditions, however, the opposition to Perón was not very effective, and he encountered serious political danger only when portions of the military began to oppose him actively.

An understanding of the treatment of political opposition during the Perón period is crucial for an understanding of the later role of opposition in Argentina. The primary goal of the Peronistas was to render opposition ineffective, either by physically suppressing opponents or by restricting their potential to communicate their ideas. Thus Perón moved early in his presidency to purge labor of possible opponents. Old-line trade union leaders were ousted from their posts, and reliable Peronistas were placed in control of the national central labor organizations, the CGT. Some of the socialist labor leaders went into exile where they formed an organization, called COASI, whose purpose was to criticize and expose the Perón government. Those trade unionists who decided to remain in Argentina were eventually defeated by the government. Luis Gay, the Secretary General of the CGT who desired to keep that organization independent of the government, found himself removed from office. Cipriano Reys, a labor leader who was an early influential supporter of Perón, and who helped form the Partido Laborista which supported Perón for the presidency in 1946, was ultimately jailed because of his disagreements with the president. Within three years of becoming president, Perón had gained complete control of the CGT. It was directed and influenced informally by his wife Evita, and its major leaders were Peronistas first and labor leaders second.

The government moved to silence oppositionist expression in the media by purchasing both newspapers and radio stations. Sra. Perón in fact became the controller of a string of radio stations. If purchase was not possible, the government resorted to other means. In some cases advertising was limited by governmental laws. This reduced the income of those papers not supported by the government. Opposition newspapers were also struck by progovernment unions, and minor health infractions were used as reasons for closing down opposition papers. The restricting of the amount of newsprint allocated to opposition papers was also an effective means of silencing the editorial opponents of the government. In 1951 the government finally forced the closure of *La Prensa*, one of the world's great newspapers, and a critic of Perón. Later *La Prensa* reopened with an editorial board composed of CGT officials and an editorial policy completely supportive of the government.

Control of communications media by the government greatly hindered anti-Perón forces from articulating their opposition. Freedom of speech continued to exist in the congress, but no newspapers printed legislative debates, and opposition arguments had no noticeable effect on the votes of Peronista legislative majorities. One source of communications which did exist was provided by Argentina's geography. It is a relatively short distance across the Rio de la Plata estuary from Buenos Aires to Uruguay. Opposition people in exile made use of this proximity to beam antigovernment broadcasts into Argentina. Clandestine presses also produced leaflets and pamphlets criticizing the Perón regime.

Although the government managed to silence most communications from the opposition, it did not convert all Argentines into its supporters. Elections in 1951 saw almost one third of the voters cast their ballots for Ricardo Balbín, a Radical, and the only opposition candidate allowed to run against Perón. All other potential candidates were disqualified under the regime's electoral laws. Balbín managed to attract votes despite strong government harassment during the campaign. He was denied radio time and printers refused to print his literature.

Under Perón there was also some opposition from workers. In 1949, 1950, and 1951 there were strikes by railroad employees and by workers in the sugar industry in Tucuman province. The government used violence to put down these strikes, and the CGT intervened and took over control of the unions.

In its early years in power the Perón government had moved to rid itself of possible opposition from the courts and the universities. Both the universities and the national court system were purged of those people who were opposed to the values of the Perón government. In addition to taking steps to reduce the strength of known opponents, the government also initiated programs to generate support for itself among uncommitted groups. Federations for students and young people were started to provide centers for sports, social events, and the dissemination of government propaganda.

Military opposition was a source of potential danger for the government. Perón constantly tried to rid the military of those officers considered disloyal, but was never completely successful. An attempted coup in 1951 was ill-planned and unsuccessful. Some factions in the military were almost always dissatisfied, however. Evita's prominence in Argentina and her close relations with the labor movement were constant irritants to military men. When it was suggested that

85

Evita might run as her husband's vice-presidential candidate in 1951, military resentment flared and the possibility of her running was quickly discarded. The very fact that the regime catered to labor rankled certain military men. Perón always faced the problem of balancing the support he got from his military and labor followers.

Perón also faced a final, external source of opposition. US officials fought against Perón's policies to increase Argentine influence in the Americas. Argentine and US representatives clashed at many international and hemispheric conferences, such as the 1948 conference in Bogotá which resulted in the formation of the Organization of American States. Argentina's position was that Latin America's basic need was for inter-American cooperation for economic development. Argentine delegates charged that the United States was only interested in creating a united hemispheric front against communism and was not interested in attacking Latin America's underlying economic and social problems. In addition to direct clashes between Argentine and US officials, the Perón government also found itself opposed by representatives of organizations friendly to the United States. These opponents of Perón tried to discredit his policies and to document the existence of political repression in Argentina. There were bitter exchanges at many international conferences, with particularly effective criticism of Perón at the ILO, where exiled Argentine trade unionists had organizational standing, and used the ILO meetings as a forum for attacks of the Perón government and its policies.

By the end of 1954, the Perón government was running into some serious political difficulties at home. Eva Perón had died in 1952. The strong support she had brought Perón through her hold over leaders in the purged labor movement and the emotional appeal she held for the lower classes had been major sources of governmental support. Without Eva, Perón himself had to manage such support. By the end of 1954, an open rift with the Church was evident, and the government accused some priests of supporting Catholic trade unions to compete with the Peronista unions. A decision to legalize prostitution also was looked upon with disfavor in Catholic circles. Perón mounted an energetic campaign against the Church, and this campaign was ultimately harmful to the president. In the process of the struggle Perón was excommunicated and Peronista followers sacked some of the major churches in downtown Buenos Aires. The most damaging aspect of the feud with the Church was the effect it had on some military men. Certain Catholic nationalists in the military began to oppose the government. Workers who were strong Catholics were also disturbed at the growing distance between the Church and their leader. Civilian politicians, long persecuted and harassed by the government, made the Perón-Church struggle into their own cause and joined together in denouncing the actions of the government against the Church.

In June 1955 naval and air force officers made an abortive attempt at a coup. The army stood firm behind Perón, and he remained in office. From June until August 1955 Perón tried a new campaign to woo support from Argentina's politicians. Political leaders, led by Artro Frondizi, refused to cooperate, and instead made demands that Perón restore freedom of the press and freedom of action for his opponents. Perón's attempt to woo the opposition ended in August when his government adopted a policy of militant opposition toward its opponents. Early in September 1955 a revolt against Political leaders, led by Arturo Frondizi, refused to cooperate, throughout Argentina. Three days later Perón was ousted from the presidency and a junta composed of military men took office.

The Post-Perón Years

The years following Perón's ouster constituted a continuation of the struggle between Peronistas and anti-Peronistas. The major political question in Argentina from 1955 to the present has been how to incorporate Peronista followers and

Peronista ideas into the Argentine political system. During much of this period, Peronistas have constituted the major source of opposition to military governments and civilian governments alike. Military men ruled from 1955 to 1958, from 1962 to 1963 (although a civilian technically headed the government), and again assumed control in June 1966. In each of these cases, the military interceded into politics at least in part because of their opposition to Peronistas. The gulf between the followers of Perón and the military has been the major cause of the political instability plaguing Argentina since 1955. With the coming to power of the military government headed by General Onganía in 1966, new elements have also become part of the political opposition in Argentina. These new elements, composed of trade unionists, certain sectors of the clergy (the Third World Movement), students, and urban terrorist organizations represent a new kind of political opposition and dissent for Argentina. The target of their opposition is the Argentine political system itself, not just the government in power. They urge that violence is the only way to bring about needed changes. Since 1968 violence has greatly increased in Argentina. There have been many bombings, raids on military and police centers, and assassinations.

The nature of the new kinds of opposition and dissent which have emerged in Argentina since 1955 can best be appreciated by tracing the political history of the country since Perón's overthrow. The leader of the coup which ousted Perón, General Eduardo Lonardi, ruled Argentina for only two months. The main source of opposition to Lonardi came from military men who charged he was too soft on Peronistas. Army General Pedro Aramburu led a coup which ousted Lonardi, and Aramburu headed a government which ruled Argentina from 1955 to 1958.

President Aramburu and Vice President Admiral Isaac Rojas (who was also vice-president under Lonardi) formed a government which mounted a determined drive against the Peronistas. Peronista trade union leaders were removed from their posts, militant Peronistas were imprisoned, and many of Perón's better known followers fled into exile. The government undertook a massive investigation into the activities of those in power under Perón and brought criminal charges against many major Peronista figures. Charges ranged from using political office for personal gain to treason. Perón himself was charged with being a traitor to the country. The government actively persecuted Peronistas during the 1955-58 period. Military men were placed in control of the unions, but by 1958 Peronistas had reasserted their control over labor. In 1956 an attempted pro-Perón coup was squashed, and its leaders were executed by the government. Such execution of political opponents is extremely rare in Argentina.

The government allowed the presidential election to be held in 1958. Peronistas were barred from nominating their own candidates. Arturo Frondizi, a lawyer, outspoken critic of Perón during Perón's rule, and leader of the Intransigente faction of the Radical party, was elected president. He won on the strength of a secret agreement he had made with the ex-dictator, who by 1958 was living in exile in Spain. Perón's followers apparently supported the wishes of their leader, and Peronista votes, added to votes from Frondizi's own followers, elected the Radical candidate as president.

Frondizi's years in office were hectic. Initially, he had the support of the Peronistas, in large part due to a major wage increase he allowed for workers, and because he had promised to try to reintegrate Peronistas into Argentine politics. At the end of about six months in office, Frondizi's policies changed in an anti-inflationary direction. Workers began to feel the pinch as the government adopted austerity measures to try to halt inflation. Frondizi also granted foreign petroleum concessions, thus causing the wrath of nationalists. Trade unionists opposed the government's economic policies.

Frondizi's major political worry during his entire time in office was the military. A number of unsuccessful coups were attempted against the wily Radical politician, but he managed to stay in office by adroitly appealing to various sectors in the military. By 1962 Frondizi's luck had run out. His decision to allow Peronistas to run their own candidates in the March elections for governors and congressmen proved disastrous. Peronista candidates won about one third of the total vote, got 41 seats in Congress, and elected governors in almost half the provinces, including the politically crucial province of Buenos Aires. In addition to his gigantic political miscalculations regarding Peronista electoral strength, Frondizi had also made several statements about the Castro regime in Cuba which the military did not like. The combination of the Cuban statements and the political blunder which resulted in Peronista electoral successes was too much for the military to accept. President Frondizi was ousted by a military coup two weeks after the March elections were held, and the election results were nullified.

A provisional government under José María Guido took office, but was controlled by the military men who had directed the coup against Frondizi. During President Guido's stay in office, the principal source of opposition came from the military itself. There were two major groups in the military with bitterly opposed political ideas. The Colorados (Reds) group was very anti-Peronista and called for a military dictatorship which would last until Peronista influence in Argentina had been eradicated. The Azules (Blues) group saw a need to somehow accept the Peronistas as a fact of national political life and wanted a return to a constitutionally elected government. In September 1962, the Azules and Colorados engaged in a short civil war. The Azules, led by General Juan Carlos Onganía, emerged the victors. In June 1963, elections were held to name a new president.

The 1963 elections clearly demonstrated the effects of the Perón and post-Perón years in Argentina. The winner of the elections, Arturo Illia, received only 26% of the popular vote. He was the leader of the faction of the Radical Party which had not supported Frondizi in 1958. Frondizi's own faction split, with many of his former supporters now supporting their own nominee, Dr. Oscar Allende. Frondizi himself tried to build an alliance with Peronista supporters, but the presidential nominees of this group were disallowed by electoral officials, and ultimately both Perón and Frondizi ordered their supporters to cast blank ballots in order to register their displeasure with the prevailing situation. There were also a number of minor party candidates running for the presidency. Thus, the political fragmentation of Argentina was quite evident in the divided state of political parties in the 1963 election.

When President Illia came to office in 1963, he had no single clear opposition, but a multitude of oppositions. As Illia's government proved itself incapable of solving any of the problems facing the nation, the range and intensity of these oppositions became increasingly apparent. The situation was hopeless for a president who could not command majority support on a single issue.

Illia was finally overthrown in a coup in June of 1966. This coup brought the so-called Argentine Revolution into office. Opposition to Illia had come from many sources. There was a split between the president and the chief of his own faction of the Radicals, Ricardo Balbín. Civil disorders in the poverty-stricken province of Tucumán led to a state of virtual anarchy in that province. Students actively opposed the government which had failed to pass a budget for 1966, thus leaving the universities without funds. Student street demonstrations led to street violence. The military opposed both student demonstrations and those civilian authorities whose ineptness had led to student violence. The military also opposed what it felt was increasing communist influence in the universities. The major issue, however, remained the Peronistas. The government had scheduled elections, and it was quite possible that Peronistas would win control of Buenos Aires province in 1967. Military leaders opposed both the portable Peronista victory and the government's questionable maneuvers to avoid such a victory. Peronistas, although themselves divided into factions loyal to Perón and those calling for a Peronism without Perón, had won some elections in minor interior provinces and shown some electoral strength. In addition, they had mounted a campaign to take over factories in 1964, and in 1965 and 1966 had engaged in a series of strikes against the nation's communications and transportation facilities. Much publicity was given to supposed political meddling and technical inexpertise in the operation of state-run enterprises. Scandals involving government officials in Tucumán and the customs operations also were widely publicized. The two leading weekly news magazines, *Confirmado* and *Primera Plana*, were stridently antigovernment, virtually calling for a revolution in every issue. In the face of so much opposition and dissatisfaction, it was no surprise when the government fell without a struggle, and with no noticeable effect on the daily routines of most Argentines.

The government that came to power following the June 1966 coup against Illia was headed by General Onganía, the same man who in 1962 had led the faction in the military which had fought for constitutional government rather than military dictatorship. In 1966 Onganía opted for military control in the face of civilian chaos and tried to speak for the nation as leader of the Argentine Revolution. The government stated that it was going to rule for as long as was necessary, probably at least ten years. One of the first acts of the government was the outlawing of all political parties and the seizing of their property on the grounds that the parties had not operated in the national interest. The government also took over control of all provincial governments, disbanded Congress, and changed the membership of the Supreme Court.

Although its initial political measures appeared severe, the government was widely accepted by Argentines. Onganía was looked on as a unifying leader for the nation. There was no great rejoicing over the fact of another military coup, but there seemed to be no great sorrow over the passing of the

Illia government either. Many Argentines were hopeful that the military government could change the situation that had existed under the Illia government, where action of any kind seemed impossible. The new government won public support from ex-president Frondizi on the grounds that a dynamic government was necessary for Argentina's progress. Ricardo Rojo, a leftist leader, also supported the government, seeing it as a step forward toward the needed destruction of the nation's sterile political party system.

Governments of the revolution have not been able to sustain their initial public support. Groups in Argentina have moved into active opposition to the government. Both *Primera Plana* and *Confirmado* have suffered closures for printing material unfavorable to the government and have not become supporters of the revolution they helped to bring about. Although political party activity has been banned, politicians have met privately to criticize the government and call for elections. The trade union movement has become increasingly split, with some factions militantly opposed to governmental policies, other factions opposed less militantly, and at least one faction attempting to work with governmental authorities. Students have gone into active opposition to the government, as have certain sectors of the clergy. New groups, waging campaigns of urban violence, have appeared to oppose both the government itself and the political system as it operates in Argentina. By 1970 the government was almost universally opposed by Argentines, whereas in 1966 it had been widely accepted, and in some cases had been praised. The net result of the period of military rule which began in 1966 has been to widen and deepen the divisions which already existed in Argentine political life, and to encourage new divisive forces to appear.

In the trade union sphere there is a factional fight for control of the CGT. The leader of one of the factions, and the strongest trade unionist in political terms, Augusto Vandor, was assassinated in 1969. José Alonso, leader of a faction opposed to Vandor, was assassinated in 1970.

Raimundo Ongaro has emerged as leader of still a third major faction in the trade union movement. His faction is the most militant of the three. Ongaro has been jailed by the government because of his opposition to its political activities. Labor groups in the interior cities of Tucumán and Córdoba have broken with national trade union leaders in Buenos Aires, and have led their followers in violent clashes with the police and military. Government economic policy in general has been to fight inflation by not allowing wage increases large enough to match price increases. The worker has seen his real wages decrease, and resents bearing the brunt of the battle to halt inflation.

Political party leaders, although far from united among themselves, all oppose the governmental policy of not calling for elections. The party leaders want a return to the system of elections which has proven ineffective since the fall of Perón. Many of the leaders are old, and no outstanding new leadership has emerged in the parties since the fall of Perón. Some sectors of the military also favor a return to civilian elected government in the near future. The military is divided over the question of whether or not to return to a civilian system of government, and the timing of elections.

The Church, which originally appeared to be a strong supporter of the highly moralistic Oganía government, had become badly split by 1969. Approximately 10% of Argentina's priests belong to a militant Third World movement in the Church which calls for drastic and immediate social reform. This militant group included several bishops in 1970. Third World priests accept violence as a legitimate means of bringing about change in some cases. There were rumors that Third World priests might have had some connection with the kidnappers and killers of ex-President Aramburu in 1970. Militant priests want wholesale changes in Argentine politics, not a return to what they consider to be a fraudulent electoral system.

Urban guerrilla groups have also emerged in Argentina to form spectacular sources of opposition to the government and the system. There are a number of these groups, apparently operating independently, and with ideologies ranging from far left to far right. These groups have engaged in numerous bombings, robberies, kidnappings, and destruction of property. They have claimed credit for some assassinations and have fought several battles with police and the armed forces. These terrorist groups have emerged since 1968. They have mounted attacks on some military camps and have taken over the control of small towns for short periods of time. The government so far has been unable to stop the activities of these terrorist groups, and the number of such groups seems to be increasing.

In June 1970 General Onganía was removed from the presidency by a coup led by a military junta which named General Roberto Marcelo Levingston as the new president. The Levingston government announced its support for "truly representative political parties" and appeared to be willing to talk with civilian politicians. It promised elections, but set no definite date for holding them. Bombings and both urban and rural violence continued under the Levingston regime. There were serious clashes between government opponents and police and military forces in Buenos Aires, Córdoba, and Rosario with some deaths resulting. Extremist groups gave no sign of heeding governmental calls for national unity.

By October of 1970 the Levingston government was taking a more "hard line" stance, and announced that no elections would be held for at least four years. On March 22, 1971, less than a year after assuming power, President Levingston was ousted from the presidency in a bloodless coup headed by General Alejandro Lanusse, the commander of the army. Political party activity, which had expanded under Levingston, increased under Lanusse. Efforts to form a coalition containing both Peronista and non-Peronista political groups were soon underway. This coalition, "The Hour of the People," called for early elections. In July Interior Minister Arturo Mor Roig announced that President Lanusse's administration intended to turn control over to a popularly elected civilian government by May, 1973.

During the latter part of 1971 the government ununsuccessfully tried to curb a sharply increasing inflation with the imposition of wage and price controls, and the devaluation of the peso. Guerrilla activity continued at a fairly steady rate. On August 8 President Lanusse hinted he might legalize the Communist party in exchange for a promise to break with radical elements advocating violence. This offer represented an attempt to deepen already existing divisions among leftist groups. In October of 1971 the Lanusse government had to contend with an attempted barracks revolt in the city of Azul. This uprising was led by an Army commander who favored the "hard line" advocated by ousted President Levingston. The attempted coup was put down without bloodshed. The Lanusse government clearly retained the support of a majority of the military. Just as clearly, however, the government was far from solving the economic and political problems which faced a badly divided Argentina.

Conclusion

Opposition and dissent have become dispersed throughout Argentina's political system. There is no single political institution which monopolizes the role of opposition. Since 1943, all sectors of Argentine political life have functioned from time to time as opponents of the government. The most powerful sources of opposition are the military and the Peronistas. Both are divided internally. Political parties have proved themselves to be ineffective agents of government since the Perón era. New sources of opposition have emerged in the form of urban and rural terrorists and Church radicals. These new sources of opposition are willing to use violence as a tactic of opposition to the prevailing political system. They are, indeed, opposed to the Argentine political system itself, not merely to the governments in power. They call for drastic changes in Argentina's political, economic, and social relationships, not merely for new faces in the government. The Perón government started to bring about such changes, particularly by attempting to integrate the working class into politics and by providing labor with a greater share of economic, social, and political benefits than it had ever before enjoyed. Since Perón, the problem of the Peronista place in society has split all political groups. Civilian governments that have attempted to work with peronistas have been ousted by the military. Peronistas themselves have served as opponents of military governments.

In Argentina, the role of opposition is difficult to define because of the extraordinarily fragmented nature of the political system. All politically active groups, including the military, political parties, students, trade unionists, and the Church, are divided. There are factions in each group which bitterly oppose other factions in the same group. The definitional difficulty involved in the idea of opposition is that opposition is usually thought of in relational terms. In Argentina there is no majority, there is no aggregating institution in the political system. In such a situation it becomes difficult to say what the opposition is opposed to. Different sectors of the opposition are opposed to different things, and there is no central focus for the opposition. The result is that opposition elements themselves become fragmented, and the opposition can offer no coherent alternative to existing governments or the existing system. Should a government be toppled, its successor would face just as serious problems as the fallen government. It would be opposed, with differing intensity, by many different sectors for many different reasons. The new government would represent a narrow segment of groups which had opposed the old government. It would not represent an acceptable solution to all groups previously in the opposition. In such a situation, civilian governments such as the Illia government will inevitably prove incapable of effectively attacking political and economic problems because they will be unable to achieve a majority of the needed legislative votes for their programs. Military governments, such as the Onganía regime, will encounter difficulties due to internal divisions among the military over the questions of (1) whether the military should return control to civilians and (2) whether policies followed by the military government are harmful to the military as an institution. When a dominant group in the military believes that the answer to either question is yes, then the existing leader will be ousted and replaced by a new military man. Usually the answer to the second question will depend on factors such as the amount of civilian unrest, the intensity of division within the military, and the results of governmental economic and social policies.

Political problems have made Argentina into one of the most unstable countries in Latin America, whether measured by the number and frequency of governmental turnovers, or, since 1968, whether measured by some indicator of internal violence. No political structure currently appears capable of performing the role of political aggregation in Argentina. In the absence of an aggregator, opposition will continue to be spread through all political groups in society and will be directed at both the government in power and the system itself. Both government and system will remain unstable. The most probable cycle will be as follows: A military government will rule. It will run into opposition from within the government over the policies it is following. A coup will occur and bring to power (1) new military leaders who promise civilian rule or (2) new military leaders promising a harder line against civilian unrest. If the new government allows elections, the elected government will be a minority government and will be unable to get support for its policies from other civilian politicians. Political and economic problems will go unsolved and civilian and military opposition to the government will increase. Eventually, the government will be toppled by a military government promising to bring order to Argentina. The cycle will then repeat.

If the coup overthrowing a military government institutes a harder line against civilian unrest, the probable cycle will be that repression of civilians will be followed by increased violence against the military. The military leaders will become split over the extent of suppression to be used to put down violence. Eventually, a coup will overthrow the government and there will again be an attempt to allow civilians to rule. The civilians will be ineffective and the cycle will repeat.

One way to break the cycle would be to have a very strong, very effective military government that would ruthlessly suppress all opposition groups. Since there is much division among the military on this issue, it is unlikely that such a very strong ruthless government will come to power. A second way to break the cycle would be to have a civilian government come to power that would purge the military and destroy the military's ability to dominate Argentine politics. It is very unlikely that the military would allow this to happen.

During the last quarter century, then, opposition and dissent have been dysfunctional in the Argentine political system. Opposition has primarily aimed at overthrowing governments, not at opposing and criticizing specific issues. Perón's treatment of opposition groups allowed the opposition no choice but to attempt to oust him. Under Perón, the opposition became the enemy, and as such was actively persecuted by the government. Since the fall of Perón, opposition groups have come to oppose the system of government as well as the governments in power. Their goal has been to change the political system so as to implement broad economic and social change and so as to allow Peronistas to again play a legitimate political role. Increasingly, opposition groups have felt that neither of these goals can be accomplished without violence. In Argentina there is no effective aggregation agent either for the governments in power or for opposition. There is opposition from all groups in the system but they are not opposed to the same things.

Consequently, there is no way to satisfy all opposition groups. Some will always be opposed, and in Argentina in the years since 1943 to be opposed means to favor the ousting of the government. Given this situation, no government can respect the opposition, no compromise seems possible. The function of opposition in Argentina is, therefore, to fragment the polity and to further decrease the possibility that an aggregating structure will emerge in the political system.

4

Patterns
of Indian
Political Conflict

Angela S. Burger
University of Wisconsin

Two distinct patterns of political conflict can be detected in India since its independence. In the first stage from independence until 1967, Indian politics was characterized, nationally and in most of the states, by a multiparty system with a dominant party. The second stage began in 1967 with the end of Congress dominance and increasing competitiveness. Still, however, after the split in the Congress, a majority party continued on the national level.

In the first stage (party dominance), the primary political conflicts seemed to be within the Congress. There was an increase in the intensity of factionalism as well as the institutionalization of factions on a statewide and national basis. Factional layers appeared, with many state leaders having their own groups but able to develop support from other factional leaders. Prominent state and national figures became known for their ability to manipulate other factional leaders. On higher levels (national and sometimes state) factions had divergent orientations in economic, linguistic, communal, and secular policies, as well as bases in regional or socioeconomic identifications. Close personal ties within factions and personality differences between them were more marked on lower levels.

The factions in Congress were competitive and cooperative; a better description might be competitive but coalescent. A major factor in the coalescence was the desire to hold office and share power. This was possible only in the Congress. The Congress was dominant and its members had seen what had happened to those who had departed in the late 1940's; they knew that Congress held the shears that had cut the locks of Samsons.

Little attention was paid to opposition parties as such; intraparty factionalism was more important. Congress factions did utilize opposition parties for their own purposes. Factional spokesmen would encourage select opposition parties to take a strong stand, replete with agitation, on a certain issue in order to strengthen the position of those within Congress favoring that stand. To better the position of their faction in the intraparty power game, leaders would provide information and encourage opposition leaders to make charges—corruption, maladministration, immorality, and the like—against specific Congressmen. Occasionally an opposition party leader might be asked to intercede with Congress officials on behalf of a specific Congress faction. A case in point occurred a few years ago in Uttar Pradesh, where a prominent Praja Socialist was asked by the dissident state Congress faction to plead its case before a particular member of the Congress High Command. There was a caste connection between the two leaders which the dissidents hoped to exploit. In this case as in others it was difficult to separate policy and factional interests. Sometimes factional leaders delighted in using a policy decision to score over their opponents, while not caring particularly about what policy position they took. At other times, of course, policy differences were real and salient. It was sometimes difficult to distinguish the occasions, and one could easily become a complete cynic.

Given the intense factionalism in the dominant party, it would seem logical to expect opposition parties to utilize that friction to promote their own policy preferences. However, in Uttar Pradesh a few years ago my queries into this kind of interaction were met with what might be described as shocked outrage. Respondents considered many tactics and strategies—including riots—to be legitimate efforts to attain a policy goal. But to play on Congress factionalism was seen as immoral, unethical, illegal, unconstitutional, and a slur on the honor and integrity of opposition parties and their leaders. The only difference in attitude between opposition and Congress respondents was that the Congressmen tended to be amused as well. Perhaps this general attitude is peculiar to Uttar Pradesh. It is certainly difficult to explain.

Basically the prime bargaining and policy opposition was within the Congress. The idea that democracy might include a dialogue with minority parties did not seem to be understood. There seemed to be a general reluctance on the part of Congress to acknowledge that opposition parties spoke for any groups. Congress leaders were aware of the importance in election victories of the personal element and the social configuration. They did not regard opposition parties as having a policy mandate. The opposition parties had to "prove" their representativeness—in this country with few and financially weak interest groups—by mobilizing people in agitations. When opposition parties could prove they did represent a large and intense group, then a policy change might result. Even here the dialogue would not be with the opposition party, however, but within the dominant party. A factional leader would take up the position, often without reference to the opposition party.

During this period the Congress declined in strength, more markedly in the states than on the national level. The reasons for the decline were legion.[1] One was the intense Congress factionalism, which led to efforts to defeat factional opponents in elections. Congress could afford to lose more than just a few seats because they had so many. P. R. Brass points out that during major factional struggles Congress membership swelled, and the Congress ranks were renewed.[2] However, it is one thing to enlist dues-paying members; it is another to recruit among different strata of society; it is another to represent interests of new groups; it is yet another to give leadership positions to representatives of new entrants. And these "others" weren't done. The Congress leadership was increasingly drawn from groups mobilized by the time of independence. Leaders of more recently mobilized groups, finding that they could not gain recognition in the Congress, increasingly turned to the opposition parties.

Congress policies adversely affected the status, role, and functions of some, and these turned to opposition parties. Where policies were not carried out, another group began turning to the opposition parties. The opposition parties were infused also by displaced leaders—those who could not survive the transition of a national movement to a governing party, either because of inability or unwillingness to discard agitational skills, or because of a lack of education, or because they did not have the backing of a politically mobilized group. These used their talents and skills in building the opposition.

The Congress had become vulnerable. Another time bomb was hidden in aggregate electoral data. In many areas, the Congress tended to win seats formerly held by the opposition parties, and the opposition parties to win seats which had been held by the Congress. As the several opposition parties extended their organizations throughout the countryside, and as they developed methods of working together, it was apparent that the process would eventually work to the disadvantage of the Congress which had more seats to lose.

In 1967 all these factors coalesced, in a setting marked by critical problems of economic development and foreign relations as well as the death of the great leader Jawaharlal Nehru, to bring about the electoral outcome of that year. The interaction of many factors trebled the vulnerabilities of the Congress and led to its debacle. To the opposition parties, of course, the electoral outcome was a resounding victory. The victory of what? The answer is still in the making.

The current stage of political conflict began in 1967 with the change in party system from one-party dominance to moderately competitive multiparty. The Congress lost its dominance and in over half the states lost its majority as well. The pattern is marked and will probably continue to be marked by political instability, fluctuations in party strength, and party schisms and realignments. Opposition leaders quickly understood that they had options open to them which before had never existed, and they seemed to choose with care which option to exercise. It would have been so easy, for example, for each of a variety of parties in several states to have formed a coalition government with the Congress—far easier than forming a coalition government of seven or eight other parties. It would have been so easy for the opposition parties to have split, with factions rushing to join the Congress and thereby transform it into a majority party once again. It would have been so easy for individuals to have deserted the party-of-election in favor of the Congress. That these events did not happen immediately tends to indicate the care with which decisions were made by individuals and parties. It also demonstrates the existence of some powerful tensions in the society.

The electoral outcome also seemed to change the political outlook of opposition parties. When far removed from power, leaders and members of opposition parties stressed the differences among themselves and often showed little desire to cooperate with one another. With control of the government now an option, under the condition of cooperation, the opposition party leaders and members began to explore the areas of likeness and showed a degree of pragmatism that had previously been absent. With the possibility of running the government now an option, some internal leadership changes were to be expected, in the direction of a rise of those with administrative rather than agitational skills, and of those with subject matter expertise rather than merely skill in emotional rhetoric. Similarly, being a government party made opposition party membership more attractive to many individuals in the society—and in the Congress.

The change in party system also affected the Congress, but many Congress leaders did not seem to perceive the constraints of the new situation as quickly. For example, the electoral outcome affected the internal factional struggles. As was mentioned earlier, one factor cementing factions to the Congress was the share of governmental power available only through the dominant Congress. Now the electoral tide had washed away that cement. In such a situation, more rather than less compromise would seem to be necessary to hold the party together. But many leaders both in the states and at the center acted as if the commitment of members to the party were even stronger than before. Initially on the state level and then nationally, factional leaders took unusually strong if not extreme measures against their opponents, with the apparent expectation that the factional opponents would accept any kind of treatment. So in Haryana, the chief minister, B. D. Sharma, decided to omit his three factional opponents and their followers from his ministry. In Uttar Pradesh, C. B. Gupta decided not to honor the agreement worked out regarding the role of Charan Singh in forming a ministry. On the national level, Indira Gandhi and the Syndicate each took grossly offensive actions against the other. "Take it or leave it" was the theme, with factional leaders seeming to believe that the others would "take it." But the commitment to the Congress had been eroded. Alternatives were open to factional leaders that previously had been closed. And in many instances the disaffected leaders exercised that option and left the Congress.

There are other interpretations of Congress schisms. One is that the Congress high command could not control the state leaders as they had previously. For years this trend had been apparent, and the deaths of Jawaharlal Nehru and Lal Bahadur Shastri marked a convenient breaking-point. Another is that the new national leaders found it difficult to act as arbiters in the states because of their involvement in and

106

identification with specific factions in the states. Closely associated with this interpretation is that national leaders in their struggles with each other needed the support of state parties, had little incentive to act as arbiters, and were forced to support only their followers in the states. Another interpretation is simply that Indira Gandhi is not the politician her father was. All these factors undoubtedly played a role in Indian politics; however, the change in the party system served as a catalyst, making the alternative of defection markedly more attractive than it had been in previous years.

The electoral results also meant that the relations between the Congress and the other parties changed. Again, some Congress leaders seemed unable to adjust to the new situation. They continued to act in the condescending manner of former years, which might help explain why they were unable to obtain sufficient support from the ranks of opposition parties and independents to form a winning legislative coalition. In some states, Congressmen had difficulty accepting opposition status. They worked incessantly to bring down the government; reports of bribery and kidnapping were not uncommon.

Another dimension of interparty relations was due to the federal structure of the Indian government. There were strains in operating a federal system with the Congress in control nationally and with non-Congress governments in many states. Many Congress leaders on the national level undoubtedly wanted to strengthen themselves by ousting non-Congress governments in their home states; many were undoubtedly pressured by state-level Congress leaders to make things difficult for non-Congress governments. Even without such pressure, relations would have been difficult. As compared with the Congress, many of the United Front Governments showed a marked difference in class, caste, and rural/urban orientation in both their composition and policies. In some states, their desires to speed up economic development, especially in rural areas, while relieving the tax burden on the rural poor and coping with near-famine conditions led these state governments to operate well in the red, and to demand additional funds from the center. Of course, the center could not possibly have obliged all, nor did it want to. In West Bengal, the support given to labor and to more violent processes created an economic problem as well as one of order.

This period was also marked by the development of a new pressure technique—the *gherao*—and by the beginning of the *naxalbari* movement, both of which carried with them insecurity and disorder. Communal and linguistic problems flared anew. There was governmental immobility in many states as their governments concerned themselves with mere survival. The result was predictable: instability and President's Rule. The Congress split raised the specter of the same kind of instability on the national level. That ghost was exorcised in the subsequent election.

A Theory of Interparty Coalition Maintenance

Some states with coalition governments enjoyed greater stability and less immobility than others. Under what conditions did this occur? Basically the problem is that of interparty coalition maintenance, which is a different process from that of coalition formation.[3] I would like to share with you, in summary form, a theory of coalition maintenance which has at least two interesting points in its favor: first of all, it does not rely on traditional factors (which can be used to explain anything), and secondly, the theory holds up thus far in cross-national testing.

The theory is based on assumptions that coalitions are desirable, that every actor—whether collective (i.e., a party) or individual—knows the possible combinations of actors which would provide a winning coalition and can rank these combinations in order of preferences, and that payoffs are controlled to the extent that collective actors (parties) cannot receive payoffs unless they enter a winning coalition. There are some specific conditions which affect the operation of the following hypotheses. One condition is the extent of internal party cohesion. In India, cohesion tends to be low, which means payoffs are uncontrolled to the extent that individual actors do not have to remain members of a particular collectivity (party) to obtain payoffs in a winning coalition. Another condition specifies the utility of maintaining membership in a particular collectivity in terms of institutionalization of conflict by parties (i.e., the relationship of electoral success-failure to party membership), ideology, tangible payoffs, and so on. As Brass has indicated, institutionalization of conflict in India varies from state to state but on an all-India basis would have to be considered fairly low.[4] In many states on the state level, utility seems rarely to involve the factor of ideology.

This theory is based on definite internal structural characteristics of coalitions. Actors in a coalition can be categorized as either essential or inessential to winning status. With a minimum winning coalition there would be no inessential actors; however, there are several reasons why actors in a parliamentary setting would try to form coalitions larger than minimal for the purpose of governing. Adrian and Press have detailed some of these reasons as the costs of information, dissonance, responsibility, persuasion, and so forth.[5] A sample of parliamentary coalitions (alternate years, 1948-68) revealed that the most frequently occurring sizes ranged from 55 to 61% of the seats in the lower house. It is quite possible for several small parties as well as independents to be inessential—not to have the numeric strength to bring down a coalition government. It is, of course, fairly easy to determine if an actor is sufficiently large to be essential or inessential.

In addition to being either essential or inessential, actors can be in favorable or unfavorable position to form a new winning coalition should the existing coalition collapse.[6] This factor should affect the behavior of the various actors in the coalition. The favorability index for this theory is based on determining, for each collective actor, the number of possible alternative winning coalitions in which it could participate, with points of being given in accordance with the preferability of different coalition sizes,[7] as well as the variable of parsimony in regard to the number of collective actors in each possible coalition. To make the task manageable, three size ranges with equal intervals were posited. Actors are given points on this basis: 15 points for participation in each possible coalition in the most frequently occurring range of 55.00% to 59.99% (hereafter called the optimal), 10 points in the second most frequently occurring range of 50.00% to 54.99% (called the minimal), and 5 points for the third range of 60.00% to 64.99% (called the maximal).[8] Most of the parliamentary coalitions (at least over the past 20 years) fall into these size ranges. The variable of parsimony is taken into account by giving an additional 5 points to each actor in a coalition of two, and 2 points for a coalition of three. In determining favorability, one other variable seemed to be important. It seemed logical to subtract points for actors less than a certain small size. Granted, a small party or even one individual can be occasionally in a critical position to make a winning or losing coalition. However, most of the time one individual or small party can be readily substituted for another (particularly if the system contains several small parties or independents). A minor consideration is that there are obvious limits to what can be offered to or requested by the very small in size when a coalition is being built. Coalition builders would be fools to offer each independent a ministerial position! So, while within each size range, and between the ranges, individual actors and small collective actors can be added or dropped in varying combinations, it would seem to be appropriate to subtract for each actor with less than 3% of the seats in the lower house, 2 points for participation in each possible coalition. The scoring system is summarized in Table 4.1. To determine favorability, the total possible score in that particular setting is figured; all actors

110

with a score in the upper 55% of the total are considered to be in a favorable position to form a new coalition should the existing one collapse, and those in the lower 45% are considered in an unfavorable position.

From these two factors, a fourfold classification results, and the behavior of actors in each category can be hypothesized and then tested.

Actors essential to the coalition and in a favorable position to form a new coalition should the existing one collapse will tend to make the highest demands, will tend to be the most intransigent, will tend to be the least willing to compromise, and will not generally provide mediators or bargainers. Theirs is the *pivotal* position[9] and they will take advantage of it. A coalition with several actors in this category is the more difficult to maintain. Conflict between or among pivotal actors will be critical and will tend to lead to the collapse of the coalition. Stability is likely only if salient differences do not occur among them. Of course, having identified the pivotal actors in a coalition, one can often predict what kinds of issues are likely to lead to intense conflict. Of course, actors might have preferences for a particular coalition, relating to the payoffs available, the

Table 4.1: Favorability Scoring Summary

| Favorability factors | Size ranges | | |
	55-59%	50-54%	60-64%
Basic points	15	10	5
Factor of Parsimony:			
Coalition contains 2	+5	+5	+5
Coalition contains 3	+2	+2	+2
Factor of smallness			
Actors with less than 3%			
of seats in lower house	−2	−2	−2

Example: Seats in lower house are distributed as follows: A = 41.46%; B = 43.09%; C = 13.00%; D = 2.45%; E = .81%.

Winning coalition of ACE (55.27) has been formed. If it

111

collapses, no combination containing ACE is allowable; the possible alternatives follow (numbers indicate the score in terms of basic points and parsimony; factor of smallness is figured in "Scoring"):

Posible Alternative Coalitions	55.00-59.00%	50.00-54.99%	60.00-64.99%
ACD = 56.10	(17)	AC = 54.46	NONE
BC = 56.09	(20)		POSSIBLE
BCD = 58.54	(17)		
BCE = 56.90	(17)		
BCDE = 59.35	(15)		

Scoring

A: $17 + 15 = 32$
B: $20 + 17 + 17 + 15 = 69$
C: $17 + 20 + 17 + 17 + 15 + 15 = 101$
D: $(17-2) + (17-2) + (15-2) = 43$
E: $(17-2) + (15-2) = 28$

Total score possible, 101; favorable if score is 45.45 or higher. In the coalition, only C ranks as favorable, and because it is essential, C is the pivotal member of the coalition. A is a mainstay and, under conditions of low cohesion, one might expect the party to split. E is inessential and unfavorable.

---

division of the payoff, inertia costs in changing a coalition, and the like. Preference can affect whether an actor withdraws completely from a coalition or withdraws from the ministry but continues to support the government in the legislature.

Actors generally prefer the status of essential-favorable, or pivotal, and will often attempt to become so. Sometimes this can be accomplished by merging with other actors and sometimes by division into two or more smaller units. When a party split would place both segments in a pivotal position, there would be few incentives to hold the party together. If only one segment would be pivotal, the other would be expected to make strenuous efforts to avoid the schism. In a system with low cohesion, as determined by low institutionalization of conflict, movements to become pivotal may characterize the activities of various parties. An opposition party eager to topple the government would be expected to encourage such movement.

The second category is composed of those actors which are essential to the coalition but in an unfavorable position to form a new coalition should the existing one collapse. These actors will make high demands but will either retreat—if the conflict is between them and a pivotal actor—or compromise if the conflict is with others in this same category. They will show displeasure and make threats, but will back down. These essential-unfavorable actors or mainstays of a coalition, will provide mediators or bargainers. In many instances, the larger parties in a coalition seem to fall into this category—just as was the case with party A in Table 1 in the example given.[10]

The third category is composed of actors that are inessential to the coalition but in a favorable position for forming another one. These will tend to show disaffection often, will actively seek alliances within the coalition, will provide mediators, etc. If they are successful in forming alliances which then are essential, they will be less willing to compromise, will not provide mediators, and often will behave as do pivotal actors. If they cannot form "essential" alliances then they will function to resolve crises, will compromise, and will try to bring about compromises. These would be the easiest to dislodge from a coalition government because of their dissatisfaction with their rewards in the government and their favorable position.

Actors in the last and least desirable category—inessential and unfavorable—will tend to grumble occasionally but will rarely make strong demands. They will seek allies, will provide mediators, and by performing functions such as communication, aggregation, and mediation will attempt to create obligations for other actors, which under social exchange or the norm of reciprocity could be returned in some tangible payoff. Individual actors such as independents are likely to fall into this category.

Under the condition of low party cohesion, with its attendant schisms, defections, and mergers, actors can be expected to change from one category to another fairly frequently. Their behavior would change with their position.

With this theory some predictions can also be made about the activities of actors in the opposition, especially in systems with low party cohesion. Actors in the opposition will attempt to nurture conflict in the winning coalition by several methods. They can attempt to remove inessential actors who, of course, perform some very desirable functions for maintenance. They can attempt to change actors in the coalition from unfavorable to favorable by different means. A schism or merger of those in the opposition may succeed in changing the classification of those in the coalition. Or they can encourage factions within a mainstay party (essential-unfavorable) to defect, thereby changing one or both segments to a favorable position. Or they could encourage merger of groups in the coalition so as to create additional pivotal actors. The purpose, of course, is to create a coalition containing numerous pivotal actors. Then issues can be raised or forced which would divide pivotal actors, and would probably lead to the collapse of the coalition. Such tactics are likely to be employed with considerable fervor where there is no tradition of alternate party rule of the government. Where this condition exists along with low party cohesion, party fractionalization and political instability are to be expected.

Coalition Politics in India

Having outlined the theory, let us illustrate it by referring to the coalition politics of a few Indian states, looking at the period closely following thy 1967 general elections. The state of Haryana provides a very clear picture of the politics of coalition maintenance with more than one pivotal actor.

In Haryana there were three distinct political periods from the 1967 elections until the establishment of President's Rule in November of that year. In the first period, from the election until late March, the Congress had a comfortable majority of the seats in the lower house. There was obviously no question of a coalition—save that the Congress itself could be viewed as a coalition of different groups. One Congress factional leader, B. D. Sharma, decided to form a ministry without his three factional opponents. Protests and pleas from the dissidents to the Congress high command were to no avail. As long as these factions were committed to Congress membership, they were clearly in an unfavorable bargaining position. If, however, a group was both willing to leave the Congress and sufficient in size to bring down the Congress, it would become essential-favorable. The Devi Lal faction and Rao Birendra Singh factions together were of that size, and they combined under the leadership of the latter, issued a twenty-four-hour ultimatum to B. D. Sharma, and, when it was not met, brought down the government. The high command apparently did nothing to pressure Sharma or placate the dissidents until the latter had actually left the Congress.

The second period began in late March when, under Rao Birendra Singh, the Haryana Congress was formed and a United Front government of all the former opposition parties was set up. (The Independents had by that time formed no party in the Assembly.)

Once this government was formed, the new Haryana Congress under Rao Birendra Singh—while essential—was no longer in a favorable position to form a new coalition should that one collapse. The Jan Sangh and the Independent Navin Haryana Janata (Independent's party) were pivotal, and both the Swatantra and Republican parties were inessential and unfavorable (see Table 4.2). In May the Swatantra party threatened to withdraw support from the government unless the minimum price of wheat was raised to 100 rupees. Their demand was not met; they did not leave the government, and after that were never reported making any demands at all. The Republicans apparently never made any demands or any threats whatsoever. The Jan Sangh, under directions from

Table 4.2: Favorability Scores of Parties in Haryana, 1967

(asterisk* denotes favorability; underlined are essential)

Parties	March 24, 1967 Total Psb: 164 Fav. − 73.80+	August 4, 1967 Total psb.: 303 Fav. − 136.35+	Sept. 12, 1967 Total psb.: 77 Fav. − 34.65+
Jan Sangh	121*	146*	77*a
Independent Navin Haryana Janata	81*	126	−
Haryana Congress	66	146	−
Vishal Haryana	−	−	30
Swatantra	44	109	−
Republican	44	109	−
Devi Lal's group (not in coalition)	−	96	27
Congress (not in coalition	122	238	47

[a]By this time the Jan Sangh was in the uniquely advantageous position of being a necessary participant for any coalition possible in the three size groups.

their national leaders, had refused to accept any ministerial positions (in part to show their disinterest in the "loaves and fishes of office"), but were noted as having great if not "undue" influence in the United Front.[11] Unfortunately the press reports do not mention the Independent party at all in this period, which in itself might indicate satisfaction. The account in the press emphasized the difficulty Rao Birendra

116

Singh had in maintaining harmony in the coalition, with the friction stemming from Devi Lal's (Jat) group within the Haryana Congress.[12] Unfortunately the press did not give the size of Devi Lal's group until it apparently left the United Front with a total of six members. Then the press reported surprise at the small size, and estimates were made that Devi Lal initially had the support of 13 to 16 members.[13] The "Devi Lal Six" were not enough to be essential to the coalition; a larger group would have been both essential and favorable. Rao Birendra Singh had twice expanded his ministry during the summer to stave off attacks by Devi Lal, and the granting of such tangible rewards was mentioned as having reduced the size of Devi Lal's following.[14]

While the newspaper accounts of the summer leave something to be desired, it is safe to assume that by early August Devi Lal's group of six had definitely left the United Front. The governing coalition was by then minimal in size; all actors had become essential and about half the legislators in the Front held some kind of ministerial position. The Jan Sangh and Haryana Congress had become pivotal; all others, while essential, were unfavorable (see Table 4.2). Defections ceased for a time and it appeared that a new configuration of forces had developed. Almost immediately in this third period, conflict arose between the pivotal Jan Sangh and Haryana Congress concerning a trucker's strike (with two of the truckers' organizations being led by Jan Sangh leaders) over a new law on goods passed by the United Front (with the support of the Jan Sangh in the government). Apparently, it was the unusual internal division in the Jan Sangh that prevented the collapse of the coalition on this issue; the press did not report on the resolution of the conflict at all.[15] In early September a group of five to eight Jan Sanghis, who were identified with the truckers' organizations and other labor groups, threatened to leave the party, and their demands on the party and the government became greater every week. The Jan Sangh then made demands on the chief

117

minister with an open threat of withdrawal unless the demands were met.[16] The chief minister countered with action—begging Devi Lal to return to the Front, opening talks himself with Congress leaders about a possible coalition, and forming a new party (the Vishal Haryana) of 29 of the 30 non-Jan Sanghis in the front. The Vishal Haryana was essential to the coalition but was not favorable; it was not, in other words, pivotal (see Table 2). The chief minister seemed to be trying to improve the likelihood of continuance by removing one of the actors from the pivotal category, whether he was conscious of this or not. However, within days there was disaffection within the new party. Some of the members possibly realized they were in a less advantageous position in the coalition. For several weeks there was manuevering within the Vishal Haryana and Jan Sangh and between them. At the end of October the tenuous relationships broke down and defections—from virtually every party to every other party—began.[17] These few weeks of rapid movement with practically each individual actor being essential and having two choices (to remain where he was or join the other side) marked the end of the period. The actual end came with the establishment of President's Rule and the dissolution of the Assembly. Realignment of politicians and parties continued unabated for several weeks.

In the Pubjab immediately after the 1967 elections, even greater friction and instability might have been expected. An eight-party coalition (minimal in size) had been formed containing the Sant Akali Dal, the Jan Sangh, and the two communist parties. Reporters pointed out that the division of the old Punjab state into the new Punjab and Haryana was largely due to the friction between militant Sikhs (in the SAD) and militant Hindus (JS), that the Jan Sangh was virulently anticommunist, and that the communist parties were two instead of one because of their inability to compromise their differences. Given this background, the comity within the coalition surprised observers. Within a

118

short time reporters began to comment on the "transformation of Punjab politics" which stemmed from the harmony
among the disparate parties. In hopes of dividing the
coalition, the Congress leaders raised the issue of state trading
in grain, a question which was important to the Jan Sangh
and the communists and on which they had taken different
stands. The ploy failed. Even the question of the status of
Chandigarh (which one would expect to be divisive inasmuch
as the Jan Sangh was a coalition partner in Haryana, the
other state claiming the city) failed to divide the Jan Sangh
and Sant Akali Dal.

A theory of coalition maintenance which related stability
to either ideological congruence or socioeconomic similarities
could not explain the accord in the Pubjab. Structurally,
however, all the coalition partners fell into the "unfavorable"
category. Some were essential, others not, but none was in a
favorable position to form a new coalition should that one
collapse (see Table 4.3). The Sant Akali Dal held the lowest
favorability score, which may help to explain why their
members accepted scanty representation in the cabinet with a
minimum of grumbling.[18] Leaders of various parties in the
Punjab acted as the theory specified. They did not make
extreme demands on each other, but compromised their
differences.

After learning that they could not separate the parties by
raising what were considered to be divisive issues, the
Congress tried a new ploy. They endeavored to split the Sant
Akali Dal by offering the chief ministership to anyone who
would bring down the government and form a winning
coalition with the Congress. As was stated, the SAD had the
lowest favorability score; in a split, however, any unit with
10 to 15% of the seats in the lower house would become
pivotal. Given conditions of low party cohesion, offer of such
a reward is likely to be a very successful method of dividing a
party or gaining supporters, and L. Gill succumbed to the
temptation. From his ministerial position, Gill began to

119

Table 4.3: Favorability Scores of Parties in the Gurnan Singh United Front Government, Punjab, 1967

(favorable: score of 481 or higher)

Parties	Favorable Score	% of Seats in Assembly
In the United Front:		
Sant Akali Dal	70	23.07
Jan Sangh	434	8.65
CPI	331	4.80
CPI-M	379	2.88
Independents*	387	5.77
Republicans	379	2.88
Master Akali Dal	347	1.92
Samyukta Socialist Party	442	.96
Not in Coalition:		
Congress	999	46.15
Independents*	379	2.88

*The Independents were divided; the numbers in each group are approximate and were derived from analysis of reports given in *The Statesman* on March 8, 22; April 4, 6; May 27, 1967.

gather a group about him in a time-honored manner. He took stands preferred by the members of the Dal—such as ruling that his office would accept only communications and petitions in Punjabi, not Hindi—which made it difficult for his own party leaders to discipline him without losing support, and which antagonized a coalition partner (in the language question, obviously the Jan Sangh).[19] When he had obtained the support of 15% of the legislators in the lower house (drawn from five different units in the coalition), he brought down the Gurnan Singh ministry and with the aid of Congress set up his own government. What he had done was to bring several persons belonging to unfavorable units into a pivotal group. The Gurnan ministry fell about the same time as that of Rao Birendra Singh in Haryana, but the politics in the two had been vastly different. Missing in the Punjab were the daily shifts of legislators from party to party, the frantic scrambling to maintain a majority, the threat of withdrawal unless demands were met, the bloating of the cabinet with new defectors, etc. The politics of Haryana had been a politics of immobility. Not so in Punjab.

Instead of analyzing other states, let me just comment on various parties and how they acted in a few states. In Bihar after the 1967 elections a coalition was formed that contained three pivotal parties. However, the Samyukta Socialist Party, the largest—and essential—party, was in the unfavorable category. Cursory analysis indicated that the reason for this unfavorable position was that it was too large. A split would increase the options available. Actions of party leaders seemed to indicate an awareness of this situation, because for several months there were successive accounts of internal friction over policies and personnel. Dr. Lobia did not behave like a leader trying to hold a party together; he denounced a faction in the party and went so far as to call some SSP ministers in the Bihar government "moral lepers."[20] A faction led by B. P. Mandal seemed equally interested in departing, and did so in August, 1967, forming the Soshit Dal. The Soshit Dal was in a favorable position to form a new coalition but was not large enough initially to be essential. The SSP was still essential, and while its favorability score had been raised, it was still not high enough to reach the favorable category. For a time each party concerned itself with either gaining or losing a few more adherents, a process that would tend to place both in the essential-favorable category. Eventually, using methods open to criticism, the Soshit Dal attracted enough support to become essential and brought down the government. Interestingly, the PSP was in the third category of inessential but favorable until the SSP split. At that point it became pivotal and began acting accordingly. Before that time there were no reports of the PSP making extreme demands or refusing to compromise;

after the change in category the PSP made demands and threatened withdrawal unless they were met.[21]

In the 1967 United Front government of Charan Singh in Uttar Pradesh, the SSP was initially in the essential-unfavorable (mainstay) category and, as in Bihar, concerned itself with internal matters. A series of what seemed to be minor shifts among several parties served, however, to change the SSP into a pivotal member. Thereafter, the conflicting demands of the SSP and Charan Singh's Jana Congress filled the *Statesman*; threats of withdrawal were made by both sides and eventually carried out.[22] By contrast, in the 1967 coalition government in Madhya Pradesh, the nonessential and unfavorable SSP members were models of decorum; there was nary a report of the kind of behavior that characterized the party elsewhere.

In Madhya Pradesh it was the friction between the two pivotal parties, the Jan Sangh and Lok Sevak Dal, which brought down that coalition. The Jan Sangh had initially been essential-unfavorable (a mainstay) in that coalition— which helps to explain why its leaders accepted less representation in the ministry than its size would warrant. Although it was the largest party in the coalition, the party had only 7 ministers as compared to the 19 given to the much smaller group of Congress defectors.[23] Not until the party became pivotal were there reports of disagreement and intransigence stemming from the Jan Sangh. Likewise, in Uttar Pradesh where the Jan Sangh was essential-unfavorable for many months, the party made demands but backed down in every conflict except when they were in alliance with a pivotal actor. Even on the occasions when the Jan Sangh made their strongest demands with threats of resignation, they said in virtually the same breath that of course they would not withdraw support from the government. The party changed its behavior when it thought it had become pivotal: its leaders apparently believed rumors that a group was ready to leave the Congress and establish a party available for

122

coalition formation. Calculations showed that if a group of the reputed size had split off, the Jan Sangh would have become pivotal in the existing coalition. It was at this point that the Jan Sangh became intransigent.[24] It was also at this point that the Praja Socialist Party—which had been inessential-unfavorable and had endeavored to mediate disputes within the coalition—became pivotal, and promptly ceased to perform a mediation function.

While not exhaustive, perhaps these few examples help to illustrate both the theory of maintenance as well as some patterns of conflict in the second state. By-elections in the states did not restore Congress majorities, but it was not until the Congress split that the possibility of restoration appeared lost. The Congress bullocks had been pulling in different directions for years, and in 1970 the leaders removed the yoke that had held them together.

The majority victory of Indira Gandhi's Congress means that coalitions will not be necessary on the national level in the near future. However, a merger of leftist parties into Mrs. Gandhi's Congress and of rightest parties with each other is improbable, given the low salience of ideology. Leaders of most of the parties have shown by their willingness to overlook ideological differences for the sake of holding office on the state level that ideology is not that important; furthermore, most of the leaders would be in a more favorable position to obtain office if they remained separate from the respective Congress organizations. There will probably be an effort in all parties to promote and reward party loyalty and to penalize defectors, in an effort to stabilize coalitions. In many of the states, the politics is likely to resemble that in pre-World War I Italy, where *transformismo* and *combinazione* were the usual pattern.

Notes

1. **Burger** AS: *Opposition in a Dominant Party System.* Berkeley,

University of California Press, 1969. For a different point of view, written before the 1967 elections but bringing out many of the same factors, see Weiner M: *Party Building in a New Nation.* Chicago, University of Chicago Press, 1967, pp 459-496.

2. Weiner, *op. cit.*, pp 468-472; Brass PR: *Factional Politics in an Indian State.* Berkeley, University of California Press, 1965, pp 26-27, 240-241.

3. Groennings S: Notes Toward Theories of Coalition Behavior in Multiparty Systems: Formation and Maintenance, pp 445-465; Schwarz JE: Maintaining Coalitions, pp 235-249. S. Groennings, E.W. Kelley, M. Leiserson, eds.: *The Study of Coalition Behavior.* New York, Holt, Rinehart and Winston, Inc., 1970.

4. Brass PR: Political Participation, Institutionalization and Stability in India. *Government and Opposition*, IV, 1 (Winter, 1969), pp 23-52.

5. Adrian CR, Press C: Decision Costs in Coalition Formation. *American Political Science Review*, LXII, 2 (June, 1968), pp 556-563.

6. The favorability concept was suggested by Riker WH: *The Theory of Political Coalitions.* New Haven, Conn., Yale University Press, 1960.

7. For this measure, "preferability of different coalition sizes" was defined in terms of frequency of size occurrence. Obviously, "preferability of different coalitions" as such would necessitate the use of many other variables.

8. Optimal, minimal, and maximal are not being used in strict definitional terms, but for ease in reading and writing this paper.

9. "Pivotal" is used in many different ways by different authors; it must be stressed that here the term means that a party is both essential and favorable, as previously defined. It does *not* mean that it was the last actor to join a protocoalition, thereby transforming it into a winning coalition.

10. This confirms Riker's finding that smaller parties were more often in a favorable position than the larger in coalition formation possibilities. See Riker WH, *op. cit.* The hypotheses developed in this paper differ substantially from those of Sven Groennings, who hypothesizes that the larger the party the greater the insistence on payoffs relative to its size, that "pivot parties" (defined as those having coalition options, with no measure of the extent of such options and no mention of essentiality—though perhaps that could be implied) will tend to be "insistent bargainers" while "captive parties" (defined as inessential to the coalition and possibly unfavorable as well, depending on one's interpretation of the definition given) will tend to be "weak bargainers." It is not clear whether "insistent" and "weak" refer to the

performance or the result of the bargaining function. Groennings, Kelley, Leiserson, op. cit., pp 464, 451.

11. *The Statesman*, June 4, 1967.

12. *The Statesman* reports that Devi Lal's group expresses unhappiness over "Ahir prominence" in the United Front on March 24, 1967, and discontent over Jan Sangh influence in the government on June 4. On June 21, 1967, *The Statesman* reports that Devi Lal's group threatens to work with the Congress to dislodge Rao Birendra Singh's government, and on June 22 reports a challenge on a vote in the Assembly. On June 23, 1967, *TheStatesman* again reports disaffection of Devi Lal over the size of the ministry. Such reports continue almost daily through July and into August.

13. Throughout July the Devi Lal group is termed "footloose." At no time is there explicit reference to a formal resignation. It is not until August 4, 1967, that *The Statesman* explicitly states that Devi Lal's group contains six members. Earlier estimates (*The Statesman*, June 22 and July 17, 1967) of 13 to 16 can be questioned inasmuch as the Haryana Congress initially totalled only 17 and contained Rao Birendra Singh's group as well as Devi Lal's. In March, 1967, there were no reports of the size of either Devi Lal's or Rao Birendra Singh's respective factions in the Congress.

14. *The Statesman*, June 21, 1967; July 13, 1967; July 18, 1967; August 4, 1967.

15. *The Statesman*, August 6 and 11, 1967; September 5, 1967.

16. *The Statesman*, September 5, October 12, October 15, October 18, 1967.

17. *The Statesman* from October 30, 1967, through November 20, 1967. There were reports of MLA's moving from the Vishal Haryana to the Congress and vice versa, from Devi Lal's group to both the Congress and Vishal Haryana, a Jan Sanghi moving to the Congress and back again, etc. By the time President's Rule was declared, 36 of 81 legislators had changed parties, with 4 having changed four times and one six times.

18. The sole reference in *The Statesman* to discontent on this issue was reported on May 19, 1967.

19. Using the labor agitations issue he divided the communists from the Akali Dal.

20. *The Statesman*, April 7, 1967, and June 4, 1967.

21. *The Statesman*, November 12, 1967; December 15, 16, 1967; January 4, 1968.

22. For a review of SSP actions, see *The Statesman*, October 8, 1967, October 14, 1967; for a daily account of one episode, see October 15-October 26, 1967; for resignation, see January 5, 6, 1968.

23. *The Statesman*, August 6, 1967.

24. Compare the behavior of the Jan Sangh, as reported in *The Statesman*, on these days: April 30 and May 3, 1967; December 1, 2, 1967; January 10, 13, 1968; and the period February 7-23, 1968.

5   The Left-wing Opposition and the Chilean Democratic System

Robert J. Alexander
Rutgers, The State University of New Jersey

For almost 40 years Chile has enjoyed a political system in which most of the members of the opposition of both Left and Right have been willing to conform to the rule of democratic politics. The politicians of the country seem to have learned what is perhaps the most fundamental lesson for Latin-American political leaders: It is conceivable that· the voters may prefer their opponents. However, at the present time, the country is going through a process of rapid and basic change that is imperiling Chilean democracy, which has for long been one of the most stable political systems in the whole Latin-American area—and in the world as a whole, for that matter.

Historical Background

Stability and relative democracy are a long tradition in Chile. Between 1828 and 1924 there was only one successful revolutionary attempt in the republic, that which overthrew President José Balmaceda in 1891. The only real dictatorship the nation has experienced in the 20th century was the administration of President General Carlos Ibañez del Campo between 1927 and 1931.

During most of the 19th century, Chile was governed by a

system of presidential government, in which the administration was completely in the hands of the president, who was elected independently of Congress, but in which a strong Senate and Chamber of Deputies were jealous of their powers to legislate. After the uprising against President Balmaceda, and until the revolution of 1924, Chile experienced a parliamentary regime in which the cabinet had to maintain the confidence of Congress in order to stay in office, and in which the rapidity and frequency of changes of cabinets were comparable to the situation in the French Third and Fourth Republics. However, as in the case of France, it was a case of *plus ce change, plus ce reste*, and the same faces tended to turn up in successive administrations.

During all of this period, politics remained a monopoly of a small percentage of the country's adult population. The rural landed oligarchy, the merchant classes, and relatively small groups of artisans and white collar workers made up most of the electorate. After the turn of the century, there was a growing number of manual workers in the major cities and even in the nitrate and coal mining areas who also became voters.

However, it was not until the election of 1920 that the votes of the middle and working classes proved decisive in a presidential election. In that campaign, Arturo Alessandri, known popularly as "the Lion of Tarapacá" was the popular candidate against Luis Barros Borgoño, the nominee of the traditional ruling classes. Alessandri's victory provoked a major political and constitutional crisis, which tested whether the tradition of peaceful change of government would be allowed to continue.

The 1920 crisis was resolved by a kind of compromise. Congress agreed to recognize the victory of Alessandri, but in return there was an accord—which apparently was never written down, but which many Chilean historians assert was actually made—that Alessandri would not menace the entrenched position of the large landlords in the rural parts of the country.

However, during this first administration of Arturo Alessandri the country passed through a fundamental crisis of power. It reached unbearable proportions in September 1924, when discontent in the armed forces brought this crisis to a boil, with the result that President Alessandri was overthrown by a military coup at that time.

The next eight years were abnormal insofar as Chilean politics were concerned. After three months of military government, Alessandri was brought back to the presidency, but was forced out once again six months later—after presiding over the writing of a new constitution and the beginning of enforcement of the country's pioneer labor and social security laws, which had been passed shortly before Alessandri's first ouster. Then, after a short interim, a new constitutional administration was elected, but in the middle of 1927 the president resigned under pressure of his Minister of War, Colonel Carlos Ibañez del Campo, who was shortly after elected chief executive in a virtually uncontested poll.

President Carlos Ibañez presided for four years over the only dictatorship Chile has suffered in this century. However, even the Ibañez regime was mild compared with some of its contemporaries in Latin America and compared with many governments that have existed in the region since that time. Some of the principal leaders of the opposition were forced into exile, including ex-President Alessandri, while others were jailed for longer or shorter periods of time, and still others temporarily retired from political activity, or conducted their politics from the underground.

The Ibañez dictatorship was overthrown in September 1931. A few months later a new constitutional regime was elected under President Juan Esteban Montero. His administration lasted only seven months, and was marked by severe strikes, a serious naval mutiny, and various other crises. Montero was overthrown by a conspiracy that involved the Air Force and its chief colonel, Marmaduque Grove, followers of Carlos Ibañez led by Carlos Dávila, former editor of the government newspaper "La Nación," and various small

Socialist parties that had sprung up since the end of the Ibañez dictatorship. This motley group proclaimed "The Socialist Republic of Chile," of which Grove became the first head. His tenure in office lasted only twelve days, however, and he was succeeded by Carlos Dávila, who succeeded in holding on for three months.

With the ouster of Dávila in September 1932, the way was paved for yet another general election. This time the victor was ex-president Arturo Alessandri. He set about reestablishing constitutional government on a sound basis, and was sufficiently successful that no government has been overthrown by force since 1932.

During the last four decades many governments have been in power. Many parties have been in the opposition. But for the most part, both government and opposition have observed the basic rules of the democratic process. Although some administrations, particularly those of President Alessandri in the 1930s and President Gabriel Gonzales Videla in the late 1940s, bore down heavily on their opponents, the latter outlawing the Communist party, such actions were exceptions. Furthermore, even in the Alessandri and González Videla regimes, the great majority of the opposition parties were able to function legally, and in both cases the opposition won elections at the end of the presidents' terms of office, and was allowed to take power.

Chile's Developing Socioeconomic Crisis

Since World War I, Chile has been experiencing her own industrial revolution. During that war the country was unable to purchase consumer goods, which an appreciable part of the population had become accustomed to using, from European countries. Local artisans and small manufacturers therefore had a protected market for the duration of the war, although in the 1920s Chilean industries suffered from severe competition when manufactured goods from Europe and

North America again entered the Chilean market.

The second government of Arturo Alessandri, starting in 1932, adopted a positive policy toward industrialization. It extended tariff protection to national manufacturing firms, but more important, it used the system of rationing foreign exchange which had been introduced because of the Depression-created scarcity of foreign currencies to favor national manufacturers.

The process of industrialization received a further boost during the three administrations headed by members of the Radical party, those of presidents Pedro Aguirre Cerda, Juan Antonio Ríos, and Gabriel González Videla. The Aguirre Cerda government established the Chilean Development Corporation, which became the principal fiscal instrument for encouraging the establishment of new industries and the expansion of old ones. It established enterprises under its own control, such as the Pacific Steel Corporation and the National Electrical Enterprise. It augmented the capital of many firms by investing in their stock, particularly in metallurgical, pharmaceutical, and heavy consumer goods firms. Other enterprises received loans from the corporation.

During this period, Chilean industrialization had proceeded in conformity with the strategy of import substitution. This is a process of building industries which make goods which were formerly imported. This strategy of industrialization has several attributes.

First of all, import substitution provides a logical sequence of priorities in industrialization. At the beginning of the process, industrial imports consist principally of light consumer goods and products needed for construction, such as cement and steel rods used for reinforced concrete structures. These are therefore the first industries likely to be established within a developing country. The construction of these industries gives rise to the need for other imports, such as semiprocessed goods which go into the consumer goods industries. By expanding the market, the process of industrialization increases the demand for imports of heavier consumer goods, such as household appliances of various sorts. Hence, it is possible to push the process of import substitution into these new areas. Finally, the proliferation of the metallurgical and other industries foments the demand for imports of basic iron and steel products, hence creating the economic possibility for the establishment of an integrated steel industry.

Chile passed through this sequence of events between World War I and the end of the González Videla administration in 1952. It moved at a particularly rapid pace between the Alessandri administration and the early 1950s. By the end of the González Videla period Chile had virtually exhausted the possibility of import substitution as the main impetus for industrialization and general economic development.

At the end of the import substitution period, the whole nature of the development problem changed. During import substitution, where to obtain a market for the products of the new industries is not a major issue, since markets have already been established by imports before the process of industrialization is begun. Several other facts follow from this basic one.

One corollary of import substitution is the fact that relatively high costs and low quality of domestic manufactured goods will not act as a major impediment to the process of development. Such high costs and relatively low quality are almost inevitable in a newly industrializing country, in any case.

A second corollary of import substitution is the fact that through it, it is possible to build up a substantial industrial sector of the economy without this sector's coming into direct conflict with the relatively backward agricultural part of the economy. The fact that this agricultural sector kept a sizable part of the population out of the market did not for a while hamper the development process, since a market already existed for the products of the new industries. The fact that the backwardness of agriculture meant that the rural sector was unable to provide for the rising food needs of the growing cities, or the requirements for agricultural raw materials of the new industries, was also not a substantial drawback to further industrialization for some time. The process of import substitution "saves" foreign exchange—for example, foreign currency which has been used for bringing textiles does not have to be spent for that purpose when a domestic textile industry has been established—and at least some of this "saved" foreign exchange can be used to bring in both needed foodstuffs and the agricultural raw materials required by the manufacturers.

However, once the possibility of using import substitution as the motor force for industrialization and general economic development has been exhausted, the size of the market becomes the primary impediment to further development. Then, if the process of industrialization is to continue, if existing industries are to grow and new ones are to be established, the market for manufactured goods must be expanded.

In these circumstances, there are two areas into which the market might be extended. One is within the country; the other is through selling the country's manufactured goods abroad. To achieve either of these objectives, however, many of the same economic, social, and political changes are required.

To expand the market, whether domestic or foreign, it now becomes important to reduce prices and improve quality. As a result, if firms are to be able to sell their products to people who have hitherto not been able to afford them, they must be able to sell them at lower prices. If a firm is to be able to expand its market by taking customers away from its competitors, it probably will have to be able to sell at lower cost and provide a higher quality product.

In order to reduce costs and improve quality, several things are necessary. Firms have to become more concerned with improving the efficiency of their management. They must also pay more attention to improving the quality and efficiency of their labor force. The industrial sector in general

133

usually needs cheaper and more adequate credit than it has had in the earlier phase of industrialization.

Furthermore, the backwardness of agriculture becomes a matter of prime importance to the further expansion of the whole economy, and particularly of industry. Basic changes are necessary in the rural sector. In Chile's case, these changes included a redistribution of the land, to break up relatively unproductive large estates and turn the land over to small farmers who would make use of it or would use it more efficiently. They also included the launching of a program of heavy new investments in agriculture.

Thus, when a country reaches the end of the import substitution phase of its industrialization, it is faced with a major crisis. For industrialization and general economic development to continue at a rapid pace, fundamental reforms are necessary in the economy, social relations, and even politics.

Chile has been faced with this kind of a crisis since the early 1950s. By that time an agrarian reform, a massive program of investment in agriculture, reforms in business administration, and programs for upgrading labor were necessary if the economic development process was to continued.

In addition, a major political reform was required: the granting of the right to vote to illiterates. This change was important to help undermine the political power of the rural landlords, who had traditionally arranged for many of their tenants, who were in fact illiterate, to vote because they could be counted upon to vote as the landlords wanted them to. Only if the illiterates were given the legal right to vote could they be expected to do so in their own interests, rather than in those of their landlords. So long as the ability of illiterate rural folk to vote depended on the tolerance of the landowners, these landlords were assured that the parties enjoying their support, principally the Liberals and Conservatives, would continue to have sufficient power in Congress to prevent the passage of any basic reforms which might imperil the rural oligarchy's control over the land.

Political Developments, 1952-1964

Essentially conservative governments remained in power between 1952 and 1964. The first president of the republic during this period was General Carlos Ibañez, the ex-dictator, who was swept into office in 1952 in a widespread revulsion against the 12 years of Radical Party control of the government. Although Ibañez had sufficiently wide political support to have launched the process of basic reforms which was required by this time, he was either unaware of the need for reform or had no desire to carry it out. Indeed, there was little general recognition at this time, even among elements of the Left, of the need for agrarian reform and other basic structural changes, so perhaps Ibañez is to be excused for not appreciating their necessity, particularly since his main preoccupation during this second period in office seemed to be to stay in power as peacefully as possible, and to live down his reputation as a dictator.

Although during the first year of his administration, Ibañez had a cabinet which had among its members several representatives of the supposedly left-wing Popular Socialist Party, these Leftists did little or nothing to try to impose upon the Ibañez regime a program of basic reform. Within a year they were out of the government, and during most of the rest of his administration, Ibañez governed principally with the Liberal and Conservative parties.

Ibañez was succeeded in 1958 by a son of the late President Arturo Alessandri. Jorge Alessandri was more famous as an engineer, successful industrialist, and financial wizard than as a politician. He had widespread popularity not only among middle- and upper-class segments of the population, but among the urban workers as well, won perhaps because of his reputation for being a very good employer.

Jorge Alessandri also governed principally with the support of the Liberal and Conservative parties. His was distinctly not a reform administration, in spite of the fact that, under the pressure of the Alliance for Progress, it passed a token agrarian reform law and carried out an extensive public housing program in the major cities.

However, it would be a false picture of the period between 1952 and 1964 if one were to insist that absolutely none of the changes needed for renewed rapid development were made. The industrialists did become very much concerned with improving the quality of management in their firms, as a result of which, with the help of the United States foreign aid program, various institutions for training young managers as well as improving the formal training of more experienced ones were established. Likewise, both the state and private entrepeneurs helped the expansion of such institutions for vocational education as the private Universidad Tecnica Santa Maria and the government's Universidad Tecnica del Estado.

Nevertheless, during most of this period the national economy virtually stagnated. In most years the increase in the national income barely kept pace with the slow rise in population, and in some years it did not even do this.

The Opposition before 1964

During most of the period between 1947 and 1964 the major elements of opposition in Chile were the parties of the Left. These included the Communists, Socialists, Christian Democrats, and during much of the period, the Radical party as well.

The Communist party was established before World War I, as the Partido Socialista Obrero. With the establishment of the Communist International, the PSO joined it, and changed its name to Partido Comunista. During the early 1920s the Communists were the major factor in the trade union movement, although they had substantial competition from the anarchists. However, during the Ibañez dictatorship, unions organized under the labor laws passed in September 1924 and, enjoying the legal recognition of the government, came to constitute the majority in organized labor, and the Communists had no influence in them.

During the early 1930s the Communists remained a minority group in the labor movement and a small factor in the general political picture. However, with the establishment of the Popular Front in the late 1930s and particularly after a Popular Front government came to power in 1938, the Communist party began to grow with some rapidity.

By 1946 the Communists were partners of the Radicals in a coalition which elected Gabriel González Videla as President of the republic. For five months the Communists served in González Videla's cabinet. During that period, they gave some indication of the way in which they might be expected to behave should they ever achieve full power in the republic. Although for some years they had conformed to the normal rules of the democratic process as members of the opposition, they acted in the González administration as if they were sharing in one of the Eastern European governments of that same period. They used their influence in the government to try to crush their opponents, the Socialists and anarchists, in the labor movement, and several minor anarchist and Socialist leaders were murdered by organized Communist bands.

However, González Videla soon became tired of the Communist presence in his administration, finding it an increasing political handicap. Hence, in April 1947 he demanded the resignation of the Communist ministers. There then began a feud between the Communists and González Videla during which the latter was convinced that the Communists were trying to bring about his forcible over-throw. As a result, he sponsored legislation to outlaw the Communists.

During most of the subsequent decade the Communists remained illegal. However, they worked together with some

137

factions of the Socialists, and through this alliance were able to place a handful of their members in the Chamber of Deputies, elected on a Socialist ticket. In 1957, shortly before the end of the Ibañez administration, the Communist party was legalized once again, in a measure passed over the president's opposition, with the support of every party in Congress except the Liberals and Conservatives.

On three different occasions during these years the Communists supported Socialist Senator Salvador Allende for the presidency. In 1952 they suggested their willingness to support Allende, then a member of the violently anti-Communist Partido Socialista de Chile, if the party would nominate him. The result was that the Partido Socialista de Chile, which had until then been perhaps the most anti-Communist political group in Chile, suddenly entered into an alliance with the Communists.

By 1958, the Communists again backed Allende, by this time candidate of the Frente de Acción Popular (FRAP), composed of the Communists, the reunited Socialists, and some smaller groups. In this contest Allende, who had been but a minor candidate six years earlier, came within a few thousand votes of defeating Jorge Alessandri. Again in 1964 Allende, with the support of the Communists, was the major opponent of the victor in the presidential race, Eduardo Frei of the Christian Democratic Party.

The Communists were not only becoming a major factor in national politics but also were assuming the position of the first force in organized labor. Partly out of fear of the possibility that President Carlos Ibañez, who was then an avowed admirer of Juan Perón, might try to establish a government-controlled labor movement, and partly because the Socialists and anarchists were intimidated by the Communists' insistence on "labor unity," Socialist, anarchist and Communist unions were united early in 1953 in the Central Unica de Trabajadores de Chile (CUT). In spite of the fact that before the establishment of the CUT, the Socialists had controlled the largest segment of the organized workers, the CUT was from its inception dominated by the Communists. Through it, they were able to extend their influence progressively among the country's trade unions, most of which belonged to the Central Unica. The Socialists' role changed significantly from 1952 to 1964. The Socialist party had been established in 1933 by the merger of a group of small Socialist groups, each of which had its own *caudillo*. Its popular base was to be found in the legally recognized trade unions which had grown up during the Ibañez dictatorship, and which had been strongly opposed to Communist influence. Hence, the Socialist party was formed virtually to give political leadership to the anti-Communist element in organized labor.

During the first two decades of the existence of the Socialist Party, its relations with the Communists varied from time to time. During the existence of the Popular Front, the two parties were ostensible allies. Thereafter, from 1940 on, their relations became increasingly cold. The high point in Socialist-Communist hostility was just before and during the González Videla administration. Early in 1946 the Confederacíon de Trabajadores de Chile, in which the two parties had shared uneasily in the leadership, split into two rival groups, each using the same name. During the first months of the González Videla regime, the Communists strongly persecuted the Socialist CTCh. faction. With the exit of the Communists, the Socialists were invited into Gonzàlez Videla's cabinet.

Socialist participation in the González Videla regime, and the issue of outlawing the Communist party, which the president demanded, split the Socialist party into the Partido Socialista de Chile, which remained with González Videla, and the Partido Socialista Popular, which went into the opposition. This was the third major split the Socialists had experienced in the 1940s. In each of these, participation in the government, the relation of the party with the Communists, and personal rivalries among Socialist leaders were the principal issues of division. These splits in the

Socialist party undoubtedly helped very much to undermine the influence of the Socialists.

Until 1952 the Partido Socialista de Chile remained violently anti-Communist, the Partido Socialista Popular somewhat less so. The PSP was marked by something new to the Socialist scene. Its major leaders proclaimed themselves to be Marxist-Leninists, although they still professed strong antipathy to the Communists. For a while they were particularly attracted to Titoism, but thereafter they continued to seek somewhat unsuccessfully for a clear definition of their political philosophy.

Meanwhile the Partido Socialista de Chile suffered violent attacks by the Communists. So long as the Communists remained legal, this was expressed in public meetings, in the Communist press, and in a variety of other forums. Even after the Communist party was outlawed, its leaders and members continued violently to attack and malign the Socialists. Some of the leaders of the party, including Bernardo Ibañez, secretary general of the Partido Socialista de Chile and of its faction of the CTCh., had their reputations so badly maligned that they never recovered, and finally withdrew from politics. This experience engendered in the Socialists of all factions a haunting fear of the power of the Communists within the Chilean Left, and largely explains their unwillingness seriously to oppose them after 1952.

After the first election campaign of Salvador Allende, the Partido Socialista de Chile and the Communists became firm allies. With the reunification of the two Socialist parties in 1957, this alliance was continued. Socialists and Communists were partners in the FRAP, and shared leadership in the CUTCh, the new labor confederation, in which however, the Communists were the senior partner.

The reunited Socialist party continued to call itself Marxist-Leninist. It insisted that politically it was to the Left of the Communists. With the open split between the Soviet Union and China, some elements in the Socialist party were strongly attracted to Peking, and a few even left the party to help establish small pro-Maoist groups. All of the party swore strong support to the Fidel Castro regime in Cuba and continued to align themselves with the Cuban leader even after relations between him and the Chilean Communist Party had become quite cold.

The history of the Christian Democrats also goes back to the 1930s. During that decade the Young Conservatives, known first as the Falange Conservadora, assumed an attitude of increasing independence from the Conservative party, culminating in 1938 in a total break and the establishment by the former Conservative Youth of a separate party, the Falange Nacional.

The Falange Nacional had a Social Christian philosophy, and although its founders were predominantly from the upper and middle classes, they began immediately to try to gain influence in the labor movement. By the middle 1940s they had come to control a few small national unions and had some support in the rank and file of other groups. During the 1950s they turned their attention particularly toward the rural workers, who in some isolated parts of the country were just beginning to try to establish unions. They had more success in this field than any other political group, although in the decade of the 1950s only very limited progress was made by any trade union or political group among the peasants.

In the meantime, two other groups of Social Christian ideology had appeared. One of these resulted from a new split in the Conservative party in the late 1940s, resulting in the establishment of the Partido Conservador Social Cristiano, headed by the widely respected Senator Eduardo Cruz Coke, who had been the Conservative candidate for president in 1946. The second was a Partido Democrata Christiano, set up by some Catholic supporters of Carlos Ibañez.

After long negotiations these three parties merged in 1957 to form a new Partido Democrata Cristiano. The first test of the new party at the polls came in 1958 when Christian

Democratic presidential candidate Eduardo Frei was a considerable distance behind the front runners, Jorge Alessandri and Salvador Allende, but gained more support than any other candidate of Christian Democratic orientation had ever received in the past.

As the presidential campaign of 1964 approached, it developed into almost a straight contest between the Christian Democratic candidate and the nominee of the extremist parties, Salvador Allende. The right-wing parties had no attractive candidate, and it was clear that in any case the Liberals and Conservatives stood no chance of winning. They first threw their support behind the Radical party nominee Julio Durán, but as the campaign progressed it became clear that he too had no chance of winning. In the face of this situation, the Conservatives and Liberals withdrew their support from Durán, and without formally endorsing Frei, undoubtedly cast most of their votes in his favor. However, Frei and the Christian Democrats gave no concessions to the right wing and the Conservatives and Liberals were merely backing him as "the lesser evil."

The last of the major opposition groups during the 1952-64 period was the Radical party. From the 1930s on, it had been the largest single party in the country. It was the organization par excellence of the middle class, although it also had some support among the organized workers, and among the landed elite. It was traditionally strongly anticlerical and therefore was almost by definition antipathetical to the Christian Democrats.

Although political opportunism was a very general characteristic of Chilean politics during the period under consideration, it was most notable in the Radical party. It might almost be said that the only thing consistent about it was that it almost always talked very Leftist and usually acted Rightist. It had for several decades proclaimed itself to be a "democratic Socialist" party, but this did not prevent it from making alliances both with the Communists and with the right-wing parties, when this proved convenient.

Perhaps the strength of the Radicals was exactly to be found in the open nature of the party and its lack of clear political definition. It included within its ranks people of the most varied political philosophy, and although discontented groups broke away from time to time to form separate parties, these dissident organizations usually did not last long, and their members sooner or later returned to the Radical fold, without any retribution being taken against them.

Characteristic of virtually the whole opposition during the 1952-1964 period was its willingness to use the established procedures of democratic government. All of the parties, whether Radical, Christian Democratic, Socialist or Communist, were organized in such a way as to facilitate their participation in electoral activity. No matter how radically the Socialists or Communists might talk, and no matter what reservations their opponents might have had with regard to what they would do if they were ever to come fully to power, neither of the extreme Left parties made any serious effort to overthrow the government in any way except through the ballot box, nor did they seem to have organizations which would have facilitated such extraconstitutional bids for power.

Perhaps even more important in the Latin-American context, the opposition did not, so far as has ever been demonstrated, seek to conspire with the military or any important segment of the military. It was generally accepted by government and opposition alike that the armed forces were not supposed to participate in active politics, that their job was to defend the constituted civilian authorities and protect the process through which power could be legitimately passed on to these authorities' successors.

However, there were economic and social trends during the 1952-64 period which perhaps presaged a coming crisis, which might provoke a change in attitudes and behavior of both government and opposition. We have already noted the virtual stagnation of the Chilean economy. Also, there was a continuing process of inflation, which "price stabilization programs" of successive governments merely slowed down temporarily. This process probably resulted in a decline in real wages during the period and generated considerable social discontent, particularly among working-class elements.

In addition, there was growing evidence that the age-long placidity of of the rural workers was coming to an end. The considerable degree to which they voted for Carlos Ibañez in 1952 and Salvador Allende in 1958, both candidates opposed by most rural landlords, was an indication of this. So was the modest beginning of rural unionism, which we have already noted.

Finally, there were influences from outside of Chile which also contributed to a growing feeling of crisis. The attempts by both Chinese Communists and the Cuban Communist leadership to penetrate Chilean politics were very important in this regard. Both the Chinese and the Fidelistas preached the need for seizing power by violence, preferably through a guerrilla war, and although they did not convince many people or any leaders of major importance within the Socialist and Communist parties of the need actively to prepare for civil war, their agitation certainly did serve to make the issue a subject of conversation and debate for virtually the first time.

The Christian Democratic Government of Eduardo Frei

Eduardo Frei was elected as the first Christian Democratic president of Chile in September 1964 with an absolute majority over his two rivals. Six months later his party succeeded in getting a majority in the Chamber of Deputies, something no party had done in more than a hundred years. There is no doubt that the Christian Democrats rode to power on a wave of popularity such as had seldom been seen in Chile.

It is now possible to make some tentative judgment as to the successes and failures of the Frei administration.

144

Certainly the record is mixed, and the balance did not prove sufficiently favorable, insofar as the voters of Chile are concerned, to make it possible for the Christian Democrats to elect a second man from their ranks as chief executive.

The Frei government was elected on a program which promised that the Christian Democratic regime would enact a law permitting legal unionization of rural workers, that it would carry out an agrarian reform, that it would "Chilean-ize" the country's mining industry, that it would stimulate the renewal of the process of industrialization, that it would enact a new general labor law which would relieve the organized labor movement of most of the governmental restrictions which have surrounded it since 1924, and that it would seriously curtail the endemic inflation. The government's success in carrying out its promises has varied considerably, according to the various key points in its program.

Perhaps the single most successful part of the Frei program has been the unionization of rural workers. Until the advent of the Frei government, it was virtually illegal to establish unions among rural workers. Even before new legislation had been passed authorizing such organizations, the Frei administration encouraged the agricultural wage earners to establish de facto unions, some of which were given legal recognition under an old law, passed in 1948, which until then had been so strictly interpreted that only about a dozen unions had been able to qualify for legalization between 1948 and 1964.

A new Rural Unionization Law was introduced into Congress by the Frei government. It provided for the establishment of local unions based on the municipality, and for the unification of these into provincial federations, which might in their turn establish national confederations. Unlike the country's basic Labor Code, this new legislation did not insist on there being only one union in each municipality, one federation per province or one national confederation, but rather allowed the rural workers to establish as many such groups on a local, regional, and countrywide level as they desired.

The rural workers were quick to take advantage of first the sympathetic attitude of the government, and then the new rural labor legislation. Throughout much of the Central Valley, the principal agricultural region of the republic, local unions sprang into existence. By early 1968 three national confederations of rural workers, two of which were under predominantly Christian Democratic, the other controlled by the Socialists and Communists, each of which had several provincial federations and many municipal unions, had been established.

Furthermore, collective bargaining began to become the pattern in rural labor relations. Through collective agreements negotiated by the various local unions and provincial federations, the agricultural laborers received dramatic increases in their real wages. It was estimated in 1968 that in the provinces in which the new unions were most strongly organized, real wages had gone up by as much as 100% in three years.

Rural unionization undoubtedly brought about the most fundamental change in both economic and social relations. Levels of living rose almost as startlingly as real wages. Workers and their families who had not worn shoes began to do so; improvements were made in the workers' house furnishings; bicycles became a popular method of transportation in the rural areas.

The social situation changed with equal decisiveness. The master-servant relationship of more or less benevolent paternalism, which had characterized the rural Central Valley since time immemorial, was increasingly replaced by a situation in which landlords and their tenants and employees dealt with one another on a more or less equal basis. In their unions, the workers had their first real experience with the democratic process. The rural tenants and wage earners became increasingly anxious to have their children go to school, something which was facilitated by the Frei government's educational efforts, which resulted in hundreds of new schools being established in the countryside.

146

Rural unionization was one half of a two-part process of transformation of the rural part of Chile's economy and society which was launched by the Christian Democratic government. The other aspect of this process was the agrarian reform which the administration got under way.

During the first half of the Frei administration, before it was able to get its own agrarian reform law through parliament, it made liberal use of the land redistribution law which had been passed by its predecessor, the Jorge Alessandri government. This law provided that land could only be taken from its owners in cases of flagrant misuse of it, or absolute failure to use it, and that all land taken must be paid for in cash. This severely limited the government's ability to launch an all-out agrarian reform.

However, early in 1968 the Frei government's own land redistribution law was enacted. It provided much broader grounds for expropriation of land. It was accompanied by a change in the Constitution which allowed the payment for expropriated property largely to government bonds.

Under the two agrarian reform laws, the Frei government expropriated a considerable number of rural holdings, known in Chile as *fundos.* On these seized holdings there were established "agrarian settlements," or *asentamientosagrarios.* These were semicooperatives, governed by groups of elected workers together with representatives of the Agrarian Reform Corporation. The settlements were supposed to last three years, after which a decision would be made as to what form the land would be given to the settlement members, and during this interim there were to be crash programs to teach the workers how better to use the land and to provide additional capital equipment for the farms.

Although during his election campaign Frei had promised that one hundred thousand peasant families would be settled on their own land under the agrarian reform, he was not able fully to carry out this promise. Estimates of the number of families actually settled vary from 20,000 to 50,000.

However, the agrarian reform and the process of rural

unionization have both gone far enough to assure that the traditional socioeconomic system of rural Chile has been destroyed, once and for all. This has had profound political impact. At the present time, the mass base of the Christian Democratic party is among the rural masses. The considerable majority of the workers who were brought into unions and who received land (or were in the process of doing so) under the agrarian reform are loyal to the Christian Democratic party, which they know very well is responsible for the transformation of their situation.

Another sector in which the Christian Democratic regime of Eduardo Frei largely carried out its promised program is that of mining. The Christian Democrats had promised "Chileanization" as an alternative to expropriation of the foreign-owned mining enterprises exploiting copper and nitrate resources, and leaving their concessions completely in the hands of those enterprises. This compromise called for the Chilean government to acquire a controlling interest in the mines, but for the foreign firms to continue to hold substantial minority ownership rights. An agreement providing for this arrangement was worked our early in the Frei administration for the holdings of the Kennicot Copper Co., the Cerro de Pasco Corporation, and the nitrate firms. However, it was not until 1969 that a somewhat more drastic settlement was finally made with the Anaconda Copper Co. The agreements also called for the reinvestment of substantial parts of the repayment price for the copper mines in the Chilean economy by the Anaconda, Kennicot, and Cerro de Pasco companies.

The Frei government was also successful in stimulating the establishment of a number of new industrial enterprises. It placed particular emphasis on encouraging the establishment or expansion of enterprises which will export a large part of their output to other countries, particularly to other Latin-American nations. These have included the paper and pulp, chemical, and metallurgical industries.

However, the Frei regime failed in two aspects of its program. These were in its handling of urban labor and in its fight against inflation. In the first of these fields, two basic measures were needed, from the Christian Democratic party's point of view: a fundamental revision of the basic Labor Code and a serious effort to establish a major labor confederation under Christian Democratic control. Neither of these was undertaken by the Frei administration.

The Labor Code, the basic elements of which were enacted in September 1924, provides for only two kinds of unions. One consists of the manual workers of a particular plant or workshop and is known as a *sindicato industrial.* The other, known as a *sindicato profesional,* can include the white-collar workers of a firm which has a *sindicato industrial,* or a group of workers from several plants none of which has 25 employees, the minimum number required to establish a *sindicato industrial.* There is no provision in the law for industrywide unions or for confederations of workers. Unions are forbidden to have paid officers, and union officials must carry on their union activities after their regular eight hours of work in their plant, office or workshop.

These provisions of the Labor Code have for long favored the Communists within organized labor. Since the legally recognized unions may not employ full-time officers, it is very difficult for union officials adequately to service their members. Since industrywide unions and national labor confederations are not recognized in the law, it is not possible for the legal unions to contribute funds for the maintenance of such organizations. As a result, it is the Communists, who have for four decades been better supplied with funds than any of their rivals in organized labor, who have been able to furnish full-time personnel to the existing legally unrecognized industrywide unions and confederations. These officials have made it a practice to intervene in any important labor dispute arising in the republic, and through their activities have been able steadily to increase their party's influence in the trade union movement.

The Christian Democrats for long had advocated basic revisions of the Labor Code. They suggested amendments which would authorize legally recognized national industrial unions and national confederations of labor. They also favored "plural unionism," altering the law to permit workers to form more than the one single union within any jurisdiction presently authorized by the Labor Code. Finally, they wanted to have the law authorize unions to employ full-time officers, who could get their income from their members rather than from their members rather than from an outside political party.

Although Frei's first Minister of Labor, William Thayer, was a strong advocate of these revisions of the Labor Code, the president did not energetically push their enactment. There are probably two reasons for this. First, there was strong opposition within the Christian Democratic ranks from the party's left wing, which insisted that it was in principle opposed to the concept of "plural unionism " and sought in party congresses early in the administration to get the Christian Democrats on record against any substantial changes in the Labor Code. A second and more fundamental reason undoubtedly was the fact that President Frei underestimated the importance of his party's problem with urban labor. In general, labor issues did not have a very high priority with him, and he did not bring the prestige of the presidency into the battle for labor law reform until it was too late.

The second policy in the labor field which many Christian Democrats urged was for the party to take advantage of the strong upsurge of sympathy among urban workers in 1964-65 to create a rival to the Communist-Socialist controlled Central Unica de Trabajadores. Certainly in the first year of the Frei administration, if the Christian Democrats had attempted to establish a second central labor federation, they could have mobilized a substantial part of the country's unions, although perhaps not a majority of the organized labor movement.

Again, Frei was largely responsible for the fact that no serious effort was made until 1968 to launch such a rival central labor group to the CUT. He underestimated seriously the political importance of Communist-Socialist control of CUT, arguing that because of the popularity of the Christian Democrats he could appeal over the heads of the labor leaders to the rank and file union members. In this he was seriously mistaken. Even though many unionists voted for Frei and for the Christian Democrats in the 1965 congressional elections, this did not necessarily mean a long-term commitment to the Christian Democrats, and it did not mean that in purely labor affairs they trusted the president more than their own union leaders.

An attempt was made in the middle of 1968 to launch a new central labor group, the Union de Trabajadores de Chile. It quite obviously had the support of President Frei. However, it failed miserably, in part as a result of the opposition within the Christian Democratic ranks from the factions hostile to the president which had developed by that time, the so-called Rebeldes and Terceristas, and who were pledged to cooperation with the Communists in the labor movement.

The final field in which the Christian Democratic regime did not succeed was in its attempts to curb inflation. Although during the first two years of the Frei administration the rate of price increases subsided substantially, thereafter, it resumed the comparatively rapid rate which had been characteristic of most of the period since the late 1940s. Although the increase in mining output which the government's program in that area and the increase in industrial output and exports which its program might be expected to generate anti-inflationary forces, these have not yet become evident. The failure in this field has caused serious discontent exactly among the labor forces which the Frei government's other policies had done little to entice.

The Opposition during the Frei Administration

During the Christian Democratic government of President Eduardo Frei the administration was faced with three kinds of opposition and what might be called the premonition of a fourth type. There was the resistance of the traditional Right to the changes inaugurated by the Christian Democratic regime. There was the opposition of the traditional Left, that is, the Communists, Socialists, and Radicals. Third, the period saw the rise of a new extreme Leftist opposition. Finally, there has been the ominous possibility, raised for the first time in nearly 40 years, of military opposition to the whole system of democratic civilian government.

The elections of 1964 and 1965 were a severe setback for the traditional Right. In the presidential poll, the Liberal and Conservative parties for the first time did not have a candidate of their own. In the 1965 congressional poll their representation in Congress was almost completely wiped out.

As a result of these defeats, the political Right decided to unify its forces. Thus, the Partido Liberal and Partido Conservador were merged to form a new Partido Nacional. Although this alliance of traditional opponents was somewhat uneasy, it was politically successful. In the Congressional elections of March 1969, the Partido Nacional made a substantial comeback, winning about 20% of the members of Congress, and emerging as the country's second largest party, substantially behind the Christian Democrats and slightly ahead of the Radicals and the Communists.

The Partido Nacional had a somewhat pragmatic attitude toward the Christian Democratic regime. Although opposed to it ideologically, it did support some of the measures which the Frei government sponsored, such as the arrangements in the mining industry. However, when the 1970 presidential election approached, it threw its enthusiastic support behind the candidacy of ex-President Jorge Alessandri. Nevertheless, in spite of the damage the Christian Democratic regime did to the interests of the landed elite which traditionally has supported the Right, there is no indication that the Partido Nacional or any other important right-wing element sought to conspire with the military to block the Christian Democratic government's program.

The Communists also played a somewhat pragmatic role during the Christian Democratic regime. They were quite definitely in the opposition, but on some key issues, such as the agrarian reform law, and the laws governing increases in wages in 1968, 1969, and 1970, the Communists voted with the government, over strong Socialist opposition. Vocally and in practice, the Communists expressed very strong opposition to any resort to force and particularly to guerrilla warfare, at least in the proximate future, as a method of seizing power.

The Communists steadily increased their influence in the organized labor movement and in general politics during the Christian Democratic administration. Luis Figueroa, a Communist, was secretary-general of the CUT during this period, and he intervened in virtually every major labor dispute. In negotiations concerning the law for wage increase in 1970, he negotiated directly with the government and reached a compromise acceptable both to the CUT and the administration. In the 1969 congressional elections, the Communists emerged as the fourth largest party in the country.

The Socialists were more consistently in opposition to the Christian Democratic regime. The party was by no means united, most of its leaders supporting the traditional policy of competing in the democratic political system, others openly advocating the launching of a guerrilla war to seize power and establish a "workers republic." However, there is no indication that any significant element of the party seriously attempted to follow such an insurrectionist policy.

The Radical party was also in opposition to the Christian Democratic administration. An outside observer might feel that it would have been "logical" for the Christian Democrats to have invited the Radicals to share in a coalition, thus assuring the government a majority in both houses of Congress after the March 1965 election. Both parties were on the moderate Left, and there was little in the program of the Christian Democrats to which the Radicals could object. However, two factors militated against such a coalition. On the one hand, the Radicals, due to their traditional anticlericalism, were alienated by the supposed association of the Christian Democrats with the Roman Catholic Church. In the second place, Frei and the Christian Democrats were determined to govern alone, without the cooperation of any other party. The only concessions they made to this idea was the move in 1968 to grant one cabinet post to the minuscule Partido Democratico Nacional, to which they had to make virtually no concession in order to acquire its cooperation in the administration.

Hence the Radicals formed part of the left-wing opposition to the Christian Democratic government. As the 1970 presidential election approached, the party joined the united front of the Left, which included the Socialists, Communists and several smaller parties, which spent several months in late 1969 trying to reach agreement on a candidate and a program to oppose the Christian Democrats and the Right. When the candidate proved to be Salvador Allende, the Socialist senator, once again, there was strong opposition within the Radical ranks to coalition in support of him, but the party finally did so.

The Radicals had already undergone a serious division in 1969. A group of party leaders, headed by the 1964 presidential candidate Julio Duran, opposed any alliance for 1970 with the Socialists and Communists, and as a result, were expelled from the party. With their expulsion an appreciable number of other national and local leaders of the party withdrew voluntarily, and the dissidents formed a new party, the Partido Democracia Radical. Although most national figures in the Radical ranks remained loyal to the original party, a sizable part of the rank and file and lower echelon leaders joined the new organization.

Finally, among the more traditional left-wing opponents of the Christian Democratic administration was a splinter group which broke off early in 1969 from the Christian Democratic party itself. Throughout most of the Frei government, there were three factions within the PDC. The *oficialistas* gave more or less unlimited support to the administration, and it represented the considerable majority of the party membership and leadership. At the other extreme, were the so-called *rebeldes,* or rebels, who virtually from the inception of the Frei government were highly critical of it, arguing that it was not carrying out the party's program of "Revolution in Liberty." In between these two groups were the *terceristas,* or thirds, who sometimes sided with the *oficialistas,* sometimes with the *rebeldes.*

Tension between the government and the *rebeldes* became increasingly great. Finally, early in 1969, Senator Rafael Gumucio, one of the principal leaders of the *rebeldes,* announced his resignation from the Christian Democratic party, and he was immediately followed by most of the other leading *rebeldes.* They were joined by a few of the *terceristas,* most notably by Jacques Chonchol, who had been one of the principal authors of the government's program in the rural segment of the economy.

The Christian Democratic dissidents formed a new party, the Movimiento de Acción Popular Unido (MAPU). It joined foreces with other parties of the Left. It participated in the negotiations for a candidate and a program for the Left in the election of 1970. It offered as its choice Jacques Chonchol, but he was turned down in favor of Salvador Allende, the Socialist senator.

In addition to the traditional right- and left-wing opposition, there developed a more extremist element on the Left which refused to accept the traditional electoral process as the means of changing goverments in Chile. This far Left received its inspiration from the Chinese and Cuban Fidelista Communists.

Several new extreme Leftist elements developed just before and during the Frei administration. Elements expelled from the Communist party, together with a few third-rank leaders from the Socialist party, established a Maoist group, the Partido Comunista Revolucionario. It insisted on guerrilla warfare as the only feasible way by which a Marxist-Leninist party could seize power. However, there is no indication that the PCR has taken any concrete measures to launch such a struggle.

More serious was the Movimiento de Izquierda Revolucionaria. This was established by a heterogeneous group of former members of other Leftist parties and groups. Originally launched by a group of Socialists, headed by one of that party's principal secondary leaders, Oscar Waiss, the MIR was soon taken over by students and other young people with little previous political experience. It was also joined by members and leaders of the Trotskyite Partido Obrero Revolucionario.

The MIR has had its principal support among the students. It has for several years controlled the university student organizations in the University of Concepcion and has some influence in several of the rest of the universities. It has won virtually no backing in the organized labor and peasant movements, although its members have sought particularly to penetrate the latter.

Although the MIR apparently has not launched any serious rural guerrilla war, it has engaged in terrorism in the major cities, particularly Santiago. Members of the MIR have been involved in several attempts to rob banks, a few of them successful. They have also placed bombs in some public buildings and other installations. However, the urban terrorism of the MIR in Chile has by no means reached the proportions of similar efforts in Venezuela and elsewhere in Latin America by Fidelista elements.

The MIR has found one of its major enemies in the Communist party. However, it has been able to maintain at least some contacts within the Socialist party and among the Christian Democratic dissidents of the MAPU. Such contacts aroused dissidence within the MIR, and the opponents of the MIR leadership argued that the party was not sufficiently strongly committed to guerrilla war. Some dissidents withdrew from the MIR to form the so-called Ejercito de Liberación Nacional (Army of National Liberation).

So far, the MIR has constituted little more than a nuisance to the government and to the major opposition parties. However, probably potentially more serious is the situation within the armed forces. Since the return to power of Arturo Alessandri in 1932, the military have not actively participated in politics and there has been no serious armed forces mutiny. However, during the Frei administration there were some indications that the tradition of military neutrality in politics might be appraoching an end.

Even at the time of the 1964 election, there was some worry upon the part of supporters of Salvador Allende that if their candidate won the election he might not be allowed by the armed forces to take power. Whether there was a danger of military intervention at that time was never demonstrated, since Allende did not in fact win the election.

However, five years later a military-political crisis did arise. Late in 1969 there occurred a mutiny by part of the garrison of Santiago, led by Brigadier General Vaux, who had recently been transferred from a post of command in the northern part of the country. The exact demands made by the mutineers remain obscure, but they certainly included an increase in military salaries, which Congress had discussed at great length but had not enacted, in spite of the fact that the pay of the soldiers had lagged considerably behind income increases of the civilian populace for some time. Those who remember that the politico-military crisis which ended in the deposition of President Arturo Alessandri in 1924 began with a demand by the soldiers for an increase in their salaries are disturbed by the parallel with the situation 45 years later.

The mutinous military men also probably included a demand for the removal of certain high military officers. Although the capital city was tense for almost two days, the mutineers finally surrendered without resort to force, and with no announcement of any concessions made to them.

However, changes in top personnel in the armed forces and prompt passage of a military pay increase bill may indicate something of the nature of the agreement that ended the mutiny. A number of those who had led it were tried by court martial.

The leaders of the 1969 mutiny, including General Vaux, proclaimed loudly that their move was not in opposition to the Frei government, or to the constitutional regime in general. They were, they said, concerned only with problems of the armed forces, and their move was a demonstration rather than a mutiny.

However, there is little doubt that this development aroused grave fears among the civilian politicians. These fears were reflected in a guarded way in the Chilean press. To many civilians, the indiscipline of the armed forces indicated the possibility that the military might go further and actually attempt to dictate government policies, and perhaps even overthrow the democratic regime.

The events of 1969 were the more menacing because of what has been occurring elsewhere in Latin America. In a number of major Latin-American countries in the last few years, the armed forces have seized power, with the avowed intention of remaining in control of the government for an indefinite period of time, and have given as their excuse the inability of the civilian politicians to carry out the kind of reforms their countries require. Where such seizures of power have occurred, the soldiers frequently have given no particularly convincing evidence that they are more willing or able to bring about basic social reforms than are the civilians. However, their example is contagious and may even affect the Chilean armed forces with their long tradition of political neutrality.

There was further fear of a military coup after Salvador Allende won a plurality in the September 1970 presidential election. His supporters feared the possibility that the military might conspire with some civilian politicians to prevent his becoming president. However, General René

Schneider, the Army commander, indicated that the armed forces intended to remain loyal to their constitutionalist traditions. A few days before the confirmation of Allende's victory by Congress late in October, General Schneider was assassinated—according to rumors by extreme right-wing elements. The murder of General Schneider seems to have strengthened the determination of the other military leaders to guarantee the ascension of Salvador Allende to the presidency. Several civilians and military men were arrested on suspicion of being involved in the assassination. Among these was General Vaux, the leader of the 1969 military mutiny.

The Opposition under Allende

The advent to power of the Leftist government of Salvador Allende, dedicated to taking Chile "on the road to Socialism," presents new perspectives for both government and opposition. The Allende government started immediately a program of very fundamental reforms. It substituted nationalization for "Chileanization" of the mines, greatly stepped up agrarian reform, and began substituting collective farms for individual land grants and began nationalizing other sectors of the economy, including manufacturing and banking. It introduced workers' participation in management of government-owned industries.

Although during its first year the Allende government maintained intact the traditional democratic liberties, there were some aspects of the government's program that aroused doubts in the opposition of the Allende regime's intentions. These included its proposals to substitute a single "Popular Assembly" for the existing Chamber of Deputies and Senate, and for politicalization of the judiciary.

The opposition to the Allende government was both to its Right and its Left. On the Right were the Christian Democrats, itself a party of the Left but more moderate than the government, and the Partido Nacional. They conducted legal, although vigorous, opposition to the Allende regime during its first year.

The Left opposition centered on the MIR. Its membership was divided in its attitude toward the Allende government. Some supported it and even received minor posts in the regime. Others, however, were very critical of the moderation of the Allende government, and organized and led land invasions in the rural areas and seizures of housing projects in the cities. During its first year, the Allende government undertook only isolated acts of resistance to these actions of the MIR.

The possible menace of a military move against the Allende government remained as a background factor during President Allende's first year in office. He sought to deal with this by energetically courting an Army and Navy. Most observers agreed that if the Allende government took no overtly unconstitutional measures, it would not be menaced by the soldiers and sailors.

Conclusion

A new chapter in the relationship of the Chilean Left and the democratic system was opened by the inauguration of Salvador Allende as president on November 3, 1970. It remains to be seen whether the Socialists, Communists, and their allies will try to use their control of the administration to destroy Chilean democracy. However, it is clear that for the first time in many years, the democratic process seems seriously challenged from two other directions: the Left extremists who seek to achieve power by paramilitary actions and eventual guerrilla war, and elements of the armed forces who may be willing, for whatever reason, to end the traditional role of the military as observers of the political scene and guarantors of constitutional legality, and assume instead an attitude of direct interference in the political process.

160

6

Sources of Political Dissatisfaction and Dissent in Japan

Ardath W. Burks
Rutgers, The State University of New Jersey

The problem of defining political dissatisfaction and dissent in contemporary Japan is twofold. First, as viewed from the outside, domestic political issues appear intimately bound up ("linked," in modern jargon) with Japan-US foreign policy. It is therefore difficult to weigh the relative influence of the Establishment of Japan, Inc., on the one hand, and the minority forces of the opposition, on the other, within a purely Japanese context.

Effects of what the Japanese called the "Nixon shock," felt in the summer of 1971, clearly illustrated the confusion. A succession of governments favoring the US-Japan Security Treaty, including the record tenure of Premier Eisaku Sato, had been described as "anticommunist," "conservative," and "like American conservatives." And the so-called progressive anti-US Security Treaty groups—some articulate in Marxist idiom, if not deeply committed to revolutionary ideology— had been pictured as "communist" and "anti-American."

With the abrupt shift in President Nixon's China policy, practically without notice to his ally in Tokyo, Premier Sato's policy of giving priority to Japanese-American relations (while neglecting mainland China) was put under great strain. Even the Sato-Nixon agreement providing for the reversion of Okinawa in 1972, regarded as a political triumph by the conservative premier, did not ease the heavy pressure

161

from within his own party. Dissatisfaction with the American dollar-defense plan, aimed specifically at Japan in ill-disguised fashion, spread through even the conservative majority. Dissent was translated into outrage over what Japanese called a "crude" and "rude" ultimatum leveled by President Nixon against the politically sensitive Japanese textile export trade. As so often has been the case over a century of stormy relations, "pro-American" conservatives suddenly reverted to "anti-American" sentiments.

Second, if we turn from the foreign policy issues and concentrate on political dissatisfaction and dissent (as slightly different from the political opposition), then we discover that unrest in Japan has been quite widespread and deep, if not alarming. Disquiet has permeated the entire society, beyond the capacity of the opposition to articulate it. Japanese dissatisfaction parallels the turbulence found throughout the modern world, in countries of the north and of the south (by the way, which is Japan?); in overdeveloped and developed as well as underdeveloped regions; in Western and non-Western societies as well as those of the similarly misnamed Third World. Dissent swirls around familiar issues: war and peace, rapid urbanization and the blight of pollution, youth unrest and university crisis.

Moreover, Japanese problems are those found in an open society, a democratic polity, a mixed and highly developed socioeconomic system—in short, the dissatisfaction and dissent characteristic of countries with a high rate of growth. Until very recently, these were characteristics seldom stressed by those observing from outside Japan. In this sense, however, Americans could have felt a strong sense of identity with Japanese.

An attempt to describe dissent in Japan and its attendant political activism might imply a comment on the bankruptcy in the study of political *institutions* as against political *behavior*. In the case of Japan, however, the political scientist can find important evidence of both stability and instability which exist *because of institutions*. In any case, he should

162

not generalize on modernization and its cost, on growth and its price, or on stability and instability in politics, without reference to the remarkable case study of Japan. Whether Japan is a model for other developing societies (the equation is cited casually and often) is not entirely clear.

To digress a moment, despite the dogmas many Japanese carry as luggage, Japanese political culture has not been derivative. The role of political institutions and their contributions to habit, political stability, and, paradoxically, the possibility of open dissent are significant.

When one considers the pendulumlike swings over the last century, he cannot help but be astounded at the relative stability of formal Japanese political institutions. They have survived "late modernization," Japan's crisis of security; then Japanese imperialism, aggression, war, defeat, the Occupation; more recently, the economic miracle, urbanization, and the consumers' durable goods boom. Three decades ago, many observers were predicting that Japan would undertake a reverse course, reacting against an alien-inspired Constitution and imposed reforms, or what Robert Ward has called "directed change."[1] As a matter of fact, the Occupation closed with a minimum of friction. The Japanese Constitution, never formally amended, has nonetheless permitted informal revision. Beginning in 1948, what had appeared to be a somewhat idealistic organic law became more and more practical. To the earliest parliamentary tradition outside the West was added a stake in the peace constitution, in democratic procedures, and in civil liberties. It was shared first by peasants, then by professors, women, labor, and students. Indeed, there is a paradox here: the forces we shall call the Establishment wanted to turn the clock back. This tendency has been opposed by the opposition which is, therefore, conservative!

Meanwhile, political behavior has caught up with the institutions. Urbanization at a geometric rate of speed, the new white-collar middle class in cities, affluence, and the plunge into the durable consumer-goods boom—all of these

163

have provided the middle-class background for the institutions established earlier. Perhaps most important, for whatever reasons, Japan is now an open modern society. One mark of its modernity is the exceptional rate of literacy, the highest in the world. The country is literally saturated with newspapers, a wide variety of magazines, a radio network, and television broadcasting. (July 1969 statistics indicated that there were 80.3 TV sets for every 100 Japanese households.) All this means that not only can the Establishment educate, inculcate, or even propagandize the public; but also, within the constitutional framework, the government cannot suppress information—it dare not ignore the opposition entirely.

Like other advanced societies, Japan is just beginning to experiment with the tensile strength of post-treaty political institutions, when they are subjected to the torque of problems such as war and peace, the gap between rural (traditional) and urban (modern) societies, and the balance between individual liberty (in the post-war era) versus community order (in the traditional Japanese sense). Finally, despite a vocal, strident minority, there is really no mainstream of ideology. Whether Japan has entered the era of the end of ideology is a moot point. It is, however, intriguing for the social scientist to speculate on developments whereby a relatively open society with democratic institutions, supported by a high growth rate in GNP, marked by a new white-collar middle class, seems increasingly scientific, pragmatic, and even apolitical, rather than dogmatic. Such speculation projects a dilemma for political theory, both in the West and in the East. What kinds of standards do we apply to questions of orthodoxy and heterodoxy in a middle-class society?

In order to understand both informal dissent in Japan and the formal political opposition, we must begin by describing majority, conservative forces. Very briefly, a century ago the Meiji modernizers engaged in what Frank Langdon has called "conservative change."[2] So successful were Japanese leaders that, by World War I, the country had become a recognized Asian power—indeed, a world power. In the interwar period there followed the disastrous flirtation with radical-reactionary political movements. These in turn led to imperialist adventure, war, defeat, and the Occupation. The largely American-led Occupation has, on occasion, been called "democratization" or "induced revolution." As a matter of fact, already by 1948 the Occupation had begun to shift its emphasis from reform to reconstruction—that is, it became increasingly conservative. By the time Japan recovered the exercise of its sovereignty in 1952, conservative forces were firmly in control.

What has been called the Establishment has been a series of conservative governments in control of Japan since the peace treaty. Sometimes also called a pluralistic hegemony, the Establishment consists of the majority Liberal Democratic party, its closely allied business and industrial representatives, and, behind the scenes, the venerable civil service, perhaps the oldest elite group among conservative forces. Noteworthy in this elite Establishment are the delegates of the reshaped *zaibatsu* (the finance clique) a new agrarian sector (after land reform), and almost a total absence of important military representation.

The Establishment has rested its political fate in two important gambles in policies. First, the series of conservative governments purchased independence (through the peace treaty) and continued security by placing Japan within the US defensive umbrella. Steps included signature of the Japan-United States Security Treaty, 1952; the treaty was renewed after a bitter struggle in Japan in 1960; and the treaty was again subject to further review (and was automatically extended) in 1970. Second, conservative leaders promised unprecedented growth rates for Japan—to double the national income in a decade. As a matter of fact, accomplishments have far outrun the most sanguine hopes of the politicians: Japan has actually quadrupled its GNP in just ten years. These gains, as we shall discuss them later, must be qualified, but the performance is little less than an economic miracle.

In the arrangement of forces since the war and the peace treaty, there is an interesting paradox. Conservative governments, who have favored the American alliance, have most openly advocated revision of the US-inspired Constitution. The opposition has regularly been able to garner a little more than one third of the seats in the Diet. They have thus been in a position to block any revision of the Constitution (amendment requires a two-thirds majority in both houses). The opposition has opposed the American Alliance, but has defended the American-inspired organic law. The Japanese public, in its political wisdom, has thus regularly returned a conservative majority, but not a sufficient majority to allow alternation of the structure of the government.

Now it is precisely in Japan's remarkable growth where one can detect certain problems, sources of dissatisfaction and dissent. Certainly Americans, of all people, can recognize this possibility of tension resulting from rapid growth.

On the one hand, the annual Japanese growth rate has averaged over 16%, resulting in a quadrupling of the GNP in just a decade. In absolute terms even the GNP per capita has annually increased by 15.3%, a rise from $388 (1959) to about $1400 (1969). Thus Japan, as former Ambassador Edwin Reischauer put it, is now a "great power." Its GNP ranks the country second (behind the United States) in the noncommunist world.

On the other hand, Japan continues at an inordinately low level of national income per capita, with a rank of 16th in the world. Moreover, wages have increased by only an average of 9% per annum (as compared with GNP per capita, which has jumped 15.3%). In case of labor's demands for a greater share of the national income, management counters that labor productivity has increased at an average rate of only 7.5%.

Even informed Japanese speak of the "shadows" of economic growth. Not nearly enough money has been spent on social overhead. For example, Japan's urban population

166

has grown from 45% (1955) to 58% (1965); and if the trend continues as expected, it will jump to 71% (1975). Rapid urbanization has been accompanied by demands for adequate housing, rudimentary sanitation, and improved transport and an insistence upon communities with good schools, recreation facilities, and access to cultural riches. Despite a sophisticated system in model, social security for the whole nation is at a low level. Japan ranks eighth both in proportion of GNP and in absolute amount per capita devoted to social security.[3]

There is a whole set of other demands on the product of growth in the Japanese economy. Two have a bearing on the forces of opposition, soon to be described. As Japan's level of expectation has risen, there has been a widespread demand by Japanese for an improved system of higher education. This is not so much a problem of quantity, as the population reaches a plateau and as the postwar baby boom subsides. It is rather a question of quality, or, as our students put it, "relevance." Japanese higher education is under assault. About one in every five four-year colleges and universities is subject to disorder now.

Finally, there is a hidden demand, one which the opposition, the Japanese dissenters, may not recognize. To the extent that Japan moves from dependence to independence; to the degree that Japan escapes from the orbit of the American defense system; to that extent there will be a need (if not a demand) for an expansion of Japan's expenditure on defense. It is not entirely a coincidence, of course, that Japan has enjoyed a sharp rise in GNP and has at the same time spent less per capita on military resources than has any other comparable great power in the world.

Growth itself, then, has given rise to some dissatisfaction in Japan. For example, all political parties have encountered an increased political apathy demonstrated by the new middle class, a studied indifference compounded of extreme pragmatism, scientism, the impact of technology, and increased bureaucratization of Japanese life. Perhaps for

167

"stability" (of political institutions), we should use the word "inertia" (of the citizenry). But even this substitution is not quite accurate, for a large, vigorous, independent press has played an important role. Newspapers have contributed to the degradation of the politician in a mass society. Middle-class skepticism has at best been kept thoroughly informed by enterprising media; or it has at worst been encouraged by a vast network of cynical *masu komi* ("Mass communications").

The conservative Establishment, of course, profits most from apathy and inertia, but the urban migration also has eroded the old coalition led by the Liberal Democratic party, the alliance of peasants and business. Many members of the new middle class have, rather than given up any allegiance, begun to float according to the mood of each successive election. Thus although the Establishment still remains firmly in power, the Liberal Democratic party, as a party, has lost power from a high of 74.5% of Diet seats (1949) and 66.1% of the popular vote (1952)—losing seats at about 1.15% per year—down to 48.8% (1967) and 47.6% (1969) of the popular vote. It should be noted that Japan, still facing the issue of reapportionment in the future, translates this popular vote into 59.2% of the lower House of Representative seats (1969).

The opposition has increased the public's skepticism in the fact that "progressives" have demonstrated little likelihood of succeeding to responsible power. They have not (except for one brief postwar moment) been tempered by holding political leadership. Thus they have viewed political behavior as a "struggle." Meanwhile, an entrenched bureaucracy stresses majority will over minority rights, so that the opposition can only denounce the conservatives for a "dictatorship of the majority." Sectors of the minority often appear to have been colored Red; indeed, they usually speak in Marxist jargon and are therefore distrusted by the Establishment elite.

Moreover, improvement in wages has similarly weakened

labor's allegiance to the socialist parties. The blue-collar worker, aspiring to status as *hoito-kara sarari-man*, is less inclined to listen to strident, ideological pleas for a class struggle.

Two new actors have most recently appeared on the scene. These include an emerging layer of elderly (over 65 years of age) retired Japanese, with a decade of life remaining to them. Relatively abandoned by their families, as compared to the situation in traditional times, they find themselves at the mercy of the urban lonely crowd. The elderly too constitute an unpredictable, floating vote.

Most explosive, of course, are Japan's youth (age group, 18-26). Permissively reared, traditionally indulged, and left free prior to settling down in the complex net of obligations, these new *ronin* ("masterless samurai") have lashed out at not only established order, but also at all discipline. All political parties, the labor federations, the universities, and Japanese families have felt the effects of this youth revolution.

Turning from dissatisfaction in the abstract to the political opposition in the concrete, first, who are the interest groups outside the formidable Establishment? Second, how are these interests articulated? Facetiously, one might hastily reply, not very well! More seriously, dissent in Japan is diffuse, as has been indicated, and the political opposition is complex, faction-ridden, and often not in touch with reality.

The so-called progressives, as we shall see, have traditionally built single-interest group parties. That is, labor unions have provided the mass support. At the prefectural level, the interlocking directorate of union officials and "progressive" party leaders is striking. One problem is that as labor has split, so have the "progressive" parties. Another difficulty is that outside labor organizations, no real mass support at the "rice-roots" level exists. The great labor federations have been characterized by rigid ideology and intense (and traditional) Japanese factionalism. Seldom faced with the necessity to fight over, bargain collectively for, and win

169

bread-and-butter gains, the unions have become intensely politicized. The two main federations of the present time are the General Council of Trade Unions (Sohyo) and the All-Japan Congress of Trade Unions (Domei Kaigi). The former has about 4,200,000 members; the latter, about 1,400,000.

It is remarkable that opposition interest groups outside these union federations are poorly represented or not represented at all in "progressive" parties. There are, for example, what the Japanese call the *interi* (the "intellectuals"; i.e., almost anyone with a college education). The older generation of intellectuals has been heavily influenced by Marxism in the course of their education. Articulate, almost arrogant in a stance astride some media, and influential in opinion-molding well beyond their numbers, nonetheless, they sometimes find themselves alienated from radical youth on the extreme Left. It goes without saying that this group (whom Vice-President Agnew might call "effete snobs") is separated by an even greater gap from the Establishment on the Right.

Then there is a miscellaneous group of dissidents—they can hardly be dignified by the name interest groups—the small merchants (on a lower level of a dual economy); the urban proletariat (sometimes called "industrial peasants"); lower-level bureaucrats; women and youth. Although they are included in the labor federations, teachers (for example, in the Japan Teachers Union) have shown a marked penchant for bowing to authority and, at the same time, embracing political radicalism.

The most extreme among youth, as we shall see, are suspicious of all interest groups, owe allegiance to no established party, and bow to no authority.

Opposition parties, to repeat, articulate these dissatisfied interests poorly and this is by the parties' own admission. First, however, let us simply list them.

The traditional opposition has long been embodied in Socialists (JSP; Social Democratic party of Japan; Nihon-

Shakaito). A product of prewar social democracy, stunted in growth under a police state, the Socialist party emerged in the postwar period already rent with factionalism. In 1952-53, significantly it split into a left wing and a right wing over signature of the peace treaty. Patched together, it split again in 1960—exactly parallel to a fissure in the labor movement—and the result was the appearance of the Democratic Socialists (DSP; Democratic Socialist party; Minshu-Shakaito). This group possibly comes closest to representing the liberal *interi*. It is, therefore, denounced by the Left as being only halfway between the Establishment's Liberal Democratic party and the true Socialists. Just as the JSP represents Sohyo strength, so the DSP is backed by Domei Kaigi, among the labor interests.

The Japan Communist party (JCP; Nihon Kyosanto) is actually only a small Diet party (but it has a larger mass membership than all the other left-wing parties combined). Like standard communist parties anywhere, it has been badly factionalized among pro-Chinese and pro-Soviet Union Communists, and neutral groups.

Finally, mention should be made of a unique party phenomenon in Japan, the Clean Government party (KMT; Komeito, political arm of the Buddhist Soka Gakkai). This group is hard to place in the political spectrum. It taps a traditional Japanese religious layer (Nichiren Buddhism); it uses the newest means of communication and organization; it commands the loyalty of many wealthy Japanese; it is most often in opposition to the orthodox Establishment (LDP); and, at the same time, it is regarded as an enemy to the death by the Japan Communists. Table 6.1 shows the distribution of votes of these various opposition parties, relative to the Liberal-Democratic party (1969); and the most recent distribution of seats in the lower House of Representatives, for comparison.

The Socialists (JSP) well represent a paradox in contemporary Japan's opposition. Thus, although it is true that many Japanese are increasingly critical of the administration led by Premier Eisaku Sato, it can also be said that they hardly believe there is the slightest chance for the JSP to lead in the formation of a coalition government. The most recent in a succession of shattered hopes is represented by reflections on the 1969 elections for the Tokyo Metropolitan Assembly.

Table 6.1: Elections to the House of Representatives in Japany, 1967 & 1969

Party	Symbol	% of Popular Votes Election		House of Representatives Seats	
		(1967)	(1969	(1967)	(1969)
Liberal-Democrats	LDP	48.8%	47.6%	277	288+
Socialists	JSP	27.9%	21.4%	140	90
Democratic Socialists	DSP	7.4%	7.8%	30	31
Communists	JCP	4.8%	6.8%	5	14
Komeito	KMT	5.4%	10.9%	25	47
(Independents)	—	5.7%	5.3%	9	16
	TOTAL	100.0%	100.0%	486	486

+After election, admission of 12 conservative independents boosted LDP total to 300.

Chairman Tomomi Narita of the JSP had stated that his party had five goals: (1) support of the "peace" Constitution; (2) realization of "disarmed neutrality"; (3) an economy "free from monopolistic evils"; (4) protection of "the people's standard of living"; and (5) encouragement of party members' "democratic activities."[4] Armed with these slogans, with no policy to implement them, the JSP nonetheless entered the Tokyo elections with a symbol of success. A few years before, Socialist-backed Ryokichi Minobe had been elected governor of Tokyo Metropolitan Prefecture. On July 19, however, the JSP suffered a shattering defeat in Tokyo. The party won only 24 seats in the Assembly, a drop to

172

nearly one half of its previous 45 seats. Indeed, the party fell to third place behind a majority LDP and the KMT (with 25). Incidentally, the JCP made a big advance to 18 seats (double its previous figure).

Secretary General Saburo Eda of the JSP tried to explain away the failure: "The decline of the Socialist party is not a phenomenon confined to Japan. Socialist movements are diversified throughout the world. Socialists are suffering from self-contradiction. They are struggling in the face of the necessity to carry out reforms. I hope that they will overcome these difficulties and make contributions to the future advance of Socialist movements. . . ." Governor Minobe, "shocked" by the crushing defeat, was somewhat more forthright. The party's defects, he said, were the so-called Narita principles, the "low caliber" of JSP Diet members, the party's "overreliance on labor unions," and the total "lack of everyday activities" at the local level.[5]

Even more damaging was the JSP-sponsored poll, a survey of 500 men and women voters (aged 20-30) living in Tokyo. The young Tokyo voters considered the JSP inferior to both rivals, the KMT and the JCP, in "aggressiveness," "youthfulness," "stability," "progressiveness," and "potentiality." The Socialists were ranked behind the LDP in every respect except "youthfulness." Perhaps most startling was a contradiction of the old assumption that whereas the LDP appealed to "conservative" rural voters, the JSP attracted both "progressive" and urban followers. Results of this and other polls clearly showed, however, that increasingly Socialist votes were coming only from farming or from suburban areas.[6]

One of the most recent significant developments is the fact that militant youth has threatened to drive a wedge into the once monolithic relationship between the JSP and Sohyo. Ironically, the Socialists and the labor federation had created, in 1965, the Anti-War Youth Committee (AYC; Hansen Seinen Iinkai) to counter a group founded by the Communists. At the core originally were young unionists, who designed machinery through which youth could campaign against the "US invasion of Vietnam" and the Japan-South Korea normalization treaty. Soon, however, the AYC was infiltrated by radical students, many of whom had in turn been expelled by the JCP because of the students' lack of discipline and their advocacy of violence as policy. In short, Sohyo argued that the ultimate aim of all AYC was to destroy the "established Left" (a magnificant irony) and to form a "new Left." The Socialists tended to be more tolerant of the youth.[7] Other disputes between the "established Left" and young radicals will be described later.

The Democratic Socialists (DSP), in some of their recent policy postures, illustrate very well the dilemmas faced by this Socialist faction. Anxious to remain a legitimate part of the opposition, the DSP has regularly denounced the Establishment as well as the JSP for extraparliamentary, undemocratic procedures. For its efforts, the DSP has in turn been denounced by the Left as a "new bourgeois" party.

An interesting development was the inauguration, on July 23, 1969, of a new society. Member organizations included, in addition to the DSP and its sister labor federation Domei, the so-called Democratic Socialism Study Group, religious organizations, and some medical societies, small business, cultural, and educational associations. All of these jointly launched the lengthily but accurately named Association for Revising the Security Treaty and Protecting Democracy (Ampo Kaitei; Minshushugi o Mamoru Kai). The Establishment, argued association members, in 1970 planned to adopt as policy the "automatic extension" of the US-Japan Security Treaty. The JSP and JCP demanded the pact's abolition. The new association advocated revision of the treaty on the basis of a national consensus. By this traditional Japanese term, the association hoped to avoid internal disorder over the treaty issue and confusion over reversion of Okinawa. Specifically, Article 6 of the Treaty (providing for the US right to maintain forces and establish military bases in Japan) would be deleted. All US bases in Japan would eventually be removed. For such bases as are required in a transitional period or as an exceptional measure, a different and new agreement should be signed. No American military would be stationed in Japan on a permanent basis. Finally, provision of the (revised) treaty should be applied in entirety to bases in Okinawa after reversion.[8]

This posture, essentially the policy position of the DSP, is moderate. Its platform is critical but constructive. Above all, the DSP as usual eschews violence in settling any policy issue. The difficulty is that the Democratic Socialists, on this as on many other policies, have had trouble in attracting a large percentage of the electorate.

The Communists (JCP) also face a dilemma. Often criticized for being too mild, the JCP has slowly but steadily gained popular support as it has renounced a policy of violence. Peculiarly, the Sino-Soviet dispute has served to strengthen its popular image, because it has adopted a policy of "self-reliance and independence" with regard to both Peking and Moscow.

The Communists' mildness has been, of course, all the more reason for denunciation of the JCP by other leftists. Tetsuzo Fuwa, Chairman of the party's Political and Foreign Policy Committee, has dealt with the familiar charge that the Communists were aiming for a one-party dictatorship. He stated that his party, unlike the JSP, "has never aimed for establishing a single-party regime. We strive for the establishment of a democratic coalition government to be followed by a people's democratic government only by the coalition of all democratic parties and forces." On other counts, too, the JCP found itself at odds with the Socialists. A JCP official recently complained that the JSP has in reality condoned the "Trotskyites," student radicals whom the Communists condemn.[9]

On the other extreme, Komeito, a rising political force with far greater parliamentary strength than the JCP enjoys, has considered the Communist party its mortal enemy.

The "Clean Government" party (KMT; Komeito) is

175

probably less well known outside Japan than its parent organization, the Soka Gakkai. The latter has received fairly widespread publicity, even in the West, where it has often been condemned as a potentially fascist organization. Actually, it has denounced both the conservative Establishment and the so-called Left Cultural Front. Tentatively, at least, it is better to try to think of the neo-Buddhist organization in its own terms, "Builders of the Third Civilization."[10] In any case, its political arm, the Komeito, is properly to be placed in the opposition. And the KMT has proved to be a formidable opponent, carefully marshalling its political resources and gradually emerging as the second most effective opposition party.

Space permits description of only one illustrative posture of the Soka Gakkai and its party arm, the KMT. In 1957 the organization's Student Department was established with a membership of a little over 500 youths. The department's rolls have since swelled to over 230,000. In July 1969 it initiated in turn a new student organization called the National Liaison Council for Smashing the University Bill (Daigaku Rippo Funsai Zenkoku Renraku Kyogikai, abbreviated "Zenkyo"). The allusion in the name was to the new university law, ramrodded through the Diet by the LDP and designed to control campus disorders. Some 1,600 representatives from 180 universities attended the first Zenkyo convention.

President Daisaku Ikeda of Soka Gakkai left it to the student leaders to define the "third road" toward ending the protracted campus conflict. Zenkyo Chairman Tadaaki Tsuda promptly declared that his group was not aiming at the university law alone. "If we make progress in organizing students, then we can take a fighting posture over the Security Treaty and Okinawa issues." The basic approach, he added, was one of "construction"; but this word was interpreted to mean "destruction" of the "old established order," that is, the "power structure" under the LDP.[11]

Student dissent, campus disorders, and university con-

176

frontations have, as a matter of fact, defied all channels of organization. So complex is this feature of dissatisfaction in Japan, within limits of space only a little coherence can be brought to the subject in this concluding section. Finally, we must take note of the remarkable fact that open dissent is engineered by a factionalized minority of students, the majority of whom are doubtless becoming depoliticized. It is difficult to winnow much hope from either tendency.

First, it should be noted that disorder among Japanese youth is, in one sense, but part of a truly worldwide phenomenon. Second, in another sense Japanese student opposition is among the oldest of the modern species; one might add, with pardonable if dubious pride, that the Japanese variety perhaps still holds the mythical world's championship for disruption. Some selected current developments will illustrate the point.

Up to August, Japanese police arrested a total of 5,984 persons (mostly students) during 1969, in campus riots and political demonstrations. The figure, according to the National Police Agency, was more than double that for the first half of 1968. A further breakdown of the statistics clearly revealed that the renowned Zengakuren (National Federation of Students Associations), viewed from outside Japan as a monolithic, radical organization of students, was itself dangerously fractured. In a sort of descending order of index of radical activism, the Middle Core (Chukaku) faction led in arrests with 807; followed by Revolutionary Marxists (Kakumaru) with 498; then the Anti-Imperialism Students League (Hantei), with 468; and the Socialist Students League (Shagakudo), with 445.[12]

Press coverage even outside Japan of the rising crescendo of confrontation has been sufficient to indicate the major trends. Suffice it to say that deep-down dissatisfaction with the traditional structure and operation of the Japanese university produced the advance wave of strikes. The prestigious Tokyo University, embroiled almost entirely through 1968 and 1969, provided a representative example.

177

What began as a protest against procedures of the medical faculty called forth the usual overreaction by the Establishment in the form of police invasion of the campus. The climax came in January 1969 and was fully aired over radio and TV throughout Japan and the world: students on camera played out the samurai drama of a 10-hour siege by riot police, culminating in the eventual capture of the famous Yasuda Auditorium tower. At Kyoto University, September 21, 1969, same tragedy, same script; some 2,000 riot police had to clear the campus of barricades and found themselves besieging the last stronghold, the clock tower.

During the year 1968, there were some 90 separate university disputes, which resulted in the arrest of 3,000 students. At the time of writing, the final score for 1969 was not yet in. In August, it is true, the LDP-led government of Premier Sato forced through the Diet over opposition boycott a University Normalization Law. By late September, "seriously ill" campuses had been reduced from 18 to 13; class work had been resumed in many colleges; some 20,000 absentee students (in the spring) had declined to 6,400 (in the fall). Meanwhile, however, the "normalization" had served only to polarize the radical opposition; new issues of foreign policy and the security posture of Japan had displaced the narrower academic disputes. Some representative developments may be singled out to illuminate the ominous facts behind the headlines.

Indeed, with the surfacing of security issues, it has recently been quite apparent that the older Zengakuren is not in the center of gravity of dissent. Most prominent in demonstrations designed to plateau in the fall of 1969 and to peak in June 1970 was the previously mentioned Anti-War Youth Committee (AYC; Hansen Seinen Iinkai). This group was said to have 20,000 individual members in some 489 subgroups. Perhaps most significantly, some 12,500 were young unionists who, since the latter half of 1968, increasingly behaved like the students (according to Sohyo). Wearing helmets (with symbols to mark off squads), face covers, and vests, they swung wooden staves, threw rocks, built barricades, and tapped the alarmingly high supply of Molotov Cocktails available in Tokyo.

Considerably smaller in size but commanding a vocal elite of youth is the Japan Peace for Vietnam Committee (Beheiren), organized in April 1965. Its total membership is estimated at about 6,500, concentrated mostly in Tokyo (where 30% of its members reside).

On September 5, 1969, all of the "radical" (in Japanese terms, anti-Japan Communist party) factions except for Kakumanu (Revolutionary Marxists) held a major rally in Hibiya Park, Tokyo, to form a "grand alliance." The new joint body was to be called the National Federation of All-Campus Joint Struggle Committees (Zenkoku Zenkyoto Rengo). Yoshitaka Yamamoto was chosen chairman but as he came up from the underground to assume leadership, he was promptly arrested by police. Plans for massive demonstrations were nevertheless projected; the Establishment could count only on the obvious fact that no coherent united front of youthful demonstrators could be constructed.[13]

By the end of 1969, the pattern of assault was clear. The October 10 *demo* (anniversary of the Haneda Airport Incident, 1967) was relatively mild, under strict police surveillance. International Antiwar Day, October 21, was more dangerous even though engineered by a minority of hit-and-run disrupters. Action was to pick up speed by November 18, date of Premier Sato's departure for Washington (for talks with President Nixon). And there was a promise that, regardless of the Establishment's formula for settlement of the issues for 1970—Okinawa reversion and the Japan-US Security Treaty—sporadic and even massive demonstrations continued right up until June 23, 1970. The date marked automatic extension of the Security Treaty.

Even the informed Japanese press occasionally raised questions about the thrust of the dissent. Why, for example, if the Communists, Socialists, labor federations, and student organizations were desirous of a prompt return of Okinawa, did the leaders of the *demo* aim to block Premier Sato's departure for Washington, where he drew up with President Nixon the final agreement on reversion? For many of the radical students, there were two answers: first, reversion was the price to be paid by the United States for automatic extension of the Security Treaty; second, passive parliamentary protest—recommended by the DSP, JSP, and even JCP—would not serve to convert these sensitive issues into instruments for bringing down the whole Establishment system.

There were, of course, even among students and youth those who actively opposed *demo* and street-fighting tactics. About 400 organizations of various sizes on the Right, comprising about 110,000 individuals, had appeared. A basic characteristic of these groups was that, until late in 1969 at least, they lacked enough cohesion to effect joint action. The Establishment could take little solace in this fact, however, for these groups too planned mass campaigns to "heighten national consciousness," to put pressure on the government to "renovate the nation" so as to make it resistent to Leftist agitation. Very general aims included educational reform (with an emphasis on *more* discipline in university life); improvement of law-enforcement functions; a "self-reliant constitution" (to replace the American-imposed "peace" constitution); outlawing the JCP; and offering state support to the Yasukuni Shrine (dedicated to dead war veterans).[14]

Such groups have come to be called the Nationalist Factions (Minzoku-ha). Significantly, they began to make their appearance amidst Meiji Centenary (1968) programs, designed to celebrate the 100th anniversary of the so-called Restoration and studiously ignored or vigorously opposed by the Left. Somewhat more specific reference may be made, for example, to the platform of the Japan Student League (Nihon Gakusei Domei; abbreviated "Nichigaku-do"): (1) overthrow the Zengakuren; (2) destroy the "Potsdam system" (imposed on Japan after surrender) and promulgate an "autonomous constitution"; (3) abolish the Japan-US

Security Treaty and establish a self-reliant defense system; (4) regain Okinawa (from the United States) and the "northern territories" (islands off Hokkaido occupied by the USSR); and (5) destroy the nuclear proliferation treaty. The thrust of the platform is more significant than the size of the organization, which consists primarily of students in Waseda University.[15]

A more sizeable group, formed May 4, 1969, is the National Liaison Council of Student Self-Government Bodies (Zenkoku Gakusei Jichitai Renraku Kyogikai; abbreviation, "Zenkoku Gakukyo"). These originated as voluntary groups, aimed at supplanting the official student associations. As of the end of August, Zenkoku Gakukyo claimed to have won control of 20 student government assosciations (a small number, of course, when compared with the hundreds on the extreme Left). The new group planned to take one more step on November 3, Culture Day, by establishing what would be called the Minzoku-ha Zengakuren (Nationalist-Faction Students Federation). Its membership goal was projected at 10,000 students. Like the other groups mentioned above, its basic ideology was obviously neonationalism (*shin minzoku-shugi*).

Despite the massive protests, even the violent *demo*, mounted by the minority of radical students, there is some evidence that Japanese youth as a whole has shown decreasing "political interest" during the past decade. In certain Japanese studies, "political interest" in this context means activism designed to alter the political system by such means as substituting for the (LDP) party in power another opposition party. Movements outside the system have been called "depoliticalization," in Japan and elsewhere. During 1968 a poll was conducted by a large Sohyo affiliate, the Postal Workers Union (Zentei), with a sample of 12,000 out of its total membership of 74,000. The sample was deliberately chosen from the 16-30 age group.

What was discovered in this, as well as similar polls, was a corollary to "depoliticalization": a decline in popular support for the Socialists, whom youth regarded as more doctrinaire and ideology-bound than the Communists. It became more apparent that, for the average young man, the chief goal in life is a comfortable home life, not the establishment of a classless society. (The current leftist epithet for this propensity is called *maihomu-shugi*, meaning "my private home above anything else" principle.)

In the poll, respondents were asked: What do you think should be done about the "capitalist society" of Japan? Over 36% answered, "Capitalism can be improved by modifications." On labor-management relations: What would you favor with regard to your own promotion? Almost 40% chose judgment according to the "merit system." Finally: Suppose you could listen to a talk by one of the following?—and a list of prominent names was appended. In startling fashion, more than one of every four chose to listen to a famous Japanese industrialist. (The list was as follows: Matshushita, 25.96%, Schweitzer, 22.78%; Lenin, 22.36%; Eda [of the JSP], 11.8%; Ishihara [former Rightist], 7.2%; Yoshida [the Occupation-period premier], 6.23%; and Trotsky, 3.15%.) The decline of socialism as an ideal among youth, concluded the postal union leaders, was owing to a widespread feeling of complacency in Japan.[16]

This is a somewhat confusing, if rather accurate, note on which to conclude. Japan's whole search for identity itself is a puzzle. Armed with one of the great economies of the world, Japan is nonetheless uneasy. Dissatisfaction and dissent are, formally, channeled into a number of organized opposition parties, but often informally burst the dikes and spill over into widespread student protest. The Establishment can, of course, boast of success, but continues to rule on the basis of inertia at least partly. None of the formal opposition organizations has been able to define and capitalize on the vague malaise. Student activism, perhaps confined to a minority, is set off against a seeming trend toward "depoliticalization" of youth.

One can only add a worry in the form of a question: in a

society prone to take important steps *not* by confrontation and division, but rather by consensus, how will decisions on the pressing issues of the 1970s be made?

Notes

1. Ward RE: "Reflections on the Allied Occupation and Planned Political Change in Japan," in Ward RE, ed: *Political Development in Modern Japan.* Princeton, Princeton University Press, 1968, p 477.

2. Langdon F: *Politics in Japan.* Boston, Little, Brown, 1967, p 8.

3. Miyazaki I: "Japan's Pressing Task: Erasing the 'Shadows' of Growth," *The Japan Times Weekly,* August 16, 1969; also Morley, JW: "Growth for What? The Issue of the 'Seventies,' " in Curtis GL, ed: *Japanese-American Relations.* Fo; the American Assembly. Washington, Columbia Books, 1970.

4. *Sankei Shimbun,* September 10, 1969.

5. *The Japan Times Weekly,* August 2; July 19, 1969.

6. *The Japan Times Weekly,* October 4, 1969.

7. (Editorial) "JSP and 'Antiwar Youth,' " *The Japan Times Weekly,* July 5; Murata K: "Militants Among the Workers," *The Japan Times Weekly,* August 23, 1969.

8. Ikeda H: "In Search fo; National Consensus," *The Japan Times Weekly,* July 26, 1970.

9. Fuwa T: "Prospects for an Independent and Democratic Japan," *Akahata* [Red Flag], July 5; Ueda K: "1970 and the Touchstone for a Progressive Party," *Akahata,* September 5, 1969.

10. Dator JA: *Soka Gakkai, Builders of the Third Civilization; American and Japanese Members.* Seattle, University of Washington Press, 1969; a more recent, sophisticated, and detailed study of the Gakkai is to be found in White JW: *The Sokagakkai and Mass Society.* Stanford, Stanford University Press, 1970.

11. Murata K: "Sokagakkai's Student Union," *The Japan Weekly,* July 19, 1969.

12. *The Japan Times Weekly,* August 2, 1969.

13. Murata K: "Student Violence on Rise?" *The Japan Times Weekly,* September 27, 1969.

14. Murata K: "Rightists and 1970," *The Japan Times Weekly,* September 6, 1969.

15. Murata K: "The 'Minzoku-ha' Students," *The Japan Times Weekly,* October 18, 1969.

16. Murata K: "Depoliticalization of Youth," *The Japan Times Weekly,* August 9, 1969. For a wide-ranging survey of dissatisfaction

and dissent, see the special issue, "University and Society," of the *Journal of Social and Political Ideas in Japan*, Vol. 2-3 (December, 1967). The title is misleading, for data on education in general, alienation, the "test hell," and student protest carry the issue well beyond the confines of the university into the society at large.

7 Opposition in the Federal Republic of Germany

Arthur B. Gunlicks
University of Richmond

Introduction

The legitimate existence of organized groups—especially political parties—that oppose, criticize, and attempt to replace the ruling elites can be viewed "as very nearly the most distinctive characteristic of democracy itself."[1] But only to a point. Twelve years after the founding of the very democratic Weimar Republic in Germany in 1919 there seemed to be "nothing but opposition"[2] to the republic and the democratic process for which it stood.

Twelve years after the establishment of the Bonn Republic in 1949 little notice was paid to the "oppositions of principle"[3] that had once destroyed democracy in Germany. The social, economic, and political milieu had changed dramatically since the days of Weimar, and the impact of this change on the German party system was significant. Indeed, the problem now seemed to be too little opposition!

What had happened to the opposition, not only in West

I wish to thank the University of Richmond and the Committee on Faculty Research for a grant which covered the expenses incurred in writing this essay.

Germany but in much of the Western world, became the subject of several important articles and books.[4] The "waning of opposition" and an "end of ideology" were said to be caused mainly by the fact that the modern welfare state and rising levels of affluence had provided solutions to formerly intractable problems. And though there was no guarantee that domestic conflicts would become less numerous in such a system, it was thought that they would be less intense.[5] In foreign policy, too, opposition was seen as waning, because of the "authority and prestige" enjoyed by "responsible statesmen" and because foreign policy initiatives and changes were either too technical or too vague to have an "appreciable impact" on voters.[6] The division of the country into East and West had the additional effect of encouraging Germans to "play down divisive elements and internal criticism and to look with suspicion on any type of criticism which is parallel with . . . that coming from East Germany."[7]

But in the late 1960s something unexpected happened. The opposition pendulum began to swing back. In one Western country after another, there emerged a "new left" opposition of principle that was perhaps related to, but certainly not identical with, the "old left" communist movements of interwar and immediate postwar days. The Federal Republic, the paragon of the vanishing parliamentary opposition, became the scene of some of the most violent and fanatic extraparliamentary new left agitation and action witnessed anywhere in the West. At the same time a new rightist movement was catching on at the grass roots level and making sufficient progress to cause both German and foreign observers considerable concern. Important changes, then, had occurred in West Germany, as elsewhere, during the last half of the 1960s.

The changes in the politics of opposition that have taken place in the Federal Republic from 1949 to the present are the general subject of this essay. These changes suggest two more specific questions: whether the waning of opposition and an end of ideology were not temporary phenomena in the Federal Republic, and whether they did not trigger a reaction by those who were not satisfied intellectually with the new politics of consensus or who felt left outside and bypassed. It may well be that by a kind of dialectic the gradual decline and disuse of regular opposition channels encourage an antithesis which takes the form of an explosion of pent-up opposition outside these channels.

An Uncertain Beginning

After World War II there was sufficient reason to be skeptical about the future of German democracy. Many opposition groups in the Weimer Republic had failed to abide by the most fundamental rules of the democratic game, and there was no guarantee that there would be a change in the Bonn Republic. For this reason a conscious effort was made in certain provisions of the West German "Basic Law" to limit the effect of potentially "irresponsible" oppositions.[8] Other important legal restrictions were incorporated in electoral laws at national and *Land* (state) levels which, among other things, place limits on the parliamentary representation of parties receiving less than 5% of the total vote. Still other obstacles exist, of course, which cannot be traced to legal restrictions. Some of these are common to other democracies as well, such as "depoliticalization" in the new Europe,[9] the postwar decline of the party-oriented press in Western Europe, and a growing concentration of the press.[10] Some are perhaps peculiar in part to the political culture of Germany. These include considerable public misunderstanding of the role of opposition in a democracy;[11] the "rise of a new type of professional politician in all parties, chiefly distinguished by his skills as a tactician and as a broker among diverse interests, rather than by the more traditional skills of agitation and advocacy"[12]; and certain events of recent years that have demonstrated to many observers the lack of unequivocal support or understanding even among important party leaders for the role and function of criticism and opposition.[13]

For these reasons it is easy to sometimes overlook the important *opportunities* enjoyed by opposition forces in the Federal Republic. The Basic Law, for example, not only guarantees the traditional freedoms of speech, press, and assembly which are essential to the functioning of opposition parties; it also grants all political parties explicit constitutional recognition and protection. The Federal Constitutional Court, the guardian of the Basic Law, has been used as a constitutional instrument of appeal by opposition parties. Other legal provisions, too, provide considerable assistance to opposition parties. Thus parties that receive more than one half of 1% pf the national vote are reimbursed for most of their campaign costs from the public treasury (public financial assistance for the parties extends even to the local level in many cases).

The mass media in West Germany provide opposition parties with numerous opportunities. German radio and television stations, publicly owned and regionally organized, offer free time to government as well as opposition parties during national election campaigns. Controversial federal or *Land* government statements carried over radio and television may become the subject of further debate by the parliamentary parties who receive free time for their responses.[14] And though most German television programs, like their American counterparts, may try to avoid controversy, there are few American network programs, except perhaps "60 Minutes," and "The Great American Dream Machine," that could compete with "Panorama," "Report," "Monitor," and "ZDF Magazin." The first of these stirred considerable controversy during the Adenauer era, while the last has aroused government indignation in the early 1970s. Though most of the German press considers itself to be politically independent, about 40% of the press, including the "serious" press, sympathizes at least to some extent with one party or another. [15] Nor can there be any doubt about the critical role of the news magazine *Der Spiegel*, which many have come to consider "the loyal opposition" in Germany.[16] Since August 1, 1968, it is no longer illegal to distribute East German Communist newspapers in the Federal Republic, and the security law, which was the authority for the action in 1962 that led to the "Spiegel Affair" (a kind of German "Pentagon Papers Affair"), has been revised and made less ambiguous.[17]

Parties and the mass media have been joined as instruments of "opposition" by a wide variety of powerful and well-organized groups, representing every conceivable interest in German society. Where others have failed, they have often succeeded in influencing the Bonn government to revise or drop policies and proposals deemed inimical to their vital interests.[18]

Because West Germany is a federation of eleven *Laender* ("states"), including the *Land* ("state") of West Berlin, opposition parties excluded from rule in Bonn enjoy opportunities to form regional governments. The experience, publicity, and self-confidence gained by governing at the *Land* level and, in particular, in the larger cities, have been of inestimable importance in the past to the "perennial" national opposition party, the Social Democrats (SPD), and at present to the Christian Democrats (CDU/CSU). And parties in opposition at the national level have not been averse to using their *Land* base to oppose the central government.

Finally, it is important to note the impact of cabinet stability on the parties and groups in the Federal Republic that serve as the outlets for opposition sentiments. The development of German parties since the establishment of the Federal Republic "has been strongly influenced by the fact that in contrast to the Weimar period genuine government majorities have been formed in the Bundestag and in most of the *Laender* parliaments." Thus parties have not been forced to "take into account a continuous change in the composition of the Government."[19]

Opposition Politics, 1949-1960: From "Loyal Opposition" to "Me Too-ism"

The first general election to be held in West Germany after the war was the 1949 election for the Bundestag (Lower House) of the newly created Federal Republic. Though many had expected the Social Democtatic Party of Germany (SPD) to win a plurality in that election, the Christian Democratic Union (CDU) and its sister party, the Christian Social Union (CSU) of Bavaria, emerged with the most votes, leaving the SPD in a very close second place. Konrad Adenauer, the leader of the CDU/CSU combination, became the first Chancellor by a margin of one vote in the Bundestag. His coalition government, comprised of cabinet ministers representating the Free Democratic Party (FDP) and German Party (DP) as well as the CDU/CSU, excluded the SPD and a number of smaller splinter parties, including the Communists (KPD). Thus the SPD was to begin with the formal establishment of the Federal Republic as the major opposition party, a role it was not soon to lose.

The story of the Social Democratic Party from World War II through the 1950s and early 1960s has been told often and well.[20] It is only necessary here to sketch in broad strokes the recent history of this party, whose origin dates back more than a hundred years and which served as the prototype European Social Democratic Party for many decades.[21]

Following the formation of the first Adenauer Government in 1949, the SPD Opposition under the leadership of Kurt Schumacher initiated a policy of vigorous opposition, directing its most vehement and bitter criticism toward the government's foreign, military, and economic policies. Whether it was the Petersburg Agreements of 1949 between the Western Allies and Adenauer; the Schumann Plan for establishing the European Coal and Steel Community; the

190

rearmament of Germany within either the EDC or NATO; or Ludwig Erhard's "free, social-market economy," the SPD fought hard against it. In the first years it opposed both European economic integration and defensive military alignments because of its fear that these cooperative ventures would be at the expense of German national interests, in particular of German reunification. The party's traditional Marxist objections to capitalism were reinforced by an allegedly discredited continental European capitalism which had capitulated before the Nazis and which was apparently incapable of providing either an ethical or economic basis for the common welfare.

In spite of, or perhaps because of, its vigorous opposition after 1949, the SPD suffered a severe defeat in the national elections of 1953. For the first time in German history a single party, the CDU/CSU,[22] received an absolute majority of the seats in the parliament, though it won less than a majority of the popular vote. The SPD also gained since 1949 in absolute numbers of votes, but because of the larger turnout, its percentage of the national vote actually declined slightly. The smaller CDU/CSU coalition partners of the first legislative period, the FDP and DP, lost both voters and percentage points. The BHE, the refugee party—really an interest group masquerading as a party—also received far less support than most observers had predicted on the basis of its relative successes in several *Land* elections between 1950 and 1953. For the other, smaller, splinter parties the 1953 elections were even more disastrous. The sharp decline of all parties other than CDU/CSU, SPD, and FDP characteristic of the German party system during the 1950s began with this election, in which the combined percentage of the total vote for the above three parties rose from 72.1% to 83.5%. Though they held a majority of the seats in the Bundestag, the CDU/SCU formed a new coalition government with the FDP, BHE, and DP in order to have the two-thirds majority required for the constitutional revisions that would probably be needed for West German entry into a Western defense force. The SPD, which was sure to object to any German participation in such a force, was left playing a very lonely role as the "loyal opposition."

Table 7.1: Bundestag Elections in the Federal Republic of Germany, 1949-1969*

Election Year	Voter Turnout	CDU/CSU	SPD	FDP	Other Parties
1949	78.5%	31.0%	29.2%	11.9%	27.9%
1953	85.8	45.2	28.8	9.5	16.5
1957	87.8	50.2	31.8	7.7	10.3
1961	87.7	45.3	36.2	12.8	5.7
1965	86.8	47.6	39.3	9.5	3.6
1969	86.7	46.1	42.7	5.8	5.4

*Adapted from Klingemann HD, Pappi FU: "The 1969 Bundestag Election in the Federal Republic of Germany," *Comparative Politics,* II, No 4 (July 1970), p 524.

After the Adenauer government brought the Federal Republic into NATO and attention was turned to the question of conscription, the SPD decided to cooperate with the other parties in the Bundestag committees in drafting the necessary legislation. The party had hinted even before that it might be willing to agree under certain conditions to West German participation in a Western alliance, but this was the first really major break with the former policy of strenuous opposition to virtually all CDU/CSU foreign and defense policy.[23] This perceptible change in direction was not purchased without cost, however; 20 SPD Bundestag deputies refused to participate in drafting the conscription law.[24] though this rare display of disunity in the ranks of the opposition was not repeated in later years, it was a preview of the intraparty discussion that was to come over "principled" versus "pragmatic" politics.

From the perspective of Adenauer and the CDU/CSU, the SPD's loyal opposition tactics in foreign, defense, and domestic affairs after 1953 were no doubt less troublesome than the "disloyal" opposition tactics of the smaller coalition parties, BHE, FDP, and DP. Almost as soon as the cabinet was formed in October 1953, FDP deputies began to openly criticize the government's Saar policy, and in 1954 the FDP was joined by the BHE in public criticism of Adenauer's foreign policies. Soon the conservative DP began complaining about both foreign and domestic policies. Important votes in 1955 then revealed differences not only between Adenauer and the smaller coalition parties but also deep divisions within the latter. These led to a split in the BHE and the decision by a majority of the party's deputies to join the parliamentary opposition.

Even more sensational, however, was the withdrawal of the FDP from the CDU-led coalition government in the *Land* of North-Rhine Westphalia in 1956. This maneuver was perhaps the best example in postwar Germany of the potential use of the *Laender* as bases of opposition to the national government. In this case, the effect was all the greater because the formation of an SPD-FDP coalition in North-Rhine Westphalia caused the Adenauer government to lose its two-thirds majority in the Bundesrat, the second chamber of the West German Parliament and the representative organ of the *Laender*.[25]

The effect was also to lead to the withdrawal of FDP support in the Bundestag for the Adenauer government. Not all FDP deputies joined the opposition, however; a sizeable minority, including the four FDP cabinet ministers, continued to support the government and left the FDP. Thus in spite of the break with two of its three coalition partners, the Adenauer government retained a comfortable majority throughout the second legislative period.

For three reasons the 1957 elections proved to be one of the most interesting in German history. First, never before had a single party received a majority of the popular vote as did the CDU/CSU. Second, all small splinter parties were unable to pass the 5% hurdle required by the electoral law so that a greatly simplified party system consisting of CDU/

193

CSU, SPD, and FDP, could emerge. And third, the SPD had again proved unable to gain more than one third of the popular vote. Against a "catch-all" *Volkspartei* like the CDU/CSU, with a Catholic wing and a Protestant wing, a labor wing and a big-business wing, a peasant wing and an urban wing, and a chancellor in firm control of the cabinet, able and willing to dispense favors to the myriad interests that made up his constituency, the SPD seemed condemned to permanent opposition and frustration.

The CDU/CSU-dominated governments had from 1949 to 1957 set the course in German foreign policy, economic policy, and social policy. It was futile to continue to oppose a foreign policy which, though failing to achieve progress toward reunification, did provide considerable military security, remarkable trade and other economic benefits, and a degree of integration with Western Europe and North America never before equaled. Nor did it make much sense to continue invoking even diluted Marxist or semi-Marxist analyses of the Erhard social-market economy (a "free" capitalist economy with a social conscience) and predicting all kinds of dire consequences when living standards had been raised to an all-time high for most West Germans and future prospects were even brighter. The CDU/CSU slogan "no experiments," used so successfully in 1957, no doubt reflected well the feelings of the majority of the electorate, hoping to preserve what they had so recently acquired and fearful of any threat that might be posed by a party bent on effecting far-reaching changes.

The shock that followed the 1957 elections was not the first one felt by the SPD. The party had been bitterly disappointed in 1949 and 1953 as well, and following the 1953 elections certain attempts were made within the SPD to analyze and discuss the probable causes of defeat. But little was accomplished.[26] After 1957, however, it was clear to all that something had to be done if the party was ever to control the reins of government and shape the future according to its own vision.

194

Some, especially the more doctrinaire Marxists in the party, urged the leadership to turn further to the left and reject the "embourgeoisement" temptations that had been felt increasingly in the party throughout the 1950s. Others, however, recognized that it was largely the old leftist image of the party that made it so suspect to the German middle classes, whose votes were essential to any party with serious intentions of capturing executive power in West Germany. In spite of its relative moderation since the end of World War II, its determined stand on German reunification, and its democratic tradition, the SPD suffered from the accusation that the party "stood in opposition to the state rather than merely to the political majority. CDU/CSU leaders in the cabinet, particularly Adenauer, frequently played on this Bismarckian image of the SPD."[27] Though the SPD had participated in the creation of the Federal Republic, that republic in the late 1950s was not the SPD s product. To the contrary, the CDU/CSU had identified itself so strongly with the new German state "that it could not only suggest to its own voters that if the SPD were to come to power it would mean the fall of Germany; also the opposition itself had almost come to 'believe' it."[28] Apparently there was agreement among the party's leaders that the SPD could not turn to the left. As an observer of the 1957 election wrote: the SPD "cannot win an ideological election, and if the issue is Christianity versus socialism it will for years to come stay cooped up within its own third of the electorate."[29]

The only alternative to "perennial opposition," then, seemed to be further retreat from the SPD tradition of radical, doctrinaire socialism. "Further," because the party had already gone to considerable lengths to dilute the classical Marxist stance of the past, having mellowed considerably by the end of and following World War II. It had been disappointed over the practices of Soviet socialism; it was well aware of the threat of aggression from the East and the protection afforded Europe by American forces; it had become wary of Marxist slogans like "dictatorship of the proletariat," because "dictatorship" had now been experienced all too closely both in the Third Reich and in Soviet-occupied East Germany; it distrusted the bureaucracy and the decline in enthusiasm for socialism which had accompanied socialization of basic industries in some other countries; and it noted with great interest the economic and social advances made by workers in the United States since the war.[30]

The culmination of the discussion, debate, and soul-searching that followed the electoral defeat of 1957 was the acceptance in 1959 by the national party conference of a new program to replace the Heidelberg Program of 1925. This new "Godesberg Program," named after the town of Bad Godesberg, near Bonn, where the 1959 party conference was held, was a remarkable document for a German socialist party. It speaks of "Christian ethics, humanism, and classical philosophy" as the roots of European Democratic Socialism. It does not even mention Karl Marx. It rejects any claims of "ultimate truths" and criticizes Communists for falsifying socialist ideas and establishing party dictatorships. But what was different—and especially controversial within the party— was the program's explicit acceptance of a free market economy, tempered only slightly by a recognition of the desirability of some degree of planning. That "socialism is no substitute for religion," and that "the Social Democratic Party respects churches and religious societies" may have surprised many of the old-school dogmatists, but to them nothing was more heretical than the contention that "from a party of the working class the Social Democratic Party has become a party of the people."[31]

Though the Godesberg Program went far toward encouraging and confirming a trend toward a politics of consensus on domestic affairs, the party did not give up its opposition to CDU/CSU foreign policy. The SPD continued to emphasize its role as the party of reunification, and in 1959, the same year in which the Godesberg Program was accepted, the party published its *Deutschland Plan*. This plan called for the withdrawal of all foreign troops from central Europe, the banning of nuclear weapons, and the reunification of Germany in three stages through negotiations between government representatives of the Federal Republic and the East German communist regime.[32] The plan was immediately subjected to scathing attack, and soon the SPD leaders themselves began to have serious doubts about their proposals. Not the least of these was the growing recognition that whatever opportunities there may have once been for SPD foreign policies, these had been lost by *faits accomplis* and a virtually irreversible course set long before by the CDU/CSU.[33]

On June 30, 1960, the SPD announced that it was ending its opposition to the foreign policy of the CDU/CSU. Herbert Wehner explained in a speech in the Bundestag that the SPD now accepted the European and Atlantic treaty systems as the basis of German foreign policy and reunification policy. The speech caused a sensation in Germany, because "in part a mere change of emphasis, the total effect was the final abandonment of the Schumacher-Ollenhauer foreign policy in favor of one hardly distinguishable from the one pursued by the CDU since 1949."[34] In effect the party was abandoning the basic assumption on which so much of the previous foreign as well as domestic policy of the party had been based: the provisional nature of the Federal Republic. From now on, reunification was still important, but more important was the security and well-being of the Federal Republic.[35]

Politics Without Opposition, 1960-1966:
Stability and Frustration

Following the endorsement of the Godesberg Program in 1959 and the Wehner speech on foreign policy in 1960, partisan politics in West Germany became quieter, less controversial, more dignified, perhaps, and a little full.

This was reflected in the 1961 elections, the first fought at the national level within the context of a politics of consensus. Sometimes to the irritation of the CDU, the SPD attempted to create the impression that there were no basic differences between the two major political forces in the country. There was even some talk in SPD quarters of a possible coalition with the CDU—a suggestion that annoyed Adenauer, who continued to hint that the "red" SPD was not to be trusted at the helm of state in any capacity. To counter the automatic association in the minds of many voters between SPD and "opposition," the campaign emphasized the experience of SPD candidates in *Land* and city governments. And with the emphasis on Willy Brandt as the party's chancellor candidate, personality replaced the party platform and program as the most important campaign instrument.[36]

Still, the results were disappointing to the SPD, which received only 4.4% more of the vote than in 1957. The FDP, on the other hand, gained spectacularly, from 7.7% in 1957 to 12.8% in 1961. Its campaign promise to join the "CDU without Adenauer" in forming a new coalition had indeed appealed to many CDU/CSU voters, for Adenauer, if not the CDU/CSU, had lost considerable support during the past two years.

Following the elections, Adenauer and the CDU/CSU entered coalition negotiations with the FDP. These proved to be difficult for both parties, because Adenauer refused to step down as chancellor, the CDU/CSU was not prepared to force him out, and yet the FDP had committed itself publicly to a coalition with the CDU/CSU without Adenauer. After weeks of sometimes bitter discussions—and a CDU/CSU sounding out of the SPD concerning the possibility of a "grand coalition"—an agreement was achieved between Adenauer and the FDP concerning a new coalition. In order to save whatever face he could for the FDP, Erich Mende, the leader of the FDP, did not join the cabinet. But Adenauer, who was to remain chancellor until some undetermined time before the 1965 elections, had all too obviously forced the FDP to eat crow.

A year later the CDU/CSU was again negotiating with the FDP—and sounding out the SPD—over a new coalition Government. The famous Spiegel Affair had broken in the fall of 1962, involving the questionable actions of the Adenauer government and especially of the leader of the CSU, Defense Minister Franz Josef Strauss, in seizing and arresting on the charge of treason the publisher and key journalists of the iconoclastic but reputable news magazine *Der Spiegel.*[37] Not even the FDP Minister of Justice had been informed of the legal actions taken against the magazine. Therefore, when the party did not receive full satisfaction either with respect to future relationships with the CDU/CSU cabinet members or to disciplinary measures to be taken against those allegedly responsible for ignoring the FDP in the Spiegel actions, it withdrew from the coalition. After a. second round of difficult negotiations, the union parties joined with the FDP again in a coalition government, but without Franz Josef Strauss. It was also agreed that Adenauer would step down as chancellor in the summer of 1963. The already uneasy relationship between the union parties and the FDP resulting from the natural antagonism between two very unequal partners, the smaller trying to remain a separate force in the minds of the voters by frustrating many of the plans of the larger party, was severely strained by the events surrounding the Spiegel Affair. But since the only alternatives were a CDU/CSU minority government or a CDU/CSU-SPD grand coalition, neither of which appealed to a majority of the union party leaders, the difficult alliance with the FDP was continued.

As the differences between the coalition parties and even between their respective wings seemed to increase following the 1961 elections, those separating the government and the SPD opposition seemed to decline. It was not as if the SPD ceased to oppose altogether; during the Spiegel Affair, for example, its criticism was vigorous, and the debate between opposition deputies and union party spokesmen—especially Adenauer and Strauss—frequently acrimonious.[38] Nevertheless, the leaders of the SPD, and particularly Herbert Wehner, were ready to join the union parties in a grand coalition that would retain Adenauer as chancellor if that proved necessary. When such a coalition was not formed, the party seemed determined to "help govern from the opposition."[39] It "sought to exercise influence on politics wherever the political system permitted it, at the Land and local level, in interest groups, on the electorate, and in the committees of the Bundestag. This blurred the distinction between the positions of majority and minority on the floor of the Bundestag. It also multiplied the foci of the political contest."[40] At the same time that the party leaders continued to express the willingness of the SPD to join the union parties in a grand coalition,[41] many of these leaders were also unwilling to exhaust their efforts and talents attempting to exert however slight an influence on national policy when they could *govern* at the *Land* and local levels where their party enjoyed majority support. Thus Willy Brandt, the party's chancellor candidate in 1961 and 1965 and party chairman after 1963, resigned his seat in the Bundestag after each election to return to West Berlin.[42]

It was not difficult to understand the SPD's change of course in the early 1960s.[43] To many observers developments in the Federal Republic were conforming to a general pattern of politics that was already well established or emerging in other democratic states in Europe and North America. This postwar politics of consensus was explained by many factors.[44] Some of these were peculiar to West Germany's postwar situation, but many were common to the industrialized states of Western Europe.[45]

The waning of the formal opposition in the Federal Republic did not mean, however, that the government was now in a position to steamroll its programs and ideas through the Bundestag and Bundesrat. On the contrary, the FDP, with its individualistic Liberal orientation, was a most difficult partner for the much larger CDU/CSU. On foreign policy it was generally in sympathy with or at least closer to the SPD, whereas it was frequently to the right of the CDU/CSU on domestic, social welfare legislation. Even within the CDU/CSU there was continuing and persistent division on a number of questions which affected differently the numerous religious, social, economic and regional groups that together are the component parts of the Union parties.[46] Voting unity was generally high in the CDU, especially on foreign policy during the 1950s, but on social policy the party was frequently divided. Gerhard Loewenberg, who has published the most comprehensive analysis of the West German Parliament, has written that on social policy "there was always the peril that the party's labor groups would vote with the SPD, and that its Protestant Members would vote with the FDP. The divisions within the major governing party thus set limits to government legislation on a major domestic subject."[47]

Opposition in the Federal Republic thus became highly diffuse in the early and mid-1960s. Government and opposition leaders were generally too busy cultivating interest groups, the mass media, their own parliamentary parties and working groups, members of the Bundesrat and key *Land* politicians to have much time or energy left for major confrontations in the Bundestag. Besides, the attraction of bargaining and compromise in the parliamentary committees—closed to the public and the mass media in order to further facilitate compromise—was very great. Because of the constructive vote of nonconfidence (Article 67 of the Basic Law), the fate of government-sponsored bills did not determine the fate of the government itself, as would be the case in the "classical" parliamentary system. This permitted the opposition—whether SPD or intraparty—to participate in the legislative process.[48] Thus "on domestic policy, the SPD participated in the enactment of an ever growing proportion of the bills before the Bundestag, voting in favor of 90% of those passed between 1960 and 1963."[49]

With the election of 1965, it appeared to many that a peculiar kind of "stability"—seen as frustrating stagnation by some[50]—had been firmly established. The CDU/CSU was too large and stable a combination, in spite of its internal divisions, for the SPD to defeat alone for the foreseeable future. Only with the help of the FDP could the SPD ever hope to replace the CDU/CSU as the dominant government party. The FDP, however, made it clear in 1965 as in 1961 that it would not join the SPD in a coalition; either it would rule with the union parties or, if the latter should receive an absolute majority, it would go into opposition.[51] The campaign slogans of the two giant parties were hardly distinguishable (SPD: *Sicher ist Sicher*; CDU: *Sicherheit fuer Alle*). And while the SPD seemed to be appealing to the voters by suggesting that it could carry out CDU policies more effectively than the CDU, the CDU emphasized the dangerous heresies of the SPD in the *past*. Personalities— Erhard for the CDU, Brandt for the SPD, and Mende for the FDP—were even more important in the 1965 campaign than in 1961. Policies were almost forgotten.

Whatever "opposition" existed seemed to be concentrated increasingly within the ranks of the CDU/CSU. Since Adenauer's departure in the summer of 1963, it had become perfectly clear that Erhard would not or could not exercise the strong leadership in government and party required to keep peace and settle disputes among the warring factions and wings of the CDU/CSU. Though a truce was declared before the campaign, the continuous struggle between Erhard and his "pro-Atlantic" supporters on the one hand and Adenauer (who was still CDU chairman) and Strauss and their "pro-Gaulist" supporters on the other hand was beginning to wear down the chancellor and seriously erode his authority in the cabinet, in the CDU parliamentary party, and in the public mind.

Nevertheless, Erhard's finest hour was the 1965 election. In spite of Adenauer's public suggestions that he was incompetent as a leader, and in spite of growing references to him as a weak "rubber lion," the CDU/CSU received a sizeable plurality (47.6%) with Erhard leading the ticket. The SPD, hoping for the first time to top 40%, had to settle for a rather disappointing 39.3%; still, it was the third modest percentage increase in a row and the largest percentage the party had ever received. The FDP, the only real "loser," received 9.5% as opposed to 12.8% in 1961.

Though there was some talk of the possibility of forming a grand coalition which would exclude the "unreliable" FDP after the 1965 elections, and though the German President, Heinrich Luebke, favored a CDU/CSU-SPD government, the coalition with the FDP was renewed. It was renewed with little enthusiasm, because relations between the FDP and CSU had been severely strained since the Spiegel Affair of 1962 and FDP-CDU relations had become less cordial in the perceding years as well. There seemed to be no alternative, however, since Erhard, the obvious candidate for chancellor, was strongly opposed to the idea of sharing power with the SPD, and the prospects of governing without any coalition party, that is, as a minority government, were not welcome.

The fifth legislative period in the Federal Republic began in the fall of 1965 with a coalition government in which there were both personality and policy conflicts within the CDU, between the CDU and the CSU, and between the CDU/CSU and the FDP. To confuse matters all the more, the various factions cut across party, religious, and regional lines, creating a situation in which government initiative and innovation in either foreign or domestic policy was blocked or seriously hampered. Growing pressures for decision-making in questions concerning the Common Market, European defense, relations with the United States and France, foreign policy toward Eastern Europe, and, in particular, the growing signs of more serious economic trouble with an already sputtering domestic economy combined to produce in the public a widespread sense of concern, frustration, and impending crisis. Dissension within the cabinet and among the numerous factions increased, while the opposition took advantage of the opportunities to press for decisions on long-smoldering problems and to criticize the government for its lack of leadership, direction, and self-confidence. Finally, in the fall of 1966, the FDP refused to accept mutual responsibility for an Erhard budget, the coalition collapsed, and for the first time since World War II the Germans faced a cabinet crisis.

The Grand Coalition and the New Opposition, 1966-1969: The Revival of Ideology

With the collapse of the Erhard government, the conditions favoring a grand coalition had finally been met. An SPD-FDP coalition would have too small a basis to govern, the CDU/CSU did not want to rule as a minority government, and the only alternative remaining was a CDU/CSU-SPD coalition. Thus on December 1, 1966, a new government was formed under the chancellorship of the former Minister-President (rather like an American governor) of Baden-Wuerttemberg, Kurt Georg Kiesinger of the CDU. Willy Brandt, the leader of the SPD, became Foreign Minister.

The establishment of the grand coalition in 1966 was an event in postwar Germany of great significance. It was significant because of the respite it would give the CDU/CSU, the social acceptability it would hopefully grant the SPD, and the majorities in the Bundestag it would guarantee for passing financial reforms, state of emergency legislation, and a new electoral law.

It was even more significant because the new "extraparliamentary opposition" of the left and the emerging National Democratic Party (NPD) of the right were given an impetus in December 1966 by the formation of the grand coalition which they would not have otherwise enjoyed, for the normal channels of discontent provided by a significant parliamentary opposition were missing from then on. The FDP, with 49 deputies or about 10% of the Bundestag representation, was simply too small to perform the functions normally expected of an opposition party.

The extraparliamentary opposition of the "new left." For several years, especially since the promulgation of the Godesberg Program in 1959, many intellectuals on the left had been bitterly critical of the SPD. Numerous writers, dramatists, professors, journalists, and others came to reject as "unprincipled," "socially treasonous," and even "undemocratic" the politics of compromise, negotiation, and cooperation with the "rightist" CDU/CSU. Increasingly during the 1960s, these opposition voices turned from the SPD and to the press, television, to the universities, and, finally, after the formation of the grand coalition, to the streets. Opposition in the universities and on the streets was led by neo-Marxists whose heroes included first Herbert Marcuse and then Ho Chi-Minh, Che Guevara, and Mao Tse-tung..

Since the only meaningful opposition party in the country had decided to join the "enemy," many of those who refused to accept the status quo in German domestic and foreign policy came to feel that the regular channels of opposition sentiment in the "so-called" West German democracy were ineffective or nonexistent. Demonstrations, the occupation of university buildings, the introduction of leftist intellectual conformity into German universities—by terroristic methods if necessary—and the resort to violence were the result. This movement soon became known throughout the Federal Republic as the *Ausserparlamentarische Opposition* ("extra-parliamentary opposition") or "APO."[52]

The German APO were confronted, however, with a momentous task. For

what *they* perceive as an unbearable situation seems sufficiently satisfying to the large majority of the population. Hence one of their main tasks is seen to be the "enlightening" of the masses and changing their "false consciousness." Some of the protest actions are deliberately intended to serve the purpose. If the

205

police, for instance, are provoked to use their power brutally, their popular image will change; if authority can be made to act repressively or to look ridiculous, respect for it will wane. With *such* an end in view, many of the protest actions are indeed shrewdly chosen and are not the infantile expressions of self-indulgent activism which some critics have judged them to be. They are efforts at establishing a self-confirming hypothesis.[53]

As in most other Western societies where left extremism has grown in recent years, there was some positive effect of "new left" agitation on the political process. There was more concern about obsolete educational traditions, concentration of the press, equality of opportunity, etc., and political talk became less banal at the higher levels.[54] But the negative effect—and again West Germany is hardly unique, in Europe or elsewhere—was perhaps greater. As "backlash" sentiment in the Federal Republic grew with every report of new demonstrations and acts of violence, so did the new party of the right, the National Democrats (NPD).

The National Democratic Party of Germany and the emerging right. The NPD was not formed as a result of the grand coalition or the APO. It had been founded more than two years before as a new effort to unite the disparate and often quarreling splinter parties and groups on the German right. Not since the Federal Constitutional Court had ruled unconstitutional the neo-Nazi Socialist Reich Party (SRP) in 1952[55] had the German right made an impact on any meaningful segment of public opinion. But a combination of factors favored this latest attempt to create an enlarged base of support for an emergent right. These included a sense of insecurity arising from a feeling of diplomatic isolation and the "long agony of the Erhard majority,"[56] the continued lack of progress toward reunification, the frustration of still unassimilated refugees and expellees from the lost territories of the East, and economic recession. Economic recession, which had been a major factor in the fall of the Erhard cabinet, was probably the most important single factor explaining the rise of the NPD in 1966 and 1967. Nevertheless, the new party was certainly given an impetus by the formation of the grand coalition and by student violence.

The rise of the NPD was a cause of growing concern among German and foreign political observers, and throughout 1967 and 1968 the CDU/CSU-SPD government came under strong pressure to "do something" about the NPD. Many urged that the government bring official charges against the NPD under Article 21 of the Basic Law. The second section of Article 21 permits the Federal Constitutional Court to declare unconstitutional "parties which, by reason of their aims or the behavior of their adherents, seek to impair or destroy the free democratic basic order or to endanger the existence of the Federal Republic of Germany. . . ." Unlike the SRP, which had been declared unconstitutional in 1952, the NPD leaders had exercised great caution in their publications and pronouncements, from the party platform (Manifesto of 1965) to the raising of the *left* hand at party meetings, avoiding at considerable effort any direct association with the outlawed NSDAP (Nazi Party). Though many of the leaders of the NPD had Nazi backgrounds, and though its appeal was—in the context of the 1960s—similar in some respects to that of the Nazis, direct evidence that the party was about to "destroy the free democratic basic order" was simply not available in amounts sufficient to guarantee a "conviction" before the Federal Constitutional Court. Thus it was feared that if the government should not be able to prove its case before the court, the party and its supporters would feel exonerated and, with its newly acquired "social acceptability," would receive fresh impetus for renewed agitation and growth. It seemed wise, therefore, not to attempt to ban the party.

Another alternative was, of course, revision of the electoral law and specifically alteration of the 5% clause. This clause permits any party receiving more than 5% of the national vote to receive membership in the Bundestag in proportion to the percentage of votes received. The CDU/CSU had long favored deemphasizing proportional representation in favor of single-member districts.[57] If the CDU/CSU could convince the SPD to go along, the grand coalition could pass a new electoral law which would effectively eliminate the chances that the NPD might otherwise have of entering the Bundestag and, incidentally, would also knock out the "troublesome" FDP. Though initially expressing cautious interest in the reform of the electoral law, the SPD leadership later indicated strong reservations[58] that helped destroy whatever hopes certain CDU leaders had of passing a new electoral law. In addition, however, it should be noted that many Germans felt it inconsistent with the spirit of a truly democratic state to resort to changes in the electoral law in order to eliminate uncomfortable competitors.

To the faint-hearted souls who expected only the worst from the German voter, the failure either to outlaw the NPD or to block its entry into the national legislature by electoral reform was irresponsible and perhaps criminal, considering German history. To others it represented a challenge to counter the political views and agitation of the NPD with "better" arguments and policies. To a considerable extent this was done, especially by the mass media. To still others, however, the failure on the part of the government to take effective legal action against the extreme right suggested an opening for the reestablishment of a party of the extreme left, the Communist party.

The reemergence of the "old left." The Communist party of Germany (KPD) had been outlawed by the Federal Constitutional Court in 1956.[59] Since then the Communist party and all organs or agents of that party have been illegal in the Federal Republic, excluding West Berlin. Nevertheless, with the efforts of German governments in the 1960s—and in particular with the efforts of the grand coalition after 1966—to improve relations with Eastern Europe, it was apparent that the atmosphere in West Germany toward

Communists had become more relaxed. A new press law, passed in 1968, had even permitted the distribution of East German newspapers in the Federal Republic, even though East Germany has refused to reciprocate. Communists in West Germany therefore decided that the time was right for announcing in September 1968 the formation of a "new" party, the German Communist Party (DKP), not to be confused with the "old"—and illegal—Communist party of Germany (KPD). In December 1968 an "electoral party," the "Action for Democratic Progress" (ADF), was formed by the new DKP with other leftist groups, such as the older "German Peace Union" (DFU). Soon after its founding, the ADF began selecting candidates for the 1969 Bundestag elections.[60]

Table 7.2: The Rise of the NPD,
as Reflected in the Bundestag Election of 1965
and *Land* Elections, 1966-1968*

Land	Date of Election	Percent NPD Vote, *Land* Election	Percent NPD Vote, Bundestag Election, 1965
Hamburg	March 27, 1966	3.9%	1.8%
North-Rhine Westphalia	July 10, 1966	—	1.1
Hesse	November 6, 1966	7.9	2.5
Bavaria	November 20, 1966	7.4	2.7
Berlin	March 12, 1967	—	—
Rhineland-Pfalz	April 23, 1967	6.9	2.5
Schleswig-Holstein	April 23, 1967	5.8	2.4
Lower Saxony	June 4, 1967	7.0	2.5
Bremen	October 1, 1967	8.8	2.7
Baden-Wuerttemberg	April 28, 1968	9.8	2.2

*Schneider F: *Die Grosse Koalition: zum Erfolg Verurteilt?* (Mainz: v Hase & Koehler Verlag, 1968), p 68. Cf Warnecke S: "The Future of Rightist Extremism in West Germany," *Comparative Politics,* II, No 4 (July 1970), p 639.

The Grand Coalition in perspective. With the growth of the NPD, the formation of the DKP, the dramatic increase in the level and intensity of "extraparliamentary opposition" in the universities and in the streets and halls of German cities, and the pessimistic assessment of the future of German democracy rolling off the domestic and foreign presses,[61] it was understandable that to many the grand coalition was symbolic of all that needed changing in German society. Few attempted to justify, defend, or at least discuss dispassionately the principle and practice of government by grand coalition.

It was not impossible to do so, even if one concentrated on opposition in the grand coalition. After all, the decline of parliamentary influence which was often attributed to the grand coalition was a development that observers had noted long before December 1966. Negotiations and compromises between party specialists in Bundestag committees, rather than continuous criticism and opposition in heated debate in the legislative chambers, had been established practice since the early 1950s. Indeed, there were signs that parliamentary influence per se was declining in *most* Western parliamentary democracies, including Great Britain. But contrary to the view that the grand coalition virtually turned the Bundestag into a rubber stamp with a 90% majority, the evidence seemed to point to an actual strengthening of the CDU/CSU and SPD parliamentary parties (*Fraktionen*)—and thus the Bundestag—vis-á-vis government ministers. Party discipline had become difficult to justify, because the government's majority could hardly be jeopardized, and interest group representatives among the deputies quickly recognized their new opportunities. Thus a center-left coalition of Social Democratic and left-wing CDU members could join in their opposition to government intentions to check social security expenditures; the right wing of the CDU and CSU could hamper government efforts to improve relations with Eastern Europe; numerous SPD deputies could support the opposition FDP proposals for modifying draft provisions of state-of-emergency legislation;[62] and on numerous occasions the CDU and SPD *Fraktion* (parliamentary party) leaders, Barzel and Schmidt, could force the cabinet to negotiate compromises with them in order to expedite important legislation. Thus, "unlike the Austrian parliament, the Bundestag ... preserved a remarkable degree of autonomy under the 'black-red' coalition."[63]

In spite of the continuing capacity of important interest groups to veto or modify legislation directed at them, in spite of the natural tendency of ministries to resist efforts to reduce their activities and subsidies whose purposes had too long gone unquestioned, in spite of the very real "control" that still existed even without a formal opposition of any size in the Bundestag,[64] the grand coalition was able to break many of the old deadlocks that had severely limited the field of maneuver of the Erhard government.[65] Important reforms covering finance and medium-range economic planning, a more flexible policy toward Eastern Europe, and the passage of long-delayed state-of-emergency legislation with more safeguards against abuse than found in most democratic countries were the most significant, but by no means only, accomplishments of the CDU/CSU-SPD majority.[66]

But to the consternation and frustration of the SPD, the results of elections held in various *Laender* after the formation of the grand coalition seemed to suggest that the voters were crediting not the SPD but the CDU for the notable success—especially in the economic sphere—of the government. Before the grand coalition had been formed in December 1966, the SPD had gained seats in the *Land* legislatures of North-Rhine Westphalia, Hesse, and Bavaria; but in 1967 and 1968 it lost votes in Berlin, Rhineland-Pfalz, Lower Saxony, Bremen, and Baden-Wuerttemberg. It made marginal gains only in Schleswig-Holstein. To make matters worse, the votes the party was losing seemed to a considerable extent to be going to the NPD!

Meanwhile, a minor revolution had occurred within the ranks of the FDP. Erich Mende, leader of the conservative wing of the party, was replaced as party chairman by Walter Scheel, leader of the "progressive" wing. There ensued over the next two years an internal struggle that was to change dramatically the FDP from a party generally to the right of the CDU on domestic social and economic issues and to the left of the CDU on foreign policy to a position to the left of the CDU on many questions of domestic reform and perhaps to the left even of the SPD on foreign policy. From a party about as "radical" as the French Radical Socialists of the Fourth Republic, the FDP had become in a remarkably short period of time about as "liberal" as the Liberal party in Great Britain.

The first major consequence of this new position was the action taken by the FDP delegates at the meeting of the Federal Assembly,[67] called in March 1969 in West Berlin to elect a replacement for the outgoing President of the Federal Republic, Heinrich Luebke. In a dramatic turnabout from its preelection commitment to the CDU in 1961 and 1965, the FDP decided to support the SPD candidate, Minister of Justice Gustav Heinemann. On the third ballot, which required only a plurality rather than an absolute majority of the votes of the Federal Assembly, Heinemann was elected by a very narrow margin over Gerhard Schroeder, the CDU/CSU candidate.[68]

Relations between the union party ministers and *Fraktion* (parliamentary party) and their SPD counterparts naturally cooled with the approach of the Bundestag elections on September 28, 1969. These elections were perhaps the most important since the founding of the Republic. The outcome was certainly awaited with greater anxiety for the future of German democracy than in the past several elections. By the summer of 1969, if not earlier, there were few even among the leadership of the coalition parties who thought that a new grand coalition was desirable. In spite of its positive contributions, the differences and disagreements involving both personalities and policies which had surfaced since the presidential election in March 1969 would make a new grand coalition difficult to form. More important, however, was the fact that extremism on both the Left and Right had grown dramatically since 1966, and there was little doubt that the grand coalition—and the opposition it aroused—was a contributing factor. A general sense of frustration had grown among political observers during the grand coalition, and the thought of its continuation after the election was depressing, if not intolerable. Though the partners in the coalition campaigned against its renewal,[69] there was reason to fear that there would be no alternative to the grand coalition after the election. If no party received an absolute majority in the Bundestag, a coalition would be necessary. But if the NPD could squeeze through the 5% barrier, as it was expected to do,[70] then an SPD-FDP or CDU/CSU-FDP combination would probably be too small a basis for a new coalition, and the only alternative would be an all-party government, excluding the NPD, or a resumption of the grand coalition. It was precisely this kind of difficulty that the advocates of electoral reform had warned against, and if it was an exaggeration to fear a "grand coalition without end,"[71] there was little cause for optimism either.

To the surprise and relief of many observers, the gloomy predictions about the future of the German party system proved to be generally inaccurate. The NPD's failure to receive the required 5% of the vote (its national total was 4.3%) for entrance into the Bundestag was the most sensational initial result of the election. (The extreme left ADF also did poorly, receiving only 0.6% of the vote.) Not only was this result important because of the embarrassment, polemic, and revival of anti-German sentiment that the Federal Republic would be spared now that NPD deputies would not be taking their seats in the Bundestag; it also facilitated the formation of a small coalition of either of the larger parties with the FDP, for the seats which would otherwise have gone to the NPD were distributed proportionately among the parties that did pass the 5% hurdle. Though the second important result of the election was the serious

213

decline of the FDP, which barely exceeded the 5% minimum, the FDP again found itself in the position of balance (*Zuenglein an der Waage*) between CDU/CSU and SPD. The CDU/CSU, with more votes and more seats (242—not counting deputies from West Berlin, who have no vote) than the SPD, naturally expected that it would lead a new coalition government with the FDP as junior partner. But the SPD and FDP interpreted the election differently. The leaders of these parties noted that with the changes that had occurred within the FDP during the previous two years and with broad preelection hints that if possible the FDP would join with the SPD in forming a new government, FDP voters had cast their ballots in full knowledge and support of the preferences of the FDP leadership. Moreover, the SPD argued, the SPD was the largest party. The CDU/CSU, Willy Brandt pointed out on election night and repeated frequently thereafter, was a combination of two parties, and the SPD was larger than the CDU alone. Needless to say, the CDU/CSU did not accept this argument, and the vehemence of their opposition which was to come could be explained in no small part by their anger over what to them seemed to be new rules of the game about which they had not been consulted.

The SPD and FDP negotiated a coalition agreement in the days following the election over the protests of the CDU/CSU, and with a narrow majority of 254 (SPD: 224; FDP: 30) of 496 Bundestag seats the new "small coalition" was formed.[72] For the SPD the grand coalition had proved to be worth the risks after all; it had, indeed, brought the party new votes in the elections and made possible a government without CDU/CSU participation.[73] It was the first SPD-dominated government since before Hitler. One of the few classical criteria of a democratic system that the Federal Republic had failed for 20 years to satisfy at the national level—an occasional "changing of the guard"—had now been met.[74]

The 1970s: The Reemergence of a "Loyal Opposition"?

When the chancellor of the new coalition, Willy Brandt of the SPD, presented the new government's program before the Bundestag, he was confronted by a CDU/CSU leadership and *Fraktion* that had never sat as the opposition since the founding of the republic. They were unhappy and uncomfortable in the new role, and they had no intention of remaining in it any longer than necessary. Their understandable pique was soon compounded by provocative remarks made by Chancellor Brandt, such as the suggestion in his initial speech to the Bundestag that German democracy was just beginning with his new government or his unsubstantiated charge preceding the June 1970 elections in three *Laender* that the CDU/CSU had conspired with management to take a hard line in bargaining with labor in order to provoke wildcat strikes and damage the image of the SPD-FDP coalition.[75] The SPD *Fraktion* leader, Herbert Wehner, also added on several occasions much fuel to the fire of overheated coalition rhetoric. The new opposition, however, did not proceed with caution, either, in hurling verbal thunderbolts at the SPD-FDP coalition. Thus immediately after the formation of the new government, the official CSU weekly, the *Bayernkurier*, accused Brandt of a "sellout" of German national interests to the Soviet Union and East Germany. On numerous occasions opposition spokesmen, especially the CSU's Franz Josef Strauss, but including newspapers friendly to the CDU/CSU, more than hinted that they considered the government'sd foreign and economic policies not just unwise or inappropriate but dangerous and possibly disastrous.

It was the government's foreign policy, in particular the new *Ostpolitik*, or "Eastern policy," that the CDU/CSU opposition most vehemently criticized. It started with Brandt's reference to the division of Germany as a condition in which one nation had been divided into two states. This was interpreted by the opposition as implying de jure recognition of East Germany and thus permanent division of Germany, an interpretation which, whether accurate or not, reflected the deep concern still felt over future reunification. Then, in November, the new government signed the Nuclear Non-Proliferation Treaty, to which the opposition objected on a variety of grounds.

In 1970 the SPD-FDP coalition began a series of negotiations with Communist representatives in East Berlin, Moscow, and Warsaw with the purpose of easing tensions in Eastern Europe, "normalizing" relations, and reaching accommodations of mutual benefit. The CDU/CSU had no objections to the announced goals of the negotiations; however, they objected strenuously to the likely cost to German and Western interests of agreements that Communist East European leaders would be willing to make with Bonn. Though the dramatic meetings between Brandt and East German representatives at Erfurt in East Germany and at Kassel in West Germany led to no immediate practical agreement, they were the subjects of lively debate in the Bundestag between government and opposition. The opposition had given its cautious support to the government's initiative toward East Germany, but it expressed its dismay over the conduct and handling of the Kassel meeting in particular. Perhaps even more controversial was the treaty of August 12, 1970, which had been negotiated by the Government with Moscow. In a heated debate within as well as outside of the Bundestag over the preliminary basis of agreement—the so-called "Bahr Paper"—which had been published through the conscious "indiscretion" of *Ostpolitik* opponents, the CDU/CSU forced the government into a defensive position before the FDP Foreign Minister, Walter Scheel, departed for Moscow for the negotiations on the final draft of the treaty. After eleven days of hard bargaining, Scheel was apparently able to secure a Soviet agreement that answered at least some of the opposition's criticisms of the Bahr Paper, specifically on the question of successful four-power negotiations on Berlin before final ratification of the treaty by the West German Bundestag.

By the time the government had negotiated a treaty with Poland, however, the opposition ranks seemed to show signs of cracking. Thus when the treaty was initialed on November 18, 1970, the CDU indicated cautious approval with perhaps mild criticism of certain details. Strauss of the CSU, in contrast, wrote that his party objected to the Warsaw treaty just as it had objected to the Moscow treaty and the Nuclear Non-Proliferation Pact: "In these three treaties the Federal Government has, without any necessity or compulsion, conceded to Moscow the fulfillment of all its political wishes it has pursued over many years."[76] Strauss and others in the CDU/CSU saw these fears confirmed when the Four-Power Agreement on Berlin was accepted by the Brandt-Scheel government in the late summer of 1971, followed by Chancellor Brandt's visit to the Soviet Union in the early fall.[77]

By the end of 1971 Franz Josef Strauss, the leader of the Bavarian CSU, became increasingly the exponent of almost total opposition to the new *Ostpolitik*. The CDU, however, showed signs of internal dissension. Though highly critical of the SPD-FDP initiatives toward the East, the CDU/CSU *Fraktion* leader, Dr. Rainer Barzel, generally took the middle position that had been the hallmark of his political career. But even as he was elected chairman of the extraparliamentary CDU in October and made the CDU/CSU chancellor candidate for the 1973 elections in November, thus combining three key leadership positions, he was constantly forced by Strauss to watch over his right shoulder to ensure that he was not being overtaken as the symbol of the new opposition.

If the SPD-FDP coalition pursed bold new initiatives that brought an unexpected diplomatic movement in East-West relations, it had no coherent or convincing economic policy that would stop rising inflation and cool an overheated economy. Knowing well the German fear of inflation, a fear based on catastrophic experiences in this century, the opposition hit hard at the inability of the government to act decisively against inflation. Nevertheless, the rate of inflation in the Federal Republic from August 1969 to August 1970 was the third lowest (the fourth lowest in the first three quarters of 1971) among 11 Western industrialized states of the world,[78] and employment remained high in contrast to the United States, which was suffering from both inflation *and* rising unemployment. The 10% surcharge on imports that was imposed by President Nixon in August 1971, however, raised new and even more serious questions about the West German economy.

In other domestic areas as well, the opposition confronted the government in the Bundestag with vigorous criticism. Government-opposition controversy over the budget, agricultural policy, urban land development, pensions, rent controls, and employee relations with management were only examples of the evidence pointing to a growing "polarization" between the CDU/CSU and right-of-center interests on the one hand and the SPD, FDP, and left-of-center groups on the other hand.[79]

As one might expect, it was the relative lack of success in domestic politics more than the new *Ostpolitik* (which in opinion polls was given strong majority support) that seemed to count most with the voters in *Land* elections which were held after the SPD-FDP coalition was formed. Thus in a series of elections in 1970 and 1971 the CDU and, in the case of Bavaria, the CSU consistently improved their positions markedly over the previous *Land* elections. The SPD, in contrast, made significant or moderate gains (largely at the expense of the FDP) in only four *Laender*: Lower Saxony, Rhineland-Palatinate, Schleswig-Holstein, and Bremen.

The FDP, on the other hand, lost votes in all but three *Land* elections and even failed to win the required 5% of the vote for admission to the *Land* legislature in Lower Saxony, the Saarland, and Schleswig-Holstein. It was therefore with great expectation that political observers awaited the results of each *Land* election in 1970 and 1971. For if the FDP were

218

Table 7.3: Land Election Results in the Federal Republic, 1970-1971*

	Hamburg 1970	Hamburg 1966	North-Rhine Westphalia 1970	North-Rhine Westphalia 1966	Lower Saxony 1970	Lower Saxony 1967	Saarland 1970	Saarland 1965	Hesse 1970	Hesse 1966	Bavaria 1970	Bavaria 1966	Berlin 1971	Berlin 1967	Rhineland-Palatinate 1971	Rhineland-Palatinate 1967	Schleswig-Holstein 1971	Schleswig-Holstein 1967	Bremen 1971	Bremen 1967
	%	%	%	%	%	%	%	%	%	%	%	%	%	%	%	%	%	%	%	%
CDU	32.8	30.0	46.3	42.8	45.7	41.7	47.9	42.7	39.7	26.4			38.3	32.9	50.0	46.7	51.7	46.0	31.6	29.5
CSU											56.4	48.2								
SPD	55.3	59.0	46.1	49.5	46.2	43.1	40.8	40.7	45.9	51.0	33.3	35.8	50.4	56.9	40.5	36.8	41.2	39.4	55.3	46.0
FDP	7.1	6.8	5.5	7.4	4.4†	6.9	4.4†	8.3	10.1	10.4	5.5	5.1	8.5	7.1	5.9	8.3	3.8†	5.9	7.1	10.5
NPD	2.7†	3.9†	1.1†	–	3.2†	7.0	3.4†	–	3.1†	7.9	2.9†	7.4	–	–	2.7†	6.9	1.3†	5.8	2.8†	8.8
DKP	1.7†	–	0.9†	–	0.4†	–	2.7†	–	1.2†	–	0.4†	–	2.3‡	2.0#	0.9†	–	0.4†	3–	3.1†	–
Others	0,4	0.3	0.1	0.3	0.1	1.3	0.9	8.3	0.1	–	1.5	3.4	0.6	1.1	–	1.2	1.6	1.9	–	4.3

*Adapted from *Das Parlament*, March 28, 1970, p 3; June 20, 1970, p 2; November 14, 1970, p 3; November 28, 1970, p 4; April 3, 1971, pp 12-13; May 1, 1971, p 9; October 16, 1971, p 1. The election in Baden-Wuertenberg will be held in the Spring of 1972.

†Indicates party did not gain admission to the *Land* legislature because of failure to pass the 5% hurdle.

‡The old KPD was not outlawed in West Berlin, where it has operated during the postwar years under the label SED (Socialist Unity Party).

to fail to receive the minimum percentage of votes required for admission to the parliaments of enough key *Laender*, there would be little doubt that the FDP was through as a viable political force. The result would be at best a weakening of the SPD-FDP coalition, which might encourage several FDP deputies to defect to the CDU/CSU as three had already done in 1970.[80] In fact there were some who predicted—or hoped for—the collapse of the FDP in the near future, with the distribution of the 27 remaining FDP deputies between the SPD and CDU/CSU determining the composition of the Government until 1973. Whether the party collapsed or not, the pressures increased greatly on FDP deputies to remain loyal or defect to the opposition, which needed only three more votes to rob the government of its majority. Perhaps it was not surprising, then, that shortly before the Bavarian election an FDP deputy claimed that he had rejected strenuous efforts by the CSU and its leader Strauss to have him defect.

Fortunately for the Government and the FDP, the party gained entry into the parliaments of both Hesse and Bavaria, doing much better at the polls than many observers had expected. Thus the SPD-FDP coalition seemed confident of its ability to withstand opposition challenges until the 1973 elections. But the CDU/CSU had been bolstered by the *Land* elections of 1970 and 1971, the results of which had inspired new hopes about forcing the government into retirement in 1973.

Conclusion

When Adenauer became the first chancellor of the Federal Republic, he was confronted by an opposition Social Democratic party which was the oldest, most tradition-bound party in Germany. The 1949 elections had been a severe disappointment to the SPD, for they had been confident of victory. They were forced to observe, however, as Adenauer and the CDU/CSU set the future course of the Federal Republic in economic, military, and foreign affairs. The opposition objected strenuously to these basic CDU/CSU policies, but to little avail either in the Bundestag or at the ballot box.

By the mid-fifties, and in particular following the promulgation of the reformist Bad Godesberg Program of 1959,. the SPD began to moderate its opposition and accepted, perhaps reluctantly, the basic foundation and, one might add, success of the domestic course set by the Adenauer governments; and in 1960 the party recognized the "reality" of West German foreign relations and international commitments.

With occasional notable exceptions, such as the Spiegel Affair in 1962, the SPD in the 1960s deemphasized its role as an opposition and began instead to "embrace" the government, concentrating on shaping and guiding legislation through the Bundestag. It became increasingly important not to present an image of a cantankerous "nay-sayer" but to demonstrate the party's moderation, cooperativeness, and problem-solving capabilities. This policy, designed to broaden the appeal of the party to groups other than the working classes, pushed the SPD toward the ideological center and made its leadership cautious or even hostile toward the more doctrinaire Marxist elements in the party. The more moderate and conciliatory the SPD became, the more blurred was the distinction between the personalities and policies of the government parties and those of the opposition Social Democrats. Finally, in November 1966, the CDU/CSU joined with the SPD in forming a grand coalition, and a formal, system-supporting loyal opposition of significance ceased to exist altogether.

It would appear that the grand coalition, which for the German left was merely the last straw in a series of steps the SPD had taken to reach an accommodation with the "CDU/CSU state" (the democratic Leviathan),[81] triggered the outburst of extraparliamentary opposition in the late 1960s. The violence and radicalism of this opposition, together with the economic recession that toppled the Erhard government, then set the stage for a revival of the German right.

With the "change of guard," however, there has been a renewal of vigorous opposition in the Bundestag, this time by the CDU/CSU. And while there has been a sudden increase in formal opposition, the extreme right has been experiencing a rapid decline since its failure to gain entry into the Bundestag in 1969. The failure of the NPD to win the required 5% of the vote in a single one of the 10 *Land* elections in 1970 and 1971 so confirmed its decline and disarray that the party's leader, Adolf von Thadden, resigned in November 1971.[82] Also the extreme left, or at least part of it which organized around the new DKP or ADF, made barely a ripple in the 1969, 1970, and 1971 elections in spite of certain gains made among radical students in 1971.

Thus, since the 1969 elections and the reemergence of a meaningful government-opposition dichotomy, the extra-parliamentary opposition in West Germany has weakened, though it has not disappeared. While there has been a renewal of genuine conflict within the established political structures over economic, foreign policy, or other issues, oppositions of principle, whether on the right, like the NPD, or on the left, like the APO, are not likely to seriously threaten the political system. A vigorous system-supporting opposition in a democratic state appears to give a somewhat hollow ring to the charges emanating from the extreme ends of the political spectrum.

221

Notes

1. Dahl, RA, ed: *Political Oppositions in Western Democracies.* New Haven, Yale University Press, 1966, p xvi.

2. The phrase used by Alfred Grosser in his essay "France: Nothing but Opposition." op. cit., p 284.

3. For a brief description of the oppositions of principle during the Weimar period, see Kirchheimer O: "Germany: The Vanishing Opposition." ibid., pp 238-240.

4. These would include Kirchheimer O: "The Waning of Opposition in Parliamentary Regines." *Social Research*, 24, No 2 (Summer 1957), pp 127-156; "The Transformation of the Western European Party Systems." *Political Parties and Political Development.* Edited by La Palombara, M. Weiner. Princeton, Princeton University Press, 1966, pp 177-200; and "Germany: The Vanishing Opposition," in *Political Oppositions,* op. cit., pp 237-259. See also Lipset SM: "The Changing Class Structure and Contemporary European Politics." *Daedalus, 93* (Winter 1964), pp 271-303; Freidrich M: *Opposition ohne Alternative? Ueber die Lage der parlamentarischen Opposition im Wohlfartsstaat.* Cologne, Verlag Wissenschaft und Politik, 1962; Waterman H: *Political Change in Contemporary France.* Columbus, Charles E. Merril, 1969: and Bell D: *The End of Ideology.* New York, The Free Press, 1962.

5. Dahl, RA: "Epilogue" *Political Oppositions.* op. cit., p 398.

6. Kirchheimer, "Germany." op. cit., p 247.

7. Ibid., p 249.

8. For example, Article 21 authorizes the Federal Constitutional Court to declare antisystem parties unconstitutional, and Article 67 provides for a "constructive" vote of nonconfidence according to which the Federal Chancellor can be forced to resign *only* if a successor is elected by a majority vote of the Bundestag (Lower House). This latter provision makes it difficult for "negative" majorities, such as the combined Communist and Nazi delegations at the end of the Weimar Republic, to join merely for the purpose of causing a cabinet to fall.

9. Lijphart A: "Typologies of Democratic Systems" *Comparative Political Studies,* I, No 1 (April 1968), pp 35-39.

10. Meyn H: *Massenmedien in der Bundesrepublik Deutschland.* "Zur Politik und Zeitgeschichte," hrsg. Landeszentrale fuer politische Bildungsarbeit Berlin. Ergaenzte Neuauflage 1970. Berlin, Colloquium Verlag, 1970, pp 58-67.

11. Kralewski W, Neunreither K: *Oppositionelles Verhalten im ersten Deutschen Bundestag 1949-1953.* Cologne and Opladen, Westdeutscher Verlag, 1963, p 15.

12. Loewenberg G: *Parliament in the German Political System.* Ithaca, Cornell University Press, 1967, p 432.

13. For a bitterly critical and emotional treatment of the postwar development of German democracy, see Jaspers K: *The Future of Germany.* Chicago, University of Chicago Press, 1967.

14. Meyn: *Massenmedien,* pp 86-88.

15. Ibid., p 44. Many newspapers, of course, are strictly partisan as in Weimar days.

16. Ibid., pp 49-50, and Bunn RF: *German Politics and the Spiegel Affair.* Baton Rouge, Louisiana State University Press, 1968, pp 3-28.

17. Meyn, *Massenmedien,* pp 17, 27.

18. Safran W: *Veto-Group Politics: The Case of Health-Insurance Reform in West Germany.* San Francisco, Chandler, 1967.

19. Bergstraesser L: *Geschichte der politischen Parteien in Deutschland.* "Deutsches Handbuch der Politik," Band 2. 11. Auflage; Munich and Vienna: Guenter Olzog Verlag, 1965, p 236. Unless otherwise indicated, all translations are by the author.

20. See for example Chalmers DA: *The Social Democratic Party of Germany: From Working-Class Movement to Modern Political Party.* New Haven, Yale University Press, 1964; Childs D: *From Schumacher to Brandt: The Story of German Socialism 1945-1965.* New York, Pergamon Press, 1966; and Schellenger HK Jr: *The SPD in the Bonn Republic: A Socialist Party Modernizes.* The Hague, Martin Nijhoff, 1968.

21. That it may still be the prototype can be inferred from comments made at the 1970 Blackpool Conference of the British Labour Party. See *Christian Science Monitor,* October 2, 1970.

22. Technically, of course, the CDU and its Bavarian affiliate, the CSU, were sister parties, not a single party. But they were and still are considered to be in many respects a single party, though especially since the early 1960s certain rather important differences between the two have become very perceptible.

23. Schellenger: *The SPD in the Bonn Republic,* pp 52-52.

24. Ibid., p 80.

25. Pinney EL: *Federalism, Bureaucracy, and Party Politics in Western Germany.* Chapel Hill, University of North Carolina Press, 1963, pp 103-109.

26. Schulz K-P: *Opposition als Politisches Schicksal?* Cologne, Verlag fuer Politik und Wirtschaft, 1958, p 17; Chalmers, *The Social Democratic Party,* pp 60, 63.

27. Loewenberg, *Parliament,* pp 398-399.

28. Narr W-D: *CDU-SPD: Programm und Praxis seit 1945.* Stuttgart, W. Kohlhammer Verlag, 1966, p 158.

29. Kitzinger UW: *German Electoral Politics.* Oxford, Clarendon Press, 1960, p 302; Chalmers, *The Social Democratic Party,* p 60.

30. Schellenger: *The SPD in the Bonn Republic,* pp 97-98.

31. For the complete text of the Godesberg Program in English, see Muller S, ed: *Documents on European Government.* New York, Macmillan, 1963, pp 148-164.

32. Schellenger: *The SPD in the Bonn Republic,* pp 55-56.

33. Cf. Ibid., p 172.

34. Ibid., p 171.

35. Narr: *CDU-SPD,* p 214.

36. Schellenger: *The SPD in the Bonn Republic,* p 179; Barnes SH et al: "The German Party System and the 1961 Election," *American Political Science Review,* LVI, No 4 (December 1962), pp 899-914.

37. For a detailed study of the background and ramifications of the Spiegel case, see Bunn RF: *German Politics and the Spiegel Affair.* Baton Rouge, Louisiana State University Press, 1968.

38. Ibid., pp 147-153, 158-162.

39. Narr: *CDU-SPD, p* 222.

40. Loewenberg:*Parliament,* p 392.

41. See Preface, *Jahrbuch der Sozialdemokrarischen Partei Deutschlands 1962-63.*

42. Cf. Loewenberg: *Parliament,* p 393.

43. Whether one *approved* of this course was, however, another question. For one who did, see Merkl PH: *Germany: Yesterday and Tomorrow.* New York, Oxford University Press, 1965, p 323. For one who had serious doubts, see Flechtheim OK: "Die Institutionalisierung der Parteien in der Bundesrepublik," *Zeitschrift fuer Politik,* IX (N.F.), Heft 2 (1962), p 103; for a detailed, highly critical examination of the pragmatic transformation of the SPD, see Narr, *CDU-SPD,* especially pp 194-208; finally, a rather superficial critique by a Marxist and former SPD member can be found in Abendroth W: *Aufstieg und Krise der deutschen Sozialdemokratie.* Frankfurt am Main, Stimme Verlag, 1964, pp 73-83.

44. Lipset: *Daedalus,* 93 (Winter 1964), p 274.

45. Ibid., Kirchheimer: *Social Research,* 24, No 2 (Summer 1957), pp 148-149, 152; and Lijphard: *Comparative Political Studies,* I., No 1 (April 1968), pp 35-39.

46. Loewenberg: *Parliament,* pp 356-357.

47. Ibid., p 360.

48. Ibid., pp 391-393.

49. Ibid., p 395. It should be noted, however, that even during the first legislative period (1949-53) the SPD voted for 84% of the bills passed (p 394).

50. The well-known Protestant leader Pastor Martin Niemoeller went so far as to call for a popular boycott of the 1965 elections to protest the lack of alternatives.

51. The only condition the FDP made in 1965 was that it would not

join a CDU/CSU coalition that included the CSU leader Franz Josef Strauss.

52. For a brief but excellent study of the APO, see Shell KL: "Extraparliamentary Opposition in Postwar Germany," *Comparative Politics*, II, No 4 (July 1970), pp 653-680. For a convenient collection of views representative of the APO, see Wilfert O: *Laestige Linke: Ein Ueberblick ueber die Ausserparlamentarische Opposition der Intellektuellen, Studenten und Gewerkschaften*. Mainz, Barbara Asche Verlag fuer politische Texte, 1968; and Glaser H, Stahl KH, eds: *Das Nuernberger Gespraech—Opposition in der Bundesrepublik: Ein Tagungsbericht*. Freiburg, Verlag Rombach, 1968.

53. Mayntz R: "Germany: Radicals and Reformers." *Public Interest*, XIII (Fall 1968), p 161.

54. Ibid.

55. *2 Entscheidungen des Bundesverfassungsgerichts* 1-79.

56. Lembruch G: *"The Ambiguous Coalition in West Germany." Government and Opposition*, III, No 2 (Spring 1968), p 203.

57. The West German electoral laws provide for a combined single-member district/proportional representation system, with each voter receiving two votes. In its effects, the system is essentially proportional.

58. One reason for these reservations was the strong negative reaction of the SPD party conference at Nuremberg in 1968, a reaction based in part on the fear that a change in the electoral law would work to the disadvantage of the SPD.

59. *5 Entscheidungen des Bundesverfassungsgerichts* 85-393.

60. For study of the origin and program of the DKP, see Baerwald H: "Die DKP—Ursprung, Weg, Ziel," in "Aus Politik und Geschichte," Beilage zur Wochen Zeitung *Das Parlament*, February 22, 1969.

61. The best known of these was probably Jaspers' *The Future of Germany*.

62. Lembruch: *Government and Opposition*, III, No 2 (Spring 1968), pp 194-195.

63. Ibid., p 195.

64. Schneider F: *Die Grosse Koalition: zum Erfolg Verurteilt?* Mainz, v. Hase & Koehler Verlag, 1968, pp 73, 78-80.

65. Cf. Lembruch: *Government and Opposition*, III, No 2 (Spring 1968), pp 200-201.

66. Cf. Schneider: *Die Grosse Koalition*, pp 80-83.

67. The Federal Assembly (*Blundesversammlung*) consists of the 518 members of the Bundestag (including the nonvoting deputies from West Berlin) and an equal number of deputies chosen by proportional representation from the *Land* legislatures. In effect, the Federal Assembly is a presidential electoral college. (Cf. Article 54 of the Basic Law.)

68. See *Das Parlament,* March 8, 1969, p 2.

69. Cf. Edinger LJ: "Political Change in Germany." *Comparative Politics,* II, No 4 (July 1970), p 554.

70. Cf. Ibid., pp 561-562.

71. Hennis W: *Grosse Koalition ohne Ende?* Munich, Piper Verlag, 1968.

72. Technically the SPD-FDP had a majority of 12 votes, 254 to 242 for the CDU-CSU. In fact, only 251 of that majority voted for the coalition; three either abstained or joined the CDU/CSU in opposing the coalition. See *Das Parlament,* October 25, 1969.

73. Cf. Klingemann HD, Pappi FU: "The 1969 Bundestag Election in the Federal Republic of Germany." *Comparative Politics,* II, No 4 (July 1970), pp 540, 546-547.

74. Werner Kaltefleiter, however, notes that the celebrated " 'change of power' in 1969 was the result of a somewhat accidental distribution of votes for the FDP and NPD; differences of less than 1% would have produced a reverse situation," that is, a return to the grand coalition, a CDU/CSU-FDP coalition, or a CDU-CSU majority. "The Impact of the Election of 1969 and the Formation of the New Government on the German Party System." *Comparative Politics,* II, No 4 (July 1970), p 595.

75. Several months later Brandt retracted the statement, but not before CDU leaders had already decided to take the issue to court.

76. "Relay from Bonn," German Information Center, November 19, 1970, p 2.

77. *Das Parlament,* October 2, 1971.

78. *Die Zeit,* October 6, 1970, p 18; October 5, 1971, p 19.

79. *Das Parlament,* October 9, 1971, p 1; *Die Zeit,* August 31, 1971, p 3 and September 7, 1971, p 1.

80. After the defection of the three FDP deputies, among whom was the former FDP party chairman, Erich Mende, the government had 251 seats, the CDU/CSU opposition, 245.

81. As described by Robert Dahl, the democratic Leviathan is a political system that is

a product of long evolution and hard struggle, welfare-oriented, centralized, bureaucratic, tamed and controlled by competition among highly organized elites, and, in the perspectives of the ordinary citizens, somewhat remote, distant, and impersonal. . . .

It is, therefore, a system like that of the Federal Republic, "that many young people, intellectuals, and academics reject,"

not because it is democratic, but because, in their view, it is not democratic enough: this new Leviathan is too remote and bureaucraticized, too addicted to bargaining and compromise, too much an instrument of political elites and technicians with whom they feel slight identification.

See his "Epilogue," in *Political Oppositions,* pp 398-400.
  82. *New York Times,* November 21, 1971, p 29.

8 Political Opposition in the United States

Ellis Katz
Temple University

Introduction

In the recent literature on political conflict and opposition in the United States, the reader cannot help but be impressed with four general conclusions. First, he is struck with the high degree of satisfaction Americans have with their political system. For example, Almond and Verba, in their five-nation study of political attitudes, concluded that Americans "tend to be affectively involved in the political system: they report emotional involvement during political campaigns, and they have a high degree of pride in the political system. And their attachment to the political system includes both generalized system affect as well as satisfaction with specific governmental performance."[1] Second, one finds that modern America is a near perfect working model of liberal democracy "in which all the active and legitimate groups in the population can make themselves heard at some crucial stage in the process of decision."[2] Third, one finds the withering of ideology, so that political conflict is tempered by a basic agreement on liberal democratic values. According to Daniel Bell, modernization has caused leftist revolutionary ideology to become irrelevent to questions of social change. "Ideology," he maintains, "which once was a road to action, has come to be a dead end."[3] Finally, one cannot escape the frightening conclusion that whatever health remains in American politics depends on the fact that those who are not committed to the system have little influence and rarely participate. Thus, the "invisible hand" of American politics is not democratic competition, but apathy.[4]

So strong is the evidence in support of these conclusions that if one never read newspapers or talked with students or Blacks, one might well believe them. I do not mean to suggest that American social scientists lie or fudge data; rather, this divergence between theoretical perspective and social reality is the result of an ideolgoical bias that values stability over change, consensus over cleavage, and the elite over the mass.[5] Furthermore, and perhaps more importantly, American social scientists are prone to define politics too narrowly, and consequently, create an artifical distinction between political conflict and social conflict that does not result in governmental decision-making.[6]

Perhaps these difficulties can be clarified if the nature of political opposition is identified in a fairly abstract manner. It must be recognized that political opposition has several different dimensions. What follows is a tentative exploration of the various aspects of opposition.

The nature of opposition. It is most useful to identify political opposition in terms of its functional, or dysfunctional, consequences.[7] In other words, attitudes or behavior that serve to promote change should be viewed as opposition. Not only does this notion serve to avoid the sticky problem of intentions, but it is broad enough to include both latent and manifest consequences and both immediate and indirect results. Furthermore, this concept of opposition makes no distinction between political change and other social change, nor between legitimate opposition and so-called illegitimate opposition.[8] To make distinctions in these latter two cases gets one in the realm of value judgments that political

230

scientists are not especially capable of making. For example, in the first instance, American social scientists have drawn a sharp distinction between the economic system and the political system.[9] Thus, political scientists have not been concerned with the great conflict that takes place over the distribution of wealth unless such conflict takes place in the governmental arena.[10] One consequence of this rather parochial view is a static concept of opposition by which the current political forces are taken to be the only political forces. In the second instance, political scientists have valued "legitimate" opposition but have feared forces that threaten the current stability and consensus.[11] The distinction does not bear analytic scrutiny and is a reflection of nothing more than the rather conservative bias of most American political scientists.

The focus of opposition. For the purposes of analysis, social scientists assume that attitudes and behavior are oriented toward something. It is this "something" that I identify as the "focus of opposition." Analytically, opposition may be directed toward one of several "political objects."[12] First, it may be directed toward the political community itself—toward the very idea that a given number of people belong to the same political unit and constitute the same political society. Second, it may be directed toward the regime, which is defined as that set of values, norms, and structures that guide political decision-making for a given society—in other words, the constitutional order. Third, it may be directed toward the authorities, defined as that particular set of political decision-makers legally empowered to make political decisions for the community. Fourth, it may be directed toward specific public policies, whether already in existence, currently being debated, or not yet on the agenda. Finally, it may be directed toward societal practices, value structures, or groups which are not clearly part of the governmental structure but which do constitute an essential component of the power structure of society.

It should be pointed out that these categories are analytical ones only, and opposition may actually occur in the form of a generalized discontent or malaise[13] which, at least for the time being, is unfocused. However, widespread "opposition" of this sort certainly creates the potential for being mobilized as opposition toward a specific political object. To neglect discontent of this sort would do serious injustice to the dynamic quality of political opposition and lead to conclusions that do not accord to social reality.

Sources of opposition. "Sources," as used here, has several different referents. First, it can be used in the rather trivial "majority-minority" sense that most public opinion polls and many survey research studies often employ.[14] Second, it can be used to refer to specific social groupings that are the underpinnings of pluralist political and social theory.[15] Third, it can be used to refer to psychological sources of opposition, as distinguished from the social and economic base of opposition.[16] Fourth, for some purposes it will be useful to focus on the attitudes and behavior of the politically influential, and for other purposes, it will be instructive to view the attitudes and behaviors of the mass.[17]

Articulation of opposition. Thus far, opposition has been defined as including both attitudes and behavior. Obviously, a distinction between the two must be drawn and this is fairly simple to do. However, one must avoid the trap of assuming that attitudes that do not result in behavior have no influence on political decision-making.[18] Indeed, the law of anticipated reaction may serve as just as much a constraint on political decision-making as does the activity of a vociferous interest group. Furthermore, as Peter Bachrach has pointed out,[19] by focusing only on activity, one excludes consideration of the possibility of nondecision-making. One must also avoid the trap of interpreting behavior too narrowly. For example, if voting is viewed as a minimal act indicating political support, then perhaps one should view the defacing of public transportation facilities as a minimal indicator of opposition. We view voting as political, not because of the intentions of the voter, but rather because of the consequences of the action for the political system. From this perspective, much antisocial behavior is political because of the consequences it has upon the political system. As Easton has reminded us, the drawing of boundaries is an empirical question.[20] Political scientists have misunderstood the nature of the issue and have excluded, by definition, consideration of behavior that is not traditionally viewed as political. Furthermore, if one insists on pushing the question of intention, he must be aware that most people do not see an immediate connection between their personal discontents and the political process. Thus, as contemporary American radicals have recognized, the development of political awareness must be an important goal early in the development of any political movement.[21]

The consequences of opposition. Usually, political scientists conclude their investigations of political opposition in terms of its impact upon the stability of the political system.[22] Such considerations are, of course, very important. However, they smack of tautology (little opposition and dissent equals great stability), and avoid the important normative questions that are just beginning to attract the attention of some political scientists.[23] Also, this conceptual limitation leads to the type of short-sighted conclusions exemplified by the works cited at the beginning of this essay. Consequently, it will be necessary to explore the policy implications of various types of opposition—or, in some cases, the policy implications of the lack of political opposition.

The Focus of Opposition

The political community. The development of a sense of

political community in the United States has been a slow and halting process that is well documented in a variety of places.[24] Examples of serious threats to the notion of political community can be drawn from almost any historical era. Even today, separatist movements among Blacks, Indians, and even Hippies constitute sources of opposition to the political community. It is difficult to evaluate their eventual impact, but it is doubtful that they will constitute a serious threat, at least in the immediate future. However, it is evident that some minorities are strongly alienated from American society and culture.

However, two distinct but related stresses in the current American system are apparent and important. On the one hand, there is the growing recognition that American society needs more central control and planning;[25] on the other hand, a significant group of theorists and activists, pessimistic about the responsiveness of large bureaucracies, call for local self-determination and even "neighborhood government."[26] Obviously, they are distinct, even contradictory goals, but they are related in that they both stem from the failure of American federalism.

The federal structure of the American political system is really an ingenious way for the national government to avoid making decisions on issues on which there is no consensus and which would be likely to create sharp cleavages in society.[27] Indeed, it leaves vast decision-making authority in the hands of the states and their localities where the citizenry is likely to be more homogeneous and where it is considerably easier to develop consensus. In other words, federalism allows the federal government to avoid those issues which, if decided, would split the society so severely that the danger of civil war would arise. Questions involving religious conflict[28] and race relations[29] are typically of this sort.

However, such a strategy works well only when the various minorities are geographically separate. But the demographic development of the rise of large, polyglot cities in almost every state has created the condition that a state is no longer a homogeneous political society.[30] Thus, urban-rural and class conflicts mark the politics of each state just as they affect national politics.[31] Out of this fact grows the two different but related alternatives of more central control and local self-determination.

The call for neighborhood government, which is so attractive to certain romantic radicals, is neither a revolution nor a possibility. Rather, it is a quasi-conspiracy by conservative interests to avoid decision-making on the national level and thus channel threats to their power into constructive, but limited, self-help programs. However, the call for more central control and public planning has the virtue of being both potentially revolutionary and possible. But it should be pointed out that greater central control and planning will undoubtedly lead to greater political conflict and even coercion as previously unresolved issues become part of the agenda of national politics.

Regime values, norms, and structures. While the national-ization of American society has probably minimized threats to the political community itself, contemporary American politics is marked by challenges to the rules of the game. The notion of regime values, norms, and structures is from David Easton's work[32] and refers to (1) the purposes for which political authority may legitimately be used, (2) the formal and informal rules for political participation, and (3) the distribution of authority roles in the political system.

It is extremely difficult to discuss the values that Americans expect their political system to serve. On one level, the vast majority of Americans support efforts by the government to deal with unemployment, job training, aid to education, and health care.[33] At the same time, substantial numbers of people feel that the government interferes too much with private enterprise and property rights, and express fears about left-wing influence and a trend toward social-ism.[34] However, perhaps political scientists are too con-

235

cerned with attitudinal profiles of this sort and there is little serious attempt to get at questions of intensity and priority.[35] Even more importantly, there is a little evidence to indicate that such attitudes play any sort of important role in the making of public policy.[36] Perhaps a better indicator of American values would to look at the impact of public policy upon various interests in American society and see which are promoted and which are not.

In this connection, Theodore Lowi has identified "interest group liberalism" as the guiding principle of American politics.[37] By this, Lowi means that the American political system delegates both policy-making and implementation functions to those groups most directly affected by the policy. As a result, legal governmental authority is delegated to established and powerful groups that had been crucial to the making of social policy even before government intervened in the particular policy area. Consequently, policy is necessarily conservative and tends to promote the economic and social interests of established and relatively powerful groups. Thus, the American political system assures that policy will reflect private rather than public interest and that powerful economic groups will dominate over citizen or consumer groups.

There are two serious consequences of interest group liberalism. First, interests that are unorganized can have little influence on the policy-making process. For example tenants, as oposed to land owners and real estate developers, have had no influence on urban land use policy;[38] consumers, as opposed to agricultural producers and distributors, have not influenced agricultural policy;[39] and the unemployed, as opposed to business and organized labor, have not influenced national fiscal and monetary policy.[40] Of course there have been recent attempts to organize such groups as welfare recipients, migrant workers, and students,[41] but they have been largely unsuccessful. Even where such organizational attempts have had some success, the actual impact upon policy-making has been marginal as the leadership of the movements has emphasized bread-and-butter issues that are rather easily accommodated within the system.[42]

This suggests a second difficulty with interest group liberalism. Groups are rewarded for organizing around a narrow conception of self-interest and are encouraged to seek "a piece of the action."[43] Thus, there is little room for ideological groups organized around a notion of the public interest.[44] In other words, while the American system accords opportunity to pursue limited and specific goals articulated within the framework of the system, there is no institutionalized opportunity for them to pursue ideological goals that might challenge the system itself. Thus, there would be little point for a Marxist-Black-Power group to testify before the Senate Judiciary Committee or for the Yippies to seek representation within the Defense Department. Consequently, groups of this sort must either engage in extra-systemic political action, or withdraw from even revolutionary politics and seek success through a cultural revolution.

The overall result of interest group liberalism as an operating principle is to foster the American tendency to equate the "is" with the "ought" by encouraging political goals that aare reflective of the distribution of power within society. *Politics is not conceived of as a process for building a just society; rather, the just society is presumed to exist and the role of politics is to reflect existing social relationships.*

While American liberal democracy is vacuous with regard to the substantive values it promotes, it claims a strong commitment to procedural norms for political participation. Indeed, the United States Constitution explicitly provides for free speech, freedom of conscience, voting rights and "due process of law." However, there is strong evidence that, when placed in the context of specific policy considerations, Americans are found to be much less committed to these liberal procedural values than one might expect.[45] For example, according to one famous study done during the 1950s, only 21% of the population would abridge the speech of a person of "questioned loyalty," but almost 70% would curtail the speech of an "admitted communist."[46] Thus it would appear that the commitment to liberal procedural values is related to substantive goals. That is to say, public attitudes are supportive of liberal procedures only when such procedures serve conservative interests.

But one need not limit these considerations to attitudinal data alone. Norms have a behavioral component[47] and a much better indicator of commitment to liberal values is the extent to which they are observed by actual political participants. Unfortunately, there is relatively little systematized data available on the actual observation of liberal political norms. Part of the difficulty is theoretical—how does one measure free speech—but it is also simply because political scientists have rarely been willing to investigate the "darker side" of American politics. However, there are strong indicators that liberal norms are often observed more in the rhetoric than in behavior. The exclusion of Japanese-Americans, the McCarthy era, the censoring of Vietnam critics, the harrassment of Black Panthers, and Vice President Agnew's recent attacks on the press are but a few recent examples of the intolerance practiced by even political elites. Much more data on less publicized events is necessary before one can reach firm conclusions on the actual observation of political norms.

Whatever the case might be, however, it must be remembered that liberal norms of procedure are both ends and means. They are ends in that they contribute to the development of the individual.[48] But this is a goal that is never realized since it depends on rational discourse and an openness of mind that is not apparent. In reality, public discussion of issues serves more to prevent action and creates what one author has called "false consciousness."[49] In addition, one must not forget that these are norms of procedure, and, as such, must be evaluated in terms of the results attained.[50] It is to this point that much of the criticism of the young radicals is directed.[51] Too often the requirements of due process mean either that no decision is made or that the decision is a compromise to such an extent that those who were led to expect great changes leave with a heightened sense of frustration. Thus, as the radicals see it, liberal politics is a mechanism to insure ineffectual participation by those who seek to change the status quo.

In conclusion, then, there is little evidence to indicate that the liberal norms of free speech and due process are observed by the political elite when their observation is not in their interest; and, second, that their observation may be a means to create a false sense of participation and prevent political action and change.

Finally, opposition to the distribution of authority roles within the system has taken a curious turn in recent years. At least since the days of Jackson, liberals and progressives identifed with the presidency and saw that office as the seat of social change.[52] However, since the beginning of American's involvement in Vietnam, liberals have come to fear expanded executive power and have actually championed increased congressional control of the president. There is no inconsistency, however, and this turn is merely an example of the fact that one cannot separate substantive policy outputs from procedural mechanisms.

More importantly, however, opposition to the current distribution of authority in the American political system follows two contradictory strains. As was suggested earlier,[53] the old left (and liberals as well) would like to see greater centralization of political authority in the United States. Their claim is that only a highly centralized state can control (or countervail) the highly centralized economy. The new left, on the other hand, influenced perhaps by the working of highly centralized regimes in the socialist countries, maintains that such centralization is inimical to popular control. Consequently, in the best Jeffersonian tradition, they argue for a return to a simpler age, in which both the economy and the government can be returned to the people.

The authorities. The heart of any democratic system is

opposition to the official holders of governmental power. Such opposition is assumed to keep the officeholders honest, progressive, and responsive to the demands of the society. Opposition to the political authorities, however, may be of two types. First, typical partisan opposition seeks merely to replace one set of political leaders with another, and emphasizes personnel rather than policy. On the other hand, one may oppose the political authorities as a social class. In other words, emphasis is upon the class background and ideological orientation of the office holders.

Partisan opposition takes place within the context of the decentralized two-party system. The system is decentralized in the sense that there is relatively little coordination of nominating, campaigning, and policy-making activities by members of the same political party.[54] Whatever tendencies toward greater centralization might be noted, the system remains one of great decentralization.[55] The two-party nature of American partisan opposition, however, needs greater discussion. First of all, it should be pointed out that it is no exaggeration to claim that America has as many party systems as it has elections. Furthermore, the two-party model fits only a relatively small number of electoral contests. Using the traditional measures of two-party competition,[56] one would find that there is no serious party competition in most electoral districts.[57] Thus, in most electoral contests in the United States, there is not even elite competition for political office. Moreover, the available data strongly indicates a low level of political knowledge among voters[58] so that, for all practical purposes, there is no electoral check on the political behavior of these elected officials. However, for many political offices, there is strong electoral competition. Competition for office is most associated with the presidency and various statewide contests rather than with congressional and local elections. But even such competition that does exist does not really provide a mechanism by which an electorate can hold its representative responsible. Such party competition takes place in districts where there is a relatively even distribution of partisan loyalties and small shifts in the electorate often determine the outcome of an election. Thus, personality, emotional "style" issues, and shifts by small blocs of voters serve to swing an election from one candidate to another.[59] Thus, even where there is party competition, elections cannot be viewed as broad policy mandates since they are most often determined by highly emotional and irrational factors, or are the result of swings by specific groups.

However, even if the American electoral system more nearly approximated the classic two-party model, there would be no guarantee that elected officials would be more responsible to the voters. This is true for several reasons. First, as was pointed out earlier, Americans, like the voters of most Western industrial nations, have an extraordinarily low level of political knowledge and involvement. Political scientists have usually assumed that this is simply a fact of political life, and that models of democratic politics based upon widespread knowledge, interest, and involvement are unrealistic and utopian.[60] This criticism somehow assumes that the degree of political interest is a function of human nature and that apathy is thus sown into the very nature of man. This assumption itself is based upon certain Freudian and biological assumptions that are not only unproven, but ideologically are undemocratic and elitist. Rather than viewing political behavior as being rooted in individual psychology, I would suggest that political scientists examine the political, economic, and social conditions that might serve to either frustrate or encourage political awareness.

The second difficulty is that many political decision-makers are not subject to election. Even within the governmental structure itself, important decision-makers such as judges, members of regulatory agencies, military and State Department officials, and a host of bureaucrats make daily decisions that affect the interests of many citizens and greatly influence public policy, and are effectively beyond the restraint of electoral politics.[61] But even beyond this, economic decision-makers within the private sector, such as corporate managers and directors and labor leaders, are often authorized to make decisions that affect people's interests exactly as if those decisions were made by decision-makers in the public sector, and yet are completely removed from public accountability. In other words, most important societal decisions are made by individuals who are not even theoretically accountable to the society. Furthermore, even where the government does act to regulate this sort of decision-making, its regulations usually serve to foster the interests of the private decision-makers, or, in effect, invest these private decision-makers with the cloak of governmental legitimacy.[62]

In sum, then, the limited partisan competition that exists in the United States fails, for a variety of reasons, to hold governmental decision-makers responsible to their electorates. Furthermore, most of the important public decisions made in American society are made by decision-makers who are not even subject to whatever restraints election does provide.

This leads to consideration of opposition to the authorities as a class. It is fairly well documented that individuals who occupy positions of authority in American society over-represent the upper socioeconomic strata in society.[63] While this is probably less true of governmental decision-makers than it is of important decision-makers who do not occupy governmental positions,[64] it is still true that important governmental decision-makers are disproportionately drawn from the higher socioeconomic strata. There are, of course, many obvious exceptions to this. The early backgrounds of former Presidents Hoover, Truman, Eisenhower, Johnson, and Nixon probably would not be sufficent information from which one could have predicted their futures. But it is important to bear in mind that each of these individuals, before attaining high political office, demonstrated his success in and acceptability to the upper socioeconomic classes. In other words, while the child born in poverty and the one of wealthy parents both have approximately the same statistical probability of becoming president, neither of them could attain the office if he did not demonstrate his acceptability to the ruling elite.

The ideal and myth of equal opportunity in American society has done much to inhibit the development of class politics in American society.[65] While this is not the place to discuss the impact of technology and affluence upon class conflict,[66] it should be pointed out that there may well be a growing awareness of class differences in American society and the possibility of class conflict should not be so easily discounted. A growing awareness of affluence, spread by television and rising expectations, may well lead people into a heightened sense of frustration and generalized discontent. Whether such discontent would lead to socialism or "Consciousness III"[67] remains to be seen.

Public policies. Social sicentists have accumulated much data on the public policy preferences of Americans. Clearly, if the data demonstrates anything, it shows that the vast majority of Americans, in terms of the operations of American politics, are liberal, and favor increased governmental activity to control the economy and deal with the worst aspects of economic inequality.[68] However, the same survey data indicate strong support for the private property system and many Americans express doubts about the growing size and power of government.[69] Thus, there is a conflict between the pragmatic "operational liberalism" of Americans on the one hand and their "ideological conservatism" on the other. In fact, according to one study, 23% of those who were classified as liberal on the operational spectrum were classified as conservative on the ideological spectrum. Furthermore, to complicate the picture somewhat further, while 65% of Americans were "operational liberals" and 16% were "ideological liberals," 29% of Americans identified *themselves* as liberals.[70]

This vast attitudinal confusion seems to stem from the fact

that Americans do not put policy questions into an ideological pespective.[71] At least they do not relate these policy questions to concepts like "liberalism," "conservatism," etc.[72] In other words, they fail to relate specific policy matters to any sort of concept of social organization. This fact in itself, however, represents a specific ideological orientation toward society.

The inability of Americans to relate individual grievances to the structure of society has been well documented. For example, in one study when Americans were asked what they were most worried about, the vast majority expressed concern about economic matters such as job security, health, and a decent standard of living. On the other hand, when asked what their political concerns were, most respondents answered in terms of international issues such as war and peace.[73] In other words, people fail to see the political relevance of their own situation in society. This ideological constraint provides an important buffer for the political system in that certain kinds of issues are not perceived as "policial" and are left for resolution to other social agencies.[74] However, just as this constraint serves to protect the political system from pressure, it also means that the problems are not dealt with. Finally, current radical movements are ideological just in the sense that most Americans are nonideological. This fact, combined with the operationally liberal orientation of most Americans will, no doubt, have a considerable impact upon American politics.

Other social structures, values, and groups. No political activity takes place in a vacuum; rather, the political process is turned to in order to accomplish various social and economic goals. Thus political conflict has its roots in society.[75] Indeed, the very purpose of politics is to either alter or secure relationships in society[76] and one cannot go very far in explaining political opposition if he neglects the societal relationships that give rise to that opposition. Nor can a political scientist assume that if he studies current patterns of political opposition he will gain a complete picture of future patterns of political opposition. It is exactly this failing that leads to the sort of static and unproductive theories and hypotheses cited at the beginning of this essay.[77] Furthermore, as has been suggested throughout this essay, government is not the only important political process in society. Educational institutions, religious bodies, and the economic order all allocate values with just as much authority as does government.[78] There are several patterns of opposition in American society that are worthy of at least brief discussion.

First, the corporate economic structure of American society has come under significant attack. This attack takes several forms and has several sources. For example, the whole concept of production for profit has become suspect as a broad range of Americans have become concerned with the social costs of production. Consumer groups have become actively interested in both the quality of goods produced and the validity of various dubious merchandising practices; environmental groups have attacked American business for its wanton destruction of the environment; and American youth has become as much concerned with the "social conscience" of a prospective employer as with the opportunity for advancement and economic security.[79] All of these forms and sources of opposition have not yet converged in a generalized attack on the profit system but the historical trend seems clear and one should not be surprised by such a turn of events within the near future.

Second, educational institutions are clearly under intense and widespread attack in contemporary America.[80] Again, this attack takes several forms and has several sources. The public educational system is challenged by urban Blacks because of its failures in educating their children. Their demands take a variety of forms, including school desegregation, community control and remedial programs. Catholics, and other defenders of religious private education, seek to divert public funds to their own purposes. And liberals and

245

other reformers challenge the whole concept of public education with their suggestions for the institution of a voucher system which would encourage school children to attend private rather than public schools. Colleges and universities are also under attack from variety of sources and for a variety of reasons. Students and faculty challenge the cooperation between their institutions and governmental and economic interests; they challenge the "irrelevance" of the educational experience; and, depending on the nature of the institution, they challenge either the impersonality of the bureaucracy or the restrictions on personal freedom that the school imposes. None of this is to suggest that those who attack the American educational system are banded together in a common cause. Quite the contrary, the critics often seek incompatible and even mutually exclusive goals. The point is, however, this opposition to the structure and purposes of American education is a political controversy regardless of whether or not it is resolved or mediated by governmental decision-makers.

Finally, there is growing opposition to the basic value structure of American society itself. On the one hand, Blacks and other racial and ethnic minorities and Marxist-oriented youth organizations pose a challenge to the whole concept of private property. While they differ among themselves over their degree of commitment to socialism, they do agree that more public control over the uses of property is necessary and desirable. On the other hand, a growing number of Americans see the problem as one of bureaucracy and technology, and seek to restructure American society around humanistic and often irrational values.[81] Within the radical movement itself, this is a growing schism and there is considerable debate over the need for political action. The politically oriented wing of the movement argues that political controls over society are necessary and that politics represents the most effective means of promoting social change. Others maintain that political action is unnecessary and that great social change can be accomplished simply by people "doing their own thing." The thesis of this essay is that whether one engages in political revolution or cultural revolution, he is articulating opposition to the political process and values of society.

Spiritual malaise: opposition without focus. The position taken thus far is based upon an instrumentalist view of human behavior which assumes that opposition is directed toward specific political objects for special political purposes. Whatever scientific purposes are served by this assumption, it certainly does not accord with perceptual reality. Such a view of behavior, for example, cannot account for widespread discontent whether that discontent is manifested in behavior or not. Furthermore, such discontent certainly may have important political consequences whether or not the individual basis of the discontent is political or not.

Public opinion survey data indicate that Americans, by and large, are happier, more optimistic, and less worried than are their counterparts in other nations—at least in the other nations included in the survey.[82] However, verbal responses to interviewers may differ significantly from actual attitudes and feelings. Indeed, political scientists and other survey researchers have not been very sophisticated in the development of techniques to probe deep-rooted and highly personal attitudes.[83] Awaiting such a methodological development, it might be more useful to focus on behavioral data to gain a crude measure of the extent of personal happiness or discontent in society.

There are a wide variety of behavioral patterns in contemporary American society that can be taken as crude indices of discontent and even political opposition. The crime statistics prepared by the FBI, for example, are replete with such data. Crimes against property are explicitly political. Indeed, some criminologists have suggested that such rational criminal activity represents an acceptance of American values and are actually supportive.[84] However, in recent years, the great increase in crime has been in the area of violence, often unrelated to the "rational" goal of acquiring wealth. Violent and "irrational" crimes represent an explicit rejection of dominant political and social values. The fact of increased drug use is a different form of the same tendency. Here, criminologists tell us, the antisocial activity is retreatist rather than violent because the individual cannot totally escape his middle-class aversion to violence.[85] Finally, rape and other sexual assaults have political significance—at least according to Kate Millet[86]—and are supportive of the Western tendency to equate power and masculinity. Thus, according to Millet, the very definition of sexual roles is a political decision.

Second, recent developments within the popular culture often have explicit political significance. Popular music, for example, has taken a clear political turn in recent years, in terms of both lyrics and melodies. While different musical groups propagate different social messages, one does find common themes which are quite political. At the same time, the melodies lack the discipline of Gershwin or Rogers and emphasize a personal freedom that is quite out of keeping with traditional middle-class taste. Even folk music, which traditionally dealt with tragedy in a stoic and personal manner, now blames society for personal ill fortune. Finally, it should be pointed out that while youth has always had its music, it has usually abandoned it at some stage for more traditional classical works. Today, this does not appear to be happening and youth's commitment to its music runs much deeper and may be a permanent fact. Record manufacturers, for example, report that they may be forced to stop producing classical records because they no longer appeal to youth, which has become the largest market for records generally.[87] But it is in the area of film that the popular arts have become most explicitly political. The characterization of the anti-hero in popular films like *The Graduate* and *Easy Rider* has had great appeal not only to the nation's youth, but to more adult middle-class audiences as well. Thus, no longer do audiences identify with an inner-directed and successful hero, but with a central figure that is buffeted by forces he cannot understand or defeat and even spiritually or physically murdered by the society in which he attempts to survive. It is interesting that it is only in television that these developments have not manifested themselves. In television, the heroes still tend to be dedicated doctors or aggressive lawyers or honest policemen. This is perhaps because television, unlike music and film, is regulated by the federal government.

Finally, one cannot neglect the development of political movements in the United States that explicitly reject the traditional framework. The Weathermen faction of the Students for a Democratic Society, the American Independent Party, the Wallace movement, and even the Eugene McCarthy for President boom all represent unfocused attacks upon American society and politics. While the McCarthy and Wallace movements were associated with specific policies and grievances, the data indicate that McCarthy and Wallace supporters were generally alienated from American society.[88] For example, while McCarthy and Wallace certainly had different programs and platforms, supporters of the two men often had little understanding of their leaders' positions. Rather, they supported the two candidates simply because they represented an alternative to traditional politics.[89] Both Wallace and McCarthy demonstrated considerable popular support. However, the data leads one to the conclusion that it would be a mistake to conclude that this was support for a particular set of programs or policies. Instead, it should be taken as another indicator of unfocused discontent with contemporary politics.

The Sources of Opposition

Social scientists have obtained considerable data on attitudes toward a variety of political objects, and if such data is reliable, then we know that the vast majority of Americans support their political system.[90] However, there are two factors that make the data and the conclusion somewhat suspect. First of all, it is not at all clear what the survey data actually measures. The fact of the matter is that people do not think very much about politics, and the only stimulation for them to form an attitude is often the asking of a question by an interviewer.[91] Furthermore, people have learned to give correct answers. Thus, there is no assurance that survey data are indicative of a deeply rooted attitude that is likely to be actually relevant to actual political behavior. Indeed, except on the experimental level, there is little data on the utility of attitudinal measures to predict political behavior. Finally, survey data represent a specific verbal response to a specific verbal stimuli. Stimuli in the real world are considerably more complex and unless attitudinal measures deal more effectively with the intensity of preferences and stimuli, then the data must remain suspect until it is verified in the real world. For example, according to the Almond and Verba study, only 59% of Americans would oppose marriage to an opposition party supporter;[92] yet approximately 90% of husbands and wives are of the same political party.[93] While this fact might be explained by a number of factors,[94] it does at least raise doubts about the reliability of attitudinal data as an indicator of actual behavior.

Second, most attitudinal surveys are not much concerned with intensity and lump respondents into simple dichotomous categories.[95] This creates the appearance that all respondents that are placed into one category are identical, and totally opposed to those that fall into the other category. Social scientists know that this is not the case, and while they have developed ranking techniques,[96] these techniques are rarely applied to survey data. In fact, elements in one category may even be more like elements in the other category than they are like each other. Even where ranking techniques are used, it is impossible to predict the behavior of elements near the ecenter of the scale. This is why party identification is not a useful predictor of voting behavior for those with weak party identification.[97] Thus, to discover that the majority of Americans support the political system is not very useful for predicting behavioral opposition to that system.

Finally, a relatively small number of Americans participate in the making of political decisions.[98] Those who do participate directly in decision-making—the elite—are even more committed to the political system than are the majority of Americans.[99] However, a democratic society generates counterelites, and there is relatively little information on their commitment to the political system. In other words, political leaders recruited through established channels have political values similar to those of the existing leadership. However, the converse may well be true about political leaders who emerge through extrasytemic channels.[100] Thus, political leaders who "seize power," such as student radicals and Black militants, might well have values which threaten the existing political consensus. Furthermore, the delicacy of American society allows for the emergence of leaders without followers, so that a relatively small number of people can greatly disrupt the functioning of social institutions. Thus, even small groups of intense dissidents can challenge the stability of society. For this reason, it is necessary to break down gross "majority-minority" measures into more useful components.

In the *Federalist No. 10,* James Madison suggested that while the "latent causes of faction are sown into the nature of man," they may or may not be relevant to political activity "according to the different circumstances of civil society."[101] In other words, at different times, and under different conditions, different characteristics of individuals will become relevant for political activity. First, race is obviously an important factor not only in terms of an individual locating himself in society, but also as a source of political conflict. Most Blacks appear to have similar political attitudes as whites—they are optimistic, committed to the system, and view society from the same nonideological perspective.[102] However, a significant number of Blacks appear to have lost faith in the ability of the American political system to deal with their needs. For example, according to one study conducted in 1964, almost 10% of all Blacks—over two million people—felt that the United States was not worth fighting for, and over 20% felt that significant violence would occur in the civil rights struggle. Even more important, perhaps, is that 42% of all Blacks felt that most whites wanted "to keep Negroes down."[103] Surprisingly, the percentages are pretty uniform nationally, with no significant attitudinal differences between northern and southern Blacks.[104] Unfortunately, the data are rarely broken down into useful categories, such as age and income, but most observers would agree that the highest degree of dissatisfaction is among urban youth.[105] Thus, if better historical data were available, one might well detect a trend toward greater dissatisfaction. While the attitudinal data is sketchy, behavioral measures do indicate a considerable lack of support for the political system. For example, low voting turnout, dropping rates of enlistment in the armed forces, high crime rates, and the inability of urban police departments to recruit Black officers, are all rough indicators that a significant proportion of Black Americans lack faith in the political system.

One of the most interesting features about the current civil rights struggle is the extent to which it divides the white population of America. Regardless of the extent of racist attitudes among white Americans, the struggle poses fundamental challenges to other American values and institutions, such as home ownership, job security, and education. What is even more significant is the extent to which some political leaders correlate other social problems with Blacks. For example, law enforcement is seen as a problem of repressing Blacks, educational reform is seen in terms of keeping Blacks out of neighborhood schools, and inflation is seen as caused by increased welfare expenditures to Blacks. Thus, regardless of the attitudes of Blacks, white hostility toward them makes their commitment to the system more and more tenuous.

A second major division in American society is along the axis of age. A generation gap of sorts is always part of every society. Indeed, in every society, youth are expected to act differently from their elders. However, all past experiences with a generation gap have always assumed (1) that youthful attitudes would change once the children passed through the appropriate rituals into adulthood, and (2) that the elder generation's authority over society was not to be challenged. Thus, the contemporary schism between youth and adults would appear to be qualititatively different from past experiences with similar phenomena.

First of all, the younger generation seems well aware of the possibility of "copping out" once they assume the responsibilities of adult existence, and have taken precautions against it. Indeed, they have created alternative institutions by which they can meet the responsibilities of adulthood without altering their life-style. Communal living, semipermanent nonmarital relationships between men and women, shared child-rearing responsibilities, and the use of inexpensive food and clothing are all means to facilitate this process. Indeed, adult society supports this alternative through such devices as predoctoral fellowships, loose requirements for welfare assistance, and the mass production of inexpensive clothing and other necessities of life.

Second, adults themselves seem unsure of their hold over the institutions of society and hold up youth as a virtue. Consequently, a curious reverse socialization process takes place by which adults are socialized into the value system of the young. Thus, American youth has been imitated by their elders in such areas as clothing and music to opposition to the Vietnam war and concern with the environment.

None of this should be taken to indicate that youth is a monolithic group; however, it does serve more and more as an important cleavage in society. Thus, for example, drug use is clearly a spreading phenomenon, and even if drugs are used by only a small proportion of young people,[106] there is every indication that that proportion is growing larger and is encompassing a wider spectrum of young people. As it spreads and affects more groups of young people, adult opposition to it has increased. This, in turn, serves to increase the gap between the generations as individuals are forced to choose sides.

A third cleavage in American society is social class. While many political scientists have tended to discount the relevance of class as an important political factor in industrialized America,[107] there seem to be several reasons why it is not likely to disappear. While the mass production of goods has brought many goods into the reach of many Americans, the advertising that accompanies mass production has created a revolution of rising expectations that is unparalleled. Thus, while many Americans can afford to buy television sets, few of them can afford to buy the image of American life that television offers them. Thus, even the middle-class American is denied access to the world of affluence, to say nothing of the genuinely poor in America.

Finally, David Apter has suggested that the basic division in modern society is between "a small but powerful group of intellectually participant citizens" and the "scientifically illiterate."[108] Thus, society is divided between a responsible and rational elite and an irrational, and perhaps ideological, mass. If Apter's description is not yet accurate, American society is certainly moving in that direction. However, Apter's view is too simplistic. One cannot separate ideology from decision-making.[109] The real distinction will be between a technically competent elite committed to an ideology of pragmatism and efficiency and a technically unskilled mass alienated from society. Clearly, the Wallace supporters in the 1968 presidential election were precursors of the alienated mass.[110] However, this image of society overestimated the affluence of Americans and underestimates the continuing importance of economic issues.

One of the major failings of American political science has been its conceptualization of political conflict and opposition only within the context of the electoral system. Political violence, extra-Constitutional actions, and even revolution are possibilities within the United States. To assume that the American electoral system provides opportunities for all dissident groups is not only false, it is dangerous. Great social and political upheavals occur not because a majority of citizens change their institutions through the ballot box; they occur because significant groups of people have lost faith in the ability of the political process to deal with their grievances.

The Articulation of Opposition

David Truman has pointed out that the structure of government is never neutral;[111] it accords advantages to some groups and disadvantages to others. Thus, when a system provides channels for the articulation of opposition, it necessarily advantages some groups over others. The channels provided by the American system include elections, political parties, and interest groups, among others. Success through the electoral system is based upon certain demographic characteristics. That is to say, to win any election, one must have the right number of people in the right place. Thus, while Republicans usually carry almost half of the total votes cast for Congress, they actually win many fewer seats than they might obtain under a different sort of electoral system.[112] Furthermore, the single-member district system puts maximum importance on successful coalition formation and minimizes the likelihood of success for a third-party candidate. This emphasis on coalition formation forces the candidate to make broad appeals within the framework of accepted ideology. Thus, as Robert Dahl has pointed out: "Opposition cannot change the institutions because of the ideology; yet opposition cannot change the ideology because of the political institutions."[113] This means that critics of the ideology must work outside of the electoral system or compromise their ideology to increase their chances of success within the system. This dilemma has long frustrated opposition from both the left and the right. In the short run, this exclusion of ideologues from power lends stability to the system; in the long run, ideologues will be forced to challenge the system from without if their substantive demands are not met. Historically, the two-party system has been able to make marginal adjustments so as to satisfy extremist critics.[114] However, the goals of contemporary extremist politics are confused and revolve as much around symbolic issues as around substantive ones. Also, for perhaps the first time, America contains strong extreme political movements on both the right and left. It is doubtful whether the current political leadership can make the stylistic changes necessary to satisfy critics from both ends of the political spectrum.[115]

However, the American system does not rely upon elections alone for the articulation of opposition. Indeed, the distinctive characteristic of the American system is the extent to which it depends upon interest groups for the articulation of demands. Interest groups, unlike parties, provide an opportunity for narrowly organized interests to articulate their demands. Also, they are not necessarily as dependent upon demographic distribution. However, even the interest group system does not provide an opportunity for all interests to be heard.

First of all, mechanistic interest group theory[116] assumes the neutrality of political decision-makers. In its most primitive form, interest group theory conceives of the political decision-makers as little more than instruments upon which the relative power of competing interests are reflected. Obviously this is not true; political decision-makers bring their own biases and orientations to political office.

Secondly, interest group theory assumes that all social interests are represented in the formation of public policy. Again, this is an unfounded assumption. Generally, interest groups are organized around economic, productive interests. Thus, while there may well be competition among interest groups over specific policy choices, it tends to be among competing productive interests, such as trucking firms and railroads, rather than among productive and consumer interests.[117]

Third, interest groups vary tremendously with regard to the amount of influence that they exert. Social status, money, expertise, and the like are power resources that are unevenly distributed among even organized groups. Thus, for example, even where welfare recipients do organize, they can provide little opposition to more powerful groups.

Finally, it should be noted that there is a vast difference between being heard and being influential. The American political system, with its emphasis upon procedural rights, guarantees that every interested party can voice his view on specific policy questions. However, this is a far cry from the actual ability to impose some sanction if his voice is not heeded. But this is precisely the situation in which many groups find themselves in American society. Consequently, finding themselves not able to sanction by withholding votes, or funds or other support, they seek to impose sanctions not viewed as legitimate within the framework of the political system. In recent years, these illegitimate sanctions have ranged from blocking traffic to kidnapping.

But radical interests in society are in the unfortunate situation of not having either the resources necessary to be effective within interest group politics or the wide appeal necessary to be successful in electoral politics. Consequently, they have developed novel methods of articulating their interests that necessarily violate procedural norms. These techniques have included demonstration, boycott, individual acts or terror and even riot. In areas where their goals have been specific, such as in the early days of the civil rights movement, they have been remarkably successful regardless of how extreme the tactic. Conversely, where their attack has been ideological and upon the social system itself, they have been met with effective repression and counterviolence. Highly individual and irrational acts of personal acts of terror have been counterproductive and it is no accident that the FBI's "most wanted" list is dominated by individuals who commit acts of this sort.

The Impact of Opposition

There can be no doubt that the lack of ideological opposition in the United States has lent great stability to the system. Ideological movements, for both cultural and structural reasons, have had little impact in altering the basic framework of American society. If stability is a virtue, then surely modern America is a virtuous society.

But this lack of ideological opposition has had other effects upon American society. According to Roger Hilsman, decision-making in America tends to follow the following pattern:

> Rather than through grand decisions or grand alternatives, policy changes seem to come through a series of modifications of existing policy, with the new policy emerging slowly and haltingly by small and usually tentative steps, a process of trial and error in which policy zigs and zags, reverses itself and then moves forward in a series of incremental steps.[118]

Since policy-makers lack an ideological perspective and are not subject to ideological criticism, policy can be made in no other way. Political decision-makers no longer consider goals but merely make marginal adjustments to deal with specific demands. There is no doubt that this sort of decision-making process cannot deal with the vast social crises that confront modern America.

Second, this lack of ideological criticism results in a kind of cultural nondecision-making.[119] Within the framework of the American value system, certain issues are not perceived as political, and as a result are not dealt with. In the past, Americans could rely upon nongovernmental officials to make political decisions dealing with the allocation of human and material resources. However, the vastness and interconnectedness of social problems require centralized and responsible political action.[120]

Finally, it is not at all clear that America can continue to avoid sharp social cleavage, ideological debate, and increased violence. On the one hand, the militant radical left has already declared the beginning of a revolution in the United States. The great tragedy of their position is that they must become more and more violent but can never succeed in revolutionizing social institutions. They can accomplish nothing but their own doom. On the other hand, the growing alienated mass to which Apter referred,[121] dispossessed of their status and denied full participation in American affluence, has already declared its dissatisfaction with contemporaty institutions.[122] The tragedy of their situation is that is exactly they whom the radical left seeks to save. Yet, the differences in life-style and in ideology set them apart as combatants.

There is, of course, the possibility that great social, and ultimately political, change can come about without political action. This, at least, is the hope of the Yippies and their allies, who would simply will themselves to be free. In all likelihood, however, like the Luddites of old England, they will find themselves destroyed by the machines.

An Afterword to American Political Scientists

Since 1950, at least, American political scientists have rejected the notion that formal governmental institutions constitute the only legitimate area of study. Rather, they maintained, the political process should be viewed as performing certain functions for society, whether performed by governmental agencies or not. However, they have neglected this important insight when examining the political processes of their own country. Consequently, their view of politics is too narrow and their concern is still essentially

259

with governmental institutions, or, at best, with those nongovernmental political institutions such as parties and interest groups, most directly related to government. But if one takes a functional approach, then there is no useful distinction to be made between politics and other social institutions. All social institutions, and especially economic ones, participate in the authoritative allocation of values, the mobilization of resources and the integration of social processes. Thus, a decision within a university on curriculum is political, not simply because it involves power relationships within a faculty, but because it has very great impact upon the integration of society. In this sense, Blacks who are critical of vocational educational programs for their children because they consign them to menial jobs show greater political sophistication than do the educational planners who make the decisions.

If American political scientists fail to broaden the scope of their activities, then perhaps they deserve the charge of "irrelevance." I hope that they will not let it happen.

Notes

1. Almond GA, Verba S: *The Civic Culture: Political Attitudes and Democracy in Five Nations.* Boston, Little, Brown and Co., 1965, pp 313-14.

2. Dahl RA: *A Preface to Democratic Theory.* Chicago, University of Chicago Press, 1963, p 137. For an elaboration of Dahl's position, see his *Pluralist Democracy in America: Conflict and Consent.* Chicago, Rand McNally and Co., 1967.

3. Bell D: *The End of Ideology.* New York, The Free Press, 1963, p 393 *passim.* For a further discussion of this issue, see Waxman CI, ed: *The End of Ideology Debate.* New York, Simon and Schuster, 1969.

4. This is certainly the conclusion reached in Berelson B et al: *Voting.* Chicago, University of Chicago Press, 1954. See also Bone HA, Ranney A: *Politics and Voters.* New York, McGraw-Hill Book Co., 1963, pp 52-56.

5. There are several good statements of this position. See, for example, McCoy CA, Playford J, ed: *Apolitical Politics: A Critique of Behavioralism.* New York, Thomas Y. Crowell Co., 1967; Walker JL:

"A Critique of the Elitist Theory of Democracy," *American Political Science Review*, LX (June 1966), 286-295; and especially Lipsitz L: "If, as Verba Says, The State Functions as a Religion, What Are We to Do Then to Save Our Souls?" *American Political Science Review*, LXII (June 1968), 527-535.

6. Indeed, it is this insight that has been the most valuable contribution to the behavioral perspective since the 1950s. See Easton D: *The Political System: An Inquiry into the State of Political Science*. New York, Alfred A. Knopf, 1963, especially pp 38-47.

7. A good, concise statement of the functionalist position is Levy MJ Jr: "Some Aspects of 'Structural-Functional' Analysis and Political Science," in Young R, ed: *Approaches to the Study of Politics*. Evanston, Ill., Northwestern University Press, 1958, pp 52-65.

8. Dahl RA, op. cit., pp 145-6.

9. For two different approaches that reach a similar conclusion, see Hartz L: *The Liberal Tradition in America*. New York, Harcourt, Brace and World, Inc., 1955; and Lowi T: *The End of Liberalism*. New York, W. W. Norton and Co., Inc., 1966, especially pp 3-28.

10. But see Lasswell H: *Politics: Who Gets What, When, and How*. New York, Meridian Books, Inc., 1958.

11. This fear is best expressed by Lipset SM: *Political Man: The Social Bases of Politics*. Garden City, N.Y., Doubleday and Co., 1963, especially pp 1-12.

12. This notion of "political objects" is taken from Easton D: *A Systems Analysis of Political Life*. New York, John Wiley and Sons, Inc., 1965, Chs 11, 12, 13. Within his conceptual scheme, Easton includes the political community, the regime, and the authorities within the definition of "political objects." My own broader conception of politics would also include specific public policies, societal practices, values, structures and groups, and malaise within the scope of political analysis.

13. For an excellent discussion of this issue, see Harrington M: *The Accidental Century*. Baltimore, Md., Penguin Books, Inc., 1966, especially Ch 5, "The Crisis of Belief and Disbelief."

14. See, for one of the more useful studies of this sort, Free LA, Cantril H: *The Political Beliefs of Americans: A Study of Public Opinion*. New York, Simon and Schuster, 1968.

15. A classic and important pluralist statement is Truman D: *The Governmental Process*. New York, Alfred A. Knopf, 1960.

16. For a perceptive use of such an approach, see Bell D, ed: *The Radical Right*. Garden City, N.Y., Doubleday and Co., 1963.

17. See McCloskey H et al: "Issue Conflict and Consensus Among Party Leaders and Followers." *American Political Science Review*, LIV, (June 1960), 406-427.

18. See the brilliant article by March JG: "The Power of Power," in Easton D, ed: *Varities of Political Theory*. Englewood Cliffs, N.J., Prentice-Hall, Inc., 1966, pp 39-70.

19. Bachrach P, Baratz MS: "Decisions and Nondecisions: An Analytical Framework." *American Political Science Review*, LVII (September 1963), 632-42. But see the rejoinder by Merelman RM: "On the Neo-Elitist Critique of Community Power." *American Political Science Review*, LXII (June 1968), 451-60.

20. On the distinction between analytic and empirical systems and the problem of boundaries, see Easton D: *A Framework for Political Analysis*. Englewood Cliffs, N.J., 1965, especially pp 25-34.

21. See Carmichael S, Hamilton CV: *Black Power: The Politics of Liberation in America*. New York, Random House, 1967, pp 34-39.

22. Dahl RA: *Political Opposition in Western Democracies*. New Haven, Yale University Press, 1966.

23. Walker JL: op. cit., for example.

24. See Lipset SM: *The First New Nation*. New York, Basic Books, 1963, especially Part I, "America as a New Nation," pp 13-98.

25. See both Lowi T: op. cit., and Harrington M: *Toward A Democratic Left*. New York, The Macmillan Co., 1968.

26. See Kotler M: *Neighborhood Government: The Local Foundations of Political Life*. Indianapolis, Bobbs-Merril Co., 1969.

27. Dahl RA: *Pluralist Democracy in America*, op. cit., pp 180-83.

28. Stedman MS: *Religion and Politics in America*. New York, Harcourt, Brace and World, 1964, especially pp 20-42.

29. Dahl RA: *Pluralist Democracy in America*, op. cit., pp 181-82. Certainly this was the impact of governmental policy after 1876. For the role of the Supreme Court in this area, see Miller L: *The Petitioners: The Story of the Supreme Court of the United States and the Negro*. New York, Random House, 1966.

30. In 1960, only 13 states had no city of over 100,000 population: Alaska, Delaware, Idaho, Maine, Montana, Nevada, New Hampshire, North Dakota, South Carolina, South Dakota, Vermont, West Virginia, and Wyoming.

31. The classic work on comparative state politics is Key VO: *American State Politics*. New York, Alfred A. Knopf, 1956. For a different perspective, see Elazar DJ: *American Federalism: A View from the States*. New York, Thomas Y. Crowell Co., 1966.

32. Easton D: *A Systems Analysis of Political Life*, op. cit., pp 190-211.

33. Free L, Cantril H: op. cit., pp 11-15.

34. Ibid., pp 24-31.

35. But see the interesting book by Rae DW, Taylor M: *The Analysis of Political Cleavages*. New Haven, Yale University Press, 1970.

36. For an interesting and suggestive study of elite misperceptions of mass opinion, see Luttberg NR, Zeigler H: "Attitude Consensus and Conflict in an Interest Group: An Assessment of Cohesion." *American Political Science Review*, LX (September 1966), 655-666.

37. Lowi T: op. cit., especially 68-85.

38. Ibid., pp 191-206.

39. Jones CO: "Representation in Congress: The Case of the House Agriculture Committee." *American Political Science Review*, LV (June 1961), 358-367.

40. See, for example, Bailey SK: *Congress Makes a Law*. New York, Columbia University Press, 1950.

41. See the limited successes of the Welfare Rights Organization, Ceasar Chavez, and SDS.

42. This has been especially true of students. The involvement of the CIA in the affairs of the National Student Association is but one example of the ease with which student groups might be dominated.

43. This suggestion came from Richard M. Nixon, in his acceptance speech at the 1968 Republican Convention.

44. Truman D: op. cit., of course, rejects this distinction. While he is right in demonstrating that the distinction is not analytically sound, he, in effect, tacitly accepts it when he develops the notion of "rules of the game."

45. See Prothro JW, Grigg CM: "Fundamental Principles of Democracy." *Journal of Politics*, 22 (Spring 1960), 276-294; and McCloskey H: "Consensus and Ideology in American Politics." *American Political Science Review*, LVIII (June 1964), 361-382.

46. Stouffer SA: *Communism, Conformity and Civil Liberties*. Garden City, N.Y., Doubleday and Co., Inc., 1955, pp 34, 42.

47. See Wahlke J et al: *The Legislative System: Explorations in Legislative Behavior*. New York, John Wiley and Sons, Inc., 1962, pp 141-42.

48. Walker JL: op. cit., Lipsitz L: op. cit.

49. See Marcuse H: *One Dimensional Man*. Boston, Beacon Press, 1964.

50. Robert A. Dahl's criticism of populistic democracy applies here. See his *A Preface to Democratic Theory*, op. cit., pp 44-48.

51. See Mark Rudd's famous "bullshit" statement in Avorn JL et al: *Up Against the Ivy Wall: A History of the Columbia Crisis*. New York, Atheneum, 1970, pp 131-141.

52. See, for example, Binkley WE: *President and Congress*. New York, Random House, 1962, pp 82-83.

53. See notes 25 and 26, supra.

54. See Key VO: *Politics, Parties and Pressure Groups*. New York, Thomas Y. Crowell Co., 1964, pp 328-30, passim.

55. See Stedman MS: "Political Parties," in Stedman MS, ed: *Modernizing American Government: Demands of Social Change.* Englewood Cliffs, N.J., Prentice-Hall, Inc., 1968, pp 107-121.

56. See Jacob H, Vines K: *Politics in the American States.* Boston, Little, Brown and Co., 1965; and Schlesinger JA: "A Two-Dimensional Scheme for Classifying States According to Degree of Inter-Party Competitions." *American Political Science Review,* 49 (December 1955), 1120-1129.

57. "In six of seven [House] elections held from 1950 through 1962 less than 100 of the 435 House seats were won by under 55%." From 1952 through 1960, "over 200 House districts combined unswervingly Democratic, and over 130 remained unswervingly Republican. Party turnover was limited to the remaining ninety-odd districts." Price HD: "The Electoral Arena," in Truman DB, ed: *The Congress and America's Future.* Englewood Cliffs, N.J., Prentice-Hall, 1965, pp 42-43.

58. See Converse P: "The Nature of Belief Systems in Mass Publics," in Apter D, ed: *Ideology and Discontent.* New York, The Free Press, 1964, pp 206-261, for an excellent analysis that reaches somewhat different conclusions.

59. For example, V. O. Key has demonstrated that relatively small groups of "switchers" can make the difference between victory and defeat. See Key VO: *The Responsible Electorate.* Cambridge, Mass., Harvard University Press, 1966. Unfortunately, Key presents data only for presidential elections.

60. Berelson B et al: op. cit.

61. Lowi T: op. cit., pp 125-156.

62. Ibid.

63. See generally Mathews DR: *The Social Background of Political Decision Makers.* New York, Random House, 1954; see also Schmidhauser, JR: *The Supreme Court.* New York, Holt, Rinehart and Winston, 1964, pp 30-64.

64. An excellent study is Domhoff GW: *Who Rules America?* Englewood Cliffs, N.J., Prentice-Hall, Inc., 1967.

65. See the interesting thesis of Potter D: *People of Plenty.* Englewood Cliffs, N.J., Prentice-Hall, Inc., 1954.

66. See Lane RE: "The Politics of Consensus in an Age of Affluence." *American Political Science Review,* LIX (December 1965), 874-895.

67. The concept is from Reich CA: "Reflections: The Greening of America." *The New Yorker,* September 26, 1970.

68. Free L, Cantril H: op. cit., pp 11-15.

69. Ibid., pp 24-31.

70. Ibid., p 46.

71. Converse PE: op. cit.

72. Bone H, Ranney A: op. cit., pp 17-18, citing Campbell, et al: *The American Voter.* New York, John Wiley and Sons, Inc., 1960, would classify only 15.5% of the voters as thinking in ideological terms.

73. Free L, Cantril H: op. cit., p 52.

74. On the importance of cultural constraints as a regulation of demand articulation, see Easton D: *A Systems Analysis of Political Life,* op. cit., pp 100-116, passim.

75. This is certainly not a new idea. See Madison J: *Federalist No. 10.*

76. Truman D: op. cit., pp 104-06.

77. See notes 1, 2, 3, and 4, supra.

78. The important question, it seems to me, is not whether the allocation can be supported by the use of legitimate force; rather, the important question is the extent to which they influence actual behavior.

79. Harrington M: *Towards a Democratic Left,* op. cit., p 28, provides the following anecdote: "Late in 1967 Albert R. Hunt of the *Wall Street Journal* summarized the trend: 'It looks as if selling refrigerators to Eskimos may be only a little harder than selling the virtues of a corporate career to today's collegians.' Hunt reported that in a poll at wealthy Stanford University only 8% of the freshman class were intending to have a business career."

80. For an interesting documentation of some of these attacks, see Gittell M, Hevesi AG, eds: *The Politics of Urban Education.* New York, Frederick A. Praeger, 1969.

81. See Reich CA: op. cit.

82. Almond GA, Verba S: op. cit., p 314. See also Free LA, Cantril H: op. cit., pp 94-112, passim.

83. However, see Osgood CE, Suci G, Tannenbaum P: *The Measurement of Meaning.* Urbana, Ill., University of Illinois Press, 1957.

84. See Merton RK: *Social Theory and Social Structure.* Glencoe, Ill., The Free Press, 1957, p 134.

85. See Cloward RA, Ohlin LE: *Delinquency and Opportunity: A Theory of Delinquent Gangs.* Glencoe, Ill., The Free Press, 1960, p 7.

86. Millet K: *Sexual Politics.* Garden City, N.Y., Doubleday and Co., 1970.

87. For an informed report on the future of recorded classical music, see Stravinsky I: "Performing Arts," *Harper's Magazine,* 240 (October 1970), 37.

88. See Converse PE et al: "Continuity and Change in American Politics: Parties and Issues in the 1968 Election." *American Political Science Review,* LXIII (December 1969), p 1101.

89. Ibid.

265

90. Some interesting uses of data of this sort include Almond GA, Verba S: op. cit.; Free L, Cantril H: op. cit.; Key VO: *Public Opinion and American Democracy.* New York, Alfred A Knopf, 1961.

91. See Lane RE, Sears D: *Public Opinion and Ideology.* Englewood Cliffs, N.J., Prentice-Hall, Inc., 1963.

92. Almond GA, Verba S: op. cit., p 234.

93. Bone H, Ranney A: op. cit., p 26.

94. For example, wives may alter their party identification after marriage.

95. One obvious exception is the concept of "party identification." However, for a general discussion of this problem, see Truman D: op. cit., pp 218-220.

96. Guttman Scaling is probably the most widely used technique. For a fuller discussion, see Green BF: "Attitude Measurement," in Gardner and Lindzey, eds: *Handbook of Social Psychology.* Glencoe, Ill., The Free Press, 1954.

97. In 1956, of voters over age 35, 45% of the weak party identifiers voted for the other party, compared with only 20% of the strong party identifiers. Campbell A et al: *The Americal Voter,* op. cit., p 71.

98. See Lane RE: *Political Life.* New York, The Free Press, 1959, pp 52-56, where he claims that only a quarter of 1% can be considered as "organized activists."

99. See McCloskey H et al: op. cit.; Prothro JW, Grigg CM: op. cit.; and Stouffer S: op. cit.

100. For an interesting study on the significance of recruitment patterns, see Wilson JQ: *Negro Politics.* Glencoe, Ill., The Free Press, 1960.

101. Madison J: "Federalist No. 10," in Earle EM, ed: *The Federalist.* New York, Random House, Inc., 1937, pp 55-56.

102. Marvick D: "The Political Socialization of the American Negro." *Annals of the American Academy of Political and Social Science,* 361 (September 1965), 112-127.

103. Brink W, Harris L: *The Negro Revolution in America.* New York, Simon and Schuster, 1964, pp 61, 126.

104. Ibid.

105. See, for example, Lubell S: *White and Black: Test of a Nation.* New York, Harper and Row, 1964.

106. The data are unreliable. But even a survey conducted by the Pennsylvania Department of Public Instruction estimated that 12% of the Commonwealth's high school students were "heavy drug users."

107. See Bell D: op. cit.; and Lane R: op. cit.

108. Apter D: op. cit., p 31.

109. See Waxman CI, ed: op. cit.

110. Converse PE, et al: op. cit., p 1101.

111. Truman D: op. cit., 296.

112. For example, in 1968, the Republicans won 48.2% of the popular vote for Congress, but won only 43% of the seats.

113. Dahl RA: *Political Opposition in Western Democracies,* op. cit., p 62.

114. See Binkley WE: *American Political Parties: Their Natural History.* New York, Alfred A. Knopf, 1944.

115. Indeed, this may be the flaw in the "Southern Strategy." See Phillips K: *The Emerging Republican Majority.* New Rochelle, N.Y.: Arlington House, 1969.

116. See Schubert G: *The Public Interest.* Glencoe, Ill., The Free Press, 1960, p 136, passim.

117. See Hacker A: "Pressure Politics in Pennsylvania: The Truckers vs. the Railroads," in Westin AF, ed: *The Uses of Power.* New York, Harcourt, Brace and World, Inc., 1962, pp 323-376.

118. As quoted in Harrington M: *Towards a Democratic Left,* op. cit., p 10.

119. See Bachrach P, Baratz M: op. cit.

120. This is the theme of Harrington M: *The Accidental Century,* op. cit.

121. See note 108, *supra.*

122. Converse PE, et al: op. cit., p 1105.

9

Political Opposition in Tanzania: Containment v. Coercion

Raymond F. Hopkins
Swarthmore College

The establishment of political power seems by its very nature to call forth opposition. Throughout history, dissatisfied individuals have expressed political opposition. Whenever men disagree over who should make decisions, what policies these decisions should represent, or what procedures should be followed in reaching decisions, opposition has had a basis to occur. In institutionalized democracies, such opposition is normally expressed through organized formal parties. Those who would change some aspect of the current political process join together to express their opposition and organize the support necessary to accomplish their objectives.[1] In one-party states such as Tanzania, formal permanent opposition is illegal. As a result, political opposition, to the extent that it occurs, must seek other avenues of expression.[2]

This paper hopes to accomplish three tasks. First, it seeks to examine why formal opposition has been outlawed by the Tanzanian regime. Second, it will review the pattern of politics in Tanzania in order to describe the various sites where political controversy occurs and to illustrate the manner

I am grateful to the Foreign Area Fellowship Program and the Yale University International Relations Council for their support of the research on which this essay is based. Some of the material discussed below is reported in greater detail in Chapters 1 and 7 of my book *Political Roles in a New State*. New Haven, Yale University Press, 1971.

in which opposition is controlled. Finally, it will discuss the elite political culture of Tanzania in which the norms and role expectations for the prominent political actors are imbedded. My major thesis is that a system of closed politics, based on an elite political culture of containment, has emerged in Tanzania, and this culture has served to regulate conflict thus far without major incidents of violence or the complete abandonment of democratic forms and procedures.

The Argument for Containing Opposition

Political opposition refers to the activities of any group, however loosely organized, which are coordinated toward the goal of altering the personnel, policies, or procedures of the incumbent regime. In Tanzania, one of the few remaining single-party states in Africa, legal opposition was never very strong. In 1965, it was officially prohibited with the adoption of the one-party Constitution. As no organized opposition is tolerated, the effective opportunities for expressing opposition remain principally within the party framework.

Before examining the character of such "internal" opposition, it is interesting to puzzle out why formal opposition was outlawed. After all, oppositions have been credited with promoting a variety of beneficial effects. Aside from benefits that may accrue to individuals in the form of personal liberty or self-development, several positive systemic effects have been noted by American political scientists. Opposition, according to David Apter, "is essential if the problems of governing new nations are not to engulf those in public office and impel them to coercive solutions."[3]

Three main virtues can be listed for political opposition. First, it can promote legitimacy by giving people a channel for expressing their ideas and grievances. Some individuals are always likely to feel unrepresented by a particular party or dissatisfied by a particular set of policies. With the expression of these feelings in the form of opposition, such individuals, when their actions are tolerated by the government, may increase their willingness to accept the government. In this sense, opposition acts as a safety valve, releasing the tensions and grievances in a nondestructive and nonviolent manner. When political structure prevents such expression, it encourages oppositionist strategies that are both illegal and risky. In order to perform this function successfully, however, political opposition must be "responsible"; that is, it must be willing to work within an established political framework, even when unsuccessful in gaining its objectives. When an opposition does not take seriously limitations on its activities, it enhances the attractiveness of the government's strategy to ignore limitations on its regulation of the opposition.

A second service political opposition may perform is to dampen conflict. Where opposition is legal and has regular opportunities to capture power peacefully, it provides incentives to its members to moderate its disagreements in order to maximize potential support. Of course, where distributions of values are bimodal, regularized opposition can have the opposite effect.[4]

The third benefit that an opposition may provide is a flow of information and criticism about policies that serve as useful correctives. The communication of tensions and cynicisms makes less likely the sudden unleashing of forces or the chronic ignoring of important grievances. An opposition can improve the quality and quantity of information available to decision makers. Hence, an opposition can enhance the self-steering and policy corrective activities of the government and insure that national goals are more effectively pursued.

If such advantages do accrue from the operation of political opposition, why has Tanzania become a one-party state with no formal opposition? The most cogent theoretical arguments justifying this move were expressed by Nyerere in his speech on "Democracy and the One-Party System."

271

Nyerere argued:

> The selfishness of a faction is ... dangerous to society ... because ... membership of a faction—particularly a political faction—may afford a useful cloak under which the selfish individual can serve his own interests while claiming to serve his fellows. [5]

This analysis of men in political life is similar to that of James Madison, who helped draft the American Constitution. Madison wrote in *Federalist No. 10:*

> As long as the connection subsists between [man's] reason and his self-love, his opinions and his passions will have a reciprocal influence on each other; and the former will be objects to which the latter will attach themselves. . . .
>
> The latent causes of faction are thus sown in the nature of man. . . . By a faction, I understand a number of citizens, whether amounting to a majority or minority of the whole, who are united and actuated by some common impulse of passion, or of interest, adverse to the rights of other citizens, or to the permanent and aggregate interests of the community. [6]

While Madison and Nyerere both view factions as evil and dangerous, their solutions are quite different. Madison's solution was to fractionalize the decision-making procedures and to organize electoral bases so that any political faction or party that sought to pursue selfish policies would be checked. Nyerere, on the other hand, thought that national unity and the public interest would best be insured by allowing only a single party to operate. Thus, Tanzania became a one-party state; or more precisely, a two-party state, with the Tanganyika African National Union (TANU) operating on the mainland, and the Afro-Shirazi Party (ASP) the sole political organization on the two offshore islands of Zanzibar and Pemba. The argument for a strong, broad-based, centralized single party rested initially on the premise that this would be a national movement (open to all), and that there were no essential differences in Tanzania upon which serious political opposition could form. It was Nyerere's view that opposition politics in the United States and the United Kingdom took place over relatively unimportant issues, and the expense of such "football-style politics" was a luxury that a poor country like Tanzania could ill afford.

My own appraisal of this argument is that it is precisely the opposite reasons that account for the movement of Tanzania and a number of other African states toward a one-party system. Tanzania is not a unified and classless society in which no division "could give rise to conflicting parties," as Nyerere claimed. Rather there are many cleavages with the potential to develop deep rifts within the body politic. Consequently, it is important that such cleavages not become a source of political controversy by which ambitious politicians can seek popular support through appeals to particular ethnic, regional, religious, or economic interests. Newly established political systems are particularly fragile and minor cleavages or the activities of a few men can produce a drastic fragmenting of the political community. When political loyalties are shallow and cross-cutting cleavages are not widely recognized or evidenced, then disruptive potential or even mild opposition can understandably appear as of staggering magnitude. Nyerere himself seems to recognize this. In 1964, he stated:

> Our Union has neither the long tradition of nationhood, nor the strong physical means of national security, which older countries take for granted. While the vast mass of the people give full and active support to their country and its government, a handful of individuals can still put our nation into jeopardy, and reduce to ashes the effort of millions.[7]

Nyerere and the party leadership have used their control of the country to define politics in such a way as to prevent those conflicts that are likely to divide the public from becoming open disputes.[8]

Thus, the establishment of a one-party state in Tanzania, with its legal restrictions on political opposition, was *not* formed because the state was *unified* and hence formal opposition would have been redundant, *but rather because the state was weakly established,* the community nascent and susceptible to fragmentation. Tanzania illustrates, I think, not that Apter was wrong in proposing that *"responsible* opposition can transform potential disenchantment with government into positive channels,"[9] but rather that it is probably naive to expect an opposition to act *responsibly* when rules and guidelines for insuring the responsibility and institutionalized regularity of the government itself are weak.

Opposition Within the One-Party System

I now want to outline the growth of power in the party and government in Tanzania's one-party system, and examine how most arenas and strategies remain closed for political opposition. My subsequent remarks are based on a study of Tanzanian politics between 1965 and 1968, and an analysis of lengthy interviews with 109 members of Parliament and high-level administrators in 1966.[10]

In 1961, when Tanzania became independent, there were only two important political organizations in the country. The first, the Tanganyika African National Union (TANU), had led the drive to independence. TANU formulated positions on national issues in a very centralized manner through a powerful National Executive Committee (NEC) and under the strong guidance of its president, Julius Nyerere. The party had been a unified organization in its efforts to attain independence. However, opposition on questions of citizenship, the need for expatriate staff, and the implications of socialism began to appear. These posed a serious dilemma for the party if it wished to maintain both unity and democratic practices. The answer to this dilemma was the one-party state in which all conflicts would be resolved within the party structure.[11]

The second political organization was the government. Although the structure of the government by 1961 had been revised—particularly at the upper levels—in preparation for independence, many aspects of the colonial regime were not susceptible to rapid change and retained much of their former character. Colonial government tended to be authoritarian and paternalistic in both its attitudes and organization, and these traits did not disappear when the veneer of British parliamentary democracy was established immediately prior to independence.

The political system, therefore, that was created represented a merger of the party and government bureaucracy. This system does not operate by the rules of parliamentary democracy so quickly erected by the British prior to their exit. The patrern of rule and decision making rather is a mixture of the hierarchical and paternal qualities of colonial rule and the pattern of closed politics developed by TANU in its formative period. Issues often are not debated in public, but in private. Decisions as to the commitment to socialism, the establishment of a national bank, the union with Zanzibar, and the nationalization of major industries, banks, and trading firms were made privately. (Consultations, of course, were made according to the president's judgment, and debate within the party's National Executive has been reported as extremely lively. Moreover, the public and the legislature were eventually called upon to ratify such decisions, though not to debate their wisdom.)

While some criticisms and constructive suggestions are welcomed, and certainly there is no state or party apparatus to control opinion, practices which are likely to bring division or disunity to the country have been avoided. There seems to be an unwritten "national ethic" which urges unity and solidarity. Unity which was the policy of TANU in the independence struggle continues not only as a description of the situation, but also a goal actively sought.[12]

This unity manifests itself mostly at a national level. That is, locally based politicians and speakers in the National Assembly dealing with local topics are much more willing to discuss political problems. Bienen, in conducting interviews with political elite at the "center," found "a strong commitment to viewing both society and the political elite as cohesive and psychologically homogeneous, even if ethnically and socially heterogeneous."[13] The interviews among the elite which I conducted revealed a similar reluctance to identify any divisions in national leadership. But there were real and important ideological cleavages among the top elite, both in elective and appointive posts. The responses to questions about the economy, for example, revealed strongly divergent views on African socialism and economic quality.[14] However, these differences are not a subject for public debate. Public dialogue exposing these differences occurs seldom, and always in the third person.

The current pattern of strong political control that has developed since 1961 can best be understood by examining how the two main political structures, the party and the government, have evolved. Government bureaucracy and the scope of its policies have experienced the greatest changes. These changes have broadened the power and scope of government and increased the authority of the executive. Local government has been modernized and placed under direct control of a central government ministry. The position of chief (often the head of former native authorities) has been abolished except as an honorary title. All land has been declared government property; freehold land tenure has been ended. Existing freehold claims have been transferred into long-term leases with the Ministry of Lands having the power to regulate and revoke the rights to land. A unified system of laws, applicable throughout the country and administered through a single judicial hierarchical organization, has been established. Drawing heavily upon the governmental innovations introduced in Ghana, regional and district administration has incorporated politicians into key posts as commissioners throughout the country. Former administrators in the civil service, a number of whom had been promoted to district commissioner, were effectively demoted to become "administrative secretaries," responsible for the administration and financing of subnational units. Since 1964, however, a number of old politicians have been replaced as commissioners by former civil servants.

The presidency now combines the executive powers of the former governor-general, the responsiblities of a prime minister for directing government, and recently created additional powers. Among these additional powers is preventive detention based on the principle that "the executive, especially in the circumstances of a new nation such as ours, must have the necessary powers to carry out the functions of a modern state."[15] The Preventive Detention Act gave the president sweeping power to detain political opponents that cannot be challenged in any court; the detainee can appeal only to an advisory committee whose decisions are not binding. The president also has received the power to "deport" citizens from one part of the country to another and to expel undesirables. Finally, under the National Union of Tanganyika Workers Establishment Act of 1964, the president may appoint the secretary-general and deputy-secretary-general of the newly established National Union of Tanganyika (NUTA). With the broad powers of detention and pardon, military and policy control, broad powers of appointment, and even the ability to summarily dismiss students,[16] the president's prerogative seems unlimited. As Nyerere himself admitted, "I have sufficient powers under the constitution to be a dictator."[17]

The Bunge, or National Assembly, has been an important forum for debating government policy, raising criticisms and objections of various sorts, and providing a platform for broader explanation and defense of government programs and policies. In spite of the criticisms that have been often voiced in the Assembly, in nearly all cases the Assembly has been concerned with ratifying decisions that have been made by some other group. Not unlike the colonial LegCo, the Assembly has been more often a sounding board and a forum for extracting approbation and applause for new government policies than a deliberative body that formulates policies or actually writes legislation.

The judiciary, while remaining independent and asserting its competence, even to imprisoning political officials[18] and having its mild sentences of army mutineers upheld, still has not had its independence and ability to make constitutional interpretation tested. Explicit decisions have been made to avoid entangling the judiciary in political controversy. Moreover, with the preventive detention act and special detention powers of regional and area commissioners, the actual role of the court in politics has remained minimal. At best it can act as a referee, as in the "treason trials" of several leading politicians in 1970-71.

The union with Zanzibar in April, 1964, resulted more in changes of personnel than in the organization of the government. In January, 1964, a revolution in Zanzibar brought to power a new ruling group that included nationalist African politicians and a number of dedicated socialists with strong Marxist leanings. Following the union, Zanzibaris were appointed as members of the Bunge and several received ministerial posts or high administrative appointments. However, the two islands of the former Zanzibar Republic retain a separate government and set of ministers. The Revolutionary Council is the governing body for Zanzibar and Sheikh Abeid Karume, a former labor leader and head of the Afro-Shirazi Party, is president of Zanzibar, as well as first vice-president of Tanzania.

The party has also experienced important changes. At the time of independence, finances declined, many of the most able members and party leaders acquired positions in the government, and the organization languished. Despite the fact that TANU claimed 1.25 million members (in a population of 10 million), "subscriptions had dried up, the enrollment of new members ceased, and attendance at public meetings was shrinking."[19]

To rejuvenate the party, several changes have occurred. Graduates of Kivukoni College have been posted to district and regional level party offices. In 1962, the party was brought directly into the government through the reorganization of provincial administration. Politicians appointed to new posts of area commissioner and regional commissioner were simultaneously assigned by Nyerere as regional and district secretaries of the Party.[20] Following the army mutiny of 1964, a cell system was introduced whereby groups of ten houses or families were clustered into a single party cell. With this innovation, TANU created a pyramidal organizaton which stretches, at least in theory, from the president down to the lowest member. Moreover, this new division, the cell, has been given specific functions, particularly in relation to security and self-help projects. In 1963, TANU was opened to Asian and European members, a move Nyerere had been promoting since 1958. Since the army mutiny, soldiers in the newly organized army have been encouraged to join the Party.[21] Political education and control of the military was entrusted to a tough minded party executive, Selemani Kitundu. In July, 1964, barriers to civil servants' joining the party were lifted, though, similar to the army, there are restrictions against their holding office.

Further changes in the party have strengthened the national structure by expanding national staff positions, funding salaries from government revenue, and asking party leaders, including the president, to have specific office hours at party headquarters. Finally, in January, 1967, under the Arusha Declaration, which was a major policy declaration, party officials were brought under closer regulation, and specifically prohibited from engaging in profit-making activity.

The most important phenomenon of the independence period has been the effect of all these changes—the consolidation of power by TANU.[22] The trade unions, cooperatives, women and youth organizations, the military, the bureaucracy, and mass media all are incorporated in the party structure or subject to its control. After the party established its dominance of other groups and institutions in society, it began to exercise control over dissent.

Opposition and dissent can be expressed in a number of arenas. Interest groups, legislatures, bureaucracy, and the courts as well as political parties may contain individuals who disagree with the government on one issue or another. The first efforts of TANU, under Nyerere's leadership, however, moved to contain within the party structure criticisms from or within any of these organizations.

The relative paramountcy and comprehensiveness of TANU's position prevents groups from directly articulating dissent or opposition. Some groups that might be influential in politics have remained unorganized. Other groups that are organized are prohibited, either formally or informally, from bringing pressure to bear on policy questions, at least not publicly.

The chief's convention, for example, dissolved itself before independence, and a year later the position of chief was abolished along with all hereditary traditional status. The Asian Association and all tribal associations have been abolished. Recognition of tribalism, even in collecting simple statistics, is discouraged. All political parties, except TANU, have been outlawed, including the African National Congress, the People's Democratic Party (PDP), and the All Muslim National Union of Tanganyika (AMNUT).

This does not mean that there are no chiefs, that tribal identities are unimportant, that Asians do not communicate special interests to the government, or that policy cleavages are nonexistent among politicians. What it does mean, however, is that these groups do not organize or communicate their feelings on policy matters to each other, the public, or the government as a group. For example, informal tribal associations exist in Dar es Salaam and, no doubt, other cities, and often aid members with personal problems such as marriage, employment, or death. But they are strongly discouraged from political activity. No tribal group as such, for example, may complain openly about the conditions of roads in their area, or the desirability of a textile mill.

Organizations such as churches, schools, cooperatives,

labor unions, and business groups also exist. Their ability to exercise influence, however, is limited. Since the party represents, in theory, the interest of all the people, several of these groups are associated with the party and have representatives on the NEC. While their spokesmen may lobby within the National Executive, they cannot thwart party will. Unions, for example, are prohibited from striking. Perhaps it is appropriate that a socialist party does not have a business group affiliate, but the fact that most businessmen are either expatriates or Asians no doubt explains in large part the absence of an organized business association within the party. There seems little doubt that businessmen, and in particular Asians, have little political influence.

Teachers, also, are somewhat alienated from politics. There are several reasons for this. First, they are prohibited from holding office and must, therefore, resign (and lose their job security) if they gain public office, even at the local level. The scope of arrests and detention (usually for a day or two only) following the army mutiny in 1964 also left teachers, a number of whom were detained, fearful of political involvement. At present, although teachers number over 13,000 and are a crucial group in the country, their political interests are completely channeled through the national labor organization controlled by the party, or through the Ministry of Education.

Thus, with many groups officially restricted and others absorbed and controlled by the party, at least with respect to their political activity, the expression of group interests is publicly muffled. On only a few occasions have groups openly taken stands designed to influence government action. One group that was organized, willing to articulate its own interests and not absorbed in the party, was the university students. Though not unaware of the informal rule condemning the expression of "selfish interests," students have been confident of their own importance. In protest against what seemed unfair treatment for them under proposed National Service legislation, in October, 1966, 393 members of the Tanzania Students' Union staged a protest on the lawn of the State House. The President expelled the students on the spot and ordered them to return to their homes. The assets of the Students' Union were handed over to the TANU Youth League, the Union dissolved, and students urged to join the TYL. Six months after the expulsion, Nyerere announced, after a formal request from the Parliament, that students who requested pardon might return to the university, but that "students who are opposed to socialism will not return to the college."[23]

The news media and election campaigns are other kinds of forums in which criticism and dissenting views can be disseminated and coalitions among like-minded oppositionists formed. These forums have also been subjected to carefully developed controls. The *Daily Nation,* a Kenya-based paper that had wide circulation in Tanzania, was banned after it continued to carry articles which the party officials felt were damaging or seditious. In 1968, a press law was passed that gave the government sweeping control. The party established its own English-language paper, the *Nationalist* (with a similar Swahili publication). In 1969, the only other English-language paper, the *Standard*, was nationalized. The government and party also regulate all the domestic radio networks.

Election campaigns also can encourage criticism and dissent. In Tanzania, elections for the National Assembly, while competitive, are carefully controlled by the party executive. It altered 16 of 101 slates in 1965 and rejected the initial list of members nominated by national organizations. The nomination of a single candidate for president is crucial to contain factionalism within the party and to prevent policy disputes from erupting into public debates, thereby forcing candidates to identify with alternative positions. The public, however, seems to prefer the notion of two candidates, as indicated by a survey in Dar es Salaam in which 58% of the respondents wanted two candidates to stand for president after Nyerere retired.[24]

The final step in containing opposition has been the

establishment of restrictions on party membership. In 1967, Part Four of the Arusha Declaration read:

> Since the founding of the Party greater emphasis has been put on having as large a membership as possible. This was justified during the struggle for independence. Now, however, the National Executive Committee feels that the time has come for emphasis to shift away from mere size of membership on to the quality of membership. Greater consideration must be given to a member's commitment to the beliefs and objectives of the Party, and its policy of Socialism.
>
> The Membership Clause in the TANU Constitution must be closely observed. Where it is thought unlikely that an applicant really accepts the beliefs, aims and objects of the Party, he should be denied membership. Above all it should always be remembered that TANU is a Party of Farmers and Workers.[25]

The party has moved to become a more distinct unit from the masses. The ideas and attitudes of party leaders (average members will probably be unaffected) are receiving closer scrutiny. This new policy reflects the favorite slogan of one cabinet minister who frequently reminded his friends, "You can't build socialism without socialists."

However, there are a number of Tanzanians whose socialist commitment is fairly weak. Since TANU membership has become an important, if till recently perfunctory, qualification for many positions in the public sector and even private business (part of which, of course, has now been nationalized), loss of TANU membership is a real and serious threat. Even greater conformity to the party's creed and rules for debate can, therefore, be expected. As one MP explained, "Your political career will pretty well be finished if you're sacked from TANU, and it will probably even hurt your business contacts." The significance of this trend in exercising party authority was manifested dramatically in late 1968, when the seats of nine dissident members of the National Assembly were declared vacant after they had been expelled from the party.[26] Thus, even informal opposition and dissent by party members is now carefully regulated.

The Tanzanian political system has evolved a set of controls that demand the exclusion of differences over "fundamentals" from political debate and the relegation of disputes over "minor issues" (such as priorities or timing) to private debate, leaving only "constructive criticism" and "helpful suggestions" to be aired publicly. Nyerere and others have frequently urged more public debate and criticism of this sort.[27]

Thus, the privacy of the NEC and the cabinet have become the principal arenas for the acceptance or rejections of policy decisions. Nevertheless, major policies, such as the Arusha Declaration, require broad support built through a hierarchy of expanding groups. When widespread public support is sought, the discussion of policy is urged upon larger groups, not by the vanquished in a struggle seeking to transfer the debate to a more favorable arena, but by the victors in a preemptive move to have it ratified at all levels. Conflict is still minimized.

The privatization of conflict is, therefore, the normal style of Tanzanian politics. The one-party system seems to require this closed character to politics that minimizes conflict through emphasis on unanimity. This does not prevent shortcomings and economic problems from being faced forthrightly. The candidness of Nyerere's speeches is quite refreshing. However, his political frankness masks the fact that he has no organized critics, and that reporting of conflict among national political leaders, both as to the nature of the issue differences and the identity of antagonists, is firmly condemned. Thus, the conflicts placed in the open are always those which will promote unity and unite the vast majority of the population against enemies such as ignorance, exploitation, or imperialists. These conflicts displace political divisions along other, lesser controversies, such as the priorities for developmental allocations, and prevent conflicts from creating any permanent divisions or alignments within the country. By deciding what political conflicts may become public, the political elite have maintained unity in a party and nation whose institutionalization is fragile.

The Elite Political Culture of Containment

The manner in which national political actors understand their own role and those of other major actors is an important factor in determining the political culture that regulates the privatization of conflicts. An investigation of this elite political culture will provide greater insight into how this formal apparatus for containing the opposition is- anchored in the political norms of the governing elite.

The norms and role expectations of elite political culture shape a political system's response to dissent and opposition. Within less developed states such as Tanzania, three general patterns of attitudes and sentiments among elite seem likely to exist. These cultures reflect variants of the general situation in partially mobilized societies which have a large mass of the population parochial in outlook and a small politically active elite.[28] Where the mass of the population is unmobilized or residual, the way in which elite members view each other and to what extent they share similar priorities and concerns are particularly important. These three types are the bargaining, coercive, and containment elite cultures.

One type of elite political culture is characterized by coercion and conflict; differences among elite tend to be transferred into hostile attitudes and patterns of nonlegal retributions and maneuvering for power. The Soviet Union, particularly during the 1930s, Ghana under Nkrumah, Indonesia, particularly after the unsuccessful coup in 1965, Dahomey, and South Vietnam constitute instances of fragmentation, coercion, and conflict among modernized elites. Students, the military, and workers regularly resort to violence in order to press demands or bring about change. Samuel Huntington has characterized this pattern of politics among elite as "praetorian."[29] The attitudes and expectations of the accompanying political culture tend to support this conflict and violence.

A second elite culture is that of bargaining. This type may be associated with the pattern of polyarchy outlined by Dahl and Lindbloom.[30] The United States and Great Britain illustrate this pattern among modernized nations, while India and Israel have been examples among less advanced nations. In this culture, groups are expected to struggle legitimately to influence policy, and elections serve to resolve open political differences, at least by offering some alternatives.

A third cultural pattern is that of containment. The set of attitudes and expectations that comprises this elite culture is particularly evident in Tanzania. It may also have been present in Turkey in the period between World War I and II. A containment culture represents a compromise between an open style of politics, supported by a culture of bargaining, and a conflict style based on coercion and reinforced by attitudes of political insecurity. Such a culture closes the public arena to discussions of fissiparous issues while providing some mechanisms for articulating dissent and for bringing about change.

In order to better understand how the containment culture shapes the pattern of responses to opposition in Tanzania, I have examined the descriptive statements of the 109 elite interviewed with respect to the expression of criticism or opposition by occupants of four key roles: citizen, administrator, legislator, and president.

The Public

While many Tanzanian elite members preferred a system with norms for participation contained in the legal system, most recognized that such a pattern of politics is impractical in the near future. For example, elite attitudes stressed that citizens' duties involved participation in local economic development projects. This was mentioned by 64% of elite, while their role as voters or critics was not widely supported—it was referred to by only 11%.

286

Only a minority of the elite expected a citizen to exercise his political influence or to make demands on the government for his own benefit. The majority defined his duties in terms of responding to governmental outputs, such as speeches which explain the need for greater efforts by citizens. A typical role definition given by an administrator was: "A good citizen is one who contributes to the achievement of the targets of planned development knowing why he does so." A cabinet minister outlined the role in a more personal and direct form. For him, the good citizen should "understand his responsibilities to his neighbors; not be tribal-minded; and be prepared to accept the national decisions, whether it is to his own economic benefit or not. In return, he deserves equal opportunities and the necessary protection against ill-treatment."

Answers to the question on a citizen's role suggested a sense of frustration and distance in the elite-citizen relationship, particularly among administrators. Their view of Tanzania's development needs seems to have brought a loneliness and sense of burden to some elite who felt their view was not understood or shared by the masses of citizens. A few examples from interviews may illustrate this point.

> His greatest responsibility is to know what is expected of him by his country, to do the things for the sake of his country. But there are very few who do this. In every person there is an element of self-interest. What is needed is that one must understand his obligations. [Principal Secretary]
>
> All of them should be as the president. That is, each should regard every problem of the country as their own problem—to feel the problem as the president does. [A Regional Commissioner]

In general, what occurs to elites, when asked about the responsibilities of an ideal citizen, are not the qualities of civic competence and participation often associated with the role of citizen in modern democratic societies, but the obligation to participate and share in the tasks of nation-building, not only through hard work and increased individual effort, but by sharing with the elite the psychic burden of the problems and difficulties of national development. Thus, the citizen is expected to be an important participant in the political process, but largely on the output side, in accepting and furthering government programs and nation-building projects. His role as a critic and voter is seldom mentioned, and his proclivity to assert self-interest is condemned.

The Bureaucracy

Role expectations for administrators were also examined. Rules for bureaucratic behavior held by administrators and politicians emphasized development rather than law and order responsibilities. While technocrats in the bureaucracy were less positively inclined toward the party ideology, they did not form a major opposition group to politicians, as Foltz finds to be the case in many one-party states.[31]

Opposition within the bureaucracy generally takes the form of noncompliance or lack of enthusiasm for party guidelines rather than public criticisms. The general operating procedure that accompanied the establishment of independents was the supremacy of the party over the administration in policy making. A number of older "veteran" administrators who had served in the colonial period espoused views opposed to the norms of bureaucratic subordination to the party. These men, in contrast to younger, better educated administrators, had significantly different outlooks on the range of their responsibilities and in their enthusiasm for TANU policies. One administrator of this genre, for example, declined to discuss his views on African socialism because "it would probably get me into trouble." Reitrements and transfers among bureaucrats since the mid-1960s, however, have resulted in the replacement of a number of those who espoused such "opppositionist" or unsympathetic views. Complaints among socialists at the university of a "bureaucratic mentality" in government have declined.

The Legislature

Role expectations and orientations also shaped behavior in the National Assembly. While criticism has been voiced in this arena since independence, it has never been major. Speeches in support of stated government positions have always comprised a large portion of the total speeches given in the Assembly. While criticism of government policies, particularly among long speeches, was frequent in the early debates of the Assembly, a content analysis of speeches from 1961 through 1966 shows that dissent dropped steadily after independence and by the 1963/64 session it reached a nadir.

An important conclusion reached by examining the careers of those MP's who were most critical is that such members have not fared well politically. Only a few members during the first two years of independence gave speeches of opposition 50% or more of the time. None has since. Those who did included Tumbo and Mkello, labor leaders who were subsequently placed in detention; Masanja, who, never a serious influence in the Assembly, defected to the ANC (a miniscule opposition party), and has since retired from politics; and Siyovelwa and Mbogo, who, though loyal TANU members, did not stand for reelection. Both were appointed area commissioners, but Mbogo was removed and imprisoned for theft. Thus none of those who were clearly and consistently critical or who opposed the government in the first five years has survived as a popular politician or MP.

In the new and expanded Bunge, elected in 1965, discussions became considerably more lively. About every fourth or fifth speaker in the new Assembly who made a lengthy contribution was critical of the government. However, among those MP's who were most critical in the 1965/66 period, by December, 1968, nine had lost their Assembly seats for political reasons. Mwakitwango, for example, in July, 1968, accused the government of "tribalism," "nepotism" and slowing the pace of Africanization. He was expelled from the party three months later. Also, Eli Anangisye, former Secretary of the TANU Youth

289

League, and F. L. Masha, who had been national publicity secretary for TANU, were among those expelled.

Thus criticism and dissent in the Assembly, in spite of affirmations about its desirability, has neither been effective in the legislative process nor rewarding for those who engaged in it. Two reasons best explain this. First, the vast majority of Assembly members are usually in agreement with the government, and secondly, for those members who might raise serious criticisms, it is very difficult to distinguish between criticizing a detail of policy and criticizing government policy itself. The latter is officially not the responsibility of a member speaking in Parliament. Policy criticisms may be raised, but only in an appropriate party, and hence closed, forum. Nyerere, for example, has explicitly stated that broader questions of policy should be the responsibility of the National Executive of the party, and not subject to legislative debate.[32]

For legislators, two important rules can be derived from the consensus of role expectations among elite. These are (1) an MP may not publicly oppose a policy decision of the party's National Executive Committee, and (2) policies passed in the National Assembly must be supported in discussions with constituents.

That this supremacy of the party has been at least partially established in the elite political culture can be illustrated in two ways. First, although MP's are an important link between citizenry and government, the party is seen as an even more important and powerful link. In a survey among the urbanized Dar es Salaam electorate in 1966, people were asked: "If you have a problem in your district which requires government action, to whom should you go first—your representative in the National Assembly or your local TANU official?" Fifty-two percent stated they would go to their local TANU official first, while only 35% chose their Assembly representative. A second illustration of the party's potency compared with that of the Assembly is through a specific comparison of the NEC with the Bunge. In the Dar es Salaam survey, people were asked: "Which do you think has more influence in the way our government is run, the National Assembly or the National Executive Committee of TANU?" Thirty-four percent said the Bunge, 40% the NEC, and 11% felt they were about equal. The same question, when asked of MP's during their interviews, revealed that every member of the government stated that the NEC was the more important organ.

The second rule is that an MP may oppose government policy in party discussion or within the Assembly before the Assembly votes, but he must support it among his constituents if it is passed. This rule emerged directly from the role expectation question concerning opposition to a government policy. It closely resembles the classic formulation by Lenin of "democratic centralism." Once a measure has *passed*, an MP must support it. He may not publicly voice his criticism to his constituents. The possible consequences for MP's violating this dictum were outlined by Second Vice-President Kawawa in Parliament. He noted that it should be illegal for a person to foment discontent or ill will and pointed out that such criticisms as those contrary to government plans would "be going against TANU and the Afro-Shirazi Party." Hence, opposition by MP's is limited within the Assembly and virtually forbidden in any outside public forum.

The Presidency
The final role examined among elite was the presidency. The pattern of elite expectations uncovered, coupled with the actions and speeches of President Nyerere, provides a basis for proposing a few rules or norms for this role.

Rule 1. The president may not violate the law.
This rule reflects the expectations of the elite that the president would not act arbitrarily against the judiciary of members of the Parliament. It is also consonant with the modal expectations that persuasion is the principal tactic to be expected from a president in resolving conflict, whether

conflicts arise from tribal cleavages in the country or from issue-oriented cleavages in his cabinet. Nyerere's own ideas and actions tend to reinforce this rule. He has stressed the rule of law in a number of speeches and has emphasized the importance of legal considerations as a constraint on his behavior. His acceptance of the weak punishment of the army mutineers in 1964 is an example. More recently, legal considerations were emphasized as an inhibiting factor in his refusal to remove Oscar Kambena from the National Assembly in response to the urgings of a delegation of elders.

Rule 2. The president must be responsible to the people, not Parliament or the administration. In case of disputes or ambiguities, the people to whom the president is responsible are embodied in the party.

Evidence for this rule comes not only from particular expectations, such as responses indicating that the president would seek popular support when turning out local leaders or dismissing dissenting members from his cabinet, but also from responses which described attributes desirable in a leader and associated with Nyerere. The most frequently mentioned attribute was responsiveness to the people. This was articulated in terms of humility and tact with the people or "the masses." Nyerere's style of making decisions independently, sometimes in the face of strong subsequent disagreement with members of his cabinet, has already been described. Following such "strong" decisions, it has been the practice to hold large public rallies at which Nyerere publicly explained his actions, and urged leaders to explain the government's policy throughout the country. These rallies were typically organized by TANU, and the crowds which have appeared regularly carried signs indicating support and solidarity for Nyerere. Parades through the capital normally precede or follow Nyerere's address. Such demonstrations of public support and solidarity behind Nyerere followed his decisions to break relations with the United Kingdom in 1965 and to dismiss protesting university students in 1966, and his announcement of the Arusha Declaration in 1967. By establishing such links between presidential action, which itself is not without controversy among politicians, and strong displays of public support and solidarity for the president, the general expectation that the president is responsible and sensitive to the people has been reinforced. He was often seen, therefore, as a man of the people, and one who was not necessarily tied to intermediate organizations such as the Parliament or the cabinet.

Rule 3. The president must be free to act unhindered by legal constraints.

This rule seems on the surface to contradict Rule 1. If so, it promotes ambiguity in political-role expectations for the president. The president, as we have noted, has been given sweeping powers outside the jurisdictions of normal legal restraints. In order to minimize potential conflicts with the judiciary, for instance, a bill of rights has deliberately *not* been included in the 1965 constitution. The *One-Party State Report* declares:

> In this transitional period the maintenance of the rule of law to which we attach the greatest importance requires particular care that occasions for conflict between the judges and the executive and the legislature should be reduced to a minimum.[33]

The president's power as commander-in-chief of the armed forces, as sole head of the executive branch unchecked by cabinet rule, and his special powers under the detention act to imprison without outside review all reflect this rule.

The interviews revealed considerable affection for and trust in Nyerere among most elite. These feelings have greatly increased the flow of power into Nyerere's hands. Some even trusted Nyerere to interpret events and ideas for them. For instance, one elite remarked with respect to African socialism, "I'm not really sure about this notion, but whatever Nyerere does about it will be right." This feeling is probably a product of the high appraisal shared by most elite of the previous strong decisions Nyerere has made. The consequence is that Nyerere has become a man whom people trust in power, who is credited with the ability to make the right decision, and whose own opinion is looked upon as a source of wisdom. Opinion formation among elite, therefore, the group who, one would expect, are most likely to have alternative sources of information and independent judgments on political matters, is closely linked to statements and cues supplied by Nyerere. It seems doubtful that any presidential successor to Nyerere would enjoy this degree of trust and position of opinion leadership. Since it does exist at present, it tends to support the generalized norm or rule that the president, since he is Nyerere, must be free to act and to exercise his wise judgment unencumbered with legal restraints. This reasoning allows the reconciliation of Rule 1 and Rule 3 which has been accomplished in general practice by providing the president with the virtual legal power of a dictator. (This is not to say that a number of legal restraints on the role of the president do not exist. There are, however, two qualifications to these legal and constitutional restraints. First, the powers that the president has at present, particularly the detention act, provide sufficient leverage to remove most, and perhaps all, legal barriers to action that might arise, without the violation of any formal law. In addition, and this is particularly true among legislators, there was a willingness to expand the president's legal powers.) Thus, the power of the president is extremely great, is limited at present more by Nyerere's own self-restraint, and serves in many ways as a linchpin holding the system of closed politics in place and reinforcing the norms of the culture of containment.

Conclusion: Causes and Consequences

Why has this closed system of politics, with its rather undemocratic features, evolved? Certainly the transition to a one-party system followed quickly the ascension of the nationalist movement to political power. The answer is not that the closed system is simply a mechanism devised by politically avaricious nationalists who, having acquired high offices, wish to preserve their positions. The attitudes and sentiments elicited during the interviews and the rapid turnover and demise of political leadership do not support such a thesis. A more tenable explanation for the style of politics emerging in Tanzania is that the one-party system with its emphasis on solidarity and unity is a reaction to feelings of insecurity. Weakness and vulnerability of political institutions in Tanzania have been well recognized and mentioned by many of the architects of the political system. Such feelings were certainly heightened by the military mutiny in January, 1964. The potential for instability is also felt by many elite. During the interviews, themes such as the illiteracy of the population, the ease with which they might be swayed by "false prophets," the weakness of the police and armed forces and their subordination to civil rule, and the general vulnerability of the system to tribal residualism or external penetration and influence were all mentioned. These characteristics were often cited as justification for the establishment of a democratic system which was "different but just as good"[34] as those in Western countries. Occasionally, desiderata of economic development were also cited as reasons for the emphasis on unity and solidarity in the political system A relationship between economic development and political structure was suggested by several elite. One MP submitted that "in 20 or 30 years, when we're more developed, two parties may emerge."

A common opinion among members of the elite was that centrifugal and divisive forces existed in Tanzania with sufficient latent strength to justify a system that could nullify and smother their effects. Frequently added to this argument was the rationale that the smothering of public controversy is in the African tradition and does not limit real expression which is possible "through proper channels." To some extent, this view reduced attitude incongruities among

295

elite who had absorbed Western norms of democracy and free expression.

Is this assessment by elite of fragility in the political order correct? Without some procedure to compare the strength of these tendencies in Tanzania with those in other countries, no answer can be definitive. It is clear, however, that the government has refrained from testing its strength on certain issues. The withdrawal of the prosecution of the popular traditional leader Chief Fundikira in 1963, the cautiousness with which integration with Zanzibar has proceeded, and the hesitancy to penetrate and alter economically regressive or fissiparous tribal patterns of activity through the use of force are perhaps indicative of weakness in the government and party. Bienen argues that, indeed, conditions in Tanzania vitiate the capacity of political institutions for transforming the economy or regulating life in rural areas.[35] However, avoiding tests of strength and the political reactions which could result might also, at least in part, indicate prudence. For instance, if a full and open debate of the Arusha Declaration had been held, it would certainly have been a lively one, with the potential of creating divisions among national elite and even local leadership, had they been invited into policy discussions. One can imagine sharp national cleavages emerging as the full implications of the policies of self-reliance and conditions of leadership were realized and challenged. But such divisions are incompatible with beliefs in a classless state; ideological disputes, therefore, have been condemned as foreign and unreal. Thus decisions were simply announced—not debated. The arenas in which the Arusha policies of nationalization and rural development were officially approved were largely a series of accolades and ritualistic ceremonies. The effective decisions had already been reached,[36] and political divisions avoided.

What are the latent divisions or cleavages against which the closed sytem of politics guards? A few have already been discussed. There is nearly an even split between Christians and Muslims (aside from a large number of adherents to traditional animistic religion). Tribal and ethnic differences are also important, with the Chagga, Haya, and Nyakusa as advantaged tribes overrepresented in important posts of the modern sector. Europeans and Asians, who still occupy many middle- and upper-class economic roles, are objects of political distrust. Yet reference to these differences in a political context is stringently proscribed by political norms. Nyerere's personal ideology of a solidaristic and socialistic community labels such differences as illegitimate and threats to the public interest. A clear extension of this outlook is the denial of ideological or fundamental cleavages.[37] However, differences in ideology do exist as the responses to economic questions by those elite members interviewed indicated. These cleavages, especially, are masked by the closed system of politics.

Among the elite at the highest levels there are at least two groups between whom the political struggle, such as it was, seems to have occurred. The description of these two groups rests largely upon an analysis of elite interviews and observations of elite behavior in 1965 and 1966. Political divisions along these lines seem to be continuing as of 1970. Neither group was formally organized. The criteria for membership was not clear, even in an informal sense. What distinguished these two groups and bound together each in an unorganized and informal fashion was their sharing of certain attitudes and concerns. The groups differed in their attitudes toward Tanzanian progress, toward the outside world, and toward each other.

The first group, for convenience, will be labeled "ardent socialists." Individuals associated with this group tend to have strong ideological commitments. Oscar Kambona, the former Secretary-General of TANU, A. M. Babu, and A. K. Hanga, now deceased, were the most prominent members of this group. For them, the term African socialism, for example, was generally felt to be a smokescreen inhibiting implementation of true socialism. They tended to reify concepts like "imperialism" and "capitalism." Identifications with the West, particularly the United States, were negative, while communist countries, particularly China, were viewed more positively. Most of the xenophobia toward the West was generalized, and friendships with Westerners were relatively frequent among this group. Some of the attitudes toward the West seemed to be reinforced by feelings of vicarious pleasure derived by symbolically reasserting the power acquired by Africans initially at independence. There was a doctrinaire rather than adaptive quality in the socialist views of some members. This group was most critical of domestic policy, at least the official policies of 1966. Criticism and disaffection by this group were expressed infrequently and in a low-key manner. One of the characteristics which justifies labeling these individuals as a group rather than simply a category is that they held attitudes toward one another as friends and toward others as enemies. Communication and interaction among "ardent socialists" was relatively high, based partially on similar intellectual interests and mutual trust. Enemies are, in some sense, the product of the ardent socialist's own analysis since these consisted mainly of individuals whose attitudes were more pragmatic and whose ascension to power would realistically be a threat to their own ambitions and aspirations.

The second group, which might be labeled "nationalist neutrals," displayed fewer characteristics of cohesion than the first. The boundaries determining who may or may not actually belong to this group are difficult to establish. The attitudes and outlooks of its members varied more widely than those among the "ardent socialists." Vice-President Kawawa and ministers such as Paul Bomani and Nsilo Swai were key figures in this group. In terms of national policy goals and evaluations of internal domestic policies, members of this group tended to concentrate their efforts on narrower, more particularistic situations and prefer less radical economic policies. Their commitment to Tanzania as a nation and the advancement of Africans was as great as in the first group, but was less ritualistically expressed. Their attitudes toward foreign nations tended more toward neutrality, but reflected familiarity and sympathy with Western styles and traditions.

Both groups were comprised of politicians from nationalist, middle-class backgrounds, and neither acted as spokesman for discontented intellectuals or technocrats. However, the "nationalist neutrals" were closer to the views of technocrats in the bureaucracy. The cleavages between these groups, if released into the political system, could exacerbate latent cleavages of an economic, tribal, or religious nature. More than any other factor, the closed system of politics has prevented this. The containment of these conflicts has been achieved by a reduction in democracy.

The containment and suppression of political opposition in Tanzania in recent years raises a question as to whether the culture of containment is in fact moving toward one of coercion. Since 1967, a number of major political leaders identified with the "ardent socialists" group have gone into exile or been jailed or executed. Oscar Kambona, along with some close associates, fled to England where he remains a rallying point for opposition. Hanga, former Vice-President of Zanzibar, along with 12 others, was sent under arrest to Zanzibar, where he and two other political prisoners were executed. In 1971, a number of Tanzanians remained in prison or preventive detention for political reasons. These actions suggest that the containment of political opposition may have exceeded the justification for containment based on system stability. Is this simply coercion of one group by another, designed to insure the political survival of personnel rather than policies or the regime?

Any answer to this question is, in part, pure speculation, since no information about the considerations which led to the political executions in 1969 has been published. Indeed, the Tanzanian government has sought not to publicize these actions. Leaving aside the problems of personal justice, two comments about whether Tanzania has moved from a culture of containment to a pattern of coercion can be made. First, the elite culture embraced wide, though probably superficial, support for democratic practices. To the extent this is institutionalized, events so far seem unlikely to have altered significantly the basic characteristics of elite attitudes. Second, the parallel suggested between Turkey and Tanzania, if accepted, suggests that limited violence need not vitiate a closed but non-Praetorian pattern of politics. It should be recalled that in the 1920s, Ataturk was responsible for the death of a number of his political opponents, far in excess of those affected so far in Tanzania. While such a comparison is in no way meant to condone political executions, it does suggest that the distinction between containment and coercion is principally one of degree.

Closed politics which seeks to contain political opposition and dissent is still a more accurate description of Tanzanian political life than the coercive political pattern with its frequent violence now found so often in other African states. Thus the culture of containment continues to shape Tanzanian politics; if it remains effective, it should serve as a check on extensive suppression and coercion of opposition.

Notes

1. As Robert Dahl has noted, however, "legal party opposition is, in fact, a recent unplanned invention that has been confined for the most part to a handful of countries." Dahl RA: *Pluralist Democracy in the United States.* Chicago, 1967, p 204.

2. For some general comments on the pattern of opposition in one-party African states, see Foltz WJ: "Political Opposition in Single Party States of Tropical Africa." *Political Oppositions in Non-Western States.* RA Dahl, ed. New Haven, Yale University Press, forthcoming.

3. Apter DE: Chapter, "Some Reflections on the Role of Political Opposition in New Nations." *Some Conceptual Approaches to the Study of Modernization.* Englewood Cliffs, Prentice-Hall, 1968, pp 72-87.

4. Dahl RA: *Political Oppositions in Western Democracies.* New Haven, Yale University Press, 1966, especially pp 348-386.

5. Nyerere J: "Democracy and the Party System." Dar es Salaam,

The Standard, 1963.

6. Hamilton A, Jay J, Madison J: *The Federalist.* New York, The Modern Library, pp 54-55.

7. "President's Speech at the Opening of University College." Dar es Salaam, Government Printer, 1964, p 17.

8. For a discussion of the regulation of conflicts and its importance to politics, see Schattschneider E: *The Semi-Sovereign People.* New York, Holt, Rinehart and Winston, 1966. He writes, "Political conflict is not like an intercollegiate debate in which the opponents agree in advance on a definition of the issues. As a matter of fact, *the definition of the alternatives is the supreme instrument of power;* the antagonists can rarely agree on what the issues are because power is involved in the definition. He who determines what politics is about runs the country, because the definition of the alternatives is the choice of conflicts, and the choice of conflicts allocates power." (p 68).

9. Apter, op. cit., italics mine.

10. The interviews averaged about two hours each. For a more detailed description of the interview format and subsequent analysis, see Hopkins RF: *Political Roles in a New State.* New Haven, Yale University Press, 1971.

11. Nyerere, "Democracy and the Party System," op. cit.

12. The "national ethic" may be found in the *Report of the Presidential Commission on the Establishment of a Democratic One-Party State.* Dar es Salaam, Government Printer, 1965, pp 3-4. The concept of unity is found, for example, in such statements of Nyerere as: "Once the first free government is formed, its supreme task lies ahead; the building up of the country's economy ... calls for the maximum united effort by the whole country if it is to succeed. *There can be no room for differences or division. . . .*

This is our time of emergency, and until our war against poverty, ignorance, and disease has been won, we should not let our unity be destroyed by a desire to follow somebody else's book of rules." From "One-Party Rule," reprinted in Sigmund PE Jr, *The Ideologies of the Developing Nations.* New York, Frederick A. Praeger, 1963, p 199. "To try and import the idea of a parliamentary opposition into Africa may very likely lead to violence—because the opposition parties will tend to be regarded as traitors by the majority of our people—or at best, it will lead to the trivial manoeuverings of 'opposing' groups whose time is spent in the inflation of artificial differences into some semblance of reality 'for the sake of serving democracy'!" Nyerere, "Democracy and the Party System," op. cit., p 15. "We want to maintain and expand the individual liberty which we now have, and to ensure for our nation the safeguards which are provided by freedom for criticism and open opposition to established policies. . . . At present, however, we have to face the fact that in general terms the freedom for all to live a decent life must take priority. Development must be considered first, and other matters examined in relation to it." From Nyerere's speech at the opening of University College, Dar es Salaam.

13. Bienen H: *Tanzania: Party Transformation and Economic Development.* Princeton, Princeton University Press, 1967, pp 77-78.

14. Hopkins, *op. cit.*

15. Act Number 60 of 1962.

16. As in October, 1966, when he dismissed 393 students who protested the National Service Act.

17. Report of Nyerere's remarks on a television program in the United Kingdom on January 20, 1966, in the *Standard* (Tanzania), Dar es Salaam, January 22, 1966.

18. For example, P. Mbogo, a former MP and an area commissioner immediately prior to his arrest.

19. Bennett G: "An Outline History of TANU," *Makerere Journal,* No. 7 (1963), pp 15-32.

20. There are 69 districts or areas and 20 regions. Sixty districts and 17 regions were created in 1962-63, by dividing and realigning the former nine provinces. The Union with Zanzibar added an additional three regions and nine areas. Each district has an area commissioner and each region a regional commissioner.

21. Another action to retain control over and support from the army was the appointment of Selemani Kitundu, a high party official, as a colonel and political commissar of the army. Kitundu continued as the regional commissioner of Dar es Salaam after his appointment in 1964 until 1967, when he took his army duties on a full-time basis.

22. As Friedland points out, the party has become "a focal institution, an institution which pervades and dominates all other institutions and society." Friedland WH: *The Evolution of Tanganyika's Political System.* Syracuse, Program of East African Studies, Syracuse University Occasional Paper No. 10, p 55. This description is at complete variance with Bienen's view that the country is undercentralized, with the center having little power to effect decisions of behavior at the local level and that national institutions, such as TANU, are "fragile." Bienen, op. cit., pp 12-14. The conflict of view is reconcilable if one considers that the first estimate is based on TANU's strength relative to other national organizations, while the second interpretation relates TANU's strength vis-á-vis the ability to effect change, especially of a developmental or integrative nature at the local level. In these terms, both assessments of TANU's strength are accurate.

23. See the *Nationalist,* October 24, 1966, and April 21, 1967. Most students were reenrolled for the term beginning in July, 1967.

24. "Dar es Salaam Election Survey," conducted by Marco Surveys in January, 1966, for Lionel Cliffe and James S. Coleman, whom I wish

to thank for allowing me to use material from the survey.

25. *The Nationalist,* February 6, 1967, p 8.

26. Two of these men lost their seats due to absence: Anangisye, who was in preventive detention, and Oscar Kambona, who fled the country in 1967. The seven others were Chogga, Kaneno, Masha, Kibuga, Bakampenja, Kassella-Bantu, and Mwakitwange. See *The Nationalist,* December 6, 10, and 31, 1968, p 1.

27. The Presidential Commission, in the *One-Party State Report,* op. cit., p 21, states: "We consider that TANU has every right to insist that members of Parliament remain loyal to the basic principles of the party. Subject to this, however, we believe that there should be complete freedom of discussion."

28. Sidney Verba has characterized these as "parochial-participant" cultures. Almond GA, Verba S: *The Civic Culture.* Princeton, Princeton University Press, 1963.

29. Huntington SP: *Political Order in Changing Societies.* New Haven, Yale University Press, 1963, pp 192-263.

30. Dahl RA, Lindbloom CE: *Politics, Economics, and Welfare.* New York, Harper and Brothers, 1953, especially pp 325-365.

31. See Foltz, op. cit.

32. Nyerere, "Democracy and the Party System," op. cit., pp 6-7.

33. *One-Party State Report,* op. cit., p 31.

34. A phrase used by one principal secretary.

35. Bienen, op. cit., passim.

36. Of course, the surprise announcement of nationalization may also be justified on grounds of economic strategy. A public debate might have caused detrimental reaction among the bankers and businessmen who were otherwise caught by surprise and were unable to respond defensively.

37. For a discussion of Nyerere's ideology, see Glickman H: "The Dilemmas of Political Theory in an African Context: The Ideology of Julius Nyerere," in Butler J, Castagno AA, eds: New York, Frederick A. Praeger, 1967, pp 195-223.

10

Political Opposition in Great Britain

Barbara N. McLennan
Temple University

Political opposition in Great Britain has, for a very long time, been merged in the public mind with a concept of party competition in an institutionalized two-party system. In Great Britain, the party in power establishes the government while the party that lost the last general election is euphemistically referred to as "Her Majesty's loyal opposition." The relationship of the two parties is aptly described by the traditional dictum "The government governs, the opposition criticizes."[1] The major functions of an opposition party are to raise questions, to be objectionable, and to hope for victory in the next general election. In Great Britain the party framework has been able to aggregate the basic demands of the general population so that large-scale social and political movements have not appeared outside the party system. Third parties have, for most of the 20th century, been very small. The important political opposition in Great Britain is voiced by politicians working within the major political parties; other groups in society pursue their demands by patronizing sympathetic politicians and not by establishing political groupings of their own.

The British political system rests on a stable legal and social basis. For over one hundred years Britain has had a mass electorate accepting the constitutional system which, while providing that there should be no formal limit to the power of a government with a parliamentary majority, still establishes the rights, privileges and duties of an accepted legitimate opposition. For this period the basic two-party framework has popularly been conceived along class lines, with each major party being viewed as theoretically representative of some major social class.[2]

* Since World War II the party system has continued in the traditional framework, but has undergone many important structural and strategic changes. Such factors as religion and regionalism are not now and for a long time have not been centrally important in British elections, but the status system upon which the British class structure has long been based has begun to erode. The postwar period has also seen the appearance of a governing Labour party with an effective popular and parliamentary majority. This is also a new event for Britain where the Conservative party has long been representative of a British elite ruling the country both socially and politically. All of these recent trends question the traditional interpretation of British politics as class-based.

The Social Basis of Party Strength

The consistency of the two-party framework in Britain is demonstrated by election returns since 1900 (Table 10.1). Except for the 1920s, when Labour supplanted the Liberals as the second major party, the two leading parties have attracted 90% or more of the vote between them.

As can be seen from Table 10.1, the Conservative party has been the only British party that can be described as a "major" party throughout the 20th century. It is also the only party ever to have received a majority of the popular vote in all this time. In the 70 years since 1900, Conservatives have participated in cabinets for more than 50 of those years; Conservatives have clearly dominated the government for more than 40 years. This record must be viewed in

Table 10.1: British General Elections, 1900-1966*

Parl.	Length of Parliament Yrs.	Mos.	Party in power	% of total vote won by party in power	% of vote held by major opposition party	MP's elected by party in power
1900-1906	5	1	Con.	51.1	44.6	402
1906-1910	3	9	Lib.	49.0	43.6	400
1910	—	9	Lib.	46.9	43.2	275
1910-1918	7	9	Coalition	Lib.-43.9; Tory-46.3		272; 272
1919-1922	3	8	(Coalition Unionist)	32.6		335
1922-1923	—	11	Con.	38.2	29.5	345
1923	—	9	Labour	30.5‡	38.1	191
1924-1929	4	5	Con.	48.3	33.0	419
1929-1931	2	3	National (Coalition)	Cons-38.2; Lab.-37.1		260; 288
1931-1935	3	11	National† (Cons. dom.)	67.0		554
1935-1945	9	6	Con.	53.7	37.9	432
1945-1950	4	6	Labour	47.8	39.8	393
1950-1951	1	7	Labour	46.1	43.5	315
1951-1955	3	6	Con.	48.0§	48.8	321
1955-1959	4	3	Con.	49.7	46.4	344
1959-1964	5	0	Con.	49.4	43.8	365
1964-1966	1	5	Labour	44.1	43.4	317
1966-1970	4	3	Labour	47.9	41.9	363
1970-			Con.	46.4	43.0	330

*ªTaken from Butler D, Freeman J: *British Political Facts, 1900-1967.* London, Macmillan Co., 1968, pp 141-144; and *British Record,* BIS, No 7, June 25, 1970, p 1.

†Conservatives dominated this goverment; Labour remained a major opposition.

‡Labour governed with liberal support.

§Labour received a higher popular vote, but fewer seats (48.8% of the vote, 295 seats).

conjunction with the fact that the Conservative party has visibly been the party of an upper class and has been controlled by individuals who have, in a sense, been trained to govern by the "best" schools and "best" families in the country. It has never been a party that had to establish itself, through electioneering techniques, as fit to govern. Since World War II, however, the Conservatives have lost this position of overriding dominance—the 25 years since 1945 have seen Labour in power for about 12 years, with the Tories in control for about 13—a roughly equal division.

Much has been written about the British phenomenon of the "working-class Tory,"[3] that laboring voter who, despite his occupational status, decides to vote Conservative rather than for the Labour party. This ability of the Conservative party to attract voters of all "classes" has variously been attributed to the deferential characteristics of British society—that is, the lower classes as much as the upper strata have presumably shared the belief that the aristocracy should govern—and via the Conservative party. Of course, it also is true that Conservative success with the working-class vote has reflected certain organizational failures and deep divisions within the British Labour movement. Nevertheless, over a long period of time the Conservative party has shown strength on a national scale from all classes at the polls, while its own leadership has characteristically been drawn generally from the uppermost segments of British society. The recruitment of Members of Parliament from the ranks of the privileged has up till the present continued to be a Conservative practice.

The sources of Labour party strength have been somewhat broadened since World War II, but most of Labour's strength has historically been and still is drawn from the working class; the Labour party today is still heavily dependent on the trade unions. The recent rise to majority party status for the Labour party seems to be associated with a statistical decline in working-class conservatism (the conversion of many working-class Liberals and Conservatives to Labour) in recent years and the ability of Labour to attract a working-class vote which in the past had been quite unpolitical, that is, unaffiliated with any party. The class alignment of both parties, however, seems to be aging, and new voters of different class backgrounds appear to be entering both major parties.[4]

As can be seen from Table 10.2, the Conservative party has consistently been represented by persons of greater property and higher educational attainment than has the Labour party. Also, the Conservatives have not, by the social characteristics of their parliamentary membership, represented the working class at all. In this respect the Conservative party has been remarkably consistent; the social description of the party in 1966 was very nearly identical to that of 1951 in all variables included in Table 10.2. This has occurred in the face of a marked trend in the Labour party parliamentary membership away from working-class individuals (a drop of 9%) and toward persons of university education (an increase of 10%). Thus if there have been changes in the British class structure,

Table 10.2: Social Characteristics of
Members of Parliament, 1951-1966*

Characteristics	Party	1951	1959	1966
University education	Lab.	41%	39%	51%
	Con.	65%	60%	67%
Working-class Occupation	Lab.	37%	35%	30%
	Con.	—	—	—
Professions or business	Lab.	44%	48%	52%
	Con.	77%	76%	75%
Median Age	Lab.	52	55	50
	Con.	47	48	48
Woman MP's	Lab.	11%	13%	19%
	Con.	6%	12%	7%

*Taken from Punnett RM; *British Government and Politics.* New York, W.W. Norton and Co., 1968, p 91; based on information in Butler DE: *The British General Election of 1951.* London, Macmillan, 1955; Butler DE, Rose R: *The British General Election of 1959.* London, Macmillan, 1960; and Butler DE, King A: *The British General Election of 1966.* London, Macmillan, 1966.

the Conservative party had not, by 1966, changed its selection process to account for these changes.

It may here be pointed out that the working class may be better served by having representatives in Parliament who have university degrees than by having only workers represent them. The change in recruitment patterns of Labour does not necessarily imply changes in policy; the consistency of Conservative party selection processes equally does not necessarily mean consistent views on domestic problems. Nevertheless, Labour made internal recruitment changes in the 1950s and showed substantially increased strength in the 1960s; the Conservatives have only since 1965 formally made any attempt to reorganize themselves for purposes of appealing to a broader and changing electorate.

British Party Organization Since World War II

The Labour party grew up in the early part of the 20th century as a coalition of socialist societies and the trade union movement. Structurally and theoretically there are more limitations on the power of the leadership in the Labour party than is true of the Tories. For example, a Labour leader must face reelection annually (in 1960 Gaitskell was opposed by Harold Wilson and in 1961 by Anthony Greenwood); such an occurrence until 1965 had no place in the Conservative party framework. Despite this, in practice Labour leaders have enjoyed greater security of tenure than have Conservative leaders.[5]

Today the trade unions are the most important element in the Labour party, accounting for five sixths of the party's membership and most of the party's funds. The National Executive Committee supervises the party outside Parliament and consists of 28 members (the leader, deputy leader, twelve trade union delegates, seven constituency delegates, five women, and a treasurer elected by the annual conference). Normally, the MP's have a small majority in the NEC, though trade-union votes have an influential position both here and in the Parliamentary Labour party (PL). Generally, the Labour party leader is able to maintain control over the NEC with the aid of union votes.[6]

Leadership and organization of the Conservative party has evolved over a long uninterrupted period and, like many other institutions in British politics, has become encrusted with tradition. In formal structure the party consists of three elements: (1) the Parliamentary party in both Houses of Parliament; (2) the Conservative and Unionist Association for each constituency; and (3) the Conservative and Unionist Central Office.[7] However, the most important and, indeed overriding institution in the party has been the party leader.

FIGURE I
ORGANIZATION OF THE BRITISH LABOUR PARTY

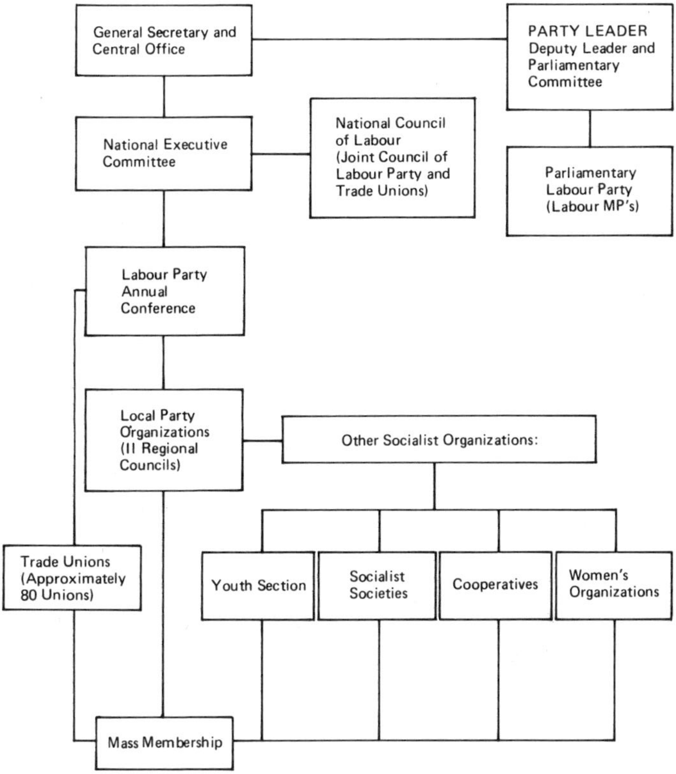

FIG. II

ORGANIZATION OF THE BRITISH CONSERVATIVE PARTY

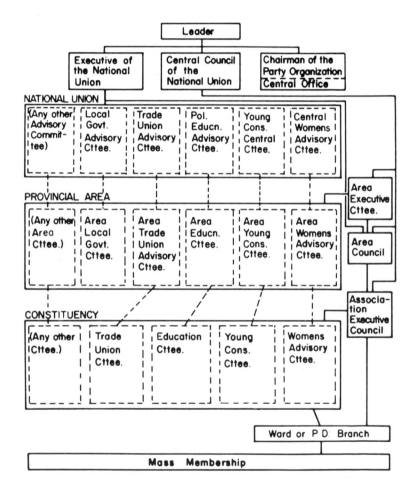

The Conservative party traditionally has vested enormous power in the leader. Once selected, he does not have to submit himself for reelection. He does not formally have to report to any party institution, either the National Union or the Parliament, and he is the final authority and interpreter of the party program.[8] As stated in a Conservative party document in 1949,

> At the head of the party there is the leader, sustained by the loyalty of the members of the party to whom he owes his position. . . . When the party is in office he is the main fountain and interpreter of policy and he is charged with the task of advising the Sovereign on appointments to the various offices in his cabinet and the remainder of the administration.[9]

The leader of the Conservative party, up till the reforms of 1965, was always the recognized leader of the party in the House of Commons and had attained this position through long experience in that body. The leader in this long period was always selected by acclamation without any formal balloting. In the early period of the party's history, frequently an individual was designated to be Prime Minister by the monarch and was only subsequently elected leader of the party. Of course, by then the choice of leader was obvious to all party members.[10]

In technical terms the party leader was historically selected at a meeting of the party's members in the House of Commons. In 1922, this procedure was broadened and Conservative Peers and prospective candidates were invited to participate in the selection of the leader. In 1937, the Executive Committee of the National Union was also invited to participate and in 1955 the National Liberal Peers, MP's, and candidates were also included.[11] In formal terms, the mass party thus selected the leader, but in practice the leader had already been co-opted by the tight elite that traditionally ran the party; new leaders were produced under the patronage of old leaders and the party meeting merely legitimized this previous selection process.

In the 1945-51 period of opposition, the Conservatives, led by Winston Churchill, maintained the traditional party structure and organization. Churchill, as leader, behaved in the accepted almost absolute manner and his choice of successor in 1955, Anthony Eden, was very much a personal choice concurred in by other members of the party at all levels. Churchill's leadership spanned a period of opposition and of government; under him no great changes occurred in terms of party personnel and structural organization. Party leadership, drawn from the wartime cabinet, was traditional in outlook and no great challenge to traditional decision-making processes occurred. The party gradually absorbed new members and made way for new leaders through basically similar recruitment procedures to previous times.

This situation was very different in the 1960s. The end of Conservative rule in 1963-64 was marked by the Profumo scandal, an event of extravagant proportions for the Tory leadership. This scandal, which called into question the integrity of certain Conservative members of subcabinet rank, coincided with the succession problem created by the retirement of Harold Macmillan. The government, considerably weakened according to the public opinion polls, resorted to its traditional tightly controlled selection processes. In 1963 the top leadership in the party selected Sir Alec Douglas-Home as Macmillan's successor in a private meeting closed to the press and the general public. Home was a peer and eligible to become prime minister by virtue of his seat in the House of Lords. He had never stood for popular election. His government generally lacked popular support and found it necessary to avoid calling the general election until the legal maximum limit—the only five-year Parliament since the World War I Coalition government. The Conservatives lost the ensuing election, though by a small margin.

The selection of Home and the loss in the 1964 election called the traditional organization into question and in 1965 after the large Labour victory in the General Election a new procedure was adopted to choose Home's successor. Home was instrumental in bringing about the changes, the persons eligible to vote for leader remained the same—Conservative MP's, Conservative Peers, candidates and members of the National Executive Committee of the National Union—only this time, the process of election was fully publicized at the Parliamentary party level.[12] In the first such election Edward Heath defeated Reginald Maudling; Heath became leader and Maudling deputy leader. Other changes accomplished at this time also affected Conservative policy and election strategy.

Party Policy and Party Discipline

The shift in Tory leadership selection procedure in 1965 was accompanied by attempts to broaden the base of the party in other ways. The party determined to focus on the young and the new professional groups that had emerged as important voting blocs in the 1950s. Rather than focusing attention on the aristocratic elements within its traditional supporters, the new strategy emphasized youth and expertise. This was an attempt to advantageously distinguish the Conservatives from old-line Labour party men who remained in public view; the average age of Labour party MP's has consistently been older than the Conservatives[13] and the Tories wished to point up and emphasize this difference.

In addition, the Conservatives established new groups of experts to help focus the party program in specialized areas. A clear choice of strategy was made—no longer would campaigns be dominated by electioneering slogans but by specific proposals. The new specialists were supposed "to systemize and sharpen opposition action on particular measures" (notably the finance, steel, and transport bills).[14] The new strategy also entailed the upgrading of salaries of professional party agents to a higher minimum and the party set a goal of 20% as an increase in the membership of the young Conservatives.[15]

Strategies of Opposition in Postwar British Politics

Structural changes in the party framework were also accompanied by a transformation in electioneering techniques as well as in policy and rhetoric. The period from 1945 to the present can be divided into three obvious periods: (1) Labour government, 1945-51; (2) Conservative government, 1951-64; (3) Labour government, 1964-70. The number of years Labour has been in office has been almost the same as the Conservatives, but the Conservatives have had two distinct periods of opposition. In all three periods, the role of the opposition was handled differently and can be assessed by analysis of activity in the total political system and changes in party policy and party cohesion.

Opposition in the First Postwar Labour Period, 1945-51: The Traditional Opposition

Under Churchill the Conservatives behaved as a traditional opposition in the traditional cabinet system; if the government governed and the opposition criticized, the Conservative opposition of 1945-51 took its criticisms very seriously. Rhetoric in this period was characterized by vagueness, slogan-mongering, name-calling, and general denunciation of both Labour's competence and motivations. There were relatively few proposals of a specific nature—very few alternatives were offered by government policy. Individual Labour party leaders were singled out by name for alleged incompetence, and the government was uniformly referred to most contemptuously as the "Socialist party."

In his general election campaign of 1945 Churchill barely noticed the Labour party as a contender. Focusing on Britain's success in surviving World War II, he made himself virtually the only Conservative party election plank and his appeal for votes seemed to merge with an appeal to patriotism. Labour was regarded as an untried entity, relying on a body of foreign alien ideology. The war became the main subject for debate, and Labour's contribution to the wartime coalition was not seriously mentioned. This was in contrast to Labour's approach in that election.

Both parties debated the same essential difficulties, but Labour was far more specific about its proposed methods. For example, with respect to employment and jobs, Churchill, in traditional political style, stated:

> To find plenty of work with individual liberty to choose one's job, free enterprise must be given the chance and the encouragement to plan ahead. Confidence in sound government—mutual cooperation between industry and the State, rather than control by the State—a lightening of the burdens of excessive taxation—these are the first essentials.[16]

In his major policy speech, Churchill did not elaborate on the above goal in any way, while Labour outlined a drastic replanning policy which would involve the establishment of a National Investment Board, nationalization of the Bank of England, and government control over the location of new factories.[17] Discussion of industrial policy took the same form—Churchill advocating a piecemeal, not terribly specific approach, and intentionally contrasting this with Labour party policy:

> As against the advocates of State ownership and control, we stand for the fullest opportunity for go and push in all ranks throughout the whole nation. This quality is part of the genius of the British people, who mean to be free to use their own judgment and never intend to be State serfs, nor always to wait for official orders before they can act.[18]

In the face of these remarks, Labour was specifically indicting the inefficiency of various industries, advocating the nationalization of fuel and power, inland transport, and iron and steel, and calling for public supervision of monopolies, the export trade, and price controls.[19] Labour linked these policies to an attempt to increase productive efficiency in a full employment economy, the stated goals of both parties. Labour in 1945 openly avowed its socialism and supported specific programs in accordance with the stated socialist ideals. Labour defeated the Conservatives easily using this tactic. (See Table 10.1.)

The remarkable feature of the 1945-50 period of Conservative opposition was the degree of cohesion and unity among the Conservatives compared to the dissension of the Labour party. The 1945 election gave Labour an overwhelming majority ensuring a workable Parliament even with the presence of rebellions over certain issues. The result was a great number of public Labour revolts, especially over foreign policy issues, compared to very few among the Conservative party. Although some changes were made in the Conservative program, no reformist group emerged among the Tories until 1950 (the One Nation group) and in all this time there were no public revolts from any of the 15 Conservative backbench committees.[20]

In 1950 a general election was held leaving the Labour party with a small majority of only five seats. Conservatives were very cohesive and united in this Parliament in the hopes of soon regaining government control. Labour had much dissension again (also mostly over foreign issues), but Attlee was still able to determine the date of dissolution.[21]

The 1950-51 Parliament found the Conservatives in opposition, and again behaving in a very traditional manner. They continued to denounce Labour in general ideological language while remaining relatively unspecific about their own plans. In fact, they admitted this openly and denounced the Socialists for trying to overplan and overorganize the state. In 1951, the Conservatives promised to undo much of the nationalization carried out by Labour and refused to issue any doctrinaire remarks explaining their purpose. Churchill openly stated, "We seek to proclaim a theme, rather than write a prospectus,"[22] and he rather obviously regarded the "socialist" opposition with contempt. As he phrased it:

We must free ourselves from our impediments. Of all impediments the class war is the worst. At the time when a growing measure of national unity is more than ever necessary, the Socialist party hope to gain another base of power by fomenting class hatred and appealing to moods of greed and envy.

Labour responded with a defense of the government's domestic record and attacked the Conservatives as capitalistic, imperialistic, exploitative and insensitive to the aims of the working class. Labour attacked the Tories as being Victorian in their colonial outlook and in favor of privilege at home. Conjuring up images of the workhouse and the Poor Law, Labour proclaimed, "The Tories with their dark past, full of bitter memories for so many of our people, promise no light for the future. They would take us backward into poverty and insecurity at home and grave perils abroad."[23]

Labour's electoral rhetoric was more all-encompassing, more ideological, and more provocative than was that of the Tories. By a rare electoral accident the Conservatives won the electoral victory, but lost the popular vote (see Table 10.1), so that it is difficult to assess the relative success of the two electoral strategies in this period. In any event, a traditional Conservative party was returned to power and Labour, the perennial opposition, was removed from office. Throughout the 1950s the roles remained intact—the Conservatives, a traditional ruling upper class party and Labour, a vocal ideological opposition.

Labour in Opposition, 1951-64

No massive changes occurred in British political strategy or organization in this period, despite important political crises such as the Suez affair. The Conservatives once more became the government and Labour, the perennial loser, once more became the opposition. Conservative election rhetoric continued to be vague and unspecific about future aims and to barely notice (except with contempt) the opposition, still

319

referring to them as the "socialists." The Tories continued to proclaim their firm faith in British initiative and the free enterprise system, blaming the "socialists" for favoring overcontrol and overplanning. They also stressed their achievement of prosperity and rising income. The Tories were for rising production, more housing, strengthened sterling and all this with lower taxation. Viscount Hailsham, chairman of the Conservative party organization, neatly summarized the party's view of its place in this system in 1958:

> There lies an even greater prize to be won than the mere tactical defeat of the Labour party. I do not believe that socialism in this country can survive a third consecutive defeat. I do not mean to suggest that the Labour party would disappear, or even that it would necessarily stop calling itself the Socialist party; but the evil fatuous spectre of democratic socialism—that contradiction in terms which has dominated and befogged the political thinking of 30 years—would have finally been laid to rest. The policy of nationalization, high taxation and controls would have virtually no adherents left, and with them too, I believe, would have gone the inverted snobbery of class consciousness, the attacks on liberty, opportunity and freedom, the persecution complexes of the maladjusted who continue to consider themselves under-privileged mainly because they are unsuccessful, years after privilege has been abolished; the whole concatenation of perverse thinking which leads men—and, in the light of recent events, I must add women—to denigrate British statesmanship, British industry, British enterprise, British imperial achievement, even British troops under fire whenever they are attacked by somebody else.[24]

The Labour party in opposition was torn apart by ideological dissension between Bevanites and the party leadership, again mostly over foreign policy issues. A cohesive rebel group, lead by Aneurin Bevan, challenged Attlee (and later Gaitskell) and caused about 30 major public rebellions. Bevan gradually lost much support with the Labour rank and file in his bid for party leadership and many critics believed that he sought publicity more than principle in his party activities.

At any rate, observers of the Labour party in the 1950s could argue that it actually was a party within a party (Labour, indeed, passed a regulation forbidding this), and that Bevan was a great Tory electoral asset. The Labour party voted to withdraw the whip from Bevan before the 1955 general election, but Bevan remained an independent for only 44 days before reapplying and pledging party unity.

Labour recognized that internal dissension had been one of the main causes of electoral defeat in 1955 and Gaitskell and Bevan made a serious attempt to reconcile their differences. Gaitskell defeated Bevan in the election for party leader, but Bevan accepted a position as shadow Colonial Secretary. The substance of the Bevanite dispute continued till Bevan's death, however, and periodically reemerged over certain specific issues. Indeed, the remnants of pacifist-neutralist left wing still are important in the Labour party today. In the early 1960s disputes became very heated and several rebels were expelled from the PLP; only with the selection of Harold Wilson as Leader (ostensibly a member of the left wing) did Labour unity reemerge in a form comparable to that of 1945.[25]

The Conservatives in this period maintained a greater sense of discipline and cohesion than did Labour (and more than Labour had when it was in power), and with much less obvious machinery for handling dissent than did Labour. No Tory was expelled from the party in this period, although there were a greater number of party disputes than in previous days. The Conservatives continually sought compromise over party issues; when Eden faced criticism over Suez he resigned rather than provoke a party power struggle. Eight Tory MP's resigned the whip over Suez and Sir David Robertson left the party to become an independent over policy toward the Scottish highlands.[26] The dissidents (except Robertson) all returned to the party after Eden's resignation. Similarly, there were a number of serious Tory rebellions over the Profumo scandal, and some important controversies over Home's succession (two former ministers,

Iain Mcleod and Enoch Powell, refused to serve in Home's cabinet) but the party was not torn into organized competing factions as was Labour.[27]

Table 10.3: Party Revolts, 1945-1964*

| | Domestic Revolts | | Foreign Affairs & Defenses | |
	Labour	Conservative	Labour	Conservative
1945-50	8	—	31	—
1951-55	1	4	14	2
1955-59	1	13	8	8
1959-64	0	15	13	6

*Adapted from Jackson RJ: *Rebels and Whips,* op. cit.

The Conservatives in Opposition, 1964-70

The 1964 election resulted in a small plurality for Labour, Wilson depending on the votes of the small Liberal party for his parliamentary majority. In 1965 he called a general election and was able to win a substantial victory for his party both in terms of popular vote and parliamentary majority.

The Labour victory of 1965 was of great proportions and had the effect of causing the first major restructuring of the Conservative party internally as well as changing the manner in which the parliamentary leader would be selected. The selection of Edward Heath as party leader and internal party reorganization also was accompanied by a basic shift in electoral strategy and rhetoric—a fundamental attempt to make the party more attractive to voters who did not identify strongly with the traditional class system. These were the young who did not recall the depression and the war and who were generally better educated and more prosperous than their elders.

While the party continued to vie with the "socialists"[28] it no longer couched its appeal in the flamboyant cliches of the

322

1940s and 1950s. The first priority had been established as restoring the British economy. The general outline of party policy was similar to the past—cut taxes, increase savings, cut waste, encourage enterprise—but within these areas specific administrative changes were proposed. For example, the party developed several prototype tax packages by testing (via computer) their effects on 22 different types of goods and services and 28 different representative households. This was described by Iain Macleod at the Blackpool conference in 1968:

> . . . we have examined 48 different tax changes. We have looked at four different income-tax systems and a number of different company tax systems. For each of these different packages we have estimated their effects on the income and expenditure of 28 different representative households, ranging from the single family pensioner to the married couple with the wife earning and a joint income of £4,000 a year.
>
> We have looked at each family's expenditure broken down into 22 different headings. . . . We have processed the whole thing on a computer using a model of the economy . . . we are at present analyzing no fewer than 50,000 separate results.[29]

Similar description was given of proposed savings schemes, new trade union legislation, and other domestic proposals. A reorganization of the secondary schools to give more authority to local bodies was proposed, as were specific reforms in the social services—with detailed reforms in housing, pensions, and family allowances spelled out.[30]

Electoral Trends and the General Election of 1970

The 1970 general election constituted an upset in the predictions of pollsters, but confirmed many general trends that have appeared in postwar British politics. Again the two leading parties were quite close—less than four percentage points apart (46.4 to 43)—and accounted for about 90% of the total votes cast. The Liberal party received only 7.4% and all other small parties received 3.2% combined. These other parties included the various nationalist parties and the British Communist party.[31] This occurred in spite of the apparent increase in regional sentiment, greater organizational efforts of regional parties,[32] voter disapproval of specific government economic policies, and general voter apathy and disinterest in the two major parties' leading candidates. Voters either stayed with the established parties or did not vote: they showed no marked shift either to smaller parties or to extraparty movements.

The 1970 general election centered about a series of issues—notably, the economy, which had showed some signs of recovery immediately prior to the election; the racial (or "immigration") issue raised by Enoch Powell in a series of inflammatory speeches; and the leading candidates. Pollsters predicted a Lahbour victory from anywhere between 2 to 8.7 percentage points, but a national swing toward the Conservatives became evident in the days immediately prior to the voting. The victory was of respectable size, but not of overwhelming proportions by British standards. The swing, however, was quite substantial and completely unexpected by professional pollsters.[33]

In retrospect the 1970 election confirmed more general trends in Britain than it questioned. Opposition in Britain is still vested, basically, in a single party. Regional problems such as the religious question in Northern Ireland, the race question, or economic difficulties in Scotland and Wales (and parts of England) have not provided substantial momentum for either minor parties or extraparty movements. This has occurred in spite of the fact that voters generally appeared quite apathetic about the established parties.

Prime Minister Wilson and his Labour party appeared to be thoroughly complacent about their presumed lead and the Labour campaign was generally considered dull and overconfident. The Conservative swing was nationwide, particularly in the English industrial midlands where the immigrant population is now as high as 10%.[34] This implies that the

324

racial issue was a factor in the Tory victory. Nevertheless, the Conservative campaign was not one calculated to win over many new voters. Mr. Heath was, as he has been in the past, aloof and shy and a rather poor speaker. His campaign was characterized by vocal criticism from within his own party of his evident inability to lead the party in the rhetoric required by a British election campaign. Heath criticized Wilson's style of government but steered clear of old-fashioned ideological indictments of Labour and "socialism." Mr. Heath's victory was therefore a negative one—he was elected because many Labour voters deserted their party or did not vote.

Britain thus remains with an extraordinarily stable alignment—a governing party with just less than half the vote, confronted by an opposition very close in electoral strength to the Government. Labour is the only national opposition and its electoral position is such that a slight swing in voter sentiment could again bring it to power. The class basis of the parties is still there, but continues to erode. Labour voters, presumably working-class persons critical of Wilson's attempt to legislate against wildcat strikes after his government had frozen wages (also at the expense of union collective bargaining power), contributed to Labour's defeat. Mr. Heath did not win over these voters but his criticism of general economic policy did attract moderate voters who simply were not convinced that Labour's domestic policy would be successful in the long run. This vote was not attracted by class or ideology, but by the policies of the day. British opposition therefore remains party opposition, but the positions and sentiments of the major parties appear to be in a state of flux.

Notes

1. For a detailed discussion of the traditional British concept of opposition see Jennings I: *Cabinet Government*. Cambridge, at the University Press, 1965, Ch XV.

2. Potter A: "Great Britain: Opposition with a Capital 'O'," in

325

Dahl RA, ed: *Political Opposition in Western Democracies*. New Haven, Yale University Press, 1966, Ch 1.

3. See McKenzie RT, Silver A: "Conservatism, Industrialism and the Working Class Tory in England," in Rose R: *Studies in British Politics*. London, Macmillan Co., 1966, pp 21-33.

4. Butler D, Stokes D: *Political Change in Britain*. New York, St. Martin's Press, 1969, Ch 4, 5, 11.

5. Punnett RM: *British Government and Politics*. New York, W.W. Norton & Co., 1968, Ch 4. The Labour party had a total of only nine party leaders before Wilson: Keir Hardie, Arthur Henderson (twice), G.N. Barnes, Ramsay McDonald (twice), W. Adamson, J. R. Clynes, George Lansburg, Clement Attlee, and Hugh Gaitskell. Attlee was unopposed for 20 years.

6. Ibid.

7. *The Party Organization*. Westminster, Conservative and Unionist Central Office, August, 1964, p 3.

8. McKenzie RT: *British Political Parties*. New York, Praeger, 1963, p 21.

9. *Interim and Final Reports of the Committee on Party Organization, 1948 and 1949*. Westminster, Conservative Central Office, 1949, p 32.

10. Ibid., pp 32-33.

11. *The Party Organization*, op. cit., p 5.

12. "Some Recent Developments," Conservative and Unionist Party, 20-2-68 (mimeo), p 1.

13. See Table 2.

14. "Some Recent Developments," op. cit., p 1.

15. *Ibid.,* p 2.

16. *Mr. Churchill's Declaration of Policy to the Electors*. London, Conservative and Unionist Central Office, 1945, p 5.

17. *Let Us Face the Future: A Declaration of Labour Policy for the Consideration of the Nation*. London, The Labour Party, 1945, pp 4-5.

18. *Mr. Churchill's Declaration*, op. cit., p 12.

19. *Let Us Face the Future*, op. cit., pp 6-7.

20. Jackson RJ: *Rebels and Whips*. New York, St. Martin's Press, 1968, Ch 3. Jackson notes that the Conservatives were more secretive than Labour over internal party dissension in this period. The Tory leadership, when the Conservatives governed the country, were able to informally persuade backbenchers to abstain on issues over which they disagreed with the leadership where Labour made much greater use of written regulations and the whip.

21. Ibid., Ch 4.

22. *The Manifesto of the Conservative and Unionist Party*. London, Conservative and Unionist Central Office, 1951, p 3.

23. *Labour Party Election Manifesto.* London, Labour Party, 1951, p 2.

24. Quoted in "Conservative Conference at Blackpool," *Notes on Current Politics.* London, Conservative and Unionist Central Office, October 27, 1958, pp 38-39.

25. Jackson, op. cit., Ch 6, 7.

26. Ibid., p 151.

27. Ibid., Ch 7.

28. See, for example, Heath's declaration *Make Life Better.* London, Conservative Central Office, 1968.

29. "Conservative Conference and Policy," *Notes on Current Politics.* London, Conservative Central Office, October 28, 1968, pp. 307-308.

30. Ibid., and *Notes on Current Politics.* London, Conservative Central Office, November 3, 1969.

31. *British Record,* op. cit., pp 1, 2.

32. Schwarz JE: "The Scottish National Party: Nonviolent Separatism and Theories of Violence." *World Politics,* July 1970, pp 496-517. Some preelection polls showed that the Scottish Nationalists had from 30-40% of the vote in Scotland.

33. Butler and Stokes havyestimated the mean national swing in British elections between 1950 and 1966 as varying between 0.7% and 3.5%; the standard deviation of swing over the same period varied from 1.4 to 2.4%. The swing in the 1970 election falls within this range again, even though it was not predicted. See Butler and Stokes, op. cit., p 137.

34. Watt D: "How it Happened in Britain," analysis by the political editor of *The Financial Times of London* appearing in the *Washington Post,* June 23, 1970, p 18.

327

11

Political Opposition in the Soviet Union

Erik P. Hoffmann
State University of New York, Albany

Political opposition is a difficult phenomenon to study. It is also a difficult concept to define. In the politics of one-party states, both of these problems are compounded. Who are the "oppositionists"? What are their purposes? What kinds of change do they desire? By what means do they try to implement their programs or beliefs? Indeed, since "Most political actions are deliberately aimed at change," or resistance to change, must one consider all such activities political opposition?[1] If not, what *are* the basic differences between oppositional and nonoppositional activities? How can one fruitfully conceptualize and study political opposition in authoritarian systems? Careful distinctions clearly have to be made. For if they are not, the term "opposition" will refer not only to the petitions of dissident Soviet intellectuals and dissatisfied ethnic, religious, economic, and professional groups, but also to the actions of countless officials in the central and regional Communist party and government bureaucracies, including even members of the Politburo and Central Committee.

Perhaps the best way to begin is to note the close relationship between political opposition and political change. Citizens who oppose certain practices and policies of their government want to see changes brought about. The questions "opposition to what?" and "change of what?" are virtually identical. Likewise, the questions "opposition *for* what?" and "change *for* what?" are basically the same. To be sure, those who strongly oppose their own political system sometimes have few concrete ideas about what kind of political order they would like to see replace the old, let alone specific plans for transforming the existing system into the desired one. Oppositionists' purposes may not be clearly formulated, their actions may not reflect their beliefs, and their activities may not achieve their aims. Sometimes opposition groups seek to resist imminent changes in government policy or to obstruct the implementation of decisions already made. But, in most general terms, oppositionists act to change important characteristics of their government's conduct, or hold the belief that major changes should be made. The researcher, then, must identify and analyze different types of change desired and, on this basis, rather arbitrarily define and distinguish among oppositional and nonoppositional activities.

Professor H. Gordon Skilling has made an important effort to conceptualize political opposition in one-party states. Skilling suggests that four main types of opposition are likely to be found in the Soviet Union and in the Communist states of Eastern Europe: "integral opposition," "factional opposition," "fundamental opposition," and "specific opposition."[2] In defining these terms, Skilling does not explicitly link the concepts of opposition and change. But, in essence, "integral opposition" consists of efforts, organized and unorganized, and desires, acted upon or passively held, to alter major structural and operational characteristics of the Soviet political system. Characteristics of crucial importance at the present time include the predominant political leadership role of the Communist party (CPSU), the tremendous influence exercised *within* the party by the approximately 150,000 professional politicians of the central and regional CPSU apparatuses, the party's numerous privileged relationships with other institutions in Soviet society, and, generally speaking, the established procedures and practices by which national policy is formulated, carried out, and legitimized. Skilling emphasizes that integral opposition may be expressed not only by overt disloyalty to the existing system or violent attempts to overthrow the Soviet "Establishment," but also "in alienation from the established order and in emotional or intellectual resistance to it, as for instance in a-political attitudes of a part of the youth, 'underground' creations of writers or painters, or the hostility of a national or regional sub-culture."[3] In short, people who feel or express integral opposition desire not only major changes in government policy, but also significant changes in the processes or institutional arrangements by which national policy is made, in the ways political leaders are recruited and selected, and in the government's most basic values, goals, and preferences.

"Factional opposition" consists of attempts to oust or discredit key policy-makers—that is, to change the top decision-making personnel of the government. Conflicts of this kind in one-party states usually take place at the highest levels of the ruling party. Important officials of other institutions, sometimes the army or secret police leadership, may play a decisive role in these intraparty struggles for position and power. The important point is that factional opposition "does not represent opposition to the communist system as such, and does not always involve even basic differences of view concerning public policies."[4] In the Soviet leadership conflicts of the 1920s and 1950s, for example, significant policy and factional disputes were closely intertwined. However, both Stalin and Khrushchev seem to have skillfully disguised many of their real policy preferences until they had accumulated sufficient power, relative to that of rival political leaders, to initiate major new programs they favored.

"Fundamental opposition" refers to disaffection with an entire set of official programs or policies along a wide front of issues. Groups and individuals expressing this opposition usually work to change important priorities of the govern-

331

ment but not to replace basic institutions. A government's priorities are clearly revealed in its national budget, in key resource allocation decisions, and in the role of the state of the economy. Priorities are also revealed in fundamental decisions concerning governmental authority and individual freedom, the role of law in society, the relationship of church and state, civil-military relations, and official policy toward ethnic, religious, and other "minority" groups (for example, the poor, ill, and aged). Briefly stated, fundamental oppositionists do not strive to change the existing governmental structure, the processes of decision-making, or to oust the chief political decision-makers; instead, their purpose is to induce incumbent political leaders to initiate major changes in the formulation and implementation of basic public policy, both domestic and foreign.

"Specific opposition" is directed toward individual policies, not toward whole clusters of policies or toward the national government's policy-making procedures or leading personnel. Opposition may be expressed toward present policies or toward policy alternatives under consideration. Communist governments, in particular instances or on an ongoing basis, encourage specific opposition on some important issues. In other words, party leaders publicly and privately solicit diverse recommendations from middle-level party officials, government bureaucrats, economists, scientists, military officers, factory managers, collective farm chairmen, and others. Even questions of such crucial importance as the proper role of the Communist party in the country's present state of economic development have been debated and discussed at length in the pages of *Pravda*. Professional and party journals and newspapers provide a public forum for much of this "loyal" opposition to specific policies. Authorized criticism and public debate take place within certain limits, however, and restrictions on discussion are eased or tightened, sometimes very abruptly, at the behest of party leaders. National, regional, and local officials also receive unsolicited, as well as solicited, advice. Specific opposition, especially of the unsolicited variety, cannot always be easily controlled, and objections to individual policies are sometimes so strenuously pursued that they may constitute, or the government may choose to treat them as, fundamental or even integral opposition.

This last observation illustrates that not all oppositional activities in the Soviet Union can be easily pigeonholed into one of our four categories of political opposition. Do efforts to achieve greater intraparty democracy (less concentration of power at the highest levels of the party) constitute integral, factional, or fundamental opposition? Do attempts to ease emigration and foreign travel restrictions on Soviet citizens constitute specific, fundamental, or possibly even integral opposition? Clearly the judgment of the researcher is crucial. Also critical is "the changing context of political action,"[5] to borrow Skilling's apt phrase. For what Soviet citizens intend to be and what party leaders regard as specific, fundamental, or integral opposition have not only differed from one another on many occasions, but both mass and elite intentions and perceptions have varied considerably over time. The very same acts, in different political contexts and periods of time, may constitute quite different kinds of political opposition (for example, Khrushchev approved publication of Alexander Solzhenitsyn's *One Day in the Life of Ivan Denisovich*, but it is most unlikely that a book on the labor camp theme could be published in the Soviet Union today). Furthermore, some oppositional activities may gradually become transformed into qualitatively different kinds of opposition in essentially the same political context. A classic example is the change from fundamental to integral opposition by some of the 19th-century Russian intelligentsia, who, in the 1850s, hoped that Alexander II would become a "socialist czar," a "crowned revolutionary," but who, in the 1860s, at precisely the time that the czar began to implement a series of major reforms, launched an underground movement to overthrow completely the Romanov dynasty and to destroy the entire czarist bureaucracy.[6] Finally, it must be emphasized that in this study the researcher assumes full responsibility for the categorization of particular statements and actions as "integral," "factional," "fundamental," or "specific opposition." No attempt has been made to categorize oppositionist activities according to the underlying *motives* of the dissidents themselves or the ways Soviet leaders *perceive* these activities.

Our classificatory scheme, then, is a point of departure. It is a good starting point, however, because it focuses attention on types of political behavior, not on groups or institutions that allegedly possess common interests or viewpoints. The latter approach usually assumes *a priori*, or on the basis of limited empirical evidence, that members of certain groups do in fact share common political interests, values, opinions, or attitudes. The present approach leaves open the very real possibility that members of the same age, occupational, economic, ethnic, or religious group may have quite different goals and beliefs, and that members of diverse groups may possess basically similar political outlooks. Indeed, in the Soviet Union today major types of political opposition are not expressed exclusively by people of similar background or by members of the same groups or institutions. Conversely, several kinds of opposition are sometimes articulated by the same person or by members of seemingly homogeneous and cohesive groups. To identify briefly the nature, sources, and extent of political opposition in contemporary Soviet society is the chief purpose of this chapter. Attention will be focused mainly on the very significant developments that have taken place in the growing Soviet dissent movement since the mid-1960s.

To recapitulate: (1) integral opposition consists of attempts to change the present system of national policy-making or deep-seated dissatisfaction with the established political order; (2) factional opposition consists of attempts to change key national and regional policy-makers; (3) fundamental opposition consists of attempts to change the major programs and priorities of the government (through the existing political institutions and with the present political leaders); (4) specific opposition consists of attempts to change individual government policies (through the existing political institutions, with the present political leaders, and without altering the government's major programs and priorities).

Integral Opposition

Let us begin by attempting to assess, in a very general way, the extent of integral opposition in the Soviet Union today. What strikes one immediately is the apparent *lack* of integral opposition. There is, to be sure, a growing underground, unauthorized, "self-published" (*samizdat*) dissent literature, which sprang up in the late 1950s and has expanded tremendously in volume and intensity since the mid and late 1960s. Probably the most important of these unofficial publications is the *Chronicle of Current Events*, since 1968 a more or less bimonthly journal or newsletter devoted mainly to disseminating accurate up-to-date information about the whereabouts, experiences, detentions, dismissals, arrests, and trials of Soviet dissenters.

However, a meticulous analysis of over 500 *samizdat* documents revealed a surprisingly few number of demands that might be termed "integral opposition."[7] Some demands for far-reaching changes have appeared in recent years, to be sure. Among the sweeping changes Soviet citizens have recommended are establishment of a multiparty system; creation of separate legislative, executive, and judicial branches of government at the national, republic, and local levels—all to be independent of Communist party control; determination, by popular referendum in each republic, of the respective spheres of jurisdiction and responsibilities of that republic and of the national government; democratic elections of party officials—with more than one candidate for each office, with candidates nominated by a fixed number of constituents (not by higher party organs), and with all candidates given equal access to the mass media to present their views on current issues to the electorate; affirmation of the inviolable rights of the individual and elimination of the "conditional" or "relative" nature of these rights as guaranteed by present Soviet law—especially abrogation of the opening proviso of Article 125 of the Soviet Constitution, which, leaving so very much open to the interpretation of party leaders, reads: "In conformity with the interests of the working people, and in order to strengthen the socialist system, the citizens of the USSR are guaranteed by law: (a) freedom of speech; (b) freedom of the press; (c) freedom of assembly, including the holding of mass meetings; (d) freedom of street processions and demonstrations."[8] All of these are examples of integral opposition.

How many Soviet citizens support demands of this kind we simply do not know. Dissidents themselves disagree. But demands of this magnitude have been openly expressed by only a handful of people and infrequently at that. Furthermore, with very few exceptions, these recommendations have been submitted by citizens who insist on their profound loyalty to the Soviet Union, to socialism, and to the goal of creating a just and prosperous Communist society. Patriotism and faith in socialism do not preclude integral opposition however. In some instances, loyalty to party, country, and social system may have been expressed primarily in the interests of political expedience—that is, to avoid possible reprisals. But even those dissidents who have expressed integral opposition to the present Soviet system— for example, those few who have overtly repudiated or challenged the privileged leadership role of the Communist party apparatus—have nonetheless displayed a strong pro-socialist and patriotic strain. To date the growing "civil rights movement" in the USSR is not in any significant sense anti-Soviet, procapitalist, or "counterrevolutionary." On the contrary, the petitions and actions of most Soviet dissenters reveal a considerable degree of idealism and human-

336

itarianism—a desire to motivate and mobilize others through exemplary behavior, a sense of personal responsibility to put forward constructive social and political criticism, and a deep-seated belief in the desirability and possibility of bringing about, through nonviolent means and *through the existing political institutions*, significant spiritual and material changes in Soviet society.

Consider, for example, a major dissent manifesto—*Progress, Coexistence and Intellectual Freedom*, by the internationally renowned nuclear physicist Andrei D. Sakharov.[9] Sakharov's famous document expresses some integral opposition. He declares, for example, in a devastating criticism of Marxist-Leninist ideas on class conflict and ideological struggle, that "any action increasing the division of mankind, any preaching of the incompatibility of world ideologies and nations is madness and a crime." There is also the statement that "the capitalist mode of production" does not lead an economy "into a blind alley," is not obviously inferior to socialism in labor productivity, and does not necessarily lead to the "absolute improverishment of the working class"; the suggestion that leading party officials sometimes place their own "caste interests" before "the genuine interests of the working class as a whole and the genuine interests of progress"; the claim that major errors in national policy are "inevitable" when crucial decisions are made by closed circles of political leaders; the affirmation that "fresh and deep ideas . . . can arise only in discussion, in the face of objections, only if there is a potential possibility of expressing not only true, but also dubious ideas"; the recommendation that international economic sanctions and United Nations military forces be employed to safeguard the civil liberties of peoples, Communist and non-Communist, whose liberties are jeopardized by their government's actions; the hope that a world government will evolve from the increasing cooperation between the United States and USSR; and others.

Nonetheless, Sakharov's views on controversial issues such

as the "convergence" of the Soviet and American systems and the development of a Soviet multiparty state are less radical than commonly recognized. Sakharov forecasts that the one-party regimes in some socialist countries, including the Soviet Union, may soon undergo significant changes. But he explicitly states that he does not consider a multiparty government to be "an essential stage in the development of the socialist system or, even less, a panacea for all ills." Also, in reference to the changing *internal* characteristics of the Russian and American political systems, he realistically contends that "both capitalism and socialism are capable of long-term development, borrowing positive elements from each other, and actually coming closer to each other in a number of essential aspects." Still less controversial is Sakharov's insistence that in *international* affairs the mutual interests of the two superpowers are becoming increasingly similar—that is, Sakharov believes that the opportunities and necessity for Soviet-American cooperation are becoming greater and more urgent. This central thesis—surely not an expression of integral opposition—is clearly manifested in Sakharov's vision of a massive, coordinated Russian-American campaign to reduce hunger, disease, pollution, overpopulation, and the threat of nuclear war in the world today.

Sakharov's strongly avowed preference for "revolution from above," for major reforms to be brought about through existing governmental institutions, is clearly articulated in a letter he and two other important Soviet intellectuals recently addressed to the highest party and government leaders:

> . . . first, at the present time it is a matter of urgent necessity to carry through a number of measures directed toward the further democratization of public life in the country . . .
>
> Second, democratization would further the preservation and consolidation of the Soviet socialist system, the socialist economic structure, our social and cultural achievements and the socialist ideology.
>
> Democratization implemented under the aegis of the CPSU in

cooperation with all sections of society would preserve and consolidate the leading role of the party in the economic, political, and cultural life of society.

Last, democratization should be gradual in order to avoid possible complications and setbacks.[10]

Forceful recommendations of this kind are a classic illustration of fundamental, but not of integral, opposition. In short, Sakharov's writings contan less integral opposition than one might expect.

Integral opposition has been expressed more directly in a major *Soviet* critique of the Sakharov manifesto. "Representatives of the Estonian technical intelligentsia" contend that Sakharov minimizes the base and irrational nature of the rulers and the ruled in Soviet society, and that he places excessive faith in technological solutions to human problems. "He [Sakharov] places too much hope on scientific-technical means, on economic measures, on the goodwill of the leaders of our society, on the common sense of people; he sees the fundamental causes of the world crisis as being outside the borders of our society...."[11] Stressing the profound importance of elevating the inner or spiritual lives of people, the need to awaken in all a greater feeling of "personal responsibility" and "conscious civic activity"—indeed, to raise "society's moral standards" and to search for "a new moral-philosophical teaching"—the critics of Sakharov conclude:

> ...we consider it necessary to expand the theses presented by A. D. Sakharov. The following are essential:
> 1. Not only the elimination of friction between hostile states, but also their positive rapprochement.
> 2. Not only coexistence and cooperation, but also positive reconciliation.
> 3. Not only a struggle against physical hunger, but also a struggle against people's moral hunger.
> 4. Not only laws on the press, but also laws which guarantee political freedoms for each person.
> 5. Not only the curbing and exposure of Stalinism, but also its positive elimination.

6. Not only an amnesty for the political prisoners, but their complete release and a guarantee of freedom of beliefs.

7. Not only a tiny economic reform, but also radical economic restructuring.

And most important of all—not only the overcoming of atomization on the surface, but inside people as well!

In conclusion we appeal to the leading minds of our society: do not confine yourselves to scientific-technical dreams, pleasant illusions and the stimulating of rosy hopes! Create new socio-ethical values![12]

Clearly a rejection of Marxist-Leninist ideology and other basic norms and elements of the Soviet political system are implicit in many of these demands.

A third major dissent document is Andrei Amalrik's *Will the USSR Survive until 1984?*[13] Here, despite protestations of patriotism, one finds a number of incisive expressions of integral opposition. Amalrik's disdain for politicians and bureaucrats is formidable ("Having become accustomed to obey orders without demur and not ask questions, in order to gain power, the bureaucrats, once having gained power, possess a brilliant capacity for keeping it in their own hands, but have no idea whatever of how to use it. They themselves are not only incapable of thinking up anything new but in general they even regard any kind of new idea as an assault on their own rights"); his prognosis about the current Soviet regime is gloomy ("To put is simply, the regime is getting old and cannot now suppress everybody and everything with the same vigor and energy as before. . . . [If] we consider the current 'liberalization' not as the regeneration but as the growing decrepitude of the regime, then the logical result will be its death, after which anarchy will follow"); he considers the prevailing mood among the workers and peasants to be one of "passive discontent" ("this discontent is directed not against the regime as a whole—most people simply have not given the matter a thought, or they think there is no alternative—but against particular features of the regime which are, nevertheless, essential elements of its existence");

he believes that meaningful cooperation between the United States and the USSR can begin to take place only when the internal characteristics or domestic politics of the Soviet system become more democratic ("Genuine rapprochement can [only] be based on a community of interests, of culture, of tradition and on mutual understanding. No such thing exists. What common link is there between a democratic country with its idealism and pragmatism and a country without beliefs, without traditions, without culture or the skill to do a job? . . . [The USSR] has betrayed all its allies as soon as it found the least advantage in doing so; it has never taken seriously any of its agreements and has never had anything in common with anyone"). Furthermore, Amalrik predicts the reunification of the two Germanies, the emergence of "desovietized" national-communist regimes in Eastern Europe, and—alarmingly—the very probable outbreak of protracted warfare between the USSR and Communist China.

Elsewhere, Amalrik declares that the political system under which he lives is "organically alien" to him, and acknowledges that many Russians may find passages in his book unpatriotic. Yet he replies that "the best patriot is not the man who papers over his country's failings but the man who exposes the wounds so that they can be cured."[14] One must judge for himself whether the motives and aims of Amalrik—and those of deeply patriotic but profound critics of the Soviet system, such as Alexander Solzhenitsyn—constitute integral or merely fundamental opposition. Amalrik, for one, is reportedly paying for his beliefs with incarceration in a labor camp north of the Arctic Circle. Also recommitted to a labor camp is Vladimir Bukovsky, who together with Amalrik and Piotr Yakir gave unprecedented taped televised interviews to an American news correspondent in 1970. Bukovsky's dispassionate but ringing declaration to an international television audience epitomizes one of the deepest currents of the contemporary Soviet dissent movement:

You have to understand first of all what is the essence of our struggle. The essence of the struggle, in my view, is the struggle against fear—the fear which has gripped the people since the time of Stalin and which has still not left people and thanks to which this system continues to exist, the system of dictatorship, of pressure, of oppression. It is into the struggle against fear that we put our greatest efforts, and in that struggle great importance attaches to personal example—the example which we give people. I personally did what I considered right, spoke out on those occasions when I wanted to, and I'm alive. . . . I can get about, I can live. For me and for many people that is very important—it shows that it is possible to fight and that it is necessary.[15]

Everything considered, the Sakharov, Estonian, and Amalrik manifestoes are heady mixtures of normative and empirical analysis—with frequent shifts from the "is" to the "ought," from the possible to the probable to the inevitable. Perhaps the least developed aspect of integral opposition in the USSR is the organizational and practical—how, specifically, to persuade, convince, cajole, coerce, or replace the men in power. Significantly, the Estonian declaration demands that all "minority groups" be guaranteed by law the right to oppose the existing government. The day when a Soviet administration accepts this idea, in theory or in practice, is not in sight. But on questions of oppositional strategy and tactics, the actions of the Sakharovs, Amalriks, and Bukovskys speak and will speak louder than words. If the recent *samizdat* literature provides any indication, a small but growing number of Soviet citizens have indeed begun to dedicate their lives to bringing about a thorough-going transformation, "democratization," or—in Amalrik's words— "a radical regeneration" of Soviet society.

In conclusion, it must be very briefly noted that systemic changes of major significance *have* taken place in the Soviet Union during the past fifty years. But the opposition that helped to produce these changes often came from *within* the highest levels of the Communist party itself. The transformation of Lenin's party dictatorship into the personal dictatorship of Joseph Stalin, and back again into the party-dominated polity of Nikita Khrushchev and his successors, clearly illustrates the magnitude of some of these changes. "Khrushchev," it has been said, "was at one and the same time head of the government and head of the opposition"[16] —and surely the same can be said of Stalin.

Factional Opposition

Factional conflict in the Communist party is a specialized subject, which will not be discussed in any detail here.[17] The study of Soviet factional opposition is sometimes called "Kremlinology." Though there is no generally agreed upon definition of Kremlinology, the term usually refers to the analysis of esoteric Communist communications for the purpose of accumulating information about leadership struggles, policy disputes, and the policy-making process at the highest levels of the CPSU. The Communist party, it must be remembered, is a self-selected elite. Key party officials are recruited, promoted, demoted, fired, and retired by *other* party officials. Disputes are not resolved by the party membership as a whole, let alone with public participation through elections or representative bodies. Factional opposition is thus an ongoing process that takes place largely within the highest organs of the ruling party. Dissidents outside of the party rarely express factional opposition. Zorin and Alekseev, for example, sharply attack the entire system of recruiting and assigning party personnel (*nomenklatura*), and Sakharov, in his book, criticizes an influential "Stalinist" official by name. But to date few dissenters have sought to participate in intraparty factional conflict—that is, spoken out on behalf of, or in opposition to, specific party officials.

Since 1921 the formation of organized factional groupings within the CPSU and open intraparty competition on the basis of separate "platforms" have been explicitly proscribed. Struggles for power and position have taken place behind a facade of "monolithic" unity. Though on some issues and in some time periods leadership conflicts have burst out into the open, factional opposition and the rules by which it is conducted have been shrouded in secrecy. These practices are reminiscent of the nominating procedure in some democratic states. But they contrast sharply with other key aspects of electoral politics, where aspiring policy-makers strive to represent various political parties, which in turn compete with one another for popular support (i.e., votes) at regular intervals of time.

During the early 1960s Western scholars engaged in a heated debate about the nature and extent of factional opposition in the Soviet system. At issue was the role of Nikita Khrushchev. Some argued that once he had emerged victorious after a majority of his fellow Presidium (Politburo) members attempted to oust him from office in June 1957, Khrushchev became the undisputed leader of the regime. The question of power apparently resolved, a greater degree of stability and less factional opposition was seen to exist in the leading bodies of the Communist party. Other observers argued, however, that leadership conflict was a pervasive and continuous element of Soviet politics, and that "Khrushchev's power and prestige were, to a far greater extent than Stalin's, dependent on the success of his policies."[18] Emphasizing the ambiguously defined division of responsibilities among the top party and governmental institutions, "the conflict school" insisted that factional opposition over power and policy had not diminished, and, if anything, considering the major reforms Khrushchev sought to implement, was likely to play a crucial role in the years ahead.

The ouster of Khrushchev from his party and state positions in October 1964 seems to lend support to the arguments of the conflict school. Two able studies have amply documented the limitations or constraints upon Khrushchev's power throughout the 1957-1964 years.[19] Yet careful analysis of the actions of Khrushchev's successors reveals some surprises: Khrushchev does not seem to have been removed primarily over policy disputes or factional infighting.[20] A number of Khrushchev's important policies have been continued by the Brezhnev-Kosygin-Podgorny regime, and remarkably few top-level personnel changes have been made. The continuity and longevity of the Soviet ruling elite suggest that Khrushchev was not the head of an identifiable leadership clique and that his ouster was not the culmination of divisive political infighting. Many Western observers believe that Khrushchev's "leadership style" was a major factor contributing to his downfall. Particularly important were his lack of careful administrative planning, his insufficient mobilization of elite support for some of his major reforms, and his growing propensity to dominate, ignore, and thereby weaken and disrupt the established oligarchic system. Growing evidence indicates that these three factors may have been the decisive ones.

Of particular significance are the unmistakable efforts of Khrushchev's successors to regularize and reduce factional conflict at the highest levels of the Communist party. Stressing the present regime's firm commitment to oligarchy, as opposed to one-man rule, Professor T. H. Rigby cites four recent developments that seem clearly designed to increase "mutual control" among the top Soviet leaders: (1) a formal decree forbidding any political leader from holding the two highest positions (First Secretary of the Central Committee and Chairman of the Council of Ministers), posts which both Stalin and Khrushchev (after 1958) held concurrently; (2) greatly reduced opportunities for patronage—especially the power to place one's supporters in influential positions in the central and regional party apparatuses; (3) reduction of overlapping membership in the top party and state organs; and (4) the establishment of "checks and balances" and "countervailing power" among the very highest party leaders.

One may conclude, then, that Khrushchev's successors have evidently given much thought to the problem of leadership, and taken a number of sensible practical measures to moderate the problem. They have acquiesced in the emergence of a "pecking order" in the oligarchy, with Brezhnev as No. 1, and this, one might expect, has made it easier to achieve coherence and expedition in current policy-making and administration. At the same time, however, and this is the most salient characteristic of their style of government, they have hedged the power and authority of individual leaders around with a number of quite formidable controls, with the object of preventing history from again repeating itself, of obstructing a new drift to one-man rule.[21]

For these and other reasons, factional opposition in the Soviet Union has been rather difficult to discern in recent years. Since 1967 the "collective leadership" has presented an unusually homogenous public appearance. Differences over policy and personnel no doubt persist, but Soviet leaders have uttered few discordant statements from which to infer these differences. A recent *Pravda* editorial, in a possible direct or indirect attack on Premier Kosygin or one of his close associates, sharply criticized an unidentified "leader" whose "empty assurances and commitments, unsupported by realities . . . only undermine confidence in them."

> Could, for example, an economic executive (*khoziastvennik*) really count on genuine respect if he promises year after year to guarantee the introduction of new technology in production and to improve working and living conditions, but practically does not do anything about it? Can the unblemished record of a collective farm chairman survive if he fights at every meeting and conference for the development of cattle-raising, but in fact does not take care of feeding and housing the livestock?[22]

The unnamed leader also allegedly "overestimated his own person," "overrated his merits," "viewed his authority as a kind of right of infallibility," and displayed "boastfulness."

Assertions such as these reflect sharp conflict and "conceit." However, the interpretation of these statements is a demanding and speculative art. The task of today's Kremlinologist is a difficult one, and this fact alone goes far toward explaining why no major study of contemporary Soviet leadership politics or factional opposition has appeared to date.

Fundamental Opposition

Legality

A distinguished specialist on Russian law has noted a major difference between contemporary Soviet and American dissent. Whereas American militants often challenge the authority of the entire judicial system and attempt to disrupt court proceedings, Russian dissidents repeatedly request that legal authorities abide by *existing* laws, in particular the Constitution of the USSR and, on occasion, "higher" international or universal law.[23] Insistence that the regime adhere to and implement existing Soviet legislation is a vital part of the current protest movement. Dissent on questions of legality and jurisprudence contains elements of integral, fundamental, and specific opposition. But legal issues will be discussed here because to date they have elicited more overt fundamental than integral opposition.

Amalrik contends that all members of the "Democratic Movement" have at least one objective in common: the establishment of a "rule of law, founded on respect for basic human rights."[24] Not all dissidents believe that a just society can be created with existing Soviet laws. Some suggest that a more democratic Constitution replace the present one (the 1936 Stalin Constitution), and that the new Constitution be approved or rejected by the entire population. Others urge that specific statutes be revised or clarified—particularly laws such as Articles 70 and 190 of the Russian Republic criminal code under whose ambiguous formulations many oppositionists have been prosecuted for allegedly "anti-Soviet" or "slanderous" allegations, writings, and actions. Still others exhort: "What is prescribed by law should not be requested; it should be demanded!"[25] And still another viewpoint is that the "lawlessness" in society is not primarily due to poor legislation, but to the government's flagrant and capricious violation of Soviet laws and unwillingness to implement them.

Perhaps most important is the oppositionist contention that the Constitution of the USSR is the highest law of the land and that the constitutionality of all other laws should be measured against this standard. What Bukovsky, Viacheslav Chornovil, Piotr Grigorenko, and others are apparently advocating is nothing less than the depolitization of the Soviet legal system—that is, the significant reduction of party control of the judicial process, adherence to the constitutional provision that "judges are independent and subject only to the law" (Article 112), and the establishment of *constitutionality*—not party fiat—as the chief criterion of legality in Soviet theory and practice.[26] The Stalin era is often cited as an example of what can happen when the state's judicial and investigatory agencies arbitrarily violate, ignore, or refuse to be bound by existing statutes.

At issue are the role and functions of law in society. A handful of Soviet dissidents, in the spirit of the Western political theorist John Locke, contend that what is crucial in a polity is not the form of government but the paramountcy of law—laws that bind both the state and the individual, laws that cannot be changed or flaunted at will, and laws that are adjudicated by men who are not beholden to the current government, but whose authority derives from the entire society's commitment to abide by legitimately established, usually written, rules. Laws are thus seen to function as a limiting or restraining force on government. In sharp contrast is the official Soviet view that written law is an instrument to serve the state, that the spirit of the law is more important than the letter of the law, and that individual rights cannot be exercised when they are deemed to hinder the goal of "communist construction." Soviet jurisprudence, in this view, is above all "a means of educating, guiding, training, disciplining, and mobilizing people to fulfill their political, economic, and social responsibilities"[27]—as the current political leaders define those responsibilities. It is ironic that during Bukovsky's recent trial the following exchange allegedly took place between foreign newsmen and a Soviet militia lieutenant:

"This is a railroad district. It is forbidden to foreigners." [Technically, all areas within Moscow city limits are open to foreigners.]
"And if we come tomorrow or next week, is that still the law?" one newsman responded.
"I don't know. There is no permanent law in any country. It depends on the circumstances."[28]

Freedom of Speech and Conscience
No less important and very frequently articulated is the elemental oppositionist demand that an individual not be persecuted for holding, expressing, or disseminating his personal beliefs and opinions. Petitioning the top party leaders, Andrei Sakharov, Valerii Turchin, and Roy Medvedev do not mince words on this issue: "Really, how can one justify detaining in prisons, camps and mental hospitals those people who are in opposition but whose opposition is legal, lying in the field of ideas and convictions?"[29] This appeal has been made again and again—by religious groups, ethnic minorities, scientists, creative artists, and others. Many dissidents believe that they have been persecuted only for their convictions or for speaking out or demonstrating on behalf of others who have been similarly treated. Harassment of this kind they consider to be illegal. In short, some dissenters contend that Soviet law guarantees all citizens certain fundamental rights and equality before the law but that party and government agencies unlawfully transgress— indeed, conspire to deprive citizens of—these rights. A petition, signed by 139 Ukrainian citizens in 1968, concludes: "the political trials held in recent years are becoming a form of suppression of those who do not conform in their thinking and a form of suppression of the civic activity and social criticism which are absolutely essential to the health of any society."[30]

349

Among the civil liberties that protesters believe should be unequivocally guaranteed by law—in theory and in practice—are freedom of conscience and the means for the public expression of opinion; freedom of speech; freedom of assembly; freedom of the press and information; freedom from arbitrary arrest, searches, and other acts of coercion; freedom of education; freedom of correspondence; freedom of mobility; freedom to choose citizenship and place of residence; freedom of worship; freedom from censorship; freedom to leave the USSR; freedom to petition all political officials; freedom to form and maintain public organizations independent of control by outside forces, including the Communist party.[31]

At the heart of the legality issue, then, lies the fundamental question of liberty versus authority: what substantive and procedural rights belong to the individual, and what rights belong to the state? In the Soviet Union today there is clearly integral fundamental opposition to official policies regarding these questions.

Religious Freedom

Attempts to defend the legal rights of religious and nationality groups have been a vital part of the current dissent movement. In the early and mid 1960s especially, Russian Orthodox and Evangelical Christian-Baptist dissenters were quite outspoken in their demands that the constitutional guarantees of freedom of conscience, freedom of worship, and separation of church and state (Article 124) be honored. Persistent government and police interference in the activities of religious organizations—including the closing of countless churches, synagogues, and mosques—has been a source of deep-seated disaffection. Interference by secular officials in the appointment or removal of clergy, in the administration of church finances, and in the activities of independent-minded religious leaders have all been strongly criticized, publicly and privately. Outspoken oppositionists have also openly challenged the government's severe reprisals

350

against some individuals who hold religious beliefs and have protested widespread discrimination, especially in educational and employment opportunities, against believers. Here too dissent has been directed mainly toward the alleged unlawfulness of the regime's sustained antireligious campaign of the past decade. Sharp criticism has also been leveled at those submissive—even "quisling"—religious leaders who collaborated with the authorities and who, through action and inaction, have helped to solidify state domination over religious organizations.[32]

Proposing an alternative to present government policy, a well-known Christian dissenter, Anatoli Levitin (Krasnov),. writes:

> The establishment of full, as opposed to imaginary, freedom of religion in our country would destroy the artificial barriers between atheists and believers and would leave room for that atmosphere of friendship and collaboration in which they could reach for the truth together.
> The struggle for freedom of religion, for freedom of atheism, and for full freedom of conscience is the olive branch that I stretch out to my friends—believers and atheists. . . .
> Long live free religion and free atheism![33]

But with the continuation of the party's vigorous antireligious activities into the 1970s, most religious dissenters appear to be deeply pessimistic about the prospects of significantly changing official policy and ever enjoying their full constitutional rights. Active opposition appears to be on the wane—temporarily at least—but passive oppositionists—those "who exhibit no discernible aspirations to change the system but seek merely to conduct religious activity regardless of whether it is legally permissible"[34]—appear to be growing in number. Both these developments are probably in large part due to the policies of the Soviet government.

Much has been written about the special position of Jews in the Soviet Union. Among Western scholars there is general agreement that Soviet Jews have been subjected to greater

351

harassment than virtually any other religious or nationality group. Significantly, some Jews who want to be *assimilated* into Russian life are apparently being harassed, as well as those who wish to maintain their distinctive religious and ethnic traditions while remaining Soviet citizens, and those who desire to emigrate to Israel. Jewish protest thus takes different forms. Jews who have little interest in their heritage seek "equal opportunity." They consider themselves first-class citizens and want to be treated as such. Above all, they desire the eradication of popular anti-Semitism, which seems to have been encouraged rather than discouraged by the regime's anti-Zionist policies and propaganda, especially after the Arab-Israeli war of 1967. Soviet Jews also want an end to discriminatory practices that curtail opportunities for professional and educational advancement. To be sure, Russians of Jewish background have reached the pinnacle of success in their respective fields. But, even in the immediate post-Stalin era, persons of Jewish origin had "virtually no access to jobs in the higher Party apparatus, the regional and district Party committees, the various central ideological organizations, the higher organs of military command, the diplomatic service, the organs of the KGB [the secret police] and the Procuracy."[35] Careful examination of today's top party and government organs suggests that changes in previous practices have not been far-reaching.

Jews who wish to preserve their "Jewishness" have been particularly unhappy with the government's hindrance of cultural, linguistic, and religious forms of expression—especially the paucity of Jewish newspapers, publishing houses, theaters, schools, Yiddish language study, prayer books, functioning synagogues, and so forth. There are only three operating synagogues in Moscow and one in Kiev, for example. Jewish cultural life, it is contended, should at least be granted the same opportunity to develop—or merely to survive—as other minority group cultures. Many Soviet Jews deeply resent the fact that the government officially regards them as a "nationality," but deprives them of privileges

352

enjoyed by other nationality groups. Moreover, the regime's anti-Zionist propaganda often depicts Jewish nationalism as "subversive" to the Soviet state.

Jews who desire to emigrate appear to have given up hope of ever attaining freedom of religion and cultural expression in the Soviet Union. Their protest therefore reflects a profound alienation toward their country and is most probably a form of integral, not fundamental, opposition. Disaffection of this kind was clearly articulated in a recent appeal from 26 Lithuanian Jews. Decrying the "rising wave of anti-Semitism" in Lithuania and post-World War II "pogroms" in the Ukraine and elsewhere, the petitioners declare: "We are confronted with a paradox here. We are not wanted here, we are being completely oppressed, forcibly denationalized, and even publicly insulted in the press—while at the same time we are forcibly kept here."[36]

Nationality Rights
Neither in theory nor practice has the present Soviet regime formulated and generally agreed upon a clearly defined policy toward the USSR's many national minority groups. Opposition to the government's nationality policy focuses on alleged "Great Russian chauvinism" in a nation whose population is becoming increasingly non-Russian—indeed, the 1970 census indicates that, if present trends continue, ethnic Russians may become a minority group (less than 50% of the population) in the not very distant future. This poses a serious dilemma for Soviet leaders because of the Stalinist precept that the Great Russian people should play a "leading role" in the multinational Soviet state. This principle has not been rejected, in theory or in practice, by Stalin's successors. One Western writer submits that the minimum goal of Soviet nationality groups is to resist extinction, and that their logically maximum goal is to achieve political independence (secession from the USSR).[37] But the chief goal of dissident nationality groups today seems to be to establish unequivocally the principle that all Soviet peoples are equal and to

ensure that all ethnic groups are in fact permitted to preserve and practice their respective cultural traditions. The ethnographic museum in Leningrad is one of the finest in the world, with displays of folk art, clothing, practical implements, and elaborate exhibits depicting the everyday life of virtually all non-Russian nationality groups. But, symbols of cultural freedom aside, fear of national and linguistic extinction persists. Forced Russification—by methods ranging from subtle forms of assimilation to territorial annexation and the deportation of entire peoples from their homeland (e.g., the Crimean Tatars)—provoked guerrilla warfare in the West Ukraine and the Baltic states in the 1940s and early 1950s and has produced sporadic but increasingly outspoken fundamental—and occasional integral—opposition since the late 1950s. Objectionable to all non-Russian nationality groups is the concept of "Russia, one and indivisible"—an officially propounded view that "one single 'Soviet nation', one single 'Soviet people' is taking shape, not in the sense of the sum total of all Soviet peoples and nations, not as a collective concept, but as some supposedly mononational or nationless synthesis which did not exist, let us say, in the 1920s or 1930s. . . ."[38]

The most important dissident nationality group is the Ukrainian. Not only is the Ukraine the second largest republic in the Soviet Union, with a population of about 30 million and an additional 10 million Ukrainians living elsewhere in the USSR, but Ukrainians have an unusually strong national consciousness and cultural heritage. Ukrainian nationalists probably comprise a formidable segment of the present dissent movement—indeed, one dissident estimates that of all the political prisoners in Soviet labor camps today, 60 to 70% are Ukrainians![39] It is not surprising, therefore, that some of the most detailed and lucid oppositionist documents to have appeared to date—ones that advocate integral, fundamental, and specific change in the spheres of politics, economics, culture, and education—have been written by Ukrainians. Consider carefully the analysis of Ivan

354

Dziuba, a young Ukrainian literary critic whose book about the nationality question fervently pleads for a return to *Lenin*'s nationalities policy. Dziuba believes that "the Ukrainian nation" is today experiencing a "crisis":

> Territorial unity and sovereignty are being gradually and progressively lost through mass resettlement . . . of the Ukrainian population to Siberia, the North, and other regions, where it numbers millions but is quickly denationalized; through an organized mass resettlement of Russians in the Ukraine, not always with economic justification and not always motivated by economic reasons . . . ; through administrative divisions that remain a formality and through the doubtful sovereignty of the government of the Ukrainian SSR over the territory of the Ukraine. This latter reason, coupled with excessive centralization and a total subordination to all-Union authorities in Moscow, makes it equally difficult to speak about the *integrity and sovereignty of the economic life* of the Ukrainian nation.
>
> A *common historic fate* is also being lost, as the Ukrainian nation is being progressively dispersed over the Soviet Union, and as the sense of historic national tradition and knowledge of the historic past are gradually being lost due to a total lack of national education in school and in society in general.
>
> Ukrainian national *culture* is being kept in a rather provincial position and is practically treated as "second-rate"; its great past achievements are poorly disseminated in society, the Ukrainian *language* has been pushed into the background and is not really used in the cities of the Ukraine.
>
> Finally, during the last decades the Ukrainian nation has virtually been deprived of the natural increase in population which characterizes all present-day nations. . . . [40]

Abundant documentation in support of these assertions makes Dziuba's study a major contribution to the analysis of the history and development of the Soviet nationalities question. However, far more radical solutions to the nationality issue have been suggested by another Ukrainian in a programmatic open letter to the deputies of the Ukrainian soviets (governmental, not party, organs). Anton Koval proposes:

To adopt a new constitution for the [Ukrainian] republic which should clearly define mechanisms that: (a) guarantee the republic the status of a sovereign nation-state; in particular, raise the significance of treaty relations among the republics in the Union and hand over the present prerogatives of the Union's ministries of education, culture, and internal affairs to the respective republican organs; (b) guarantee popular representation by means of democratizing elections (nomination of several candidates for a single post and an extensive discussion of candidates during the election campaign); (c) protect the Soviets from having their power usurped by bureaucracy.[41]

In short, Soviet nationalities policy since Stalin has produced considerable overt and passive opposition. It is a very live issue and likely to remain so for a long time.

Creative and Artistic Freedom

The issue of creative freedom provides another important source of fundamental and integral opposition. The *samizdat* literature is replete with demands that writers be allowed "to write the truth as they see it, to exercise their creative abilities, and to experiment with various literary forms independent of the regime's ideological dictates."[42] Requests such as these contrast sharply with the official view that art is an instrument that must serve the state, that artists have a professional and moral obligation to help construct a communistic society, and, implicitly, that political leaders have the capacity and right to judge whether the above two conditions are being fulfilled. In a statement with profound implications, Khrushchev's chief ideological specialist declared to a group of 400 leading creative artists in 1962:

There should be complete clarity in the question of freedom of creation . . . genuine freedom [is] freedom for the people, [not] *freedom from society, from duty to the people.*

We have complete freedom to struggle for Communism. We do not and cannot have freedom to struggle against Communism.[43]

Over the years these official views have been challenged

explicitly and implicitly from various quarters. Still the sharpest and most incisive critique is Andrei Sinyavsky's essay "On Socialist Realism." Sinyavsky observes the extraordinarily purposeful and teleogical nature of all human activity in official Soviet theory. Poets, musicians, agronomists, engineers, laborers, policemen, lawyers, theaters, machines, newspapers, guns—all are considered means of hastening the inevitable outcome of the historical process, of fulfilling its ultimate "Purpose"—the building of communism. Work toward this end is allegedly an individual's reason for living, his *raison d'être*. But Sinyavsky is devastating in his analysis of what can happen to societies whose governments claim to act "in the name of Purpose." Insightfully he declares that "true faith is not compatible with tolerance. Neither is it compatible with historicism, i.e., with tolerance applied to the past." Then, in a scathing indictment of his country's recent history and of its goal-oriented art, culture, and social institutionsns, Sinyavsky lashes out:

> So that prisons should vanish forever, we built new prisons. So that all frontiers should fall, we surrounded ourselves with a Chinese Wall. So that work should become a rest and a pleasure, we introduced forced labor. So that not one drop of blood be shed any more, we killed and killed and killed.[44]

Soviet creative artists, then, have expressed profound dissatisfaction with their political system, with their government's policies, and especially with the key tenets of "socialist realism"—the official doctrine that legitimizes extensive censorship and that views art "as a means of illustrating truths attained in some way other than through aesthetic cognition."[45] Solzhenitsyn, for one, has demanded the abolition of all censorship, and has been ejected from the Union of Soviet Writers for his efforts. Also, Mstislav Rostropovich, the enormously talented Russian cellist, asks: "Why in our literature and art do people absolutely incompetent in the field so often have the final word? Why are they given the right to discredit our art in the eyes of our people?"[46]

It is easy to imagine a kind of relationship between regime and artist that Solzhenitsyn and Rostropovich would favor. But the recent policies of the Brezhnev-Kosygin-Podgorny administration reflect, if anything, a renewed campaign to establish ideological orthodoxy and to keep in rein allegedly unreliable, nonconformist, or "apolitical" authors, playwrights, composers, sculptors, film-makers, etc. Yet opposition to official policies will probably persist as long as creative artists have the courage to express their own personal vision of the truth, regardless of whether they are allowed to publish or publicly display their work in their own country. To paraphrase Solzhenitsyn, it is unlikely that the artistically talented will ever accept the dictum that art can and must be put into categories "permitted" or "not permitted," "about this you may express yourself" and "about this you may not."[47] But it must be remembered that very few Soviet intellectuals have publicly supported Solzhenitsyn's call for the abolition of *all* censorship (clearly an expression of integral opposition). Most dissenting intellectuals apparently acknowledge the need for some kinds of censorship—Sakharov and the Medvedevs have done so explicitly—and advocate merely the reduction of censorship or the elimination of particularly odious types of government control (fundamental opposition).

Economics
The issue of economic development is a final important source of fundamental opposition. In the *samizdat* literature dissenters have made some but not many radical economic demands. For example, wages and prices should not be centrally determined, but should find their respective levels through supply and demand. Group ownership and management of light industry and agricultural associations should be established. Private ownership of local industry and individual farms should be encouraged (clearly integral opposi-

358

tion). Service industries should be run primarily by groups and private individuals. State owned, collectively owned, and privately owned enterprises should enjoy equal rights and work in free competition with one another. The right to strike should be guaranteed by law. The state should reduce its monopoly over the economy and concentrate on only crucial or strategic sectors—particularly heavy and medium industry, defense, foreign trade, transportation, communications, and state farms. Furthermore, dissenters also advocate the reduction of military and defense spending. Political leaders are exhorted to "transfer the greater part of our national resources from the construction of a military machine to cultural and economic construction."[48] In short, a few Soviet dissidents have not only expressed unorthodox views about the *ownership* of the means of production, but also about a wide range of economic policy issues.

The *samizdat* literature is not the only source of opposition on economic questions. In the field of economics, probably more than in any other, the party has encouraged, even solicited, expressions of fundamental and specific opposition. A classic example is the spirited debate over economic reform that took place in the early and mid-1960s. To be sure, some basic issues were not raised at all, and others had been discussed in the specialized economic press for a number of years. But from 1962 to 1965 a wide range of opinion *was* expressed on many important questions—the general role of planning and the market in a socialist economy, the merits of enterprise autonomy and centralized versus decentralized decision-making in various spheres, problems of resource allocation, distribution, and supply, the concepts of "profit," "profitability" (return on capital), "optimality," "success indicators," "interest," and "rent," the price system, incentives for production and innovation, and many others.[49] Also important was the growing criticism of the reform after it was inaugurated in 1965. Opposition to many of its complex and contradictory provisions was expressed not only in the party and professional journals and newspapers, but also in the actions of numerous factory managers who chose not to change old patterns of behavior, and in the obstructionist tactics of the rapidly increasing number of state bureaucrats, many of whom, for various reasons, felt they had a vested interest in hindering the chief aims of the reform.[50]

Most of these discussions and debates have been conducted by academic economists, state bureaucrats, and enterprise and party officials writing in the national and specialized presses, or speaking formally and informally at professional meetings, ministerial offices, technical institutes, etc. The different views articulated constitute "loyal" opposition, but the issues at stake—that is, the potential changes explicitly or implicitly under consideration—involve very significant policy alternatives and priorities.

Concluding Remarks

Fundamental opposition, then, takes many forms. Rarely is it officially sanctioned, and often it is vigorously stifled. But attempts to suppress fundamental opposition have to date only produced even greater fundamental opposition. The trial of Andrei Sinyavsky and Yuli Daniel in 1966—the first major political trial in recent Soviet history—produced an outpouring of dissent that appears to be growing to this day. Subsequent trials and increased publicity of dissident activities by *samizdat* have further fueled protest on controversial issues. *"Radizdat"*—foreign radio broadcasts that describe the latest *samizdat* literature to Russian listeners—has also played a major role in disseminating information about dissenters' activities. Hence more Soviet citizens are actively and passively participating in what is developing into a very earnest series of "great debates." Few ground rules have been agreed upon, for a key issue is whether the debates shall take place at all—that is, whether or not oppositionists *have* the right to dissent.

Opposition is being expressed not only toward policies the

government has taken, but also toward policies the government has not taken. Foremost among the latter is the issue of Stalin, and the apparent reluctance of the present regime to repudiate certain Stalinist policies and practices. Roy Medvedev's important book *Let History Judge: The Origins and Consequences of Stalinism* is the first comprehensive analysis of the entire Stalin era by a Soviet citizen; Anatoli Marchenko's *My Testimony* is an autobiographical critique of today's Soviet labor camps; and Zhores Medvedev's essays are an empassioned demand for greater international scientific cooperation, freedom to travel abroad, and privacy of correspondence.[51] Thus, with the significant curtailment of Stalinist terror, constructive critics feel freer to offer unsolicited advice and recommendations to Soviet leaders, and to raise fundamental political issues whether asked to or not. To date the party has responded by selectively prosecuting, with a minimum of publicity, the most outspoken of the "non-Establishment" dissenters. But through the *Chronicle of Current Events* especially, details of arrests and trials are widely disseminated. Whether it is possible to silence *samizdat*, whether government agencies will ever make an all-out attempt to do so, and whether greater publicity about the fate of dissidents will deter or increase fundamental opposition are unanswerable questions. It is to be hoped, however, that Soviet leaders, instead of ignoring or repressing most fundamental opposition, will establish, maintain, and above all legitimize additional channels through which constructive social criticism may be expressed.

Specific Opposition

Specific opposition has increased tremendously in recent years. This development has resulted in part from the groundswell of *samizdat* literature—protests, petitions, newsletters, manuscripts, poetry, ballads, etc. But also of great significance has been the rise of specific opposition from *within* the party and state bureaucracies, and from established professional, military, technical, and academic institutions and groups. "Opposition" from these organizations, it must be emphasized, is loyal and officially sanctioned. Party leaders in recent years have invited more constructive criticism, and more has been offered, solicited, and unsolicited. Increased specific opposition does not necessarily reflect greater "pluralism" or greater "interest articulation" in the Soviet system. Instead, it merely attests to the policymakers' growing need for and willingness to solicit potentially useful information, and to consider the recommendations and suggestions of those who possess special skills, who administer national policy, or who are directly affected by present policies or policy alternatives under consideration.

The Dissidents

Let us first examine the activities and proposals of political dissidents. In general, the broad issues on which they express fundamental opposition are the same as those on which they express specific opposition: legality, freedom of speech and conscience, religious freedom, nationality rights, creative freedom, economics. Since dissenters have criticized so many of the government's specific policies and actions, a few examples from each of the issue-areas above will have to suffice.[52]

Legality. On the question of legality, dissidents have made countless demands concerning specific substantive and procedural violations of Soviet law and the Soviet Constitution. Among the most often criticized practices are the KGB's illegal searches and seizures and the courts' secret (in camera) trials of political dissenters. Physical and mental intimidation of the accused, and the presumption that defendants are guilty, not innocent, have also been vigorously protested. Intimidation has allegedly taken place during the

362

court proceedings, the preliminary investigations, and, in some cases, through warning from the KGB even *before* a "crime" has been committed—that is, in anticipation of a misdemeanor that *might* be committed.[53]

Examples of specific legal demands are legion—telephone wiretapping, interference with the mails, the seizure from one's residence of books, manuscripts, tape recordings, letters, or personal belongings should be strictly forbidden, in accordance with the constitutional provision that guarantees "the inviolability of the homes of citizens and privacy of correspondence" (Article 128); trials should be open to the public and should be well publicized; defendants should be given every opportunity to prove their innocence in court, including the opportunity to present evidence, call witnesses, and obtain assistance from a defense lawyer who is permitted to defend his client to the best of his ability without hindrance or persecution; and so forth. In short, dissidents contend that rights explicitly granted to all Soviet citizens by law are flagrantly denied to some in practice. Specific opposition is very largely directed toward *existing* laws, and toward the arbitrary violation or nonimplementation of those laws by the investigative and judicial organs of the state. In fact, much specific opposition consists of seemingly minimal demands, such as requests that persons held in pretrial custody should not be detained longer than the nine-month period prescribed by law, or that sanitary conditions in labor camps should be improved.

Freedom of speech and conscience. On questions of freedom of speech and conscience, oppositionists have repeatedly affirmed that all citizens should enjoy the right to disagree with generally accepted views and official doctrine, and to hold and disseminate their own beliefs and opinions. Bukovsky insists: "Freedom of speech and of the press is, first of all, freedom to criticize. Nobody has ever forbidden praise of the government. . . . We do not need freedom 'pro' if there is no freedom 'anti.' "[54] In this vein numerous

363

dissidents have justified their actions—meetings, demonstrations, petitions, attempts to make public illegal treatment of others, etc. Intellectual dissenters contend that the rights constitutionally guaranteed to all Soviet citizens cannot legitimately be taken away from them either by the arbitrary actions of judicial and investigative agencies or by laws that contravene these rights and make it impossible for people to exercise their freedoms.

But official actions of this kind take place, and laws of this kind exist. Hence, especially since the Sinyavsky-Daniel trial in 1966, citizens' complaints have been frequent. They include letters to the authorities and to the dissidents themselves questioning the prosecution of well-known nonconformists for expressing or propagating their political and philosophical views; petitions protesting the incarceration of certain individuals in psychiatric hospitals; an occasional recommendation that the KGB be abolished, and numerous proposals that its powers be curtailed; requests that a law be passed that would amnesty all persons currently imprisoned for their political or religious beliefs; insistence that all Russians be allowed to exchange ideas with foreigners, in person or by mail; suggestions that Soviet schools and universities should encourage students to be independent-minded (to think for themselves) and to develop more fully their analytical and creative faculties; and many others.

Religious freedom and nationality rights. Some specific-demands on religious and nationality questions have already been mentioned in our discussion of fundamental opposition. The recent *samizdat* literature also includes the following requests: persons holding religious beliefs shall have the right to attend religious services and meetings; believers shall have the right to receive, to read, and to disseminate *all* religious literature including literature that is compiled in the Soviet Union and abroad, freely and regularly; parents shall have the right, guaranteed by law, to give their children religious instruction; churches, monasteries, seminaries, and religious printing/publishing houses that have been closed shall be reopened and shall remain active while the respective parishes, religious orders, and church organizations have the means and express the will for their upkeep; churches and cultural buildings and monuments must not be subject to arbitrary closure, whether for political reasons or on the pretext of "progress" (highway construction, etc.); cultural and religious monuments must be preserved as a vital part of the country's cultural heritage; religious groups shall have the opportunity to hold legal title to their respective places of worship and shall no longer be forced to rent from the state; religious institutions must not be subject to exorbitant taxation.[55]

Dissidents have also expressed opposition to many of the government's specific policies and practices on the nationalities issue. Dziuba, for one, is deeply concerned about at least eight manifestations of Great Russian chauvinism: since Lenin's death the gradual distortion of 18th- and 19th-century Russian history, whereby "imperialist" territorial aggrandizement, "colonial banditry and campaigns of conquest," and "the rapacity, perfidy, and shameless trickery of Russian czardom" are glorified and represented as "the bravery of the Russian people" and "the brilliant successes of Russian diplomacy"; the "colonizing" and "contemptuous" attitudes of many politically and socially influential ethnic Russians who today live in non-Russian republics, mostly in the cities; the deliberate or unintentional confusion of the idea of a "*Union* of Soviet Socialist Republics" with the idea of "Russia, one and indivisible"; the practice of attributing to Russians what has been accomplished by all of the peoples of the USSR; "pseudo-internationalism" or "pseudo-brotherhood" as a subtle form of chauvinism; Ukraino-phobia; the need for centralized direction of the economy as a chauvinistic rationalization; and, perhaps most important, the official practice of branding those who question or challenge any of the above manifestations of Russian chauvinism as a "bourgeois nationalist."[56]

Another Ukrainian offers an even more specific list of proposals: to "Ukrainize" the educational institutions of the republic; to ensure, in practice, that the business of government agencies be done in the Ukrainian language; to eliminate discriminatory measures concerning the cultural heritage of the Ukrainian people; to actualize the laws, directed against actions which impede the development of the cultures of national groups (Moldavians, Jews, Hungarians, Greeks, and others), and actions which instigate and spread national and racial hostility (especially contemporary anti-Semitism); to eradicate the existing secret instructions limiting the admission to universities in the eastern Ukraine of graduates from the western Ukraine and Jews; to end the prosecution of the leading figures of Ukrainian culture who have committed no state or social crimes, and who suffer civil restrictions (dismissal from jobs, denial of opportunities to publish or to speak before the workers) merely for participation in public activities devoted to the growth and development of culture (specific names are listed, including that of Ivan Dziuba); and so forth.[57]

Creative and artistic freedom. One could cite numerous examples of specific opposition on the question of creative freedom. Literary dissent was the chief form of specific and fundamental opposition in the 1950s, and only in the mid 1960s did the nature and range of dissident demands break significant new ground (with the important exception of religious dissent, which was most clearly and forcefully articulated in the early 1960s, but which was to a considerable extent silenced after 1966 by the government's selective persecution of key spokesmen). Creative artists' dissent is most frequently expressed in their work. Writers and artists have also challenged official policies in letters, petitions, and self-defense at trials. But the basic issue is always the same: does the state have the right to interfere in the work of the artist, and, if so, in what manner and to what extent shall the artist's independence be curtailed? The integral or fundamental oppositionist may repudiate any form of governmental interference and may reject entirely the view that art and culture are instruments to serve the state, not ends in themselves. Specific oppositionists are more likely to challenge individual aspects of Soviet literary theory or certain practices of the bureaucratic organs that control Soviet cultural life. For example, the prosecutor at the trial of Yuli Daniel reportedly inquired: "Who is your positive hero? Who expresses your point of view in the story?" Daniel responded: "I told you once before in our preliminary talk that the story has no entirely positive hero and that there doesn't have to be one."[58] In addition to this principle of *tipichnost'* ("exemplariness")—the idea that "typical" behavior is that which promotes progress toward new and improved conditions—Soviet cultural theory also stresses the concepts of *ideinost'* (ideological content), *partinost'* (respect for and an elemental faith in the Communist party), and "socialist realism" (the demand that a writer or artist "truthfully portray reality in its revolutionary development"). With loose formulations such as these playing such an important part in relations between the regime and the artist, it is not surprising that the artistically talented often disagree with cultural bureaucrats in evaluating specific works of literature, art, music, sculpture, etc.

Other specific demands of creative intellectuals relate to censorship, the role of organizations such as the Union of Soviet Writers, publication, copyright, and royalty procedures. These range from suggestions bordering on integral opposition—for example, that publishers and publishing houses be free to choose what they publish without interference from the state—to more modest requests—for instance, that writers or artists have personal contact with the censors of their work and that they be granted the right to appeal to higher censorship agencies, and finally to the government, if they have grievances against their censors. Particularly significant is the appeal that no work of fiction be subject to censorship or to interpretation as "anti-Soviet slander."[5][9]

Economics. Dissenters have articulated relatively little specific and fundamental opposition on questions pertaining to economics—for example, demands for a "market economy" or a "free enterprise system" are rare. Requests for higher wages, pensions, and social security benefits are common, however. Also to be expected are the complaints about the excessive difference between the highest and lowest paying jobs, especially when bonuses and other fringe benefits are taken into consideration. Especially interesting, because it raises the subject of inflation in the Soviet Union, is the recommendation that pension levels should correspond to changes in the cost of living. Also significant is the suggestion that Five-Year Plan directives should "not be implemented through administrative-bureaucratic dictate, but solely through the use of such methods as capital investments and credit, a taxation system, and *recommended*, rather than mandatory, guidelines."[6][0] But, perhaps most unusual and significant of all, is the protest implicit in Dziuba's recital of the following *official* statistics:

"In 1960 the total turnover tax in the territory of the [Ukrainian] Republic amounted to 5,442 million rubles. From this sun 1,509.4 million rubles, or 27.7% were allotted to the state budget of the Ukrainian SSR, and 3,932.6 million rubles, or 72.3%, to the Union budget." But, perhaps, this revenue is refunded to the Republic? The book *National Income of the Ukrainian SSR* gives the following answer. In 1960 the Ukraine handed over to the Union budget the said 3,932.6 million rubles plus other deductions, giving a grand total of 5,288.8 million. At the same time she received 1,113.0 million through redistribution from the budget. This leaves a balance in favor of the Union budget of 4,175.8 million. In 1959 this balance amounted to 3,886.7 million, in 1961 to 3,664.8 million, etc.[6][1]

This example, like many others, illustrates the multifaceted nature of some of the dissidents' recommendations for change, as well as the difficulty of categorizing particular statements and actions as "specific," "fundamental," "factional," or "integral" opposition.

"Within-System" Opposition

Little is known about the policy-making process in the Soviet Union, and information-gathering by party and government officials is an important aspect of that process. The recommendations of some groups and individuals may be requested on a regular basis, while others may be ignored or never solicited. Or, not surprisingly, the views of industrial or agricultural specialists may be sought on some questions (for example, economic planning), but their opinions will not be solicited or kindly received on other issues (for example, Soviet nationalities policy). Moreover, it must be remembered that technical specialists often disagree with one another and that technical expertise once solicited will not necessarily have a significant influence, let alone outweigh political considerations, in shaping public policy. Caveats aside, it can be confidently stated that specific "within-system" opposition has increased considerably in the past decade. The principal reason is that the Soviet regime has encouraged and legitimized constructive criticism on certain issues, and thus recommendations, suggestions, and petitions for policy changes have emanated from a wide range of sources.

During the post-Stalin era there has been little specific opposition from within the party and state bureaucracies on the issues of freedom of speech and conscience, religious freedom, nationality rights, or creative freedom. Differences of opinion on questions of legality and constitutionalism have been much more common. For example, since 1959 a lively debate has been taking place in government and academic circles regarding the constitutional relationship and respective legislative authority of the USSR Supreme Soviet and its 37-man Presidium, or "executive committee." Some argue that the smaller body can and should participate actively in the legislative process. Others contend that "the Presidium persistently violates the Supreme Soviet's exclusive constitutional right to legislate and that there is no practical, governmental need for it to do so."[62]

Soviet legal theorists have also debated the merits of many kinds of proposed legislation. These discussions have taken place in private, in professional journals, and in testimony before the legislative committees of the Supreme Soviet. For instance, there was considerable debate among Soviet jurists in the mid and late 1950s over "the presumption of innocence"—that is, whether the new fundamental criminal codes should explicitly state that a defendant be considered innocent until proven guilty. (It was decided not to state this explicitly.) Also, there has been much discussion over family law, the role of the "comrades' courts," and the antiparasite laws," under which dissidents and numerous other noncon-formists have been prosecuted. In short, members of the Soviet legal profession articulate specific opposition on many issues, and often advise and seek to influence party and government officials. But it must be emphasized that Soviet jurists do not devote most of their efforts to changing existing laws and policies. "On the contrary, the main role of the Soviet legal profession is to implement and secure existing policies, and the main source of its influence is the fact that it is needed to help maintain stability and order in the society, and not only to help effectuate change."[63] Hence Soviet jurists are not likely to criticize publicly laws that have been recently adopted, but they avidly will debate and reformulate statutes that the political leadership has indicated might need to undergo revision. Particularly during the preparation of basic legislation and law reform, criticism and debate "are carried on not only in the universities and legal research institutes, but also in ministries, individual factories, jurists' associations, and elsewhere."[64]

On economic questions, above all, the Soviet "Establish-ment" makes abundant and continuous recommendations for policy changes and improvements in policy implementation.

Three illustrations will suffice. First, it must be remembered that although the present party leaders are firmly committed to the idea of centralized economic planning, they have not created a single, all-powerful central planning agency. Indeed, many party and state organs participate in the planning process, and thus the powers of *Gosplan*—in theory *the* planning agency—are limited and circumscribed. What this means is simply that innumerable recommendations and suggestions are articulated, and that many party and state bodies significantly influence the making and carrying out of specific economic policies.[65]

Second, academic economists also express, and have been encouraged to express, diverse viewpoints and opinions. A relatively freer atmosphere prevailed during the nationwide discussion of the Liberman proposals in the early 1960s, and an even more open atmosphere has developed in professional economic circles since that time. Interestingly, the impetus for involving economists more directly in the solution of practical problems did not come from the economists themselves. Instead, "important pressure for improved criteria for rational decision-making [came] from scientists, technologists, and engineers . . . [who] helped convince the party leadership that the fruits of technology would go ungathered without improved economic criteria and incentives."[66] Yet the important point is that Soviet economists—of different ages, mathematical proficiency, and institutional affiliation—are now *expected* to put forward diverse proposals and to offer constructive criticism of current policies and practices.

Third, regional Communist party secretaries are a highly unlikely source of integral or fundamental opposition, but on questions concerning the appropriation of funds, the relative priority of policies or projects, and the economic interests of different geographical regions, even the provincial party leaders disagree considerably with one another. In competition for funds especially, "the key groupings are usually formed along functional lines [e.g., different branches of agriculture or industry—E.P.H.], as the party secretaries ally themselves with, and defend the interests of, state officials over whom at other times they exercise control."[67] Much of this competition takes place privately, but some of it is expressed publicly in the national, provincial, and specialized presses. Soviet officials communicate with one another through newspapers and journals for very specific purposes, and one of their chief aims is to mobilize party and specialized elite support for or against policy changes under consideration. Opposition of the kind described in these three illustrations is certainly "loyal," but the stakes for particular programs, industries, officials, and regions can be very high.

Countless attempts to initiate specific policy changes emanate from the central and regional party and government bureaucracies and from specialized professional groups (most of whose members are employees of government ministries) such as the jurists, economists, educators, industrial managers, and the military. Due to the increased activities of the standing committees of the Supreme Soviet and to other factors, there is probably even more specific opposition under the Brezhnev-Kosygin-Podgorny administration than there was under Khrushchev, despite the frequent nationwide discussions of major policy issues in the Khrushchev era. Indeed, it would seem that John Hazard's speculation of almost ten years ago has proven to be quite accurate:

> . . . future decisions on matters such as reorganization of industrial management, alteration of the structure of primary education, change in the length of the working day, or revision of attitudes toward birth control [may] be initiated and made on the basis of proposals coming from specialists employed in the state apparatus rather than from party generalists moved to action by disappointment felt after an inspection tour or on reading a report. There will be no more surprise commands unrelated to specialists' advice and based solely on personal prejudice.[68]

Specific opposition, then, is widespread. Not only are political initiatives articulated by intellectual, ethnic, and religious dissenters, but they are also proferred, especially on economic questions, by "specialist advisors or bureaucrats seeking to further their own view of the 'national interest,' " and, perhaps especially on legal issues, by those who possess a "more or less disinterested concern for the national interest."[6][9]

Conclusion

What has been attempted in the previous pages is surely presumptuous. Imagine the difficulty of analyzing the nature, sources, and extent of integral, factional, fundamental, and specific opposition in the United States today. Even with the benefit of survey research, this task would be practically impossible. But, thanks in large part to the outpouring of *samizdat* literature, one can make some tentative assessments about *some* aspects of the contemporary Soviet dissent movement.

Among the most important questions that *samizdat* does *not* shed much light on are the following: How many active dissidents (integral and fundamental oppositionists) are there in the Soviet Union today? How widespread is popular support for key oppositionist ideas? How intense is this support? What are the socioeconomic and occupational characteristics of the dissenters and those who sympathize with them? How much discontent is expressed in action, and what kinds of action? To what extent have dissidents formed small cohesive groups or embryonic organizations to fight for common goals? What strategies are being pursued to achieve specific ends?

More than anything else, the *samizdat* documents do tell us something about the goals, ideas, and hopes of Russian dissidents. These strivings have been quite diverse. Amalrik contends that a key feature of the recent dissent movement is

373

that at least three "ideologies" have emerged as alternatives to the official ideology: "genuine Marxism-Leninism," "Christian ideology," and "liberal ideology."[70] All are political doctrines, and all, perhaps *because* of their amorphous character rather than in *spite* of it, enjoy considerable support among Soviet dissenters. Proponents of these respective viewpoints probably include Ivan Dzuiba and Ivan Yakhimovich (a collective farm chairman who protested to top party leaders on behalf of political dissidents and against certain government policies, such as the intervention in Czechoslovakia); Anatoli Levitin and members of the disbanded All-Russian Social-Christian Union for the Liberation of the People; Andrei Sakharov, Pavel Litvinov, and Roy and Zhores Medvedev. Still another dissent "ideology," which Amalrik does not discuss and about which little is known, is that of the militantly nationalistic, anti-Western, anti-Semitic, racist, protofascist, and primitively religious "super-patriots," who advocate an even more centralized, repressive, and Russified state. The neo-Stalinist and neo-Slavophile ideas of these "russites," as they are called, are not only expressed in a growing number of their own *samizdat* publications, but also are reportedly held by some responsible government officials, perhaps chiefly in the state security agencies.[71] In short, there is no ideological unity whatsoever —to say nothing of organizational unity or common goals and strategies—in the current Soviet dissent movement.

Judgments about the extent of different types of opposition are necessarily very tentative, especially if one broadly defines "opposition" to include beliefs, values, attitudes, opinions, and passive as well as active opposition. But one can tentatively conclude that in the past decade integral opposition has increased slightly; factional opposition has declined slightly; fundamental opposition has risen considerably; and specific opposition has risen greatly. Of course, it could be that there is no more dissent today than there was in previous decades, but that current opposition is simply better publicized and that we know more about it.

However, the evidence presented earlier suggests that more dissent and more kinds of dissent were publicly voiced in the 1960s than in any other decade of Soviet history, with the possible exception of the 1920s. Large *samizdat* and *radizdat* audiences, widespread petition-signing, and the constitutionality argument, for example, are basically new phenomena.

Many further questions could be raised about the relationships among dissent, authority, legitimacy, interest articulation, and the sources of popular support for the present Soviet political order.[72] Why, for example, is there so *little* political opposition and dissent in the Soviet Union? This may well be the most important question of all, and the most difficult to answer.

Notes

1. Rustow D: "Communism and Change," in Johnson C, ed: *Change in Communist Systems*. Stanford, Stanford University Press, 1970, p 356; also Dahl R, ed: *Political Oppositions in Western Democracies*. New Haven, Yale University Press, 1966, especially the preface and Chapters 11, 12, 13; Dahl R: *Polyarchy: Participation and Opposition*. New Haven, Yale University Press, 1971; and Dahl R, ed: *Regimes and Oppositions*. New Haven, Yale University Press, forthcoming.

2. Skilling HG: "Background to the Study of Opposition in Communist Eastern Europe." *Government and Opposition*, III, 3 (Summer 1968), pp 297-301 ff; Skilling HG: "The Party, Opposition, and Interest Groups in Communist Politics: Fifty Years of Continuity and Change," in London K, ed: *The Soviet Union: A Half-Century of Communism*. Baltimore, Johns Hopkins Press, 1968, pp 119-149.

3. Skilling, "Background to the Study of Opposition in Communist Eastern Europe," op. cit., p 298.

4. Ibid.

5. Ibid., p 311 ff.

6. On political opposition in 19th-century Russia, see Venturi F: *Roots of Revolution*. New York, Knopf, 1960; Yarmolinsky A: *Road to Revolution*. New York, Collier Books, 1962.

7. Von Doemming G: "A Guide to Proposals for Systemic Change in the USSR Offered by Soviet Citizens," Radio Liberty Reference Handbook No 82, August 1971. The following list is drawn from von

Doemming's highly useful compilation and categorization of demands voiced in the recent *samizdat* literature.

8. Denisov A, Kirichenko M: *Soviet State Law.* Moscow, Foreign Languages Publishing House, 1960, p 405.

9. New York, Norton, 1968.

10. Sakharov A, Turchin V, Medvedev R: An open letter to the party-government leaders of the USSR, *Survey,* No 76 (Summer 1970), p 160.

11. "A Reply to Academician Sakharov by the Estonian Technical Intelligentsia," in the collection of documents appended to Bohdan Bociurkiw, "Political Dissent in the Soviet Union," *Studies in Comparative Communism,* III, 2 (April 1970), p 146.

12. Ibid., p 148.

13. *Survey,* No. 73 (Autumn 1969), pp 47-79; also published in book form (New York, Harper & Row, 1971). The following quotes are from the *Survey* translation, pp 56, 60, 61, 74.

14. Amalrik A: "I Want to be Understood Correctly." *Survey,* No 74/75 (Winter-Spring 1970), p 108. For additional forceful expressions of integral opposition, see Zorin S, Alekseev N: "Vremiia ne zhdet" ("Time Does Not Wait"), (Leningrad: 1969); and *Programma demokraticheskogo dvizheniia Sovetskogo Soiuza (The Program of the Democratic Movement of the Soviet Union).* Amsterdam, The Herzen Foundation, 1970. A very good analysis of these, and other programmatic dissent documents is presented in Frederick Barghoorn, "The General Pattern of Soviet Dissent," paper in Potichnyj O, ed: *Papers and Proceedings of the McMaster Conference on Dissent in the Soviet Union.* Hamilton, Ontario: 1972, pp 3-35.

15. Bukovsky V: Televised CBS broadcast, July 28, 1970, reproduced in *Survey,* No 77 (Autumn, 1970), pp 144-145.

16. Sormani P: "Dissidence in Moscow," *Survey,* No 79 (Spring, 1971), p 14. See also Meyer A: "The Soviet Political System," in Hendel S, Braham E, eds: *The USSR after 50 Years.* New York, Knopf, 1967, pp 39-60.

17. Hoffmann EP: "Methodological Problems of Kremlinology," in Fleron FJ Jr, ed: *Communist Studies and the Social Sciences.* Chicago, Rand McNally, 1969, pp 129-149. For full-length studies of factional opposition in the Soviet Union, see especially Linden C: *Khrushchev and the Soviet Leadership, 1957-1964.* Baltimore, Johns Hopkins Press, 1966; Tatu M: *Power in the Kremlin from Khrushchev to Kosygin.* New York, Viking Press, 1969; Ploss S: *Conflict and Decision-Making in Soviet Russia.* Princeton, Princeton University Press, 1965, and Daniels R: *The Conscience of the Revolution: Communist Opposition in Soviet Russia.* Cambridge, Mass., Harvard University Press, 1960.

18. Linden, op. cit., pp 3, 15 ff.

19. Linden, op. cit., and Tatu, op. cit.

20. See especially Rigby TH: "The Soviet Leadership: Towards a Self-Stabilizing Oligarchy?" *Soviet Studies*, XXII, 2 (October 1970), p 173 ff.

21. Ibid., pp 175, 186-187 ff.

22. "Avtoritet rukovoditelia" ("The Authority of a Leader"), *Pravda*, October 14, 1971, p 1.

23. Berman H: Address at Union College, Schenectady, New York, November 11, 1971.

24. Amalrik, *Will the USSR Survive until 1984?* in Survey, op. cit., p 52.

25. Grigorenko P: Speech to a gathering of Crimean Tatars, in Brumberg A, ed: *In Quest of Justice: Protest and Dissent in the Soviet Union Today.* New York, Praeger, 1970, p 212.

26. For a fuller analysis of these issues, see Weiner S: "Socialist Legality on Trial," in Brumberg, op. cit., pp 39-51; and Sharlet R: Book review, *Columbia Law Review*, LXXI, 7 (November 1971), especially pp 1346-1348.

27. Berman H: "What Makes 'Socialist Law' Socialist?" *Problems of Communism*, XX, 5 (September-October, 1971), p 30.

28. Charlotte Saikowski, "Soviets Snare Dissidents One by One," *Christian Science Monitor,* January 6, 1972, p 12.

29. Sakharov, Turchin, R. Medvedev, op. cit., p 165.

30. "Our Proposals," in documents appended to Bociurkiw, op cit., p 128.

31. This list of demands is drawn from von Doemming, op. cit., p 19. Only because so many of these rights are in fact guaranteed to all Soviet citizens by law—albeit conditionally—does it make sense to treat demands of this magnitude as fundamental, rather than integral, opposition.

32. See, for example, Bourdeaux M: *Patriarch and Prophets: Persecution of the Russian Orthodox Church Today.* New York, Macmillan, 1970.

33. Levitin A: A note on freedom of religion and atheism, May 30, 1965, in Brumberg, op. cit., pp 239-240.

34. Fletcher W: "Religious Dissent in the USSR in the 1960s," *Slavic Review*, XXX, 2 (June 1971), p 300 ff.

35. Medvedev R: "Jews in the USSR: Problems and Prospects," *samizdat* document, *Survey*, No 79 (Spring 1971), p 188. Cf. official Soviet publications such as Rabinovich S: *Jews in the Soviet Union.* Moscow, Novosti Press Agency Publishing House, no date (c 1970).

36. "An Appeal from the Lithuanian Jews," in documents appended to Bociurkiw, op. cit., pp 134-136.

37. Szporluk R: "Dissent and the Non-Russian Nationalities," in

Potichnyj, op. cit., pp 163 ff; and "Nationalities and Nationalism in the USSR," *Problems of Communism* (special issue), XVI, 5 (September-October 1967); and Frederick Barghoorn, *Soviet Russian Nationalism.* New York, Oxford University Press, 1956.

38. Dziuba (Dzyuba) I: *Internationalism or Russification?* London, Weidenfeld and Nicolson, 1968, p 46.

39. Masiutko MS: Letter to the Ukrainian SSR Supreme Soviet, in documents appended to Bociurkiw, op. cit., p 125 ff.

40. Dziuba, op. cit., p 14 ff. See also Chornovil V: *The Chornovil Papers.* New York, McGraw-Hill, 1968.

41. Koval A: Open letter, in documents appended to Bociurkiw, op. cit., p 131.

42. Von Doemming, op. cit., p 51.

43. *Pravda*, December 22, 1962 (italics in original), reprinted in English in Johnson P, ed: *Khrushchev and the Arts.* Cambridge, Mass., MIT Press, 1965, p 116 ff.

44. Sinyavsky A ("Abram Tertz"): *The Trial Begins* and *On Socialist Realism.* New York, Vintage Books, 1965, pp 156, 162 ff.

45. Swayze H: *Political Control of Literature in the USSR, 1946-1959.* Cambridge, Mass., Harvard University Press, 1962, p 13.

46. Quoted in Gwertzman B: "Soviet Arts: Persisting Restraint." *New York Times,* November 14, 1970, p 6.

47. Solzhenitsyn A: Speech to Fourth Congress of Soviet Writers, May 16, 1967, in Brumberg, ed: op. cit., p 247.

48. Von Doemming, op. cit., p 34. The final example and quote is from the "Estonian" reply to Sakharov, in Bociurkiw, op. cit., p 148.

49. See, for example, Zaleski E: *Planning Reforms in the Soviet Union, 1962-1966.* Chapel Hill, University of North Carolina Press, 1967.

50. See, for example, Schroeder G: "Soviet Economic Reform at an Impasse." *Problems of Communism,* XX, 4 (July-August 1971), pp 36-46.

51. Medvedev R: *Let History Judge: The Origins and Consequences of Stalinism.* New York, Knopf, 1971; Marchenko A: *My Testimony.* New York, Dutton, 1969; Medvedev Z: *The Medvedev Papers.* London, Macmillan Ltd., 1971.

52. Many of the following examples are cited in von Doemming, op. cit.

53. For example, Litvinov P: Letter to seven Russian and foreign communist newspapers, in van het Reve K, ed: *Dear Comrade.* New York, Pitman, 1969, pp 3-17.

54. Bukovsky V: Final trial statement, September 1, 1967, in Brumberg, ed: op. cit., pp 83, 88.

55. The entire foregoing list is drawn verbatim from von Doemming,

op. cit., p 44.

56. Dziuba, op. cit., pp 60-113 ff.

57. The entire foregoing list is drawn verbatim from Koval, in Bociurkiw, op. cit., pp 132-133.

58. Hayward M, ed: *On Trial: The Soviet State versus "Abram Tertz" and "Nikolai Arzhak"* (the transcript of the trial of Andrei Sinyavsky and Yuli Daniel. New York, Harper & Row, 1966, p 64.

59. All of the above examples are drawn from von Doemming, op. cit., pp 49-51.

60. Ibid., p 34.

61. Dziuba, op. cit., pp 106-107.

62. Little DR: "Legislative Authority in the Soviet Political System." *Slavic Review*, XXX, 1 (March 1971), p 66 ff.

63. Barry D, Berman H: "The Jurists," in Skilling HG, Griffiths F, eds: *Interest Groups in Soviet Politics*. Princeton, Princeton University Press, 1971, p 330 ff.

64. Ibid., p 320.

65. For some details, see Zaleski, op. cit., Chapter 2.

66. This entire illustration is drawn from Judy R: "The Economists," in Skilling and Griffiths, eds, op. cit., pp 227-228 ff.

67. Hough J: "The Party Apparatchiki," in Skilling and Griffiths, eds, op. cit., p 77 ff.

68. Hazard J: "Has the Soviet State a New Function?" *The Political Quarterly*, No 4 (October-December 1963), p 398.

69. Rigby TH: *Communist Party Membership in the USSR*. Princeton, Princeton University Press, 1968, pp 25-26 ff.

70. Amalrik: Will the USSR Survive until 1984? *Survey*, op. cit., p 51 ff.

71. See "A Word to the Nation," *Survey*, No 80 (Summer 1971), pp 191-199 (a "russite" manifesto); also Scammell M: "Soviet Intellectuals Soldier On," and Harris J: "The Dilemma of Dissidence," *Survey*, No 78 (Winter 1971).

72. For example, Rudolph Tőkes, "Authority and Dissent in Soviet Politics," paper presented at the 1971 annual meeting of the American Association for the Advancement of Slavic Studies, Denver, Colorado, March 25-27, 1971.

12

Cross-National Comparison of Political Opposition and Conflict

Barbara N. McLennan
Temple University

Political opposition, if broadly defined, exists in some form in every political system. The institutional forms it takes may vary from time to time and place to place, but no political system has long existed without some recognition of differing political interests and prospective sources of political conflict.

As already noted, Western political philosophy has, since Plato and Aristotle, been enriched by attempts to clarify and compare the nature of political opposition in varying political systems. The best known recent attempt to deal with the phenomenon appears in Robert Dahl's *Political Oppositions in Western Democracies.*[1]

Dahl intentionally restricts his field of study to established Western democratic systems where conflict has been institutionalized into national elections and party competition within national legislatures. By narrowing his focus Dahl has thus selected a fairly uniform constitutional setting for the context in which he draws his comparisons. All political systems in his sample share a kind of consensus based on democratic election procedures and the legitimacy of popular representation in legislative bodies.

Within this generally uniform context Dahl is able to distinguish oppositions cross-nationally. He states that

oppositions differ in six ways.[2]
1. The organizational cohesion or concentration of the opponents.
2. The competitiveness of the opposition.
3. The site or setting for the encounter between opposition and those who control the government.
4. The distinctiveness or identifiability of the opposition.
5. The goals of the opposition.
6. The strategies of opposition.

Dahl, using these concepts derived from descriptive accounts of a series of Western democracies, then categorizes party systems (i.e., systems of opposition) in terms of competition, cooperation, and coalescence in elections and legislative politics. He then presents a typology of patterns of political opposition: (1) Nonstructural opposition (pure office-seeking parties, pressure groups, policy-oriented parties); (2) Limited structural opposition (non-policy-oriented political reformism); and (3) Major structural opposition (comprehensive political-structural reformism, democratic social-structural reformism, revolutionary movements). Each of these types of opposition may pursue different goals, according to Dahl. They can oppose the personnel of government, the specific policies of government, the political structure, or the socioeconomic structure. In any event, the goals and strategies vary with the type of opposition.[3]

Dahl's analysis is basically descriptive. He attempts to isolate conditions in the systems under investigation which help to explain the varying patterns of opposition. Conditions in his subject of investigation are broadly similar, making more practical the construction of hypotheses distinguishing one pattern of opposition from another. Dahl finally comes up with five such conditions or variables:
1. Constitutional structure or electoral system.
2. Widely shared cultural premises.
3. Specific subcultures.
4. The record of grievances against the government.
5. Social and economic differences.

It is noteworthy that Dahl does not include fear of repression (or its lack) as one of the conditions contributing to the pattern of opposition. By restricting the scope of his comparison to the Western democracies, he has avoided the difficulty of comparing competitive systems to noncompetitive ones, where repression is either very real or threatened. Clearly, opposition can exist in such systems, but Dahl's approach, so dependent on the descriptive analysis of particular Western states, offers no clue as to how to proceed to broaden the realm of comparison to include these noncompetitive states. Also, Dahl's approach does not consider nondemocratic features (e.g., suppression of opposition through voting manipulation within otherwise democratic states).

Another attempt to establish a general theoretical model by which systems of opposition can be compared appears in Anthony Downs' *An Economic Theory of Democracy*.[4] Downs presents a model of an ideal democratic system which emphasizes the structural role of political parties in a kind of free political marketplace. Like Dahl, his analysis is intentionally restricted to the nuances of competitive Western democratic systems. He views politics as the interaction of profit-seeking—i.e., vote-seeking—entrepreneurs whose only calculations are based on the free interplay of competitive argument and party organization. Thus, Downs hypothesizes that:

1. Parties are motivated chiefly by the desire to hold public office; they formulate their policies as a means of holding office rather than seeking office to carry out preconceived policies.
2. Both parties in a two-party system agree on any issues that a majority of citizens strongly favor.
3. In a two-party system, party policies are (a) more vague, (b) more similar to those of other parties, and (c) less directly linked to an ideology than in a multiparty system.
4. In a multiparty system governed by a coalition, the

government takes less effective action to solve basic social problems, and its policies are less integrated and consistent, than in a two-party system.

5. New parties arise when (a) a change in suffrage laws sharply alters the distribution of citizens along the political scale, (b) there is a sudden change in the electorate's social outlook, or (c) there is a split caused by a radical faction of one of the major parties.[5]

Like Dahl, Downs does not regard repression or changes of constitution as difficulties for his analytic scheme. He conceives only of perfectly stable democratic systems. He does take note of such possible occurrences as a change in election laws, but he never conceives of them as weapons that frequently are used by governing parties against their opponents. Redistricting and gerrymandering can, however, be instituted in such a way as to make the political marketplace imperfect, reducing the difficulties of open competition for the party or coalition in power. This, as already noted, can be a force for suppression of opposition, not a necessarily legitimate result of the free interplay of democratic party activity. Such suppression has obviously occurred in many apparently democratic political systems, even to the extent of making elections fraudulent and changing the democratic nature of the system. Downs, like Dahl, does not address himself to this question.

Another approach to the analytic study of political conflict can be found in the work of the game theorists, of whom William Riker is probably the most widely familiar to political scientists. Drawing upon mathematical theory, Riker devises a series of theoretical proporitions which are said to govern the procedures by which political coalitions and oppositions are formed.[6] Riker is similar to Downs in that he views political actors as rational "economic" men always seeking to maximize their individual positions. He embellishes this original assumption with the more complex details of game theory. Thus, he views politics as a *zero-sum* game, i.e., a conflict where one player's gain is equal to the others' losses (that is, the total of all the payoffs is equal to zero). This is to be distinguished from the *non-zero-sum* game where all players may gain, while no one loses (e.g., the economic market place).

Riker views games as two-person or n-person, and his use of game theory allows him to consider a multiplicity of political possibilities. However, many of his hypotheses are restatements of those made by Downs because of the underlying assumption of rationality and drive for efficiency. Strategies in coalition building and opposition formation follow the configuration of the actors and the information available to each of them. Riker recognizes that some games may be quite unfair, with resources being unevenly distributed. He also recognizes that the rules of any given game might change and that this is likely to affect the outcome. He thus acknowledges that all political actors use whatever means at their disposal to maximize their positions and that this can include undemocratic measures as well as typically electoral choices of strategy.

Game theory is extremely general and can be used to explain the development of particular political systems over time. It can be used comparatively and cross-nationally only when one assumes that the basic rules of the game are similar in different systems. Then one can compare differences in strategy and coalition formation as the product of particular types of political behavior.

In essence, the game theorists would group political systems in much the same way that Dahl and Downs have done. Game theory separates democracies from dictatorships as the proverbial arithmetic problem separates apples from oranges. They are not to be treated the same way, because the underlying assumptions of each system are viewed as different. One can describe the nuances of each type of system strategically and one can describe the transformation of one system into another by discussing changes in the rules of procedure; but one cannot compare strategy formation in one type of system to another because the actors are different and they are playing by different rules.

A Cross-National Model for the Comparison of Political Oppositions

The above theories of political opposition are generally elegant in their individual abstract calculations. They do not view opposition as caused or affected by a series of variables, but as a condition created by the general context and strategies of political actors. It is the choice of specific context that makes it difficult to use these theories comaparatively.

If one transforms this basic approach and views political opposition as an empirical pattern of political behavior that is the product of a series of specific sociopolitical variables, it is possible to view the phenomenon in less elegant but more comparative terms. The loss in accuracy and technical detail is sacrificed in favor of a scheme that views opposition across national lines and discusses opposition movements from a general and comparative viewpoint.

Such an approach can be found in an application and reinterpretation of psychological conflict and equilibrium theory.[7] This model views political opposition as a function of political stability, political output, the fear of repression, and the capacity of a regime to resort to political sanctions. This relationship is depicted graphically in Figure 12.1:

The model represents a series of equilibrium positions. PQ, the axis labeled "Political sanctions," and RS ("Maximum political output") represent opposite poles which as ideal types are both negative. This means that it is assumed that political actors will behave in such a way so that there always exists a certain tendency for them to avoid both poles. The behavior of political actors in this conflict model is labeled "Opposition." The lines TO_1, TO_2, TO_3, TO^1_1, TO^1_2, TO^1_3 all depict theoretical levels of opposition.

Opposition here can be defined in both formal and

FIGURE I

POLITICAL OPPOSITION AND POLITICAL EQUILIBRIUM

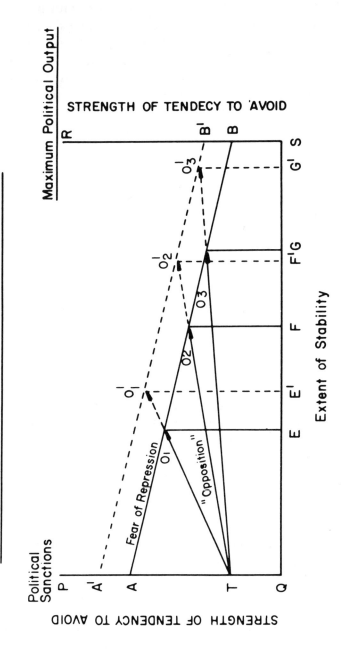

informal terms. If one were concerned with political party conflict in Western democracies (as for example is true of Dahl and Downs) opposition could be defined as a function of the division of votes or seats in legislative politics or in national elections. If one is concerned more with the general condition of informal, noninstitutionalized opposition which exists in all political entities, democratic and nondemocratic, one can define opposition as a function of cultural criticism, popular movements, and general behavioral patterns demonstrating disrespect for the established regime.

The model assumes that political opposition always exists in some form and that point T cannot be equal to zero (point Q). In other words, every system normally utilizes political sanctions, at least to some moderate extent, if only to silence extremists or lunatics. The model depicts the level of opposition as the *slope* of a line. Thus TO_1 depicts a higher level of opposition than TO_2 or TO_3.

The line AB represents "Fear of Repression" in the political systems being compared. Repression may, like opposition, be very broadly defined to fit both democratic and nondemocratic systems. While the activities of police and military authorities are widely recognized to be threatening or repressive, so can official changes in elections laws, redistricting, more stringent regulation of the mass media, and legal changes in ordinances governing methods by which persons can organize and petition the regime. Fear of repression, like opposition, is a psychological phenomenon as well; it is closely related to the level of frustration existing in the society. A high level of frustration may decrease the fear of repression in the system, even though there is no great change in the political capacity or character of the established regime. Like opposition, it is assumed here that fear of repression always exists in some form, that is, every government is believed to be capable and willing to utilize some political sanctions as a normal course of action (B is never zero).

This model represents an *equilibrium* theory because it

assumes that in a given conflict situation, the level of opposition will meet the fear of repression level at some point and settle there. Any activity to the contrary will, over time, result in the same interacting position, here labeled "Extent of stability." Thus TO_1 meets AB at point O_1; in this instance the distance QE represents the extent of *political stability* in that given conflict situation.

In this theory political stability refers to a government's ability to carry out its decisions legitimately over time. Stated differently, this model compares the level of stability as the product of political opposition and the fear of repression in the conflict arena. If opposition declines (say, from TO_1 to TO_2), stability is increased (from QE to QF). Also, it can be seen that government action to raise the fear of repression line also increases stability. In other words, raising AB to A^1B will result in greater stability for all levels of opposition.

This is an important concept because it is well known that even democratic regimes (for example, France's Fourth Republic) have used repressive means, broadly defined, simply to maintain the equilibrium stability position of the government. Governmental instability over a long enough period of time, because of widespread opposition, can turn into regime instability. Opposition can be so great that the only means of dealing with it may be restructuring the constitution so as to disenfranchise the opposition—an admittedly repressive strategy, but one which has been used in a variety of countries, many of which are loosely described as democracies.

A Comparison of Political Opposition: Hypothetical Application of the Equilibrium Model

How can the various political opposition movements discussed in this book be analyzed and compared, utilizing a uniform language and set of concepts? One possible approach is to utilize the equilibrium model presented above. As even casual observers can empirically conclude, all states discussed here have the major variable utilized in the model in varying degree.

It is clear, however, that each of the states varies in terms of the individual levels of political opposition, the prevalence and intensity of fear of repression, and consequent levels of political stability. If we were to view the problem from the point of view of the political actor, we could hypothetically conceive of three "Fear of repression" lines—a very high one for the USSR; a moderately high one for Fifth Republic France, Tanzania, West Germany, India, and Argentina; and one with relatively low levels for Great Britain, Japan, Chile, and the United States. On the other hand, the levels of empirical opposition differ from one country to another as well—with high levels of opposition in Argentina, India, and France; moderate levels in Chile, the United States, Japan, and perhaps West Germany; and with relatively low levels in the USSR, Tanzania, and Great Britain. The corresponding levels of political stability, i.e., the capacity of government to take independent action without fear of dire long-term consequences, also differs from state to state. This relationship is depicted in Figure 12.2:

It should be obvious that precision in this hypothetical model depends upon a valid, testable mathematical formula for expression of the various slopes of the "Opposition" and "Fear of repression" lines. While no such mathematical formula is presented here, it can obviously be worked out through the use of election statistics (for democratic states) or through a systematic content analysis of relevant political information. The model in Figure 12.2 merely presents the logical levels of these variables derived from the chapters presented in this volume. It assumes fear of repression and opposition to be linear, but obviously it is possible that the mathematics may in fact point to a curve to represent one or both of the two variables.

At any rate the model does categorize the political systems

390

FIGURE II

A COMPARISON OF POLITICAL OPPOSITION AND POLITICAL EQUILIBRIUM POINTS

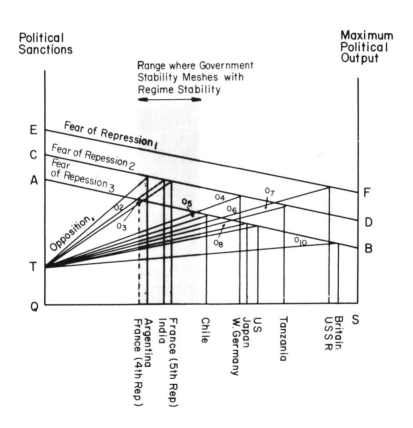

391

according to level of political stability. Thus, for example, in comparing Great Britain and the USSR, both nations appear to have very high and very similar levels of political stability. Their levels of opposition are somewhat different, Britain's being somewhat lower, but this is generally made up for by the greater fear of political repression in the USSR. Tanzania is somewhat lower in stability because this regime is somewhat less capable of political sanctions than the other two more developed states. Similar levels of stability are found in the United States, Japan, and West Germany, with broadly similar values for the two variables.

An interesting feature of the model is the ability to compare changes within a system, according to change in the use of political sanctions. Thus the constitutional change from Fourth Republic France to the Fifth Republic results, according to the model, in a higher level of political stability, basically because of a raising of the "Fear of repression" line (from AB to CD). The shaded area represents the range of equilibrium points where government instability is so weak that, in fact, the constitutional regime is threatened. France, Argentina, and India are within this range, with Chile being close but probably just outside it.

The Value of the Comparative Model

The use of this type of model allows us to compare the nature and results of political opposition across national boundaries. It allows us to view countries, provided we are thorough and accurate in our interpretation of the meaning of opposition, without respect to their geographic locations or peculiar political histories. We can compare different forms of constitutional structures, because we have assumed these institutions to be irrelevant to basic nature of political behavior which we have in fact labeled "political opposition." The behavior patterns—oppositionism and fear of repression—are empirically universal. Their effect on politics

392

is also universal and deserves to be treated as a general phenomenon not tied to any particular context.

Notes

1. Dahl R: *Political Opposition in Western Democracies.* New Haven and London, Yale University Press, 1966.
2. Ibid., p 332.
3. Ibid., p 338.
4. Downs A: *An Economic Theory of Democracy.* New York, Harper and Row, 1957.
5. Ibid., pp 296-297.
6. Riker W: *The Theory of Political Coalitions.* New Haven and London, Yale University Press, 1962.
7. The model presented here is adapted from the work done by Somers GS: "Bargaining Power and Industrial Relations Theory," in Somers GS, ed: *Industrial Relations Theory.* Ames, Iowa State University Press, 1969, pp 39-54.